Lady Gaga

This book is a multi-faceted, interdisciplinary examination of the music and figure of Lady Gaga, combining approaches from scholars in cultural studies, art, fashion, and music. It represents one of the first scholarly volumes devoted to Lady Gaga, who has become, over a few short years, central to both popular (and, indeed, populist) as well as more scholarly thought in these areas and who, the contributors argue, is helping to shape—directly and indirectly—thought and culture both in the fields of the "scholarly" and the "everyday." Lady Gaga's output is firmly embedded in a self-consciously intellectual pop culture tradition, and her music videos are intertextually linked to icons of pop culture intelligentsia like Alfred Hitchcock and open to multiple interpretations. In examining her music and figure, this volume contributes both to debates on the status of intertextuality, held in tension with originality, and to debates on the figuring of the sexualized female body, and representations of disability. There is interest in these issues from a wide range of disciplines: popular musicology, film studies, queer studies, women's studies, gender studies, disability studies, popular culture studies, and the burgeoning sub-discipline of aesthetics and philosophy of fashion.

Martin Iddon is Professor of Music and Aesthetics and Head of School at the University of Leeds, United Kingdom.

Melanie L. Marshall is a Marie Curie International Outgoing Fellow, a visiting scholar at New York University, USA, and a musicologist at University College Cork, Ireland.

Routledge Studies in Popular Music

Lady Gaga and Popular Music

Performing Gender, Fashion, and Culture

**Edited by Martin Iddon
and Melanie L. Marshall**

Routledge
Taylor & Francis Group

NEW YORK AND LONDON

First published 2014
by Routledge
711 Third Avenue, New York, NY 10017

and by Routledge
2 Park Square, Milton Park, Abingdon, Oxfordshire OX14 4RN

First issued in paperback 2016

*Routledge is an imprint of the Taylor & Francis Group,
an informa business*

Library of Congress Cataloging-in-Publication Data

    Lady Gaga and popular music : performing gender, fashion, and culture
/ edited by Martin Iddon and Melanie L. Marshall.
      pages cm. — (Routledge studies in popular music ; no. 3)
    Includes bibliographical references and index.
  1. Lady Gaga—Criticism and interpretation. 2. Gender identity in
music. 3. Popular culture—History—21st century. 4. Fashion—
History—21st century. 5. Popular music—2001–2010—History
and criticism. 6. Popular music—2011–2020—History and
criticism. I. Iddon, Martin, 1975– II. Marshall, Melanie L.
  ML420.L185L33 2014
  782.42164092—dc23
  2013023600

ISBN 13: 978-1-138-63048-2 (pbk)
ISBN 13: 978-0-415-82452-1 (hbk)

Typeset in Sabon
by IBT Global.

Contents

PART II
Gaga and Representation

Figures

Introduction

Martin Iddon and Melanie L. Marshall

In 'Telephone', Lady Gaga, Beyoncé, and the anonymous body of dancers wear US-flag inspired outfits to dance in a diner filled with their victims' bodies: regular Americans who died from consuming toxic diner food. Red, white, and blue figure-hugging outfits usually mark superheroes who expend their energies saving citizens, not murdering them. And despite the implied critique of (US) consumerism and excess consumption, Gaga's exuberance is gleefully co-opted to tell stories of international repression and censorship: her shows are confined to adults only (South Korea), or authorities ask for 'toned down' shows (Indonesia), or laws against promoting homosexuality result in editing of her songs (Malaysia). In the US media, stories of foreign authorities going gaga over, or perhaps more precisely not going gaga for, Gaga shore up a popular nationalist narrative of the US as one of the few countries where people are free. Stories of Gaga censorship within the US, such as the censoring of her language on *American Idol* in 2011, do not get the same mainstream press coverage; corporate censorship is apparently acceptable. These issues and others like them—and their intermingling, the apparently frivolous with the clearly serious, the high and the low, the adult and the, perhaps, childish—are the focus of the present volume, in which Gaga is taken both as subject in her own right and as a site where ideas are imbricated, where, somehow, things happen.

Lady Gaga's output is firmly embedded in an intellectual pop culture tradition. Her music videos are intertextually linked to icons of pop culture intelligentsia like Alfred Hitchcock and so on (with her approach to fashion, too, classic Louboutin and Versace rub shoulders—almost literally—with Formichetti's infamous 'meat dress'), and they are open to multiple interpretations. This is to say, it is the kind of pop culture that tends to appeal to people who like to 'make meanings' rather than have them made for them: people who like to think. In academic terms, what Gaga does thus intersects with the interests of a wide range of disciplines: popular musicology, to be sure, but also film studies, popular culture studies more broadly, and the burgeoning sub-discipline of aesthetics: philosophy of fashion.

Lady Gaga's appeal to queer fandom originates in her celebration of her (quite deliberate) difference, her refusal to be 'closeted', alongside her support of gay pride events and her gratitude to her gay fan base. This is particularly clear in her song 'Born This Way', her most overt musical statement to date, though this has formed an integral part of her self-construction, it seems, from the outset. Queerness, too, is an important factor in Lady Gaga's performances, alongside, but clearly not collapsed into, the pro-LGBT stance of 'Born This Way'. Queerness is construed more broadly here. The openness of any of Lady Gaga's performances—the way in which she is always already performing herself, or the continuing ambiguity of her own sexual and gender identities—opens the path to any number of queer reading strategies. This is precisely the terrain which is central to current trends in both performance research and theatre studies, especially as they pertain to technologies of the self.

Lady Gaga's interactions with interviewers position her on the side of interrogating prejudices in an intellectually engaged way. Indeed, she has arguably been interested in using interviews to expose the nature of the interview itself. This self-reflexive operation in public is not only performative in the ways mentioned above, it is also a performative examination of the ways in which the 'pop star' in the contemporary world is, or becomes, mediatized. Her engagement with 'her' public demonstrates topics which remain integral to cultural and media studies. It is hardly insignificant here that, as of August 2010, Gaga became the world's most followed member of the Twitterati, her principle means of contact with her 'little monsters', as she affectionately describes her fans.

All of these areas are central to the present volume, but it should not be thought that the contributors are without a critical edge. As well as contributions which regard the impact of Lady Gaga on culture as positive—not only, but perhaps particularly, in a political sense—other contributions are more sanguine. Examinations are made of, for instance, whether Gaga's figuring of disability, far from opening a space in which disabled bodies are recontextualized, perpetuates tropes of women's bodies as somehow 'damaged' or uncontrollable. Elsewhere, the challenge that Gaga represents little more than 'warmed-over Madonna' is examined (and only to a limited degree contested). Thus, we hope that the volume contributes both to pop cultural debates on the status of intertextuality, held in tension with originality, and to debates in women's and gender studies on the figuring of the sexualized female body.

From the outset, we conceived the volume to be wholly inter-disciplinary and international. Contributors come from a variety of disciplinary backgrounds, including music, to be sure, but also, importantly, from cultural studies, art, and fashion studies. Within those contributions which might be conceived of as 'strictly' musical, there is, too, a variety of approaches, from those considering principally the immanent trace of music's sounding surface, through those examining how sound and imagery interact, to considerations of various forms of musical reception. Indeed, the breadth of the volume (and of the interest its subject enjoins) is perhaps indicated by the fact that several of the contributors—the editors included—are writing at some distance from the scholarly concerns with which they are probably most associated. As well as their disciplinary variety, scholars also operate from around the Anglophone world: Australia, Ireland, the United Kingdom, the United States of America are all represented. The volume is divided into two large sections: the first is concerned with the sorts of contexts that Lady Gaga exists within in and creates; the second focuses both on what and how Gaga represents and is represented, though, inevitably, there is some crossover between these broad themes.

In the first section, two chapters look at specific tracks. Hawkins present a thick account of 'Judas', looking in particular to show the way in which the particular production decisions taken within the track shape both what 'Gaga' means and how this is imbricated with notions of camp and flamboyance within pop more broadly, as well as considering what sort of ways in which empathy *for* Gaga might be evoked in listeners in ways which encourage—or demand—particular forms of consumption. By contrast, Colton uses 'Telephone' as a way of placing that singular track in the context of 'telephone songs' more generally. Colton explores, in particular, the way in which women (and women's voices) have are intertwined with the history of the telephone and the way in which the telephone (and telephone songs) figure particular sorts of intimacy, placing Gaga's 'Telephone' into the context of other tracks by Meri Wilson, Cyndi Lauper, and Kraftwerk, among others. Those women's voices are vital here, especially in the context of the production of those voices in ways that manipulate and distort them.

Gray and Rutnam examine the way in which Gaga's identity has been constructed through her imbrication through cultures of fashion, through dress and coding. In particular Gary and Rutnam focus not only on Gaga's moulding of herself (and, for that matter, her *self*) in this context, but on the ways in which that self is imbricated with the fashion system and cannot be disentangled from such modes of presentation, to the extent that, for Gray and Rutnam, the 'authentic' Gaga *is* just this performance of Gaga. For Gray and Rutnam this performance of Gaga is, too, an intervention in the fashion system, shaping, re-imagining, and re-creating its possible futures. One particular example, the Fernandez and Formichetti meat dress worn by Lady Gaga to the 2010 MTV Video Music Awards, is selected by O'Brien as a site from which to reflect upon how these modes of presentation are imbricated with other modes of radical feminist protest which have foregrounded, quite literally, the fleshly, particularly in the work of Linder Sterling (but also Carolee Schneemann, Judy Chicago, Karen Finlay, Jana Sterbak, Helen Chadwick, and Tamara Kosianovsky), asking at the same time whether feminism can survive its own imbrication with the pop mainstream, or whether such a motion becomes near enough an empty signifier in such a context. O'Brien, too, considers the context of female performers and musicians within which Gaga is situated—or has situated herself—looking to parallels with Debbie Harry, Rihanna, Tori Amos, Christina Aguilera and, of course, Madonna.

For Owens and Hegarty alike, Gaga represents a site at which to reflect upon what she might be able to say about those contexts in which she is situated: for Owens, this is a question of celebrity; for Hegarty, it is one of the erotic. Owens's chapter triangulates Gaga, the figure of the zombie, and Deleuze and Guattari's Body without Organs to generate the notion of a Celebrity without Organs, an abnormal, monstrous assemblage, intersecting and suturing the literal and the figurative. Hegarty starts from an examination of the heel—especially those particular heels on display in the 'Paparazzi' and 'Bad Romance' videos—to discuss limits: the limits of the human—as Hegarty formulates them, erotic, mortal, animal, machine—but with a particular focus on the relationship between the height of Gaga's body, as it, or she, is raised and lowered, and the limits of the erotic. Hegarty's stress, like Owens's, is on how Gaga thinks (or can be used to think); it is not, he demands, the representation of love, death, and the erotic that is at stake but, rather, the representations are ways of playing out the various possibilities for being in the world. The deaths, legs, knees, toes and heels of 'Bad Romance' and 'Paparazzi'—not least the claw-like ten-inch armadillo shoe of the former video—are central, as are the various physical positions adopted by numerous possible Gagas: pod Gaga, nude Gaga, slave Gaga, wide-eyed Gaga, armadillo(-shod) Gaga.

In the second section, two complementary analyses are offered—the first by Lori Burns and Marc Lafrance, the second by Carol Vernallis—of the videos for 'Paparazzi' and 'Telephone'. Burns and Lafrance emphasize in particular the ways in which intersections between the 'strictly' musical and visual create productive new meanings and frictions to a seemingly rather greater extent than they seem mutually supportive, while Vernallis considers what sorts of narratives are played out in thee videos, wondering, especially, whether the forms of narrative played out by Gaga and Jonas Åkerlund conceal at least as much as they reveal. The presentation of Gaga on screen is the central focus of Warner's contribution too, though here, in slightly surprising guise, since his interest is in the ways in which Gaga is (re-)presented within the framework of the show *Glee*, particularly asking to what extent the edges of Gaga are capable of radicalizing the conservative world of primetime TV (and to what extent Gaga finds herself somehow watered down in this context). The two episodes Warner specifically looks at, 'Theatricality' and 'Born This Way', he suggests, use Gaga not only as a way of filling the various musical slots for McKinley High's fictional glee club, but also as a frame in which the various characters of the show are able to renegotiate their identities in more flexible and fluid ways than would ordinarily be the case, even in the show's hardly wholly realist narrative world.

How Gaga presents her*self* is central to Apolloni and Geller's contributions alike, the latter examining the broadly progressive gender politics exhibited in Gaga's performance of her *alter ego*, Jo Calderone, while the former is concerned, in more critical fashion, with the way in which Gaga figures disability. The disabilities Apolloni considers are both those of the physical disabilities Gaga (literally) performs—appearing on stage and video on crutches or in a wheelchair—but also the 'vocal damage' which is often technologically added to the way in which she *sounds* in those performances. While Apolloni argues that Gaga makes disability visible in ways which have a potentially progressive political dimension, she is concerned, too, that Gaga seemingly romanticizes a certain discourse around disability, in ways which simply repeat troubling norms. By contrast, Geller's approach to Jo Calderone takes him as a paradigmatic example of what J. Jack Halberstam has recently termed Gaga Feminism, which takes Butlerian gender performativity to what feels like its full form: a form of feminism which demands that, if gender must be a thing that is *done*, it be done according to activity, according to *action*, where that word has retains the connotations both of its Latin etymology and the political undertones it has more latterly acquired (as well, in the context of such a performance, of the command of the film director). Marshall points to a more troubling nexus of cultures of consumption and whiteness that lie at the heart of what Gaga is and does, as well as what 'we' do to Gaga, considering the imbrication of Gaga with trends as seemingly, one might expect, distant from ideas of pop stardom as ice cream and (amateur) cake baking. Recalling Owens's zombies, both 'we' and Gaga are complicit in an analysis which suggests that Gaga's 'capitalism with a human face', as Žižek would have, gets eaten up until there is nothing left.

Finally, Iddon's closing 'supplement'—intended in the Derridean sense both to reflect upon the volume without necessarily concluding it, as such—suggests that the way in which the 'authentic' Gaga exists only in presentation, combined with the ways in which the absence of any authentic self is persistently stressed by her *in* that performance, might begin to hint at a reconciliation between modern and postmodern forms of artistic practice: even where the modern tilts at presence and the postmodern at absence, the postmodern can still *reveal itself* in just the same way as the modern once seemed to and, in doing so, can still be 'truly' art.

Inevitably, any edited volume is always already the work of many hands and the editors are hugely grateful to all those whose words do not appear here, but without whom the contributors would not have delivered such finely nuanced and insightful chapters. We hope that they, and the contributors too, will be pleased with what they find within. For our part, those *sine quibus non* must be, as ever, Martin's wife Kate, Melanie's husband Han. Melanie and Han's daughter, Asha, arrived in the middle of preparing the final manuscript. Though she's probably not ready to read it yet, this volume is dedicated to her, for when she is.

Part I
Gaga's Contexts

1 'I'll Bring You Down, Down, Down'

Lady Gaga's Performance in 'Judas'

Stan Hawkins

One of the biggest hits of 2011 was 'Judas', a song that embodies everything pop is about. It comprises rousing compositional ideas: memorable chord sequences and hooks, catchy verse-chorus sections, and, most of all, a brash production. Lady Gaga's performance in this song is compelling. It is thoroughly littered with clichés in a highly polished musical production that bashes out three huge memorable melody hooks. In all her performances she re-invents herself and appropriates a wealth of musical styles. A crucial part of her act is her playfulness. Throughout this chapter aspects of subjectivity are mapped against camp display in both the pop song and video of 'Judas'. The critical approach undertaken accounts for performance strategies through style and agency. Questions posed are of a musicological kind: what features characterize the Gaga idiom, how do the details of music production shape her flamboyancy, and what is it about pop that promotes a camp aesthetic?[1]

STAGING THE TRACK

If Jesus represents the good in Gaga, then Judas Iscariot certainly wreaks havoc in her life. Exposing the motives of an ex-lover who has cheated on her, she sets out to bring him down. Through her multiple personae Lady Gaga goes on the rampage in the name of pop. Her idiosyncrasies are sculptured by musical innovation, and inextricably tied to her production is a quest for originality and surprise. In 'Judas' there is a sense that pioneering production techniques layer and color-wash the storyline. This is achieved by the meticulous treatment of sounds and effects within a highly active audio image. Indeed, Lady Gaga's brand of electropop represents a maze of sonic details that define her performance. Destined for the dance floor, her recordings simulate the ambience of a large space: the space of a crowded venue. Much of this is due to sonic density in the production. Textural layering, multi-timbral effects, contrasting dynamics, timbres, and a strident groove distributed over various tracks, all contribute to a high saturation of vivid musical ideas.

To start with, I am keen to probe at the production qualities that profile the song's aesthetics. Made meaningful through the act of listening and interpretation, pop songs emphasize pop personalities through the dramaturgy of audiovisual imagery. It is precisely this that Philip Auslander argues: 'Part of the audience's pleasure in pop music comes from experiencing and consuming the personae of favorite artists in all their many forms, and this experience is inseparable from the experience of the music itself'.[2] Feeling for an artist therefore involves empathy. Lucy Green's theorization of *delineation*, now a standardized model for understanding denotation and connotation in music, is useful for gauging this.[3] Preferences for a specific style, Green has maintained, are predicated upon on a sense of familiarity and empathy that relates to the complex process of listening competence and identification. So what makes the productions of Lady Gaga instantly recognizable? And how does her music work empathically?

Much of pop's appeal is down to the production of a song. One's first impression of 'Judas' verifies this. When experiencing the song for the first time it is clear that a dazzling array of technologies are invested in the recording process. The way Lady Gaga's voice is produced and treated in the mix is of particular musicological interest. All the conditions for featuring her persona depend on the communicative relationship she has through her voice with her fans/listeners. On this matter, I would suggest that a central part of her vocal aesthetic is linked to the dimensions and technological manipulation of her sonic space. By this I am referring to the specific arrangement of tracks and sound processing, as much as the regulation of dynamics, texture, timbre, and the control of reverb and echo. Contingent on engineering and production, Lady Gaga's songs signify an illusion of physicality, not least through the technical manipulation of the voice.[4] Consequently, the qualities of vocal recording are integral to patterns of reception. In an earlier study I argued that the recorded voice constitutes the most personal arena for pleasure because of 'the sonic qualities of the body' that implicate listeners in powerful forms of emotional response. One of the main strategies of the pop performer, after all, is to persuade the fan to believe that they have direct contact with the singer's 'real self'.[5]

Although the recording (or what I have referred to previously as the 'pop score') is fixed, it is likely to be perceived differently on every hearing.[6] In the production of 'Judas' there is a sense that musical ideas randomly fly in and out of the audio space. This is a direct result of the handling of audio technology. Regulating the spatial aspects of sound in the engineering process is a crucial part of the overall aesthetics of a recording, and with 'Judas' it is the rapid turn around of events that makes the song appealing. In other words, sonic events (in the shape and form of, say, instruments, rhythmic loops, vocals) entering and exiting the mix at different rates heighten the musical interest. The organization and manipulation of musical ideas relates directly to the technical design of the audio space. All in all, the multitude of creative possibilities that occur in a Lady Gaga recording has to do with control and shaping the audio image. And it is the aesthetic choices the producer(s) come up with that make a Gaga track what it is.

MONSTROUS BY REPRODUCTION

Lady Gaga's soundworld is discernible in every second of 'Judas'.[7] Written and produced by Lady Gaga and RedOne (a prolific Moroccan-Swedish producer and songwriter),[8] this song, lasting just over four minutes, consists of numerous stylistic features set against an inexorable rock beat. The song is similar to earlier tracks produced by Lady Gaga and RedOne: 'LoveGame', 'Bad Romance', 'Alejandro', and 'Poker Face'. Soaring vocals, programmed beats, cathedral-like synthesizers, and a pounding bass line reinforce the song's anthemic feel. With a swirling instrumental eight-bar introduction and a contrasting staccato passage, consisting of intervallic fifths on the line *Judas- Jud-a-a. Judas–Jud-a-a*, Lady Gaga hurls herself into the first verse grounded by the C Aeolian root chord, C minor. Close inspection reveals that the effect of textural layering is compositionally decisive: one colossal textural block of sound ushers in the next, forming a glittering sonic mosaic. Already in the first 32 seconds of the track (16 bars) four textural changes occur:

1. a simple melodic line with synthesizer underlay and strident pitch shifts in lower register, evoking a calm, tranquil yet foreboding mood (8 bars [15"]);
2. a wall of *a capella* multi-vocals, chorused with a high dose of effects (4 bars [8"]);
3. bass synthesizer timbres positioned to the fore of the mix, imitating the octave motif from the previous section (4 bars [5"]); and,
4. a block of vocals in unison with the previous motif expand the timbral spectrum and pitch register (4 bars [5"]).

These textural blocks help regulate the tension levels in the music's dramaturgy. One vivid example occurs in the space opened by the second textural change (see preceding list), where the vocals, without warning, are left raw and exposed. Cleverly, the engineering and textural coloration of such an *a cappella* gesture contributes to the unfolding of the song's narrative. Textural control thus constitutes a major part of the musical composition, and is a direct outcome of the production techniques.

Lady Gaga is part of the generation of super songwriter-producers who deliver large-scale productions, and 'Judas' is bound up in an array of sonic gestures activated within a 'perceived performance environment' (PPE).[9]

Indeed the material conditions of Lady Gaga's musical style—dance-pop with influences of house, techno, dubstep, disco, and Eurovision *schmaltz*—provides a vibrant sense of physical presence, albeit in many different variants. When it comes to creating a sense of space in the pop production, the performance environment is contingent on the technical regulation of sonic width and depth. William Moylan describes width as 'defined by the furthest right and the furthest left sound (lateral localization)' and depth 'by the most distant sound source and the closest sound source'.[10] Essentially, it is both of these aspects of sonic design that determine the spatial radius of the audio image.

The studio production of any pop track invariably involves a high degree of teamwork and influences by other artists. Lady Gaga has continuously emphasized her affiliations with pop artists, producers and fashion designers. In the case of 'Judas' she has acknowledged Bruce Springsteen's 'rock n' roll/metal sound [*sic*]' despite the dance track's 'hardcore upbeat'.[11] The influence of other artists abounds in all her songs: Madonna, Freddie Mercury, Whitney Houston, Iron Maiden, Kiss, Queen, TLC, Pat Benatar, and En Vogue. Perhaps of relevance here is the idea of recycling, and the inextricable bonds that exist between a constructed subjectivity and music production. If autonomy is a crucial aspect in the selling power of an artist, Lady Gaga's identity is marketed through the channels of state-of-the-art music technology. Notably, the glossy production of 'Judas' is mirrored in other hits, such as 'Bad Romance', 'Poker Face', and 'LoveGame'. Lady Gaga's inclination towards highly processed tracks discloses her role as producer, and, as I read it, this is one of her trump cards as she re-negotiates the female's presence in the pop industry.[12]

As I am suggesting, countless details characterize Lady Gaga's musical expression, with her tracks slotting into an audio space that is hyperbolic: exaggerated melodic hooks, monstrous bass lines, infectious rhythmic riffs, lavish arrangements, and catchy chord progressions. In compositional terms, embellishments make a song's arrangement effervescent, with a barrage of effects designed to titillate and energize the listener. One might describe the effect of this as *sonic bombardment*, emanating from the rapid stacking up of ideas that define Gaga's signature. Take the juxtapositioning of her voice (in all its guises) in the recording: through the details of processing, the voice distils a vibrant sonic image that is captivating. Certainly, vocal multidimensionality is rendered possible by digital technology, a prime signifier of production that is contingent on processes, such as pitch shifting, compression, echo and reverb, flanging, and panning.

Staging the voice is a major part of the pop production, and in all her songs, Lady Gaga's subjectivity is defined by her unique approach to singing. This is integral to communicating with her fans. As Simon Zagorski-Thomas claims, the spatial function of produced events is closely associated with the ways in which audiences perceive a performer.[13]

Manifested in the idiosyncrasies of compositional production, Lady Gaga's subjectivity is the sum total of creative thinking and collaborative work. RedOne's credits in 'Judas' consist of songwriting, producing, vocal editing, vocal arranging, audio engineering, instrumentation, programming, recording and even backing vocals. In an interview from 2008 with DJ Ron Slomowicz Lady Gaga enthuses:

> RedOne is like the heart and soul of my universe. I met him and he completely, one hundred and fifty thousand percent wrapped his arms around my talent, and it was like we needed to work together. He has been a pioneer for the House [*sic*] of Gaga and his influence on me has been tremendous. I really couldn't have done it without him. He taught me in this [*sic*] own way—even though he's not a writer, he's a producer—he taught me how to be a better writer, because I started to think about melodies in a different way.[14]

RedOne knows what makes Lady Gaga tick and vice versa. In every moment of 'Judas' it is as if his musical ideas converge with hers as they both regulate levels of tension and excitement. There is a sense that with the arrival of the first sixteen-bar chorus musical events reach a plateau; the volume is turned high as the texture changes. Lady Gaga's voice is treated quite differently from its penetrative and monstrous quality in the verse though with a high dose of multi-layering, dynamics, and reverb. In such moments the musical editing works in bold contrast to the verse. Generally speaking, verses need to contrast with choruses in pop, and are regulated by subtleties in production and engineering. Back to the chorus section. Lady Gaga's voice is over-dubbed and juxtaposed with a standard rock groove, which, with all its contours and changes, profiles a strident, regular beat. Built into the formula of this groove are the fine variations in compression, eq-ing, reverb, echo, and so on. A main function of this chorus is to lock the vocal part into the subdivisions of the groove. This involves moving the voice to the fore of the mix as Lady Gaga rides the groove and proclaims her love for Judas, albeit admitting she is just 'a holy fool'. Such compositional devices permeate the Eurosong-type arrangement that thumps out the four-on-the-floor beat as a veritable cliché. Furthermore, the chorus extracts the impassioned tone of an artist, marking an arrival point in the song's storyline. As with choruses from Gaga's other songs, this one functions primarily to brighten up and broaden out the tone. Much of this is down to the employment of chorus-effects and marginal tempo increases, all of which accentuate the electropop idiom. In a track that comes over corny at the same time it is pioneering, Lady Gaga's trajectory is one of humor and self-reflexivity. Quite ingeniously, the meticulous control of audio events fortifies her pop subjectivity, with the polished production operating as a mechanism for shaping glamour.

AUDIOVISUAL PERFORMATIVITY: TRANSGRESSING NORMS

The 'Judas' video is crammed with religious innuendoes, and not surprisingly this sparked off some strong reactions when it was released.[15] Lady Gaga is never Gaga without a good deal of controversy. She knows full well what she wants to get out of her music videos: they have to sell, provoke, and entertain. Besides, they often transgress a range of norms. In the visuals of 'Judas' the storyline is intentionally blurred, with a lurid mix of religion with sex, narcissism, and violence.

The opening scenes are of Lady Gaga as part of a motorcycle gang, comprising Jesus (Rick Gonzalez) as leader and Judas (Norman Reedus) as bad boy. In the role of Mary Magdalene, Lady Gaga is divided in her attraction to both these males. Seated on a bike behind Jesus who wears the crown of thorns (Figure 1.1), she lovingly has her arms placed around him, protective and reassuring. Representing the Twelve Apostles, the motorcycle gang speed down the freeway towards their hideout, the 'Electric Chapel'. Next, Lady Gaga is filmed moving (clothed in a red sarong and bikini top) with a troupe of dancers. While protecting Jesus from the ensuing brawls and his imminent betrayal, she is witness to Judas's arrival at the biker club and his involvement in a fight. Interspersed with scenes of dancing, the action in this scene climaxes with Lady Gaga, ever so camply, pointing a gun to Judas's face out of which a stick of red lipstick slowly protrudes as she smears his face and lips. Her decision not to shoot Judas through the heart is followed by a scene with her in the bath with him and Jesus (Figure 1.2). At this point the breakdown section grinds to a halt as the music is replaced by natural sounds: waves, wind, and white noise. The frame now depicts Lady Gaga washing and cleaning the feet of Jesus and Judas with her hair. This sequence is juxtaposed with a different shot of Lady Gaga standing alone on a rock as waves threaten to cover her. The intertext here is Sandro Botticelli's famous *Birth of Venus* from 1485, which idealizes the voluptuous, pale, blonde goddess of the Italian Renaissance. Botticelli's luxurious lighting, gentle colors, and especially the streaks of gold leaf he highlighted Venus's long flowing hair with are in stark contrast to the crass illumination of Gaga in color tones of hard blue, grey, white and black. Whereas Gaga is perched on a dangerous rocky cliff, which threatens to collapse under a forceful rush of water, Venus is mounted on a giant seashell, in classical antiquity a metaphor for the female vulva.

Before the music commences again, the scene shifts to Jesus walking towards his destiny. This frame then dissolves back to the bathtub, with Judas throwing beer into it. What follows is a shot of Jesus surrounded by his disciples with Lady Gaga kneeling before him, his hand placed on her head. Judas, annoyed, diverts his gaze. It is in the next frames that Judas delivers the fateful kiss on both cheeks of Jesus in a lingering and sensual moment that is nothing less than homoerotic. Like a rag doll, Lady Gaga crumbles to the floor dressed in a Lacroix bridal dress, with gloves, black and white creepers, and a crown. This final scene could hardly be more over-the-top.

Figure 1.1   Lady Gaga with Jesus (Judas to the right behind).

Figure 1.2   Anointing the feet of Judas and Jesus.

The visual sequence of events holds a vital clue to what impressions of the music are intended. The numerous layers of this video accentuate the vitality and diversity of a performance that is all about the self-fashioning of the pop artist. The tactics of engineering and design that assemble such an iconic look can be interpreted in relation to existing cultural conventions. There is evidence enough that Lady Gaga draws on a rich array of stylistic influences to play out the diverse range of characters in the narratives of each of her songs. As well as the choice of musical style, substantial effort is invested into the details of the roles she adopts in terms of appearance and mannerism. Because her characters are implicated in the roles of protagonist or narrator in every one of her songs, she chooses to change her stage persona from the context of one video or live production to the next. Attention to make-up, coiffure, costume, and accessories is meticulously complemented by the physical markers of dance, gesture and facial expression. These switches in appearance are of key importance in understanding Lady Gaga. Although something in her persona remains constant, her portrayal of different characters is what audiences have come to expect.

When it comes to a consideration of gender politics I would suggest that Lady Gaga turns to drag.[16] As one of the central ingredients of pop, drag often connotes rebellion and political disorder. Strategically, drag creates distance between the pop singer's personality and her performance 'act'. There is little doubt that Lady Gaga resists and, moreover, ridicules the structures that normalize gender and sexuality in society. Turning to drag, her 'womanliness' is sized up against the male gaze, as she sides with the male drag artist. Knowingly, she parodies femininity through a line of attack, which, as psychoanalyst Joan Riviere insists, demonstrates that women can 'avert anxiety and retribution from men'.[17] Lady Gaga's construction of femininity threatens by exaggerating stereotypes, which, arguably, becomes a strategy for embodying the maternal and nurturing her monsters.

The point I am arriving at is that Lady Gaga's performances expose the erroneous quality of gender by destabilizing its binary alignment. As *femme fatale* she makes genderplay her boldest intention. Teasing mannerisms can be construed as subversive and, as Judith Butler has insisted, genderplay repudiates power structures by ridiculing the normativity of cultural expressions. This is why gendered representations are politically strategic; they are about repetition, a copy of a copy that, as Butler claims, does not presuppose an original. Gender therefore implies performativity in progress; it shapes the subjectivity it aspires to.

Lady Gaga's gendered performance amounts to something complex and multifaceted. She prompts new ways of experiencing parody through musical expression. To delve into this a little further: the unity between her brand of feminism and her fans' solidarity can be read as a threat to sexism and homophobia. Choosing to parody the drag queen undeniably advocates a set of sexual politics. In a sense this activates a vision of the carnival of the oppressed. The distinction between appearance and reality is full of twists and turns in pop texts, with drag muddying the picture. The category of *woman* put on display can function convincingly as a transgressive category whereby femininity is parodied. If drag highlights the ambiguities of gender binaries, it also makes the female body politically pertinent. This is borne out by Lady Gaga's brand of femininity, which signifies a transgressive move that is often uncompromising. It is common knowledge that media coverage is rife with speculations about her biological sex; is she, some have even asked, indeed a 'female'? To date her most biting response is epitomized in a notorious appearance at the MTV Awards in 2011, where dressed as her fictional male alter ego, Jo Calderone, she yelled out: 'She left me! She said it always starts out good and then the guys—meaning me, I'm one of the guys . . . we get crazy. I did, I got crazy. But she's fucking crazy too, right?' Fans and critics alike were aghast.[18]

Troubling gender norms through drag, Lady Gaga becomes Jo Calderone to undermine the heterosexual matrix. By mocking the male/female binary distinction, she exposes the precarious fault lines of gender duality. I would argue that such a degree of reflexivity is necessary for camp to function. Closely aligned to the strategies of drag, camp is contingent on the juxtapositions and transformations of norms. Theorizing camp in recent years has been influenced greatly by Butler's model of gender performativity and Susan Sontag's seminal essay, 'Notes on "Camp"' (1964).[19] In the 'Judas' video performance and mannerism transport all the accoutrements of camp. The trademark of the Haus of Gaga, based upon the concept of Andy Warhol's Factory, is the combined efforts of a team of creative people from all over the world. Proof is in Lady Gaga's clothes, make-up and accessories in 'Judas': a purple silk cape (by Perry Meek) worn with an ornate bejewelled crown and jewellery pieces by Erickson Beamon; nail art designed by Aya Fukuda; an all red outfit with velvet bra and panties, topped with a flowing skirt (by Raquel Allegra) and red boots; a lavish black corseted jacket and white dress; black bra and panties, leather jacket (by Schott) and tights (by Carpezio) and laced tight-boots (by Alexander McQueen); a blue leather outfit (by Alex Noble); black catsuit and head-piece (by Perry Meek), red faux fur (by Adrienne Landau), with a big cross ring (by The Dragon Lady); a long golden gown (by Sally LaPointe); a gold Versace bracelet; a white Christian Lacroix wedding dress with crown (by Erik Halley), gloves (by Lacrasia) and black and white creepers (by Underground). Thoroughly over-ornate, the fashioning of her attire helps extract the song's narrative.[20]

Lady Gaga's campness is grounded in her being-as-acting-out-a-role, something that distances her from the very stereotypes she appropriates. Wittingly, she makes blatant the point that gender roles are all a charade. Yet, her enactment of the pop celebrity, especially through drag, does not quite eliminate the problematics of traditional sex-roles. Rather it unsettles the stereotypes within a particular social context though musical performance. In her discussion of camp (through fascinating readings of Liza Minnelli and Liberace), Freya Jarman-Ivens asks 'to what extent do we read these performances as camp because of the contexts in which they exist?';[21] identifying camp in music reveals no separation between the textual, contextual and performance elements. Lady Gaga's propensity for undermining social conventions draws attention to the actual construction of her performance. In other words, her strategies of performance are bound up in structures of narrativity. So, what types of emotions are triggered in 'Judas'? What of the depiction of Mary Magdalene and the blasphemous tirades against Christianity? And how is an ironic-tragic narrative invoked?

Camp display in 'Judas' arises from a vocabulary of elaborate production, fakery and 'low brow', where the artificiality of putting on an act winks at normality. In Jarman-Ivens's opinion it is in 'camp's relation to popular culture that it is at its cleverest'. Camp seeps in as 'valueless' while at the same time 'presenting a parodic challenge' to a wide range of norms.[22] With this, I want to turn to the body and how it is encoded as camp.

In the dance sequences of 'Judas' Lady Gaga's movements are clunky and quite distinguishable from mainstream divas, such as Madonna, Britney Spears, Beyoncé, Rihanna, and Shakira. Above all, her way of dancing is exhibited through a repertoire of movements that mirror her own ideas of personhood. For example, her technique of 'vogueing' is a prime marker of this type of sensibility, which, as I read it, is linked to camp. In her study of Cher, Kay Dickinson has pointed out how camp 'has always been about making do within the mainstream, twisting it, adoring aspects of it regardless, wobbling its more restrictive meanings'.[23] Similarly, Andrew Ross has argued that camp is often enjoyed at the expense of others: 'this is largely because camp's excess of pleasure, finally, has very little to do with the (un)controlled hedonism of a consumer; it is the work of a producer of taste, and "taste" is only possible through exclusion *and* depreciation'.[24] The borderline between political appeal and characteristics of social preference, as Ross insists, often 'joins forces in the fully commercialized forms of bad taste'.[25] Lady Gaga exemplifies this wonderfully by exposing the fantasies of pop culture through the motions of dance. These she accesses through the festivities of the body in dance, hinting at a utopian world. In the 'Judas' video there is a sense that she subverts conservative values by showing us that traditions, norms and religious narratives are not without their contradictions and prejudices. Historically, the carnivalesque, which involves all types of dance, has been greeted in certain circles with condemnation and chastisement. As with Madonna, provoking harsh reactions is one of Lady Gaga's main missions. In the video of 'Judas' one of the Bible's most profound stories is re-historicized to disclose that identities are deeply rooted in (un)truths and signs of (in)stability. Treading a fine line between camp and vulnerability, Lady Gaga marches in as a chief ambassador of pop culture.

CAMP AND THE GROTESQUE

Grotesque bodies are nothing new in popular culture. Throughout history representations of abject excess have destabilized normative codes in ways that vent hostility as much as enjoyment. Inscriptions of the glamorously grotesque body often carry with them the trademark of camp. In pop genderplay is found in female camp icons, such as Grace Jones, Eartha Kitt, k.d. lang, Dusty Springfield, Tina Turner, Annie Lennox and others. Since the late twentieth century camp has emerged as one of the favorite options for performativity in pop. On what basis then is camp expressed in any given context, and how is this received? On first glance, Lady Gaga's resistance to heteronormativity promotes solidarity with the Other: her camp sensibility functions as a prime constituent of her act. In the entertainment industry, elements of social consciousness and moral authority negotiate the merits of a disposable culture. As Ross puts it, 'camp is a rediscovery of history's waste';[26] it liberates the past and re-creates surplus value.

So far I have been suggesting that musical expression is integral to understanding how camp operates in a pop song. Given that recordings reproduce the artist in ways unattainable outside the studio, the pop performance is quite extraordinary.[27] The recorded voice is dependent on a range of technological considerations, such as the choice of microphones, eq-ing, compression, reverb, overdubbing and so on. Production techniques contribute considerably in shaping vocal timbre and texture and playing with sonic imagery. Often overstated and extravagant, Lady Gaga's vocality mediates a spectacle that is provocative at the same time it is contrived and excessive.

Eloquently phrased tessitura in melodies work in ways that are hyperbolic. Virtuosic vocal posturing articulates Lady Gaga's ideals: her voice is mocking, embodying the theatrics of her act. This reinforces the idiosyncrasies of her audio signature. Here I am referring to the minute characteristics that instantly make an artist and producer identifiable. How Lady Gaga revisits any number of strategies from one song to the next is through her voice. Wordplay and reiteration of vowels and consonants are discernible in all her tracks, regularly used to signal attitude and temperament. In addition to her enunciation of Judas ('Juda-a-a-as'), exclamations, such as 'oh-o-o-o' and 'ah-a-a-a' are highly charged. With a disco-driven energy, Lady Gaga capitalizes on a spectrum of affected mannerisms and witty banter. Indeed her vocal *manière* stages her role as a disco queen, and musically, this is what enables her to upset a stack of appellations.

In earlier studies I have theorized the correspondence between musical codes, authenticity, and gendered performance, which evoke empathic response on the part of the fans.[28] Worth stressing is artificiality, a main ingredient of Gaga's stylization. Keen to dwell on this point, I want to consider a number of the elements that mediate this. In order for her to 'play out herself', her vocal production needs to individualize her in a convincing manner. A prime task of the pop artist is therefore to win over our aural senses. The seductive tug of the fan into her world thus becomes a prime objective. As aesthete Lady Gaga seduces us through glamorous intent and playfulness. By this I am referring to tactics that designate the glamour of authorship. Made expressive through language, gender, ethnicity and nationality, the highly produced voice makes public its origins. The sung voice is therefore central to any inquiry into stylization.

Born and brought up in New York and attending the Tisch School of the Arts, she made a decision to pursue a musical career. By 2007 she had signed with Streamline Records, one year before the release of her debut album *The Fame*. The singles 'Poker Face' and 'Just Dance' helped make this album an international success, one that was quickly followed by the 2009 album *The Fame Monster*, with hits, 'Alejandro', 'Telephone', and 'Bad Romance'. This album would express many of Lady Gaga's sentiments through a monster metaphor that she exploited in her *Monster Ball Tour*. And with the release of *Born This Way*, in 2011, featuring tracks such as 'Judas', she would demonstrate that musical versatility (as her critics have claimed) is about being crazy, audacious, and extravagant. The experimental dimension of her performance act is rooted in a neo-burlesque style that draws on parody, travesty and caricature (through go-go dancing to striptease). The aspects of glamour linked to American burlesque are dance-oriented and racy, and in all her videos at the time of writing this chapter she flaunts her sexuality with a defiance that is ironic. What stands out in her constructed look is an aesthetic that borders on the monstrous and grotesque. Narcissistically she uses performance to challenge a set of norms. In this way her aesthetic goes some way in opposing normative representations of feminine beauty. Lady Gaga also panders to the queer fan by reveling in the delights of being a 'fag-hag'. Her mode of camp embraces a rich vocabulary for self-description, and is exploitative and stylized for commercial gain. Illustrative of this is her coinage of the term *retrosexual*:

> Retrosexual—I came out with that a long time ago. Me and my buddy Tom were hanging out one day in the studio and we were talking about metrosexuals, because he had bought a pair of boots and I said 'Those are very metrosexual'. And he was like 'I don't know, I think they're kind of retro'. And I said 'So you're retrosexual'. It was a kind of a joke. The more I thought about it—I'm so obsessed with things retro, the 70s and 80s. I don't know, that word just kind of flew out of my mouth one day, and stuck with me. I often do that—I coin terms, they'll become like the centerfold of my entire project or an entire record.[29]

If a retro-style defines her personality, look, sexuality and gender, this then suggests a set of politics that raise the issue of recycling. How then does this inscribe her identity? On the matter of retrosexuality, Camille Paglia declares that in Gaga we have the 'death of sex'. Paglia describes her as the world's first massive internet icon: 'despite showing acres of pallid flesh in the fetish-bondage garb of urban prostitution, Gaga isn't sexy at all—she's like a gangly marionette or plasticized android'.[30] Paglia probes at Lady Gaga's over-conceptualized identity and absence of 'genuine eroticism', something that signals the end of the sexual revolution, hence the death of sex. In particular, Paglia picks up on Lady Gaga's limited repertoire of facial expressions, which 'repeatedly thrust that blank, lugubrious face at the camera and us; it's creepy and coercive'. While artists like Madonna and Marlene Dietrich might have suggested something pansexual, 'Gaga, for all her writhing and posturing, is asexual' rather than retrosexual. This type of sexual dysfunctionality, Paglia argues, signifies a 'trend towards mutilation and death'. Paglia subsequently turns to Lady Gaga's voice:

> Generation Gaga doesn't identify with powerful vocal styles because their own voices have atrophied: they communicate mutely via a constant stream of atomised, telegraphic text messages. Gaga's flat affect doesn't bother them because they're not attuned to facial expressions.

From a pop musicologist's standpoint, Paglia is quite off the mark in her disparaging assertions of the voice. Conversely, I would argue that Lady Gaga's vocal affect is made potent by its highly produced effect: it is neither 'flat' nor powerless. Rather she possesses a dramatic *contralto* voice that brims with emotion and heartfelt sentiment.[31] Furthermore, Lady Gaga's low tessitura is made palpable through a distinct approach to delivery that is well equipped to perform dramatically. This voice type is rendered capable through a strong, raucous mid-register, where there is a tendency to oscillate between *natural* and *artificial*-sounding timbres. In 'Judas' different variants of her voice are executed through melodies that range from the mechanically distant to the warm and close. This is how Lady Gaga's vocality is made dramatic and in continuous flux.

Returning to Paglia's assertions, one should not underestimate the aesthetic choices of vocal morphology in pop, which involve masking, foregrounding, chorusing, panning, and instrumental location. As I have already pointed out, the spatial placement of the voice in the recording of 'Judas' is maintained by meticulous production and engineering devices that extract the artist's timbre. What is important here is how vocal timbre conforms to stylistic norms and expressive function along a song's durational continuum. This becomes apparent in the verse sections of the song, where the rock style prompts harsh half-sung, half-rapped melodic phrasing. The melody has a menacing quality, consisting of only one single pitch (F) in the singer's low register. Enhancing this is Lady Gaga's put-on Jamaican *patois* accent (only used in the verses when she half-raps). This alone prompts various interpretations, as all the blog sites on 'Judas' verify. There can be little doubt that Lady Gaga consciously turns to the cultural associations of this accent when importing it into her performance. More correctly described as a *creole* language, Jamaican *patois* is derived from the native languages of the Caribbean, such as Spanish, Portuguese, Hindi, Arawak, Irish, as well as African and English languages. From Old French, mid-seventeenth century, *patois* relates to 'rustic speech' and stems from the verb *patoier*, to handle something awkwardly. Given Lady Gaga's deliberate (if not awkward) use of this in her verses, one might consider her solidarity with the Other through identification with an English that is not her own. Connotations of uneducated or broken speech in the use of this form, provides Lady Gaga recourse to evaluating her ethnicity and nationality. Arguably, the effect of appropriating Jamaican *patois* is contrived and crass. Notably, in popular culture, this *patois* is present in mainstream films, such as *Pirates of the Caribbean: Dead Man's Chest* and *Meet Joe Black*, and Jamaican films, *The Harder They Come* and *Rockers*, where much of the dialogue has been subtitled in English.

In appropriating this accent, Lady Gaga enhances the snarling quality in her vocal expression during all the verses, which works in stark contrast to the sugary and demure vocalizations of the choruses (laced by her natural American accent). Timbral fluctuations are not solely down to the production, but also Lady Gaga's style of vocal articulation and ornamentation. A thin divide therefore exists between what is 'produced' and what is 'naturally sounding' in her tracks. For instance, in the verses of 'Judas' an inflated use of instrumentation in the arrangement bolsters her tone. Distorted guitars and 'fat' synthesizer lines in unison produce a sound that is foreboding the same it is dirty. The function of this is to accentuate the contrapuntal activity between Lady Gaga's part and the more melodic bass phrase that drives her voice. Her melody here is more characteristic of a bass line than a vocal line. From this it would seem that the desired effect is one of highlighting the vocal and instrumental lines as two competing melodic strands.

All instruments are recorded in a similar dynamic range to Lady Gaga's voice, meaning that the effect of her bursting into a sonorous angular melody in the next section (the Europop chorus) forms a dramatic contrast; such techniques disseminate the gist of the storyline. The objective is to situate the voice within the mix in ways that create interest and focus attention on the lyrics. Regulating depth when it comes to vocal placement is significant in most pop productions. The central aspect of depth is to do with the movement of sound within a given space and time duration. In comprehending depth there is also the matter of distance, which has a major impact on the sense of performance environment. Usefully, Allan Moore identifies the difference between depth and distance: *distance* is the distance between the 'front' of a sound-source and a listener, while *depth* acknowledges that there can be a 'back' to that sound-source, and the difference between front and back delivers depth'.[32] Moore makes the observation that, while locations of sound within the audio image are relatively mobile during the course of a track, 'sounds move far less than the technology enables'.[33] This is particularly evident in the voice's mobility within a mix, where the sense of spatiality, especially in terms of depth and distance, can be deceptive. Lady Gaga's voice is located at variable distances and depths within and between the sections of the song; during the chorus it is more at the fore of the mix than in the other sections, and its constant movement is subtle in variations. On close inspection, vocal placement becomes instructive as it discloses the intentions of the production team and performer. Creativity in in the control of sonic movement and location, as much as timbral and textural change, help defines Lady Gaga's presence in the mix.

In sum, the aesthetics of the 'Judas' video are about flaunting the grotesque female. Historically, as Julia Kristeva has noted, capable women do not easily escape the category of grotesque:

> And there you have the music just as she is after two thousand years of art and religion. A muse in the true tradition of the lowly genres—apocalyptic, Menippean, and carnivalesque. The pitiful power of the feminine, however, be it drive or murder, is in fact unleashed only with the help of masculine degradation or bankruptcy—a bankruptcy of the father and manly authority.[34]

Kristeva's astute reading of the role of the grotesque female verifies that the fear of emasculation is omnipotent, one of the reasons why abomination persists. Judgment prevails over the wretched representation of the woman who seeks inspiration from an imbalance that traditionally requires correction. For example, by exhibiting the monstrous aspects of femininity that foreground the strange, ugly and absurd in extraordinary ways, Lady Gaga releases a subversive energy. Her act becomes a tool for dramatizing the fallen man and triumph of the female temptress. Artfully, she alludes to being one of Jesus's groupies through an ironic take on the suffering Magdalene. Yet her iconography is based around a tradition of monstrous femininity that is regarded by many as deceitful, gruesome and erotic. Dark fantasy allows her to discover the tensions between disciples and masters in an environment that is patriarchal. The narrative of betrayal therefore signals an ongoing dialogue with patriarchy through the plurality of her voices.

As with the details of her sound production, her visual display shifts its textural tone continuously: from the foreground to the margin, sideways, backwards, and then to the front again. Audio and visual production helps stage the master narrative of 'Judas' through the rhetoric of Lady Gaga's take on Christianity. Blasphemously, her representation of divinity heightens suspicion, and her positioning alongside Christ and Judas in the secular context of the pop video symbolizes the wretchedness of the 'good and natural'. It is creative impudence of this kind that fuels the enormous fanbase that has grown up around her.

CONCLUSION

Lady Gaga's flight of fancy in 'Judas' entails a soaring of the imagination. Of course, any suggestion of a dialogue between Jesus and Judas is a daydream, and this is something she knows that we know is far-fetched. But all this is pulled off in the name of entertainment. This happens through a build up in empathy between performer and fan. Lady Gaga's style of entertaining is endemic to an over-stylized enactment of the performer; she provides the paradigm of an aesthetic that typifies pop music culture. A pre-condition of her aesthetic is that of full absorption, of all the sentiments and experiences that entice and delight through musical expression. It is from the vantage point that she administers her role as pop diva. Within the confines of her sophisticated productions, the song 'Judas' belongs to the listener in the present (on every new listening) while to her in the past.

The produced voice, as I have argued, connotes something tangible and intimate even though it is illusory. Camp, an integral part of the Gaga construction, permits the fan access into an extraordinary persona that revels in a sensibility that is ostentatious and frivolous. Cunningly, she tempts her audience into her world, audibly and visually, playing upon every second of her detailed performances to keep us on hold. Her sophisticated display, her *je ne sais quoi*, suggests denial and subversion through her various roles. In the end, 'Judas' mobilizes a wide range of sentiments that are gender coded in different representations of masculinity and femininity that are only decipherable through the listener. Experiencing a song is based upon the singer's self-positioning, which, in the case of Lady Gaga, occurs through a mode of address that reasserts her ego.

Finally, 'Judas' is an edgy story of sexual jealousy, betrayal, and revenge, doused with the colorations of electropop. Through eroticized vocal display Lady Gaga vows to bring her ex-lover 'down, down, down'. A taunting of patriarchy is initiated through narcissistic desire and humorous intent, which is acquired through the sound of her many voices. Everything builds up in 'Judas' to the extended instrumental dance-break, where the voice suddenly drops out. In such moments its absence mirrors the listener's own fragility. As a lifeline between the pop artist and fan, the voice is guarantor of security, intimacy and centeredness. It mediates a story by a person who is narrator the same time she is protagonist.

By recounting an untamed tale, Lady Gaga's omniscience is empowering and audacious. Much of this boils down to the musical production, which becomes an enunciation for the biblical content of 'Judas'. As I have pointed out, the diegetics of technical production construct a concept of who Lady Gaga actually wants to be in the time-scale of a four-minute song. The pleasure derived from this brings fans in touch with her sensuousness and a brazen passion that confirms an idealized construction, a self-image that consistently alludes to the exciting possibility of transformation. Knowing that musical performances prompt all sorts of identification, Lady Gaga strives to deliver on every song, video, album or concert. She understands that the prerequisite of a polished performance, after all, is to convince the fan who the artist is, and a lot more.

NOTES

1. Compare Richard Dyer's discussion of Judy Garland's camp aesthetic through appearance and gesture in his *Heavenly Bodies: Film Stars and Society*, 2nd edition (New York, NY: Routledge, 2004).

2. Philip Auslander, 'Musical Persona: The Physical Performance of Popular Music', in Derek Scott (ed.), *The Ashgate Research Companion to Popular Musicology*, (Farnham: Ashgate, 2009), 308.

3. See Lucy Green, *Music on Deaf Ears* (Manchester: Manchester University Press, 1988).

4. For a study of different kinds of sonic space in actual or abstract spatial environments, see Ragnhild Brøvig-Hanssen and Anne Danielsen's 'The Naturalised and the Surreal: Changes in the Perception of Popular Music, *Organised Sound*, vol. 18, no. 1 (April 2013), 71–80. In this article, attention is also given to the 'vocal space', where what is perceived as naturalized is not necessarily the case. Experiences of sound can be both surreal and naturalized simultaneously.

5. Stan Hawkins, *The British Pop Dandy: Masculinity, Popular Music and Culture* (Farnham: Ashgate, 2009), 85.

6. See Stan Hawkins, *Settling the Pop Score: Pop Texts and Identity Politics* (Aldershot: Ashgate, 2002).

7. 'Lady Gaga's Producer Says "Judas" is "The Holy Grail": The MTV News Quote of the Day' (online at: http://newsroom.mtv.com/2011/03/01/lady-gaga-born-this-way-single-judas/) <accessed: 29 August 2012>.

8. Nadir Khayat (known as RedOne) was born in Tétouan, Morocco, in 1970. He moved to Sweden when 19, and has established a career as one of the most famous producers of his generation, writing and producing hits with Jennifer Lopez, Nicki Minaj, Porcelain Black, Pitbull, Enrique Iglesias, Shakira, and many others.

9. This term relates to a concept of space introduced by Moylan, where the geometry and dimensions of the performance space are static while the features of a song unfold (see William Moylan, 'Considering Space in Recorded Music' in *The Art of Record Production*, ed. Simon Frith and Simon Zagorski-Thomas (Farnham: Ashgate, 2012), 179–180).

10. *Ibid.*, 164.

11. See the entry for 'Judas' in the online *Gagapedia* (online at: http://ladygaga.wikia.com/wiki/Judas_%28song%29)<accessed: 30 August 2012>.

12. For a detailed discussion of the female artist/producers role in popular music since the 1950s, see the section I edited in Sheila Whiteley, Andy Bennett, and Stan Hawkins (eds.), *Music, Space and Place: Popular Music and Cultural Identity* (Aldershot: Ashgate, 2004), with contributions from Jacqueline Warwick, Emma Mayhew, and Kay Dickinson. This deals specifically with gender divisions in creative labor, and the politics surrounding the positioning of the male producer and female pop artist.

13. Simon Zagorski-Thomas, 'The Stadium in Your Bedroom: Functional Staging, Authenticity and the Audience-led Aesthetic in Record Production', *Popular Music*, vol. 29, no. 2 (May 2010), 257–258.

14. Ron Slomowicz, 'Lady Gaga Interview—Interview with Lady Gaga' (online at: http://dancemusic.about.com/od/artistshomepages/a/LadyGagaInt.htm) <accessed: 11 September 2012>.

15. See, for example, 'Lady Gaga dresses as Mary Magdalene and Takes a Bike Ride with Jesus Christ in 'Blasphemous' New Video for Judas Single', *Mail Online*, 6 May 2011 (online at: http://www.dailymail.co.uk/tvshowbiz/article-1384131/Lady-Gaga-Judas-video-Star-dresses-Mary-Magdalene-rides-bike-Jesus-Christ.html) <accessed 5 October 2012>.

16. See Stan Hawkins, 'Dragging Out Camp: Narrative Agendas in Madonna's Musical Production', in *Madonna's Drowned Worlds: New Approaches to Her Cultural Transformations, 1983–2003*, ed. S. Fouz-Hernández and F. Jarman-Ivens (Aldershot, Ashgate, 2004), 3–21, as well as Gray and Rutnam in this volume.

17. Joan Riviere, 'Womanliness as a Masquerade', in Henrik M. Ruitenbeek (ed.), *Psychoanalysis and Female Sexuality* (New Haven, CT: College and University Press, 1966), 210.
18. See, especially, Geller in this volume, as well as Gray and Rutnam.
19. See Judith Butler, *Gender Trouble: Feminism and the Subversion of Identity*, 2nd edition (London: Routledge, 1999) and Susan Sontag, 'Notes on "Camp"', *Against Interpretation and Other Essays* (New York, NY: Anchor 1990 [1964]), 275–292.
20. See Gray and Rutnam in this volume.
21. Freya Jarman-Ivens, 'Notes on Musical Camp', in Derek Scott (ed.) *The Ashgate Research Companion to Popular Musicology* (Farnham: Ashgate, 2009), 202.
22. *Ibid.*, 193.
23. Kay Dickinson, '"Believe?": Vocoders, Digitalized Female Identity, and Camp', *Popular Music*, vol. 20, no. 3 (October 2001), 345.
24. Andrew Ross, 'Uses of Camp', in Fabio Cleto (ed.), *Camp: Queer Aesthetics and the Performing Subject: A Reader* (Edinburgh: Edinburgh University Press, 1999), 322. (Ross's emphasis.)
25. *Ibid.*
26. *Ibid.*, 320.
27. This is debated thoroughly in an investigation of Prince's musical performativity and aesthetics by Sarah Niblock and Stan Hawkins (*Prince: The Making of a Pop Music Phenomenon* (Farnham: Ashgate, 2011). In this study we contemplate the skills invested into the studio production that transfer into live events, which uncover issues of mannerism and musicianship.
28. See Hawkins, *Settling the Pop Score* and *The British Pop Dandy*.
29. Slomowicz, 'Lady Gaga Interview'.
30. Camille Paglia, 'Lady Gaga and the Death of Sex', *The Sunday Times* (12 September 2010) (online at: http://www.thesundaytimes.co.uk/sto/public/magazine/article389697.ece) <accessed: 6 May 2012>).
31. The contralto voice is the lowest of the female singing voices, extending from the F below middle C (F3) to the second G above middle C (G5). Of course the voice can reach extreme points outside this range. It is worth stressing that there are contralto voices that are lighter than that of Lady Gaga, where the range is higher and extensive coloratura on high notes is sustainable.
32. Allan F. Moore, *Song Means: Analysing and Interpreting Recorded Popular Song* (Farnham: Ashgate, 2012), 37.
33. *Ibid.*, 38.
34. Julia Kristeva, *Powers of Horror: An Essay On Abjection*, trans. Leon S. Roudiez (New York, NY: Columbia University Press, 1982 [1980]), 169.

2 Not a Piece of Meat

Lady Gaga and *that* Dress. Has Radical Feminism Survived the Journey?

Lucy O'Brien

In 1980 the counterculture rock critic Lester Bangs wrote, rather uncharitably, about Debbie Harry:

> If most guys in America could somehow get their fave-rave poster girl in bed and have total licence to do whatever they wanted with this legendary body for one afternoon, at least 75 per cent [. . .] would elect to beat her up. She may be up there all high and mighty on TV, but everybody knows that underneath all that fashion plating she's just a piece of meat like all the rest of them.[1]

Bangs highlighted the fact that despite a new-found independence female pop performers were subject to misogyny; that despite 1960s rock n' roll, punk, and women's liberation, Debbie Harry was still considered 'just a piece of meat.' Although since then artists as varied as Chrissie Hynde, Madonna, Bjork, M.I.A., Missy Elliott, Adele, and Lily Allen have exercised considerable control over their careers. There is a persistent music industry presumption that a woman has to turn herself into a sexual object to succeed.

Thirty years after Lester Bangs' observation, Lady Gaga echoed this theme with one of her most memorable images to date: the meat dress. She appeared at the 2010 MTV Video Music Awards wearing a Franc Fernandez dress cut together from slabs of raw meat. This outfit echoed the controversial meat bikini she had worn a few months earlier for the cover of Japanese *Vogue*. As a daring and visceral visual effect, it could have made a powerful feminist statement, but Gaga diluted its impact by giving a muddled message afterwards.

When interviewed by Ellen DeGeneres, Gaga said that her meat dress was a political statement, mainly in support of gay US soldiers who had been discharged due to the 'Don't Ask, Don't Tell' policy. She also referred to animal rights, saying: 'It's certainly no disrespect to anyone that's vegetarian. It has many interpretations, but for me this evening it's, "If we don't stand up for what we believe in [. . .] pretty soon we're gonna have as much rights as the meat on our bones". And,' she added, almost as an afterthought, 'We're not just a piece of meat'.[2]

Once Gaga was asked on an Australian talk show what qualities she most looked for in a man. 'A big dick,' she replied, unsmiling.[3] If she had said, '[w]e're not just a piece of meat' with the same confidence and lack of ambiguity then she would have become a true feminist heroine. The shock art concepts that drive her visual presentation, the beautiful couture meat dress allied with a strong anti-pornography slogan almost 1970s style in its radicalism, all this would have upset her record company, her sponsors, and the music industry as a whole. In one fell swoop Gaga could have destabilized the cozy hypersexualized relationship that the music industry and its female stars have developed over the last decade.

The meat dress symbolized consumption of the female body in the popular media and entertainment. Instead of capitalizing on the semiotic strength of the meat dress, Gaga dissipated it and lost an opportunity. Like Woody Allen's character Zelig, she has a protean ability to adjust her persona and her message to appeal to different cultures and markets. On *The Ellen DeGeneres Show*, she forefronted a gay issue while at the same time signaling support for animal rights campaigners, feminists and mischief-makers in general. This raises the question of whether Gaga's interview was a strategy influenced as much by a market-driven ethos as personal belief. There is a history of radical imagery being appropriated for the commercial market, whether it's Zandra Rhodes on a late 1970s catwalk with bejeweled safety pins and delicately torn evening dress or corporations such as Nike, Sprite or Diesel approaching Culture Jammers and Adbusters and offering lucrative contracts in return for partaking in ironic promotional campaigns.[4] If Gaga wore the meat dress for general notoriety or a risqué marketing tool rather than with one specific protest message, her stance was a reactionary one. There is a confusion of ideas around what could have been a seismic pop moment. *Time* magazine named the dress the Fashion Statement of 2010, but punk artist Linder Sterling was less impressed: 'Feminist history isn't just a dressing-up box. Feigned cultural amnesia is never very attractive,' she remarked.[5]

Thirty years earlier when she was lead singer with punk band Ludus, Linder covered herself in meat entrails and performed onstage at Manchester's Hacienda: 'At the Hacienda they were showing lots of soft porn and they thought it was really cool. I took my revenge. I got meat from a Chinese restaurant, all the discarded entrails. I went to a sex shop and bought a large dildo.' Just before the show she and some female friends decorated the club, tying tampons to balconies and handing out to the crowd giblets wrapped in pornography. 'The Hacienda was still this male preserve. They were panicking—"It's going to mark the floors", they said.' Then Ludus played the gig with Linder upfront, covered in meat. At a crucial moment she pulled off her skirt to reveal the shiny black dildo: 'I remember the audience going back about three foot. There was hardly any applause. And that was a crowd who thought, "nothing can shock us, we see porn all the time, we're cool." But even they were stunned.' Through the use of meat and tampons she was showing the reality of womanhood, and with the dildo: 'Here's manhood, the invisible male of pornography. That it can be reduced to this, a thing that sticks out like a toy'.[6]

In 2010 Lady Gaga presented a bowdlerized version of this: instead of raw entrails she wears a high fashion meat dress, and instead of a dildo she sports her pleasuring tool, a glitzy disco stick. Linder's meat outfit was a clear and pointed comment about sexual exploitation. In the 1970s she was exploring as an artist themes of gender and pornography. She designed album covers for the Buzzcocks, and made John Heartfield-style photomontages with pornographic images and pictures from *Woman's Realm*. Her graphic montage for the Buzzcocks' 'Orgasm Addict' record cover, for instance, depicting a 'glamour' nude with a household iron for a head and her nipples replaced with gleaming teeth, has become a feminist classic.

Gaga has taken inspiration from many diverse sources, including Linder. According to singer Morrissey, Gaga once had one of Linder's photomontages hung in her dressing room.[7] Gaga situates herself in the pop mainstream as a provocative performance artist, but how much of the original radical message from which she draws is really conveyed? In one way Lady Gaga's meat dress shows how far female pop stars have come: that a woman at the heart of the pop mainstream can display subversive imagery. But does the feminist message survive the journey? Or is the message a more complicated one about women's alienation within postmodern pop?

Linder created some of the most enduring images of punk. Although Gaga says she is influenced by 'shock art' and punk, Linder has argued that current artists presenting a highly commercial version of that movement are not punk's natural descendants. 'The legacy of punk has bred a lot of envy in people who'd like to be pretenders to punk's throne. Punk was never funded and never subsidized. Also, we trusted no one,' she said.[8]

According to art historian and theorist Griselda Pollock, there is an issue of forgetfulness. In an email interview with the author in June 2012 she said: 'I feel that the use of the meat dress without the knowledge of or reference to the artists who had explored this radically in the past makes the gesture empty. There is a problem of forgetfulness and I feel that one of the hallmarks of feminism is a deep awareness of the traditions and cultures of women.'

EATEN ALIVE

In assessing the cultural impact of Gaga's meat dress, it is useful to remember here the rich legacy of feminist artists working with food and issues of the body.

1964:

Carolee Schneemann critiques the misogyny she sees in the art world, using her nude body in her art to challenge notions of gender and representation. First performed in Paris, her piece *Meat Joy* revolved around eight semi-nude dancers playing with raw chicken, cattle organs, sausage, and fish. Improvised like an avant-garde Fluxus-style happening, this piece was described by Schneemann as a Dionysian 'erotic rite' using flesh as material.[9] As art historian Robert C. Morgan observes, Schneemann's work was a proto-feminist exploration of 'the spectrum between eroticism and politics. It is difficult to think of her work as separate from this tension: what is erotic has political significance, and what is political is transformed into the erotic.'[10]

1979:

Judy Chicago lays a dinner table in the San Francisco Museum of Modern Art with thirty-nine ceramic plates decorated with butterfly-vagina sculptures representing female pioneers throughout history. Originally conceived as 'Twenty Five Women Who Were Eaten Alive', her piece is a comment on how women's achievements were eaten up and disappeared in history and the male canon.

1986:

Onstage in Los Angeles Karen Finlay shreds and smears her body with liverwurst, ice cream, and yams. According to Jill Dolan, she offers herself 'already consumed. She appears as refuse from an exchange of sexual power that is completely self-contained. What remains of the body and sexuality has already been digested, processed and regurgitated'.[11]

1987:

Jana Sterbak creates the sculpture, *Vanitas: Flesh Dress for an Albino Anorectic,* a work made out of cured flank steak. The flesh dress is a still life comment on power, sexuality and control. When it was exhibited it was pre-salted to mimic the ageing of the body. After six weeks it hardened rather than decayed, becoming a metaphor for unyielding vanity.

1989:

Helen Chadwick's devises *The Meat Abstracts*, large visceral photographs of meat juxtaposed with leather and fabric that explore desire, lust, identity and humanity. She questions the decorative role of the female body in art, turning it back from a symbol of seduction to raw human flesh.

2010:

Tamara Kosianovsky exhibits *No Guts, No Glory*, artificial slabs of meat hung on butchers' hooks, beautifully sewn and rendered from her own clothes. Some of the carcasses resemble the human form and the emptiness of fashion and vanity, with hour-glass figures that look like dressmakers' dummies.

Even though she delivered a vague message about its meaning when questioned, the imagery of Gaga's meat dress could be seen as part of a feminist tradition commenting on the relationship between female body, food, sexuality and consumption. As Epstein observes, 'actual food acts foreground women's physical bodies in profound ways'.[12] Food use in performance draws attention to women's material reality and physical embodiment. Helen Chadwick's 1977 London show In the Kitchen, a feminist performance/installation, included female friends strapping themselves in a canvas model of a cooker. In 1994, as part of a comic monologue entitled Kentucky Fried, Ann Arbor-based performer Hilary Ramsden gorged herself on McDonalds and Burger King buns as a comment on cultural dislocation of women, eating and fast food consumption. In her 1990 exhibition We Keep Our Victims Ready, Karen Finlay made explicit the connection between women's bodies and meat production with 'Why Can't This Veal Calf Walk', a drawing of a trussed and bound calf. And lesbian performance artist Holly Hughes resisted the notion that women are just 'fuckable meat [. . .] in a consuming sexual economy' when in her 1990 piece World Without End she asked: 'Do you know who you are porking?'[13]

Examined in this cultural context, Gaga's meat dress statement could be seen as a commodification of past feminist ideas, albeit ones gleaned superficially and second hand. Even if Gaga isn't fully clued-up on art history (in an *NME* interview in 2011, for example, she seemed unaware of Orlan, the French artist whose facial modifications are very similar to Gaga's 'Born This Way' look), many of her collaborators come from an art school background. Her long-term stylist Nicola Formichetti, for instance, calls himself an 'art director' rather than a stylist.[14] He went to architecture school in London, worked as Creative Director for Dazed & Confused, and in 2010 became Creative Director of Parisian fashion house MUGLER. Gaga has become Formichetti's muse; he was the one who styled her in a high fashion meat bikini for the cover of Japanese *Vogue*. And it was as a result of the *Vogue* cover that designer Franc Fernandez made her a couture dress out of 50 pounds of sturdy Argentinian steak and built it on a corset. The dress was very heavy, but with the weight distributed around her chest, Gaga said it was very comfortable and sweet smelling. Draped on her curves in an elegant, sensuous way, the dress was matched with bound meat platform shoes.

In describing her dress, the main adjectives used by media critics were 'smart' and 'clever': 'I think it's a commentary on the music industry—no-one buys music anymore, everyone downloads these days, so the only thing about [Gaga] that has any value is her appearance and what she's wearing. She's very, very smart,' said fashion design academic Andrew Groves. Blogger Lori Penny enthused: 'It is all very cleverly done and very calculated. This is a woman in control of herself and her image', while Richard Noble, head of the art department at Goldsmiths College, observed: 'If Lady Gaga really is referencing Sterbak then it's quite a smart thing to do'.[15]

The dress works well within an ironic, high fashion global pop media. It is tasteful and witty: provocative without being too confrontational, and presented as it would be on a commercial catwalk. Epstein's work on food and feminist embodiment is relevant in this instance: 'the body must sell itself for the actor to eat. Bodies must be appetizing, performances in good taste. Thus bodies get packaged [. . .] as consumer desire, consumer sex'.[16]

Gaga is a perfect example of pliable postfeminism. She operates in a pop cultural milieu where it is clumsy to be too literal, where the past has little significance. One of the few influences Gaga comfortably acknowledges is Warhol. She adores Pop Art and has referred to her work as: 'Part pop show, part performance art and part fashion installation'.[17] Her Fame Ball tour was a triumphant show of consumption and regurgitation, described by Gaga as an 'avant-garde-performance-art fashion installation, put in a blender and vomited out as a pop show'.[18] There is a steady traffic of images from underground or performance art into the mainstream, and Gaga, with her Haus of Gaga team, adopt these with an industrious, magpie-like intensity. As Huyssen notes: '"Pop art" is a postmodernist cultural form', one that is 'specific and contingent upon the cultural field in which it operates.'[19]

In this context many argue that it doesn't matter whether Gaga has authorial intention, what's significant is how the audience reads it. However, artistic authenticity is a key part of Gaga's public identity. 'I'm not created,' she maintains. She wants to be culturally relevant and make music that cracks 'some massive historic moment'.[20] In an interview with NME she bristled at the suggestion that she had copied Madonna's song 'Express Yourself' with the melody line of 'Born This Way'. Although her song does sound uncannily like Madonna's, Gaga claimed that the song wasn't a homage. 'When I homage, I fucking homage with a big sign saying I've done it.' She went on to declare: '[I'm] devoted to my identity, devoted to my craft. And if that isn't fucking art I don't know what is'.[21]

Gaga's defensiveness on this issue shows that authorial intention does matter to her. Other musicians she admires acknowledge their sources as a way of enhancing their artistic reputation. Madonna, for instance, has cheerfully referenced (among others) Tamara de Lempicka, Frida Kahlo, Martha Graham, and Georges Bataille, while Bowie drew on Burroughs, and Marilyn Manson has been inspired by David Lynch and Lewis Carroll. There is a contradiction in Gaga declaring herself to be an artist yet showing unawareness of her influences. The question here is whether ideas like the meat dress are Gaga's own and she is hiding her influences, or whether she is a genuinely naïve, instinctive icon molded by her stylists.

Without a fixed meaning, the dress makes sense as part of the postmodern popular culture that John Fiske celebrated in his work on Madonna, the obvious template for Gaga. It creates 'pleasure in the processes of making meanings', liberating and intensifying consuming pleasures.[22] Like Madonna, Gaga's 'cultural populism requires a very nuanced account of [...] relations between cultural markets and cultural products'.[23] She claims subversion while at the same time promoting market forces. There is no disjuncture with her record label, the global conglomerate Interscope. When they signed her back in 2007, the company was so excited by her marketability as an artist they 'threw the building at it.'[24] Gaga's postmodern feminism is femininity as masquerade and Baudrillard-style simulation. As Kaplan argued, there is no essential self and the essential feminine is a cultural construct.[25]

THE DEATH OF HISTORY

Maybe it is wrong to mistake Gaga's individual play as social intervention or any kind of feminism. Her meat dress could therefore be considered part of life's 'plastic possibility [...] undetermined by history'.[26] However, it is problematic when the transmission is blurred. What do her young female audience make of it; does it matter that the message is confused? 'Anything post-Warhol is a pastiche. We're in a pop art culture, artists shouldn't be held to account,' Eva Barlow, a blogger/journalist and Gaga fan, told me in a phone interview in June 2012. 'Having said that, maybe she shouldn't have tried to explain the meat dress. The outfit on its own would have said it'.

However in a pop culture where feminist ideas are often downplayed or devalued Gaga's gesture needs to be interpreted amid a fresh discourse on women as sexual objects. It is interesting that the tropes of feminist art discourse are being resurrected now, albeit in a haphazard form. Amelia Jones writes of a nostalgia for radical 1970s and 1980s feminist art, and a drive to recuperate past activisms.[27] When Gaga wears the meat dress or Rihanna sports a tee-shirt with the slogan 'Cunt Life', they are evoking the feminist debate around 'body as battleground' and the Cuntpower of 1960s counterculture magazine *Oz*.[28] While Gaga's meat dress provides a distant echo of the politics of Schneeman and Sterbak, its significance is lessened when the influence of such artists is unacknowledged. This is a regrettable side effect of the fact that Gaga is a pop act unused to being asked about performance art history.

As Jones argues, gestures like the meat dress appropriate strategies from earlier feminism without the politics: 'The strategies are replicated either without knowing of the earlier models or by knowingly repeating them, but in new contexts in which they do not have the same political effect. The circuits through which images of self-display travel in 2007 are vastly different from those active in the 1970s'.[29] Pollock echoes this view:

> The conditions in which Schneeman was working in the 1960s with the use of her own body and materials is radically different from the post Madonna and post Spice Girls popular music scene. The sexualization of women is far greater now than twenty or forty years ago. Indeed the lack of integration of earlier feminist critique means that women are more subject to the disciplining of the body and sexualization even than when Madonna played with it.[30]

Many established feminist critics are nervous about how the process of consumer capitalism has led to a sense of discontinuity, displacement and decentering of the subject.[31] In this context Gaga's meat dress is a fanciful performance of feminism, a political smorgasbord that includes high camp gay activism and a nod to animal rights. However, it is useful to consider a young audience to whom second-wave feminism is limited by a seemingly simplistic political agenda. Maybe Linder's lumps of meat on the Hacienda dance floor would now be considered too outré and obvious a comment on pornography, and have less resonance to a generation with a sex positive stance and a hyperstimulated sense of media effects.

I would argue that Gaga's work is representative of a paradigm shift, but we won't find it in the meat dress. It is more useful to look at the music and videos contingent with that event. In 2010, at the time of Gaga's appearance at the MTV Awards, her single 'Bad Romance' was a global pop hit. It is the videos and sound of 'Bad Romance' and 'Paparazzi' that Gaga communicates a more nuanced, in-depth comment on female alienation and the music industry today.

GOT MY FLASH ON

Gaga's meat dress symbolizes the body as something to be consumed, the 'piece of meat'. It has a physical, tangible quality, something that photographs well at an awards ceremony, and makes a visceral statement. Her videos at the time, however, were less about external consumption for a mass audience and more about the fetishistic gaze of self-consumption. In order to understand the kind of alienated feminism she expresses in these videos, it is important to look at her precursors—artists like Debbie Harry, Cyndi Lauper, and Madonna—and the journey from an inclusive 1970s punk populist feminism to twenty-first century individualism.

When Blondie were at the height of their success in 1980 Lester Bangs may have considered Debbie Harry to be acting 'high and mighty'. However, Harry was wrestling with feelings of deep insecurity. The band emerged from the Lower East Side punk scene of the mid-1970s, and their aesthetic was driven by pop art. Harry described their pop style as 'deliberately uncool, very influenced by cartoon art. That brevity, that abbreviation, the knowledge that everyone understands'.[32] Gaga cites Warhol as an influence; to Harry he was a personal friend. 'I'd say Andy was the svengali of the downtown scene,' she told me during an interview in London in July 2007. 'He was very in touch with what was going on, and excited by it. He was very kind to Chris [Stein] and myself, he invited us to a lot of different things. He was a social butterfly, that was part of his ritual.'

Although Bangs dismissed Harry as 'a piece of meat like the rest of them', Harry thought very carefully about her presentation, adopting a punk approach. Much of the time, for instance, she didn't really dance, she was an anti-dancer, making small, erratic movements or tilting her head at awkward angles. 'I didn't want to be showbiz, I didn't like the idea of choreographed routines. I found that nauseating. I wanted to do something jerky, that was sexual but accentuated the lyrics somehow. It didn't concern me that I should be on the right foot with the right beat. That was part of the contrariness of what we felt Blondie was.' Uncomfortable with being marketed as a sex object, Harry was 'highly offended at everything the record company did,' recalling the Chrysalis promotional poster for their single 'Rip Her To Shreds', which read: 'Wouldn't you like to rip her to shreds?' 'That's the problem of art and commerce,' says Harry. 'We came from the New York City underground. We were trying hard to be artists. We didn't have any idea about marketing. The whole thing was a complete, gigantic shock and smack in the face. We felt we were losing our identity. My God, what's happening? There's no getting around it.'

Despite her subcultural independence, Harry was caught off-guard by the ruthless marketing of the mainstream industry. By the mid-1980s, female artists were learning how to take more control of that marketing process, to a degree steering it for themselves. With her thrift store clothing, sparky personality and ebullient voice, Cyndi Lauper led a new kind of popular feminism. Her song 'Girls Just Wanna Have Fun' was a global hit in 1984, and she followed that up with 'She Bop', a pop song about female masturbation. She had been dyeing her hair since the age of nine and always had an eccentric fashion sense. 'I wanted success out of anger,' she says. 'People would give me grief about the way I dressed, then Boy George's success opened the door for me. At the time of "Girls Just Wanna Have Fun" I was shocked at the reaction. I'd go out on stage and the audience would be filled with girls screaming, ripping at my clothes. I'd never heard girls screaming over a woman before'.[33] Madonna too, had a fervent following of teenage girls. 'She emitted a kind of bisexual vibe. She was open and honest in her songwriting. Girls wanted to be like her because she was the free spirit in their minds. They admired what she was possessed by,' recalls her former manager Camille Barbone.[34]

More than Harry or Lauper, Madonna was the first female artist to push through what Genz and Brabon define as Do-Me Feminism and Raunch culture.[35] Early on, she planted the seed in the audience's mind that what she was doing was illicit and forbidden. Relatively mild sexual moves would be reinterpreted as lustful and adventurous, because of the fantasies in her psyche. 'She pretended her audience was a peeping Tom,' says Barbone.[36] She exhibited a narcissism that drew people in because it was about the self, and self-pleasure.

That sense of voyeurism was tempered, though, by the fairly sympathetic narrative of her stories. Each album release had a strong autobiographical thread, from the young married love of *True Blue*, to the Catholic girlhood of *Like A Prayer*, to the themes of motherhood and spiritual transformation in later albums like *Ray of Light* and *American Life*. There has been an enormous focus on Madonna's selling of a hyper-real sexuality, but this is woven through with a warm sense of human relationships and a robust romantic idealism. Madonna was part of the second-wave feminist generation—in favor of no-nonsense equality, anti-patriarchy, clear about women's rights to self-determination. One of her favourite tutors at the University of Michigan, for instance, was the ardent activist feminist Gay Delanghe.[37]

However the main element that performers have persistently extracted from Madonna's work ever since is that 'self-policing narcissistic gaze'.[38] Madonna created a collision of sexual objectification and liberation that singers like Christina Aguilera and Britney Spears felt compelled to imitate. This voluntary objectification of the self was accentuated by the dynamism of Girl Power and groups like the Spice Girls, where a twenty-first-century power feminism propelled 'girlies' to an 'insider position within consumer culture'.[39] Girl Power energy became linked to the endorsement of products and designers, so pop stars were encouraged to think of themselves as a brand with a unique selling point. This in turn influenced the current wave of hypersexual female artists like Rihanna, Nicki Minaj, Katy Perry and, of course, Gaga. The shift from Blondie's all-inclusive 'Rapture' or Cyndi Lauper's 'Girls Just Wanna Have Fun' is the shift from the collective action and ideals of second wave 'sisterhood' to Gaga's provocative postmodernist individualism. Now current feminist ideas are located in a strangely unsettled in-between space.[40]

Genz and Brabon argue that this unsettled postfeminist space can have a positive effect; that rather than being the illegitimate offspring of feminism, postfeminism is a process of resignification, a concept that requires a 'more nuanced and productive interpretation'.[41] Gaga, therefore, is a resignification of the Madonna phenomenon. Madonna used sex as a marketing tool, Gaga has brought it more explicitly into what Brian McNair defines as the pornosphere, or the appropriation of the conventions of pornography by the popular media. McNair sees this as a liberating influence, leading to a 'less regulated [. . .] more pluralistic sexual culture',[42] though there is an uneasiness about the relentless commodification of a porno chic sexuality. As Caitlin Moran wrote in her debunking bible of new popular feminism *How To Be A Woman*: 'hardcore pornography is now the primary form of sex education in the Western world.'[43] Challenging the notion that sex work equals sexual empowerment, Moran asks: 'what are strip clubs, and lap-dancing clubs, if not "light entertainment" versions of the entire history of misogyny?'[44]

Some current female pop performers see this pornosphere as a return to Harry's era when women were viewed as pieces of meat. Since 2000, the technological revolution and a digital download culture has created an increasingly fragmented, overcrowded market. As a result, young pop divas have opted for post-Madonnaesque scales of sexually explicit music. 'Gaga, Beyoncé, Rihanna, they're pushing it into a new field,' says Eva Barlow. 'They are pushing each other further, like a top tier of tennis players'.[45] This scenario dismays Tahita Bulmer, lead singer with indie electro pop band New Young Pony Club. When I interviewed her in London in January 2012 she said: 'To succeed in the pop world now you have to have a streak of ruthlessness. I have seen girls reliving the casting couch. In the wake of ladette culture and a hypersexualized world—all the stuff we looked down on as teenagers, everyone seems to accept now as part of the journey. That saddens me. My generation have been brought up by feminists who camped outside nuclear power stations and had a strong political identity. Women were brought up to be treasured. So much of that has been compromised in the noughties'. Katy Perry, for instance, diluted the throwaway lyrical cool and rock 'n' roll vocal delivery of her song 'I Kissed a Girl' with a video dripping in pink purple burlesque images of fantasy lesbian sex. Her video for 'California Gurls' features girls wrapped up like sweets, girls with cupcakes on their bikini tops, and Perry naked on a cloud like a latter-day Marilyn Monroe. Perry admits that this high fashion vampy glamour requires a lot of upkeep. In reality, she says, 'I'm every woman. It takes a village to make me who I am'.[46]

On one level these hypersexual videos are just exaggerated representations of pop femininity, but on another level there is a sense of deep alienation. Although they may not be explicitly feminist, these artists are finding a way to express their autobiography: what the industry has done to them, or made them do. Early Rihanna videos, for example, show her singing a lilting reggae pop on sun-kissed Bajun beaches. The further she moves to the mainstream global success, the harder and more accentuated her videos become, from the shiny metal and erotic tease of 'We Ride' to the cascading water and abstract affects of 'Umbrella'. Then, in 2009, she suffered a trauma that had a dramatic effect on both her looks and her music, when she was beaten and hospitalized by boyfriend Chris Brown. Pictures of her with a battered face and split lip were leaked onto the internet. Brown pleaded guilty to felony assault and was put on five years probation. Although Rihanna physically recovered, the trauma surfaced in her next album *Rated R*, with songs like 'Russian Roulette' and 'Hard'. She shaved half her head, dressed up as a soldier, danced with the Barbadian flag and sang aggressive, sexually explicit lyrics in the song 'Rude Boy'. She pared her music down to rude girl basics, using the bald talk of dancehall as the foundation of what was loosely termed porno pop. For her 2010 album Rihanna took her rebellion a step further with the song 'S&M', a celebration of the joys of sado-masochism, and 'Man Down', in which she shoots an ex-lover dead. This rebellion is about a detached, vengeful performance of sexuality and sexual agency, where she is the one in control.

It is interesting how many female performers at the peak of their fame find a way to express their alienation from the process by destroying their beauty, or making a troubled comment on it. They reflect back to the public a dysfunctional view of their own objectification. Debbie Harry did this in the early 1980s. As the band outgrew their New Wave roots, Harry felt trapped by her Blondie creation, and she pursued a solo career. The H.R. Giger-designed cover of her 1981 album *Koo Koo* featured Harry with pokers stuck through her face, a stark statement against the image that had propelled her to stardom.

Madonna, too, killed off the perfect iconic blonde goddess of the *True Blue* era with the trailer trash B-movie porn look of her *Sex* book and *Erotica* album. In one picture for the *Erotica* album sleeve she sits astride a table, bound and gagged, the image cut with scratched blue tint. She was worth millions, but here portrayed herself as worthless. Singer/songwriter Tori Amos (who sang of her experience of rape in 'Me and a Gun') believes that many women artists feel the need to pillage their repressed selves: 'Maybe on your path to self-discovery and the transmutation of a domineering ideology, you need to allow yourself to be defecated on. You can choose to explore that, it's part of your damage. Many women play it out behind closed doors [. . .] [some] choose to do it in public in front of voyeurs'.[47]

Christina Aguilera destroyed the Mickey Mouse popstrel by wearing leather chaps and singing 'Dirrty', Britney did it by shaving her head in front of the paparazzi. At the level of global pop commodification, female artists signal their buried distress in a variety of ways, but it is often through the body. As Bordo argues: 'Bodies have become alienated products, texts of our own creative making, from which we maintain a strange and ironic detachment'.[48] The body, the 'piece of meat' on those pop posters and promotional packages, is an airbrushed, culturally mediated form. Their identities don't express an authentic core self but are the dramatic *effect* (rather than cause) of (their) performances.[49] With many top female performers, their video bodies express the sense of a fractured psyche.

The most distinctive of current female pop performers, Gaga illustrates this to distorted, dramatic effect in her videos. In tracing her personal journey there is a marked disjuncture between the earthy, sensuous Stefani

Germanotta with long brown hair and cowboy boots, singing Led Zeppelin covers in New York dive The Bitter End, and her alter ego Lady Gaga, turning herself into a sex robot fetish during *The Fame Monster* era.

In order to amplify this change, it is useful to look at Gaga's personal history. She started out as a fairly orthodox Catholic girl from the Upper West Side, pursuing a career as a piano rock singer/songwriter and balladeer. One night she was performing to an unruly, talkative audience who ignored her. In desperation, she stripped down to her underwear, and immediately seized their attention. Since then, her look has evolved from semi-pornographic burlesque to her trademark eccentric wide-shoulder pads, no pants, and impossibly high heels, a key example of McNair's striptease culture.

Gaga's transformation paralleled her rise within the music industry. She had a difficult relationship with a record producer many years her senior, and an abusive boyfriend who would undermine her talent and criticize her achievements.[50] In her early career she was dropped by Def Jam, and then signed by global conglomerate Interscope, home of the Pussycat Dolls. Her record company may have 'thrown the building at it [*i.e.* her]', but in so doing, Gaga had to wrest with single-minded focus some control over her image and her career.

She has done this in outlandish ways: the gigantic hair bows, the red rubber masks, the Kermit frog cloak, and, of course, the meat dress. But her strongest statement on what it means to be a woman in the business is through her videos. For early promos she experimented with a few ideas: 'Just Dance' is party scenes of dancing and drugged abandonment; 'Poker Face' has a 1970s sexploitation feel, shot by a Hollywood pool with glistening California bodies and techno sunglasses; 'Love Game' features her tongue-in-cheek disco stick. But it is with 'Paparazzi', in 2009, that Gaga produces work that is a striking and innovative reflection on the media industry that she both exploits and that exploits her. In a video encompassing mutilation, murder and horror, Gaga's diva character is thrown off a hotel balcony by her boyfriend when she won't cooperate with his staging for the paparazzi. She ends up disabled, dragging herself across the floor on crutches as she sings.[51] Like a deranged Geisha from a Japanese horror film, she then poisons the boyfriend who exploits her.

Gaga's music, too, shows this alienation, in her ability to move effortlessly between sweet, girlish melody lines and a gruff, masculine robotic voice, a skill that fuelled speculation that she was intersex. Gaga prefers to call her style androgynous. This is the root of her success: rather than being a pristine beauty, Gaga has an awkward, self-deprecating misfit quality that many fans identify with.

She consolidated this aspect of her persona with 2009's *The Fame Monster* album and the ensuing Monster Ball tour, where she referred to her fans as 'Little Monsters'. Her message has always been one of inclusion; all the freaks, deviants and marginalized are welcome in her world. This is captured most poignantly in the video for 'Bad Romance', a high-concept dystopia where body-suited space aliens emerge from shiny white coffins and dance with Gaga to a stern-faced male audience. Gaga dances amid a shower of diamonds and crystals before being engulfed in flames. The final shot shows Gaga lounging on a burned bed, covered in ashes and bruises, the charred skeleton of her former boyfriend beside her. It is a perfect example of pop schlock horror.

In Gaga's world men are sex toys or dance mates. Rather than traditional romance, the focus of her gaze is on the damaging effects of celebrity and media sex. Her imagery is tilted towards a gay male sensibility, and a voyeuristic sexuality that is lit in a cold futuristic world saturated with white light. Here Gaga has turned herself into a postfeminist cyborg. She is now in a virtual post-gender world, a post-human cyberspace, which has echoes of William Gibson's *Neuromancer* and Sadie Plant's utopian cyber-feminism. In this context, 'cyberspace offers a particularly liberating site for women as it has the potential to sever their links with the female body'.[52]

Cyborgs are hybrid entities that refashion our thinking. The female is 'artificial in both mind and flesh, as much woman as machine, as close to science as to nature [...]. As a metonym, she embodies the impossibility of distinguishing between gender and its representation'.[53] Gaga's cyber identity suggests a dissolution of gender boundaries. Through her futuristic masque she reinvents Stefani Germanotta as a multimedia avatar. Like Rock Hudson's character Arthur Hamilton in the 1966 science fiction movie *Seconds*, rejecting his former life for a new one after undercover plastic surgery, Gaga is a 'reborn'. 'You will be your new dimension,' Hamilton is told by Mr Ruby, the shady company director who provides him with a new identity. Likewise, Gaga has created a second life, her 'new dimension', but it is one that involves a culture of forgetting. Which brings us back to the meat dress.

The feminist message of Gaga's meat dress was muted because she didn't seem confident in talking about it or exploring its historical resonance. Her gesture pinpoints a disjuncture between feminist generations: she benefits from former radical ideas while making them invisible. Older feminists feel their ideas devalued and what they have achieved taken for granted. Gaga was more comfortable with an unconscious feminism, a perspective that emanated from her immediate experience as a young female performer. 'Bad Romance' and 'Paparazzi' marked a specific moment in her career, a point where she reflected on herself as a commodity. This was taken a step further with the lurid 'lezploitation' video 'Telephone', where she and Beyoncé starred in a *Thelma & Louise* style scenario of escape and revenge.[54] With her subsequent album *Born This Way* she moved into a more conventional rock/pop presentation, playing with glam metal and zombie imagery that continued the monster theme, but was less about her role as a woman in the industry.

Maybe it requires amnesia to become a global pop entity, to cast one-self adrift in that 'strangely unsettled in-between space'. But at the same time, there is strength in embedding oneself in history. If Gaga had fully owned that statement: 'we are not just a piece of meat', she would have cemented the link between previous radical feminist artists like Schneeman and Sterbak, and herself as an artist. For now she floats in an individualistic bubble, her postfeminism typical of the shift 'from a socially prescribed life story—constraining in particular for women who historically have been disadvantaged by the fact that they are female—to a biography that is self-produced.'[55] But even though Gaga is wary of locating herself in a literal feminist tradition, her reuse of the meat dress brings the work of artists who came before her into a conversation that enables a two-way reading of ideas. The meat dress is a symbol that has huge potency above and beyond Gaga wearing it to an MTV bash. She may not be aware of women like Helen Chadwick and Karen Finlay, but her dress is part of a powerful discourse about women, consumption and body image. Even if Gaga's meat dress wasn't a conscious feminist choice, the confluence of image and idea lends itself to a feminist reading.

That in itself creates opportunities for an ongoing critique about female representation in pop music. As Barlow says, 'Gaga's whole vision is hyper-sexualised for no one but herself. She is a sex symbol, but not for a male audience. Some of her visuals are so out there and grotesque, they are not a turn-on mechanism'.[56] Also when someone is read in a politicized way, they can respond to that reading. Although Gaga initially gave a confused message when she wore the meat dress, she later seemed to become aware of the significance and power of the statement she had made. An interesting development to this story is the fact that during her summer 2012 'Born This Way' tour Gaga revisited the meat concept by wearing a meat corset on stage in Romania. In contrast to the high-couture glamour of the 2010 dress, Gaga had gained 25 pounds and this flesh corset was stretched in an unflattering way over her fuller figure.

Sensitive to media criticism of her weight gain, Gaga protested: 'I really don't feel bad about it, not even for a second'.[57] She confessed to past eating disorders, posted unglamorous photos of herself in underwear online and started a Body Revolution movement on her Little Monsters website, encouraging fans to embrace their flaws. 'To all the girls that think you're ugly because you're not a size 0, you're the beautiful one. It's society who's ugly,' she tweeted.[58] In a moment of 1970s-style consciousness-raising, Gaga moved away from the hypersexual cyborg image to one rooted in real female experience. What had started out as a commercial appropriation of feminist art in 2010 shifted to a grittier, more personal statement two years later. It took a while, but maybe the radical message did survive the journey. Maybe Gaga has something in common with Linder and her punk entrails after all.

NOTES

1. Greil Marcus, *In The Fascist Bathroom: Writings on Punk 1977–1992* (London: Viking, 1993), 107.
2. *The Ellen DeGeneres Show*, NBC Universal, 13 September 2010.
3. Paul Lester, *Looking for Fame: The Life of a Pop Princess Lady Gaga* (London: Omnibus, 2010), 89.
4. Naomi Klein, *No Logo* (London: Flamingo, 2001), 298–299.
5. Ana Finel Honigman, 'Now Showing | Linder Sterling's Fashion Turn', *T: The New York Times Style Magazine*, 14 October 2010 (online at: http://tmagazine.blogs.nytimes.com/2010/10/14/now-showing-linder-sterlings-fashion-turn/) <accessed 17 March 2013>.
6. Lucy O'Brien, 'The Woman Punk Made Me', in *Punk Rock: So What? The Cultural Legacy of Punk*, ed. Roger Sabin (London: Routledge, 1999), 197.
7. Finel Honigman, 'Now Showing | Linder Sterling's Fashion Turn'.
8. Lucy O'Brien, 'The Girl, The Bad and The Ugly,' *The Guardian*, 19 February 2000.
9. Carolee Schneemann, 'The Obscene Body/Politic', *Art Journal*, vol. 50, no. 4 (Winter, 1991), 28.
10. Robert C. Morgan, 'Carolee Schneemann: The Politics of Eroticism', *Art Journal*, vol. 56, no. 4 (Winter, 1997), 98.
11. Jill Dolan, 'The Dynamics of Desire: Sexuality and Gender in Pornography and Performance', *Theatre Journal*, vol. 39, no. 2 (May 1987), 162.
12. Marcy J. Epstein, 'Eating Acts and Feminist Embodiment', *TDR*, vol. 40, no. 4 (Winter, 1996), 21.
13. *Ibid.*, 28.
14. Sam Voulters, 'Nicola Formichetti', *Vice* (November 2011) (online at: http://www.vice.com/read/nicola-formichetti-738-v18n3?Contentpage=2) <accessed: 18 March 2013>.
15. Denise Winterman and Jon Kelly, 'Five Interpretations of Lady Gaga's Meat Dress', *BBC News Magazine* (14 September 2010) (online at: http://www.bbc.co.uk/news/magazine-11297832) <accessed: 18 March 2013>.
16. Epstein, 'Eating Acts', 22.
17. Lizzy Goodman, *Lady Gaga: Extreme Style* (London: HarperCollins, 2010), 19.
18. Johnny Morgan, *Gaga* (New York: Sterling, 2010), 109.
19. Andreas Huyssen, *After The Great Divide: Modernism, Mass Culture and Postmodernism* (Bloomington, IN: Indiana University Press, 1986), 47.
20. Peter Robinson, 'Lady Gaga: Freak or Fraud?', *Esquire* (7 June 2011) (extract online at: http://www.esquire.my/InTheMagazine/Sneak-Peek/article/Lady-Gaga-freak-or-fraud) <accessed: 18 March 2013>.
21. Robinson, 'Lady Gaga: Freak or Fraud?'
22. John Fiske, *Television Culture* (London: Methuen, 1987), 239.
23. Simon During, 'Introduction', *The Cultural Studies Reader* (New York, NY: Routledge, 1993), 18.
24. Maureen Callahan, *Poker Face: The Rise and Rise of Lady Gaga* (New York, NY: Hyperion, 2010), 153.
25. E. Ann Kaplan, 'Madonna Politics: Perversion, Repression or Subversion? Or Masks and/as Master-y', in *The Madonna Connection: Representational Politics, Subcultural Identities, and Cultural Theory*, ed. Cathy Schwichtenberg (Boulder, CO: Westview, 1993), 160.
26. Susan Bordo, *Unbearable Weight: Feminism, Western Culture, and the Body* (Berkeley: University of California Press, 2003), 156.

27. Amelia Jones, '1970/2007: The Return of Feminist Art', *X-Tra: Contemporary Art Quarterly*, vol. 10, no. 4 (Summer 2008) (online at: http://x-traonline.org/issues/volume-10/number-4/19702007-the-return-of-feminist-art/) <accessed: 18 March 2013>.

28. Liz McQuiston, *Suffragettes to She-Devils* (London: Phaidon, 1997); Germaine Greer, 'The politics of female sexuality', *Oz*, no. 29 (May 1970), reprinted in *eadem, The Madwoman's Underclothes: Essays in Occasional Writings* (New York, NY: Atlantic Monthly, 1986), 36–37.

29. Jones, '1970/2007: The Return of Feminist Art'.

30. Griselda Pollock, personal communication with the author.

31. Bordo, *Unbearable Weight*, 283.

32. Debbie Harry, personal communication with the author.

33. Lucy O'Brien, *She Bop II: The Definitive History of Women in Rock, Pop & Soul* (London: Continuum, 2002), 228.

34. Lucy O'Brien, *Madonna: Like an Icon* (London: Bantam, 2007), 52.

35. Stephanie Genz and Benjamin A. Brabon, *Postfeminism: Cultural Texts and Theories* (Edinburgh: Edinburgh University Press, 2009), 92–98.

36. O'Brien, *Madonna*, 52.

37. *Ibid.*, 31.

38. Rosalind Gill, *Gender and the Media* (Cambridge: Polity, 2007), 258.

39. Genz and Brabon, *Postfeminism*, 79.

40. *Ibid.*, 105.

41. *Ibid.*, 65.

42. Brian McNair, *Striptease Culture: Sex, Media and the Democratisation of Desire* (Abingdon: Routledge, 2002), 11.

43. Caitlin Moran, *How to Be A Woman* (London: Ebury, 2011), 50.

44. *Ibid.*, 171.

45. Eva Barlow, personal communication with the author.

46. Lisa Robinson, 'Katy Perry on Her Religious Childhood, Her Career, and Her Marriage to Russell Brand', *Vanity Fair* (2 May 2011) (online at: http://www.vanityfair.com/online/daily/2011/05/katy-perry-on-her-religious-childhood-her-career-and-her-marriage-to-russell-brand) <accessed: 18 March 2013>.

47. O'Brien, *Madonna*, 183.

48. Bordo, *Unbearable Weight*, 288.

49. Judith Butler, *Gender Trouble: Feminism and the Subversion of Identity*, 2nd edition (London: Routledge, 1999), 173.

50. Maureen Callahan, *Poker Face: The Rise and Rise of Lady Gaga* (New York, NY: Hyperion, 2010), 95; 128.

51. See Apolloni in this volume.

52. Genz and Brabon, *Postfeminism*, 147.

53. Judith Halberstam, *In a Queer Time and Place: Transgender Bodies, Subcultural Lives* (New York, NY: New York University Press, 2005), 454.

54. See Colton in this volume.

55. Genz and Brabon, *Postfeminism*, 170.

56. Eva Barlow, personal communication with the author.

57. Joyce Chen, 'Lady Gaga embraces fuller figure after 25-pound weight gain: "I really don't feel bad about it, not even for a second"', *New York Daily News* (23 September 2012) (online at: http://www.nydailynews.com/entertainment/gossip/lady-gaga-embraces-fuller-figure-25-pound-weight-gain-don-feel-bad-article-1.1165856) <accessed: 18 March 2013>.

58. Rennie Dyball, 'Lady Gaga Shows Off Curvy Figure in Paris', *People* (22 September 2012) (online at: http://www.people.com/people/article/0,,20632406,00.html) <accessed: 18 March 2013>.

3　Her Own Real Thing
Lady Gaga and the Haus of Fashion

Sally Gray and Anusha Rutnam

Fashion saved my life. When I was young, I was laughed at in school because I dressed dramatically. [. . .] When I moved downtown it was complete liberation. I found all these shops on Eighth Street and I integrated fashion into my life in a healthy way because it made me feel powerful, ambitious and much more resilient.[1]

As fashion offered salvation to a young Stefani Germanotta, her creation, Lady Gaga, has proved to be an incendiary force both within the fashion world and as a performer who uses fashion and dress in highly inventive ways. Lady Gaga is, herself, a fashion phenomenon and has become part of fashion discourse itself. She has appeared on numerous covers of fashion and style magazines including US *Vogue*, US *Harper's Bazaar*, *Rolling Stone*, *Vogue Hommes* Japan, *i-D*, *Vanity Fair*, *Elle*, and *Esquire*, among others. Lady Gaga displays familiarity with fashion history and with the deployment of dress and adornment in film, popular music, and art. Exhibiting the cool savvy of the fashion insider, unintimidated by fashion's secrets and vanities, Gaga is no fashion victim, but a participant in fashion's endlessly sophisticated appropriations, quotations, inventions, flights of fantasy and imagination. She is in tune with fashion's relentless, tyrannical engagement with the present. Gaga's creative team is referred to as the 'Haus of Gaga', the name evoking the idea of a 'fashion house'—the House of Dior or Chanel for example—and the idea of the fashion *atelier* in which visual and conceptual ideas are brought together with craft skills and a range of materials to make clothing and adornment. These resources are pooled to fulfill the creative vision of a central figure, in this instance Lady Gaga.

This chapter is interested in both Lady Gaga's use of fashion itself and her wider sartorial practice beyond the borders of what Roland Barthes called *The Fashion System*.[2] Fashion and adornment are an integral part of Lady Gaga's performative enactments. The performance doesn't stop when the fans leave the stadium or the cameras stop rolling and as a result Gaga blurs the line between costume and fashion. Gaga's unrelenting dedication to fashion is typified by her appearances at airports, fresh off twelve-hour flights, in gargantuan heels with full-face makeup and elaborately coiffed hair.[3] Coverage of Gaga in the mainstream media will invariably reference her 'outré approach to costuming' in tones of amazement, respect, gushing enthusiasm, or dismissal.[4] On stage or on screen, her approach to fashion and dress are as important as choreography, music, voice, staging, and lighting. We examine the way in which Gaga uses fashion and dress to simultaneously enact, problematize, and queer, questions of 'fame', 'beauty' 'sexiness', 'femininity', and 'blond female famousness'.

FASHIONING THE LADY GAGA PERSONA

Lady Gaga's outfits and her modes of inhabiting them are not just part of her 'look'; they represent an evolving conception of a performative self. Early on in her career as pop singer, Lady Gaga designed and made her own outfits, such as the disco-ball, faceted-mirror bra she made and wore for her act at Lollapalooza in 2007. Referring to this during a December 2009 concert in Vancouver, she said:

> We used to spend hours getting dressed and we would make our own clothes together. So, you know, like the Disco Bra from the 'Just Dance' video? I made that myself and I made it in my apartment with Lady Starlight, and we were watching a Marc Bolan video [. . .] and it was funny because when I went to make the 'Just Dance' video, the record label said: 'Oh don't you want to wear something new? Don't you want to wear something that we get from a stylist or a designer, something brand new—a brand new Gaga.' And I said, 'No. This has sentimental value.'[5]

Gaga displays a crafted, personal artfulness in the way she puts together things to wear, retaining from her career's beginnings a desire to maintain control of her visual persona and to collaboratively bring it about. Her 'little monster' fans are inspired to similarly design and make their own outfits, turning up to her concerts in their self-created odes to their idol and mentor, both emulating her, and participating in the creation of Lady Gaga's global following. As the *Sydney Morning Herald* reported after one of Gaga's Sydney tours:

> There they were like precious jewels, hundreds of eager shimmery fans dressed up in their DIY Gaga contraptions fashioned from yesterday's pizza boxes, milk crates, sequins and glitter.[6]

These 'precious jewels', her fans, are part of Gaga's collective practice, part of an evolving cultural phenomenon of dressing, not in order to be attractive, but to be amazing.

STYLE AND THE HAUS OF GAGA

The Haus of Gaga is a team of Gaga's 'coolest friends' and collaborators, who create many of the garments, props, prosthetics, and hairstyles worn by Lady Gaga. [7] Notable among the members of the Haus are former creative director Matthew Williams and fashion director Nicola Formichetti.[8] They have helped put together vestimentary looks, outfits, live performances, and videos. The Haus is partly derived, in Gaga's eclectic appropriative way, from the precedent of the Warhol Factory—both creative studio and site of social and cultural innovation—and also the 'Haus' of the Bauhaus, a model of interdisciplinary collaborative creativity. Gaga took inspiration from the way the Bauhaus school of design in 1920s and 1930s Germany combined the hand-crafted with industrial production models.[9] The Haus of Gaga mixes both home-made DIY costuming and couture in a practice which—in its female-centeredness— avoids the male domination that characterized both the Warhol Factory and the Bauhaus.

The idea of a creative individual or team directing artisans and technicians, for a particular fashion brand, is mirrored in the way the Haus of Gaga operates, collaboratively leading the conceptualization of Gaga's dress, imagery, performance and staging, creating unique performances both on stage and off. The idea of the Haus of Gaga resonates with the notion of the *griffe* (label or brand) which recognizably marked the quality and style of a particular 'fashion house' in the system inaugurated in Paris by the House of Worth in the late nineteenth century. The notion of 'house' also resonates with the drag balls of *Paris is Burning*, whose divas organized themselves into fashion-style 'houses' to 'read and shade their sisters into oblivion'.[10] Gaga often states that she has retained the team of collaborators she has worked with from the beginning, in forming the Haus of Gaga, which, as mentioned, is in part a group of friends. Nicola Formichetti styles his role in relation to Gaga as 'Fashion Director'. Formichetti is a Tunisian, based in Paris, and has become a significant player in the fashion world, with stints as a Fashion Director for *Vogue Hommes* Japan, and Fashion Director for UNIQLO.[11] Largely through the reputation and fame he garnered as Lady Gaga's stylist Formichetti was also appointed as creative director at Thierry Mugler. Gaga herself had creative input into Mugler's Fall 2011 fashion show, as well as modeling in it.[12]

Lady Gaga's tattoos, on her wrist, her shoulder, back, and inner arm, include the universally recognized 'peace sign' (created in 1958 by Gerald Herbert Holtom, in the context of the UK's Aldermaston anti-nuclear marches), and a quote from the German-language poet, Rainer Maria Rilke.[13] The latter, from Rilke's *Letters to a Young Poet* of 1903, was inked in curling script inside Gaga's left arm in Osaka, Japan and reads:

In the deepest hour of the night, confess to yourself that you would die if you were forbidden to write. And look deep into your heart where it spreads its roots, the answer, and ask yourself, must I write?

Gaga's tattoos are both a form of body-art and a type of *griffe* or mark, of the Lady Gaga brand of progressive politics and ambitious artistic reach.

WITHIN AN EVOLVING FASHION SYSTEM

Roland Barthes outlined, in the 1960s, the codes—as observed in French fashion magazines—which make up what he called the *fashion system*, that is the way fashion production and dissemination is structured and coded.[14] He was especially interested in the kinds of language used to describe garments and the notions of change involved in fashion. Barthes admitted that his analysis was out of date almost as soon as he made it.[15] Today the *fashion system* has extended the way collections are presented and disseminated through fashion shows, mainstream media, video, blogs, and the internet generally, and the way fashion inserts itself into other discourses such as, in this case, pop music. Gaga's performative persona references the *fashion system* itself in an inventive series of quotations and *hommages*.

Lady Gaga wears the designs of the world's best-known fashion creators, often working alongside them in the invention of modes of self-presentation for her public appearances. In November 2009, her video 'Bad Romance' was released, the song having premiered earlier, during the presentation of Alexander McQueen's Spring 2010 collection, *Plato's Atlantis*. This show was videoed by SHOWstudio's Ruth Hogben and live-streamed on Nick Knight's SHOWstudio.com.[16] In the video, the song, including the lyrics 'Walk, walk fashion baby', accompanies images of Lady Gaga wearing head-to-toe McQueen from *Plato's Atlantis*, including the infamous 'armadillo' heels, vertiginous shoes that several high-profile models refused to walk in for the McQueen show, so concerned were they about the risks of falling over.[17] Lady Gaga was herself friends with McQueen and following his suicide in 2010 she was quoted as saying, 'Right after he died, I wrote "Born This Way". I think he's up in heaven with fashion strings in his hands, marionetting away, planning this whole thing'.[18] Later, in 2011 Gaga released the 'Born This Way' video. Even more than in 'Bad Romance', there is a sense of creative homage to McQueen's *Plato's Atlantis* collection. The symmetrical prints of that collection inform the entire visual effect of 'Born This Way', which is directed by Nick Knight. Facial and body prosthetics in the video are strongly influenced by McQueen's collection, though Gaga herself wears no McQueen garments.

It is evident that Lady Gaga is known, and admired, by important players in the fashion world including major fashion creators. Having designed costumes for her Monster Ball tour, Giorgio Armani said of Gaga: 'No other artist would give me the opportunity to devise such original and way-out creations. Lady Gaga's costumes are a pure creativity exercise that allows me to design spectacular, almost surreal pieces'.[19] The President of the Polaroid camera company was similarly effusive when in 2010 the company gave Lady Gaga the title of Creative Director.[20] It would be naive, however, to view these examples as purely creative transactions. Lady Gaga is indubitably part of a long tradition of celebrity endorsement. The March 2011 issue of US *Vogue* on whose cover she appeared was the only fashion magazine to show an increase in sales in the first half of that year. [21] Forbes magazine noted that Gaga 'isn't the music industry's new Madonna. She's its new business model', putting particular emphasis on her online presence.[22] She is adept at working in this new virtual terrain and because of this has been recognized as a powerful player in the fashion industry.

GAGA'S FASHION UBIQUITY

Gaga has been endlessly photographed by the biggest names in fashion photography: Nick Knight, Mario Testino, Annie Leibovitz, Inez and Vindooh, and Hedi Slimane. She recently collaborated with Terry Richardson on a book of portraits (by him, of her).[23] She has appeared in original *couture* dresses both vintage and current, and ready-to-wear, by the most powerful names in fashion: Alexander McQueen, Chanel, Yves St Laurent, Christian Dior, Versace, Giorgio Armani, Prada, Thierry Mugler, Marc Jacobs, John Galliano, Viktor and Rolf, and the list goes on. Hats are by Philip Treacy, Piers Atkinson, and Stephen Jones; shoes are by Christian Louboutin and McQueen. Sunglasses are by Paloma Picasso, Gianni Versace, Chanel, Gucci, and Dior. In 2011 the Council of Fashion Designers of America presented her with its Fashion Icon Award.[24]

One of the most revealing insights into Gaga's fine-honed appreciation of fashion is the 2009 live webcast SHOWstudio interview with Gaga, videoed by Ruth Hogben.[25] Lady Gaga fields live-streamed, probing questions from people as diverse as milliner, Stephen Jones, and performance artist, Marina Abramovic, with wit, aplomb, and the knowledge of a fashion insider. In the video, Gaga's look and persona channels a 'sweet' but confidently postmodern Marilyn Monroe—with traces of the ineffable *luxe* of Daphne Guinness—in Gaga's imaginative form of appropriative originality. Both the caliber of the questioners (as well as their questions) and Gaga's eloquent responses reveal her status as an authoritative fashion commentator, visually positioned within Hogben's luxurious filmic style.

As well as routinely wearing both couture and ready-to-wear designer clothing in her video performances, and in her everyday public performance of her celebrity, Lady Gaga quotes visual tropes from current elite fashion and from fashion history, including the history of film and television costume. In her first fashion column for *V Magazine*, Gaga talks explicitly (and sweepingly) about this interest:

> Glam culture is ultimately rooted in obsession, and those of us who are truly devoted and loyal to the lifestyle of glamour are masters of its history. Or, to put it more elegantly, we are librarians. I myself can look at almost any hemline, silhouette, beadwork, or heel architecture and tell you very precisely who designed it first, what French painter they stole it from, how many designers reinvented it after them, and what cultural and musical movement parented the birth, death, and resurrection of that particular trend.[26]

Highlighting the question of Lady Gaga's creation, rather than simply dissemination, of forms of fashionability, both *Time* in 2009 and 2010 and *Forbes* in 2011 voted her one of the 100 most powerful and influential people of those respective years.[27] Gaga, as a fashion savvy celebrity, *makes* fashion, in the sense that her saturation presence in the world's media declares what is fashionable in the wider sense—both clothing and dress and beyond—she has constantly created forms of fashionability. Gaga's inventive sense of the zeitgeist expresses itself in her anticipation of forthcoming fashion trends. Christophe Decarnin's Spring 2009 collection for the fashion house Balmain (publicly presented on 28 September 2008) was described by *style.com* as presenting 'a brilliant new shoulder with a bump-peaked swagger on jackets and dresses. (The eighties never looked like that.)'[28] Lady Gaga had pre-empted this trend when her short film, *The Fame: Part One*, was uploaded to her official YouTube channel on 15 August 2008 (though shot some time before that). In this video she wears pointed shoulders with a similar profile to the Balmain collection presented a month later.

UNFOLDING FASHION FAME: GAGA'S DESIGNER CLOTHING AND COUTURE APPEARANCES

Fashion itself provides one of the principal drivers of the constantly unfolding visuality of Lady Gaga's on- and off-stage performances and is indispensable to the globally recognized persona she has evolved. Gaga's modes of wearing differ from those of the celebrity who makes routine red-carpet appearances in borrowed *couture* or who appears with fashion stars, adding to their mutual charisma, such as Nicole Kidman's appearance with Karl Lagerfeld at the 2004 Chanel Spring Season show.[29]

Lady Gaga makes these appearances too, but she is also herself a creator of costume, and a fashion originator, not simply a clotheshorse for the big names in fashion. In 2009 she attended the MTV Video Music

Awards wearing a red lace dress from the Alexander McQueen archives. Her access to prestigious fashion-house archives is itself a measure of her fashion-world status. The dress was worn with an apparently matching red crown that was in fact created by Gaga's own design team, The Haus of Gaga.[30] This is emblematic of the somewhat irreverent manner in which she wears important fashion pieces, including *haute couture* garments, with her personal inventions. For her 2011 Sydney tour she gave the team at local costumier Nigel Shaw Costume Design four hours to work, with her, to conceive and complete a black PVC fishtail dress for that evening's performance.[31]

Lady Gaga's public appearances are always highly styled and choreographed events and form an essential part of her fashion persona. However, her music videos present a distilled expression of her fashionable trajectory. As we have seen, the clothes in her early videos were largely made by the Haus of Gaga or Lady Gaga herself. The cost of high fashion items, as well as their exclusivity, easily explains their absence from these early performances. An early high fashion inclusion is the pair of logoed Chanel heels, which fill the screen in the 'LoveGame' video, shot in early 2009. [32] Arguably these are not particularly significant fashion pieces but they are among several fore-shadowings of her high fashion future. In the 'Beautiful, Dirty, Rich' video, shot in 2008, for example, layered gold chains and a white lace corset seem to quote the lavish, baroque early 1990s designs of Gianni Versace but the absence of logos—most notably Versace's Medusa head—indicates that this ensemble was not likely to contain authentic Versace pieces.[33] By 2011 Gaga was being given unprecedented access to the Versace archives by Donatella Versace herself, evidence of her increasing cachet as a serious fashion player.[34]

Lady Gaga's sixth music video, 'Paparazzi', shot in April 2009, is the first in which she wears a significant piece from an established designer.[35] This was the Spring 2007 Dolce & Gabbana 'metal' corset dress (actually made from leather and silicon), which has featured in exhibitions at the Metropolitan Museum of Art, New York, and the *Musée des Arts Décoratifs*, in Paris. For 'Paparazzi' Lady Gaga was styled by B. Åkerlund, wife of the video's director, Jonas Åkerlund. An established stylist, Åkerlund's access to high fashion garments meant that the 'Paparazzi' video uses a number of important fashion pieces not accessible to a more run-of-the-mill pop star. Åkerlund said of the video:

> I don't like to pull fashion; I like to make fashion. I feel like Gaga and I are alike in that respect [. . .]. If that means pulling from old resources of designers we like, or archives of things, or whatever it is. It doesn't matter as long as it feels right. [36]

Featured in the video are several garments from the Thierry Mugler archive, along with accessories by John Galliano, Chanel and Christian Dior. There are also several pieces in 'Paparazzi' created by Jeremy Scott especially for Lady Gaga, the designer having been present on the video's set.[37] Scott's youthful and somewhat comical pieces might have appeared a good match for Gaga at the time but it is the armor-like Dolce & Gabbana dress, with its aggressive silhouette and unlikely fabrication, that really foreshadows the direction in which her fashionable expression would later proceed.

BEYOND THE FASHION SYSTEM

Lady Gaga's vestimentary performance, while being a major fashion intervention, is not limited specifically to *fashion* itself. Barthes' idea of a *fashion system* is useful, given that Gaga's vestimentary performances, while located within the domain of fashion itself, simultaneously exceed it. Lady Gaga excels at *fashion* itself on its own terms, and also exceeds the *fashion system* by bringing fashion into a vestimentary performance, which is usefully compared with performance art.

Gaga's appearance in numerous fashion magazines and mass media, photographed by famous fashion photographers, wearing the most revered designers' clothes and accessories—all religiously named by the publications and by Gaga herself—is a specific *fashion* engagement, but the uses to which Gaga puts fashion, costume and dress, exceed fashion's boundaries. Gaga's artistic practice harnesses fashion and other forms of sartorial expression in a creative endeavor which works in the rich spaces of potentiality among categories of art and fashion, male and female, straight and gay.

FROM 'CAMP TO GAY TO QUEER'

One of the aims of this chapter is to locate Lady Gaga's sartorial enactments in the context of her long-term cultural embrace of queerness. Her dress enactments are informed by the late twentieth century's unsettling of firm ideas of gender and sexuality, under different rubrics—including from 'camp to gay to queer'.[38] Gaga's sartorial enactments encompass all of these: the 'camp' sensibility referred to in Susan Sontag's famous 1964 essay, 'Notes on Camp', [39] the notion of 'gay' as a liberationist ideology and cultural practice, and 'queer', a postmodern unsettling of fixed gender and sexuality, expounded by theorists such as Eve Kosofsky Sedgwick and Judith Butler.[40]

Lady Gaga's sartorial performances display the 'love of the unnatural: of artifice and exaggeration' that Sontag identifies as the essence of camp.[41] 'The way of camp', says Sontag, 'is not in terms of beauty but in terms of the degree of artifice, of stylization'.[42] This sensibility has been a consistent part of Gaga's costume and dress, from when she appeared in the consciously retro, glittering 'disco-ball' bra of 2007 to her present endlessly inventive approaches to dress and adornment.

Eve Kosofsky Sedgwick wrote of queer as a mobile form of subjectivity exceeding received categories pertaining to sexual identity or practice. She proposed that queer is not linked to fixed sexual identities, or practices, or an innate sexual nature. Queer, for Sedgwick is: 'A continuing moment, movement, motive—recurrent, eddying, *troublant*'[43] In other words it is in motion and continual formation, not a fixed state or category. Tracing an etymology of the roots of the word 'queer' in English she writes: 'The word "queer" itself means *across*—it comes from the Indo-European root— *twerkw*, which also yields the German *quer* (transverse), Latin *torquere* (to twist), English *athwart*'. [44]

Judith Butler sees sex and gender as 'regulatory fictions' and 'contested sites of meaning'.[45] For Butler, gender is 'an effect' rather than a natural or 'real' phenomenon.[46] Following Simone de Beauvoir, she sees 'woman' as 'a term in process, a becoming [. . .] an ongoing discursive practice' brought about by repeated acts of gender.[47] We see Lady Gaga's fashion and dress practices as an example of those 'repeated acts within a highly regulatory frame',[48] which both perform gender and draw attention to its illusoriness and instability. Lady Gaga's hyperbolic 'femininity' and varied enactments of 'sexiness' serve to parody and to queer the stability of sex and gender.

Gay Liberation inaugurated a set of cultural tropes relating to dress, which Gaga has been happy to appropriate along with the liberationist import of the movement. The Gay Lib Movement had its symbolic foundational moment, in the events at the Stonewall Inn, in lower Manhattan in June of 1969, and the drag queens who fought back at Stonewall are one of many antecedents of Gaga's 'outrageous fashion sense'.[49] Lisa Robinson in *Vanity Fair* notes that Lady Gaga has been 'described in thousands of press clippings as *bizarre, a drag queen, fierce, a hermaphrodite, a gay man trapped in a woman's body, a self-parody, outlandish, hard-core, trashy, genius, futuristic, grotesque*', placing an emphasis on queer performative tropes both in Gaga's enactments and their reception.[50] Gaga's exaggerated parodies of gender and often also of fashion recall the vogueing performers in *Paris is Burning,* the iconic documentary of 1980s Harlem Drag-balls.[51] According to Lisa Robinson, Gaga had been introduced to the film by her former lover, Matthew Williams, who later became creative director of the Haus of Gaga.[52] The development of a 'gay lib' cultural sensibility also included recovered tropes of hyper-masculinity, including military and biker sartorial aesthetics, which Gaga has employed in her videos. In the 2010 'Alejandro' video, militaristic outfits were custom made for Gaga's male dancers by Emporio Armani. In his review of Emporio Armani's Spring 2011 Menswear collection, the fashion writer Tim Blanks wrote that

> black leather dominated the collection, and a clip from Lady Gaga's 'Alejandro' video that played at the finale was a reminder that Giorgio

and Gaga collaborated on her latest. It was presumably the S&M erotica of that new hit that provoked one particularly dark group [in the Armani show], with wild-boy models glowering through heavy eye makeup and sporting slave chains, studs, and grommets.[53]

Similarly, in an earlier video clip, 'LoveGame', a leather biker aesthetic dominates, with bare-chested male dancers wearing leather jackets and distressed denim jeans. 'Alejandro' also features men in inter-war German athletic underwear and Italian fascist-inflected male sartorial aesthetics: black-shirts, leather jackets. But instead of military-steps we see *Paris is Burning*-style queeny mincing, the whole ensemble making parodic, aestheticized links between eroticism and violence.

Post-gay, S&M and fetishistic elements are a common motif in Lady Gaga's fashion. In 2009 she met Queen Elizabeth II wearing a red latex gown created by Atsuko Kudo. The Scottish designer Rachael Barrett has also created latex garments for Gaga, notably for the 'Bad Romance' and 'Telephone' music videos. Studs and leather underwear also make frequent appearances. This, along with the endurance of camp, provided part of the cultural framing for Gaga's early performances for predominantly gay male audiences, her first consistent club fans, as she often remarks.[54] In wearing the famous 'Meat Dress' to the 2010 MTV Music Video Awards, Gaga sought to draw attention to the Don't Ask Don't Tell policy of the US military, which required that gays in the armed forces remain closeted.[55] The day after the awards Gaga explained the meaning behind the dress to talk-show host Ellen DeGeneres, saying, 'If we don't fight for our rights, pretty soon we're going to have as much rights as the meat on our bones'.[56] Gaga has consistently advocated equal marriage rights and proselytises on a range of issues relating to sexual freedom and open-ended approaches to gender. 'I look like a transsexual', she says, and she is more than happy to embrace 'androgynous', 'confusing', 'robo', 'weird', and 'uncomfortable' readings of her sartorial performance. [57] She is happy to be thought of as 'unsexy', unsettling the idea that hetero-normative forms of 'sexiness' in dress and appearance are what pop stars should naturally aspire to. Gaga declines to repeat familiar tropes of 'femininity', 'sexiness' or 'blondness' performed by pop stars and celebrities such as Britney Spears, Paris Hilton, or at times Lindsay Lohan, instead queering them with her tangential camp sensibility and her sexy-unsexy wackiness. Employing all of the tropes of 'sexy-fame-princess'—body-revealing corsets, leotards and bras; super-high heels and ripped fishnets; black leather, latex, S&M and fetish accoutrements; batted eyelashes, pouting mouth, pelvic thrusting and lunging—Gaga's knowing parodic performance of blonde pop princess makes transparent the notion that all gendered performance is itself parodic.[58] As singer, Christine Aguilera, says of Lady Gaga: 'I'm not sure who this person is, to be honest. I don't know if it is a man or a woman. I just wasn't sure'.[59] This confusion echoes Jack Halberstam's notion of 'gaga feminism'—working off Lady Gaga's radical excess and willful category confusion—offering new, fluid possibilities beyond 'normal'.[60]

Gaga's costume, off-stage dress, and experimental visuality of the body are enlisted in a queering of the normative. At the Tisch School of the Arts, Lady Gaga took art history courses, wrote a thesis on various pop artists and was particularly influenced by the work of Andy Warhol.[61] Warhol's permanent sartorial performance of strangeness and queerness and the queerly inflected vestimentary performances of David Bowie, Leigh Bowery, and Klaus Nomi in the 1970s and 1980s have been important to Lady Gaga's evolving queered femininity. Her double-edged, against-the-grain quotations from traditional femininity or sex appeal are what make her so engrossing as a performer.

In her early videos, gender parody, while not as overt nor as aesthetically challenging as it later becomes, is nonetheless there. For example, in the 2009 music video, 'Eh Eh', the clothes help enact a kitsch parody of scantily dressed blond pop-stars. She *could* have been another Britney; tanned, blonde, and scantily-clad. But everything is over-saturated, her hair too peroxided and styled (at one point it is shaped into a bow, which would become one of Gaga's motifs), her skin too orange and her clothes too kitsch. This knowing camp enactment playfully satirizes rather than seduces. Her sartorial performance queers notions both of originality, and normative gender and sexuality, placing her in Sedgwick's *transverse* spaces-in-between normative categories. In her imaging of a 'self', Gaga queers culturally inscribed concepts of 'good girl' and 'bad girl raunchiness' unlike the straightforward 'bad girl' acts of Pink or Avril Lavigne.

Postmodern cultural theory, including queer theories of subjectivity, upset the secure idea of a fixed and 'real' subjectivity, instituting the idea of a more mobile, unfolding notion of a self; one which is constantly in the process of forming itself.[62] Lady Gaga's sartorial performance is not an enactment by the 'real person' Stefani Germanotta. As Lady Gaga herself claims, she, Lady Gaga, is the only enactment. Lady Gaga says there is no other 'real', 'everyday' person, aside from the Lady Gaga persona, with its 24/7 sartorial enactments. This unsettles not only the media tradition of looking for and recording the 'real, sincere, and at-home-casual' person, 'in civvies', behind a celebrity, but also assumptions of Western cultural tradition which hold that human subjectivity involves a unitary 'depth model' of identity, that is a solid identity which resides within the core of the person. Jonathan Dollimore argues that camp, as a cultural strategy, 'undermines the depth model of identity from inside, being a kind of parody or mimicry which hollows out from within, making depth recede into its surfaces'.[63] Gaga's performance exceeds received categories of 'authentic' feminine identity, creating, through her multiple sartorial enactments, a more mobile queerer form of subjectivity. With her endless quotations and appropriations from art, fashion and cinema history she implicitly unsettles notions of originality, constantly sidestepping the criticisms of those who fail to read her postmodern quotational sensibility, requiring of her something—be it 'sexiness', 'femininity', 'authenticity', 'originality'—arising from a cultural framing to which she does not aspire.

DRESSING AND UNDRESSING THE BAD GIRL

Gaga's invested performance is as much about what she takes off as what she puts on. The titillation of the conventional 'sexy star's' lasciviousness around exposure/covering is not what Gaga is about. Lizzy Goodman quotes Gaga thus: 'the truth is me and my big dick are all out there for you', and Goodman adds: 'Unlike other pop stars, who tease us with a nip-slip here, and a panty line there, Lady Gaga is a sure thing. She's going to take it all off. And what she asks for in exchange is that we watch'.[64] The famous 'no pants' question is a case in point. The media obsession with her lack of knickers and exposure of her labia, extended to questions of whether she was a hermaphrodite.[65] In the 'Telephone' video, she simulated exposure of her (reputedly male) genitalia in a way that resembles more the campery of a drag queen/ king performance than hetero-normative pornographic clichés. Her parodic bad girl repertoire extends to stage-diving and crowd-surfing with exposed breasts and ripped fishnets.[66] Gaga's gender provocation, as evidenced elsewhere in this chapter, is not designed to sexually attract, arouse or please, but to inhabit her own body in a way that refuses to concede to pre-set cultural limits.

She, queerly and confusingly, is 'blond', she is 'petite but not cute', she is 'attractive' but not 'pleasing or 'appealing', she is daring and powerful but *twists* raunchy, she is 'outrageous' but not 'sexy'.[67] Lady Gaga is fully cognizant of the domain she occupies in her parodic play, saying that, 'The last thing a young woman needs is another picture of a sexy pop star, writhing in sand, covered in grease, touching herself'.[68] The idea of being 'Gaga' and Haus of 'Gaga', a term she reputedly appropriated from Queen's song 'Radio Ga Ga',[69] embraces the vernacular idea of being, or acting, slightly mad, or as she says 'weird', and like other queer performers before her—Warhol, ACT-Up AIDS political activists in the 1980s–90s—she is more than happy for her against-the-grain enactments to be 'misunderstood'.[70] As Sontag makes clear, it is persona not depth of character that is camp's speciality.[71]

SARTORIAL ORIGINALITY, QUEERING ORIGINALITY

Gaga is endlessly accused of pillaging pop cultural and fashion history, of creating nothing new.[72] In her 'Alejandro' video a Dolce & Gabbana vest and Francesco Scognamiglio pantsuit echo Madonna's 1990 video for 'Vogue' (itself laden with references to vintage Hollywood in general, and

Marlene Dietrich in particular). Camille Paglia was happy to pontificate on notions such as who, of Madonna and Gaga, is most original and a 'true heir to Dietrich', a redundant notion in relation to a wide-ranging and frankly appropriative, practice such as Gaga's.[73]

Gaga has been accused of overt plagiarism, specifically of Hussein Chalayan's Spring 2007 'Bubble dress'.[74] Gaga's dress was indeed an apparent replica of Chalayan's design. The wearing of the fake bubble dress reflects a period in which Gaga had not yet attained the status of a pop star and fashion icon to whom designers would lend significant fashion items. In fact since 2009 Gaga has worn many of Chalayan's creations. She appeared on the cover and in a four-page feature in US *Harpers Bazaar*, in October 2011, wearing a custom-made Chalayan dress. Most famously, she arrived at the 2011 Grammy Awards, in an egg-like plastic capsule, created by Chalayan, described by Nicola Formichetti as a 'womb'.[75]

This question of originality is an interesting one though, and it goes to our discussion of the queer import of Gaga's performative enactments. Pre-occupations with questions of originality are implicitly located within the Western cultural trope of 'authenticity': the idea that we have a true, 'authentic' nature, or subjectivity, and that, by extension, creative originality comes out of this authentic, original self. Without trivializing intellectual property issues arising from overt plagiarism, postmodern thinking places less emphasis on a naïve notion of the original creative genius, whose ideas have no precedent. Creative originality is partly seen, in present-day image ubiquity, as the capacity to inventively re-use ideas from the past. Gaga's parodic approach to fame, sexuality and gender, expresses itself through fashion quotation of the kind that inaugurates items like the perverse wheelchair, emblazoned with the interlocking 'Cs' of the Chanel logo, made by The Haus of Gaga for the 'Paparazzi' video. In a similar vein Gaga 'mashes-up' the cultural (and financial) capital embodied in an Hermes 'Birkin' bag by having the Canadian artist Terence Koh write all over it with felt-tip pen. In the 'Judas' video, shot in April 2011, Lady Gaga wears several *haute couture* pieces, including a gown by Christian Lacroix.[76] Of the video, which is steeped in religious imagery, Gaga says with a camp refusal to accede to a culturally 'straight' speaking position: 'In my opinion, the only controversial thing about this video is that I'm wearing Christian Lacroix and Chanel in the same frame'.[77]

FASHION AND POST-FASHION

As mentioned previously, Lady Gaga's creative engagement with dress is both within and beyond fashion, and beyond that represented, for example, by Madonna's famous Jean-Paul Gaultier 'Cone Bra' of the Blond Ambition tour of 1990. Madonna may be a precursor of Lady Gaga but Gaga's work sits in another context altogether both temporally and culturally. Gaga's is a total enactment which employs dress as one of its principal modalities. The 'Telephone' video, shot in early 2010, features both exclusive high fashion garments such as a vintage Thierry Mugler *haute couture* suit and re-appropriates visual tropes from Gaga's own earlier videos.[78] For example, a custom-made outfit by Brian Lichtenberg, fabricated from crime-scene-tape, recalls a garment constructed from rolls of film worn in the 'Paparazzi' video. Similarly she wears Haus of Gaga studded underwear, like that seen in the 2009 'LoveGame' video. Madonna as a performer realized the potential of her appearance in the context of the advent of music video which came to prominence, as she did, in the early 1980s with MTV. By contrast the exponential global dissemination of moving image and sound, via the internet, was a given when Gaga created her first performances. The introduction of video for fashion shows was also a major temporal turn, relevant to the styling of Gaga's videos, bringing a new kind of visuality to fashion. Fashion writers and photographers alike have noted how the introduction of video cameras to fashion shows radically altered the interface between fashion collections and fashion publics. When Nicola Formichetti styled Lady Gaga for the cover of *i-D* magazine in 2010,[79] with photography by Nick Knight, Gaga was in the elite company of those who were working on new ways of visualizing fashion through photography and film. Fashion photographer, Nick Knight had started SHOWstudio in 2000 specifically to bring a radical photographer's eye to the moving-image presentation of fashion in a new hybrid, fashion-film.

ART, FASHION AND GAGA'S GESAMTKUNSTWERK

Gaga's interface with fashion-film and music video creates a forum for her unique blending of visual forms. Her performances are a form of *Gesamtkunstwerk*. That is to say that all aspects of her performance—dress, image, body-props, music, sound, staging, photography, fashion-film, music video—come together under her creative direction to create a whole art work.

'Fashion is everything', she said in June 2008:

> When I'm writing music, I'm thinking about the clothes I want to wear on stage. It's all about everything altogether—performance art, pop performance, art, fashion. For me, it's everything coming together and being a real story that will bring back the super-fan. I want to bring that back. I want the imagery to be so strong that fans will want to eat and taste and lick every part of us.[80]

The term *Gesamtkunstwerk* was used in the context of nineteenth-century opera to denote the way that opera-theatre can bring all aspects of creative endeavor together in a 'total work of art'. Importantly for this discussion, the idea of a 'total work of art' was brought into currency in both the interdisciplinary Bauhaus in the 1920s and 1930s and in the context of radical performance art in the late 1960s and 1970s, when the notion of a 'total work of art', *Gesamtkunstwerk,* was employed to describe performances, happenings and installations, in New York and other centers of avant-garde art.[81] Lady Gaga is well aware not only of the Bauhaus, and the Warhol Factory as creative models, but also of the work of avant-garde performance artists of this period, citing several of them— Yoko Ono, Marina Abramovic and Cindy Sherman—as major influences on her creative practice.[82] These artists deployed their own bodies in a range of strategies to unsettle aspects of gender and raise issues regarding human embodiment itself. Abramovic's solo performance-art oeuvre, and her collaborative work with fellow artist Ulay, such as *Imponderabilia,* first performed in 1977, confronted the operation of the gendered body in space. Yoko Ono's *Cut Piece,* first performed in 1964, among her other performances in the sixties and seventies, drew attention to the implications of the fact that her body was clothed and gendered female. Cindy Sherman's *Untitled Film Stills,* from the late seventies, consisting of sixty-nine photographs of herself in the guise of different self-invented stereo-typically female film 'characters', similarly unsettles culturally formed notions of femininity. These artists brought the sexualized and gendered body to the fore as a site of artistic investigation. Their work resonated with the sexual and counter cultural politics of the 1960s and 1970s just as Lady Gaga's work resonates with new gender forms and notions of post-normal.[83]

Lady Gaga has an informed facility with the history of performance-art and the unsettling use of unconventional performance modes in artistic avant-gardes such as Dada in the early twentieth century. She is on record as stating that as well as the strong influences of the female performance artists mentioned above she attended avant-garde art performances at Lower East Side art spaces when she was a spaced-out teenager.[84] Lady Gaga writes a column, 'From the desk of Lady Gaga', for *V Magazine,* on fashion, fame, art and culture, which echoes the rhetorical style of early twentieth-century art manifestos; the columns are presented as numbered 'Memoranda' and hold forth with culturally encompassing manifesto-like utterances.[85]

JO CALDERONE: WHAT IS THIS THING CALLED GENDER?

Lady Gaga acknowledges the importance of queer readings of her work, and notes the significance of the gay community to her early success: 'The turning point for me was the gay community', she has said. 'I've got so many gay fans and they're so loyal to me and they really lifted me up.

They'll always stand by me and I'll always stand by them. It's not an easy thing to create a fan-base. Being invited to play [the San Francisco Pride rally], that was a real turning point for me as an artist'.[86]

Gaga's enactments of queer, and queer readings of her work, are not simply an extension of her progressive politics. True, she is pro-gay-rights and has embraced her gay fans and sees them as her base audience.[87] But importantly, a queer sensibility, as Mark Turner says, may also lead us to 'think outside the grand narratives that continue to see terms such as "men" and "women" in more or less uncomplicated ways'.[88] As he puts it, this has the potential to 'get us beyond binary thinking ("gay" and "straight"), of the sort that has defined so much of the way urban modernity is understood'.[89]

As we have claimed throughout this chapter the Lady Gaga persona queers notions of femininity, fame, and female sexiness. For this she has been accused of hermaphroditism and she herself has been happy to throw out the power of her 'big dick' as we have noted. Jo Calderone is an achingly handsome man brought to sartorial performative embodiment by Gaga. She says of Jo:

> In a culture that attempts to quantify beauty with a visual paradigm and almost mathematical standard, how can we fuck with the malleable minds of onlookers and shift the world's perspective on what's beautiful? I asked myself this question. And the answer? Drag.[90]

Drag, as we have said, was an important visual and political element in the symbolic foundation of Gay Lib at Stonewall. Esther Newton's work on drag influenced Judith Butler's notion of queer performativity which sees drag as an important cultural trope for thinking queerly, the parodic enactment of gender in drag bringing to consciousness the notion that all gender enactments are parodic.[91]

Jo Calderone was created by Gaga and Nick Formichetti, as Gaga recalls:

> Nick and I photographed [Gaga as] Jo, omitted his biological sex, and shopped the photographs around to men's fashion magazines. The cover of *Vogue Hommes* Japan, a major Japanese men's publication, was a coup to say the least, exciting mostly because we had convinced the editors that Jo Calderone was a male model and had sold his look as the next big thing.[92]

Jo Calderone also features in the video clip for 'Yoü and I'. Through the use of special effects. Jo plays the lover of Gaga herself. At the 2011 MTV Video Music Awards Gaga performed as Jo. Styled by Nicola Formichetti he wears a Haynes-style white t-shirt recalling James Dean, but in this case by UNIQLO, his pants are by Dior Homme and boots by Chanel.[93]

THE MEAT DRESS

Lady Gaga's enormous cultural capital and her spectacular commercial success has meant that she has access to a type of fashion that can't simply be bought, including clothes that have yet to be presented on a runway, and those lent from a designer's archive.[94] Nevertheless she continues to wear pieces created by the Haus of Gaga, 'homemade' designs that constituted the bulk of Lady Gaga's performing wardrobe prior to her astronomical rise to fame. The 'Meat Dress', which Gaga wore to the September 12, 2010 MTV Video Music Awards (one of many outfits she wore that night), is perhaps her most notorious outfit, to date, generating global, shocked and admiring, publicity, including the BBC placing interpretations of the dress on its website.[95] Cher who presented Gaga with her MTV award and embraced her on stage, said afterwards, on Twitter, 'Meat Dress was So INTERESTING Up Close & The way it was cut & Fitted to her body was AMAZING! Meat purse was genius! As Art piece it was astonishing!'[96]

The 'Meat Dress' brings together several of the themes raised in this chapter regarding Gaga's approach to her sartorial performance. It was preceded by the 'Meat Bikini' in the September 2010 issue *Vogue Hommes* Japan: a special pin-up poster insert featured Gaga wearing the 'meat bikini', with photography by Terry Richardson. Gaga, as Jo Calderone, was also featured on the cover of the same issue.[97] Both the bikini and the dress were made by Franc Fernandez, an Argentinian-born designer, who has designed several outfits for Gaga. After the sensation of the bikini, Fernandez was contacted by Nicola Formichetti, who as the magazine's fashion director, had styled the *Vogue Hommes* Japan cover, to make a full dress of meat.[98]

The 'Meat Dress' quotes fashion history in its resonance with Elsa Schiaparelli's 'Tears Dress', a silk and viscose evening ensemble, of 1938, which presented a *trompe l'oeil* effect of 'tears' in the fabric, printed to resemble pieces of flayed skin, revealing both the underside of the 'skin tears' and the pink 'viscera' underneath. The dress was created in dialogue with the Surrealist artist Salvador Dali, who designed the fabric, and it forms part of Schiaparelli's engagement with illusion and metaphor in luxury dress. It also resonates with Gaga's interest in the history of avant-garde art referred to above, evoking some of the feelings engendered by the visceral and bloody body-works of the Viennese Actionists in the 1960s. The 1987 work by Canadian artist Jana Sterbak, 'Vanitas: Flesh Dress for an Albino Anorexic', was acknowledged by Franc Fernandez as part of the genesis of his design for the meat outfits.[99] This didn't stop the *LA Times* claiming another case of Gaga plagiarism while reporting that the Sterbak work, was made from '50 pounds of raw flank steak, stitched together into a slowly rotting garment and displayed, to a sizable hue and cry, in a 1991 exhibition at Canada's National Gallery'.[100] Chinese 'body-artist', Zhang Huan, has also created a steak suit for his work 'My New York' at the Whitney in 2002, a work which sits within the trajectory of radical performance art from 1960s onwards, so influential on Gaga's 'total work of art'.[101]

CONCLUSION

Nothing in popular culture or fashionable discourse is a given; all is up for interpretation. The Lady Gaga persona is a sartorially engaged embodiment of a series of concepts and ideas, inviting—and receiving—commentary from multiple interpretive viewpoints. It is the principal argument of this chapter that all invested (*i.e.* 'dressed') performances are conceptual enactments which have little to do with the 'true personality', or the 'natural' person. Gaga's sartorial performance is not a product created by the music industry, or the fashion industry for that matter, but a creative, continually unfolding, enactment employing all of the apparatus and tropologies of the artist. The most engaging aspect of Gaga's sophisticated and informed approach to fashion and dress—aside from its visual complexity, excess and daring—is the way it is used to *queer* fixed notions of gender and sexuality, her on- and off-stage performance enacting her camp refusal to accede to a culturally straight subjectivity. We have argued that Gaga's appropriative approach to all forms of visual culture, including myriad aspects of fashion, unsettles gender and sexuality while, like fashion itself, enticing the sensibilities of viewers and observers with its luxury, inventiveness and complex intersections with the ever-changing present.

NOTES

1. Elio Iannacci, 'World Gone Gaga', *Flare* (December 2009), 108–113.
2. Roland Barthes, *The Fashion System*, tr. Matthew Ward and Richard Howard (London: Jonathan Cape, 1985 [1967]). This is discussed further below.
3. As told by Gaga in an anecdote about Jimmy Iovine. 'In Camera: Lady Gaga', SHOWstudio, (21 August 2009) (online at: http://showstudio.com/project/in_camera/session/lady_gaga <accessed: 6 May 2012>.
4. 'Passnotes No 2843', *The Guardian* (09 Septermber 2010), 2 (online at: http://www.guardian.co.uk/music/2010/sep/08/pass-notes-lady-gaga-meat-bikini <accessed: 6 May 2012>.
5. Lady Gaga, spoken during her *Monster Ball* tour (10 December 2009) (online at: http://www.youtube.com/watch?v=Vg2SgI3ByBM) <accessed: 18 March 2013>.
6. Andrew Hornery, 'Much ado about Lady Gaga', *The Sydney Morning Herald*, (16 July 2011) (online at: http://www.smh.com.au/lifestyle/private-sydney/much-ado-about-lady-gaga-20110715-1hhqe.html) <accessed: 6 May 2012>.
7. Hugh Fielder and Malcolm Mackenzie, *Lady Gaga: A Monster Romance*, (London: Flame Tree, 2012), 75.
8. Brian Hiatt, 'Lady Gaga: New York Doll Lady', *Rolling Stone* (6 November 2009) (online: http://www.rollingstone.com/music/news/lady-gaga-new-york-doll-20090611) <accessed: 6 May 2012>; Lisa Robinson, 'In Lady

Gaga's Wake', *Vanity Fair*, (January 2012) (online at: http://www.vanityfair. com/hollywood/2012/01/lady-gaga-201201) <accessed: 6 May 2012>.

9. Ralph Geisenhanslüke, 'Lady GaGa ist keine Bühnenrolle', *Zeit Online* (4 May 2009) (online at: http://www.zeit.de/2009/19/Traum-Gaga-19) <accessed: 12 November 2012>.

10. David McDiarmid, 'A Short History of Facial Hair', a 1993 performance essay which was recreated as a film and shown at 'The Fashion Space' gallery London College of Fashion, University of the Arts, London, in 2011, co-curated by Sally Gray and Magda Keaney.

11. The role of Nicola Formichetti in the creation of Jo Calderone is discussed below.

12. Cathy Horyn, 'At Mugler, Genius and Its Limits', *The New York Times* (23 March 2011) (online at: http://www.nytimes.com/2011/03/24/ fashion/24NICOLA.html?pagewanted=all) <accessed: 6 May 2012>.

13. Nicolai Hartvig, 'Lady Gaga Shows Off New Rilke Tattoo', *The Huffington* Post (10 August 2009) (online at: http://www.huffingtonpost. com/2009/08/10/lady-gaga-show-off-new-ri_n_255320.html) <accessed: 6 May 2012>.

14. Barthes, *The Fashion System*.

15. Andy Stafford and Michael Carter (eds.), *The Language of Fashion: Roland Barthes* (Sydney: Power, 2005), 101.

16. Sarah Mower, 'Review: Alexander McQueen Spring 2010 Ready-To-Wear', *style.com* (6 October 2009) (online at: http://www.style.com/fashionshows/ review/S2010RTW-AMCQUEEN) <accessed: 6 May 2012>.

17. Amy Odell, 'Models Refused to Walk Alexander McQueen's Spring 2010 Show Because the Shoes Terrified Them', *New York Magazine* (22 December 2009) (online at: http://nymag.com/thecut/2009/12/models_refused_to_ walk_alexand.html?) <accessed: 6 May 2012>.

18. Derek Blasberg, 'LADY GAGA: THE INTERVIEW', *Harpers Bazaar* (US edition) (May 2011) (online at: http://www.harpersbazaar.com/magazine/ feature-articles/lady-gaga-interview) <accessed: 6 May 2012>.

19. Robin Givhan, 'Armani Goes Gaga', *Newsweek* (06 March 2011) (online at: http://www.thedailybeast.com/newsweek/2011/02/06/armani-goes-gaga. html) <accessed: 6 May 201>.

20. Alison Powell, 'GAGA, INC', *Billboard, suppl. SPECIAL EDITION: THE 2011 BILLBOARD MUSIC AWARDS* (May 2011), 62–65; Nathan Bell, 'Stand apart and then go Gaga', *Sydney Morning Herald* (11 June 2011), 15 (online at: http://www.smh.com.au/money/stand-apart-and-then-go-gaga- 20110610–1fwpx.html) <accessed: 6 May 2012>.

21. Amy Wicks, 'Tough Times at the Newsstand', *Women's Wear Daily* (9 August 2011) (online at: http://www.wwd.com/media-news/media-features/ fashion-magazines-fall-at-newsstand-5048220?module=today) <accessed: 12 November 2012>.

22. Dirk Smillie, 'The Business Of Lady Gaga', *Forbes* 25 November 2009 (online at: http://www.forbes.com/2009/11/25/lady-gaga-music-business- entertainment-marketing.html) <accessed: 12 November 2012>.

23. Lady Gaga and Terry Richardson, *LADY GAGA x TERRY RICHARDSON* (New York NY: Grand Central, 2011).

24. Hilary Moss, 'CFDA Awards 2011: Lady Gaga, Marc Jacobs & Proenza Schouler Take Top Honors', *The Huffington Post* (7 June 2011) (online at: http://www.huffingtonpost.com/2011/06/07/cfda-awards-2011-lady- gaga-marc-jacobs-proenza-schouler_n_872257.html) <accessed: 6 May 2012>.

25. 'In Camera: Lady Gaga', SHOWstudio.

26. Lady Gaga, 'V MAGAZINE MEMORANDUM No. 1', *V Magazine* (May 2011) (online at: http://www.vmagazine.com/2011/05/from-the-desk-of-lady-gaga/) <accessed: 6 May 2012>.
27. Lisa Robinson, 'Lady Gaga's Cultural Revolution', *Vanity Fair* (September 2010) (online at: http://www.vanityfair.com/hollywood/features/2010/09/lady-gaga-201009?printable=true#ixzz1SkBDtc7P) <accessed: 6 May 2012>; Time Staff, 'The 2010 TIME 100 Poll', *Time.com*, (1 April 2010) (online at: http://www.time.com/time/specials/packages/article/0,28804,1972075_1 972078_1972195,00.html) <accessed: 6 May 2012>; Dorothy Pomerantz, 'Lady Gaga Tops Celebrity 100 List', *Forbes.com* (18 May 2011) (online at: http://www.forbes.com/2011/05/16/lady-gaga-tops-celebrity-100–11.html) <accessed: 6 May 2012>.
28. Sarah Mower, 'Review: Balmain Spring 2009 Ready-To-Wear', *style.com* (28 September 2008) (online at: http://www.style.com/fashionshows/review/S2009RTW-BALMAIN) <accessed: 6 May 2012>.
29. Suzy Menkes, 'Paparazzi! At Chanel, Lagerfeld and Kidman star', *The New York Times* (09 October 2004) (online at: http://www.nytimes.com/2004/10/08/style/08iht-rchanel.html) <accessed: 6 May 2012>.
30. Nicola Formichetti, 'MTV MUSIC AWARDS—LADY GAGA' (n.d.) (online at: http://www.nicolaformichetti.com/2009/09/14/mtv-music-awards-lady-gaga/) <accessed: 6 May 2012>.
31. Personal communication from Nigel Shaw Costume Design Sydney to the author, 10 October 2012.
32. Whitney Pastorek, 'On the Scene: Lady GaGa's "LoveGame" video', *EW.com* (03 March 2009) (online at: http://popwatch.ew.com/2009/02/03/on-the-scene-la/) <accessed: 6 May 2012>.
33. '*Beautiful, Dirty, Rich* release date information', *Interscope.com* (online at: http://www.interscope.com/artist/releases/detail.aspx?pid=1572&aid=599) <accessed 6 May 2012>.
34. Dhani Mau, 'Exclusive: "Edge of Glory" is the First Time Donatella Opened the Versace Archives for a Music Video', *Fashionista.com* (17 June 2011) (online at: http://fashionista.com/2011/06/ege-of-glory-is-the-first-time-donatella-opened-the-versace-archives-for-a-music-video/) <accessed: 6 May 2012>.
35. Jocelyn Vena, 'Lady Gaga "Very Pleased" with New Music, Video', *MTV.com*, (11/05/2009) (online at: http://www.mtv.com/news/articles/1611042/lady-gaga-very-pleased-with-new-music-video.jhtml) <accessed: 6 May 2012>.
36. Kee Chang, 'Q&A with B. Åkerlund', *AnthemMagazine.com* (09 June 2009) (online at: http://anthemmagazine.com/b-Åkerlund/) <accessed: 6 May 2012>.
37. *Ibid.*
38. McDiarmid, 'A Short History of Facial Hair'.
39. Susan Sontag, 'Notes on "Camp"', *Against Interpretation and Other Essays* (New York, NY: Anchor 1990 [1964]), 275–292. There are many relevant post-Sontag analyses of the cultural politics of camp, including an exhaustive recent exploration of camp sensibility in David Halperin's *How to be Gay* (Cambridge, MA: Belknap, 2012) but Sontag is the original source on this question.
40. See, for instance, Eve Kosofsky Sedgwick, *Tendencies* (Durham, NC: Duke University Press, 1993) and Judith Butler, *Gender Trouble: Feminism and the Subversion of Identity* (New York, NY: Routledge, 1990).
41. Sontag, 'Notes on "Camp"', 273.
42. *Ibid.*, 277.

43. Sedgwick, *Tendencies*, xii.
44. *Ibid.*
45. Butler, *Gender Trouble*, 32
46. *Ibid.*
47. *Ibid.*, 33
48. *Ibid.*
49. Megan Gustashaw, 'Happy Birthday, Lady Gaga!: Behold The 7 Most Fabulous Outfits From Your 25th Year', *Glamour.com* (28 March 2012) (online at: http://www.glamour.com/fashion/blogs/slaves-to-fashion/2012/03/happy-birthday-lady-gaga-behol.html) <accessed: 6 May 2012>.
50. Robinson, 'Lady Gaga's Cultural Revolution'. Italics in original.
51. *Paris Is Burning*, dir. Jennie Livingston (Off White Productions, 1990), 71 mins.
52. Robinson, 'Lady Gaga's Cultural Revolution'.
53. Tim Blanks, 'Review: Emporio Armani Spring 2011 Menswear', *style.com* (20 June 2010) (online at: http://www.style.com/fashionshows/review/S2011MEN-EARMANI) <accessed: 6 May 2012>.
54. Joshua David Stein and Noah Michelson, 'The Lady Is a Vamp', *Out.com* (9 August 2009) (online at: http://www.out.com/entertainment/2009/08/09/lady-vamp?page=0,1) <accessed: 6 May 2012>.
55. Don't Ask Don't Tell was the official United States policy on gays in the military between 21 December 1993 and 20 September 2011, when it was formally abolished. This meant that from the latter date gays and lesbians who identified themselves would no longer face automatic discharge. See David Lerman, 'U.S. Military Ends "Don't Ask, Don't Tell" Policy for Gay Troops', *Bloomberg.com* (20 September 2011) (online at: http://www.bloomberg.com/news/2011–09–20/u-s-military-ends-don-t-ask-don-t-tell-policy-for-gay-troops.html) <accessed: 18 March 2013>.
56. *The Ellen DeGeneres Show*, NBC Universal, 13 September 2010. See also O'Brien's commentary in this volume on the same statement.
57. Whitney Pastorek, 'Lady GaGa: Bonus quotes from the dance-pop queen!', *EW.com* (9 February 2009) (online at: http://popwatch.ew.com/2009/02/09/lady-gaga-inter/) <accessed: 6 May 2012>.
58. Butler, *Gender Trouble*, 31–33.
59. Charlie Amter, 'Five Minutes with Xtina: Christina Aguilera Takes a Look Back at a Decade on Top', *Los Angeles Times* (11 November 2008) (online at: http://latimesblogs.latimes.com/music_blog/2008/11/five-minutes-wi.html) <accessed: 6 May 2012>.
60. J. Jack Halberstam, *Gaga Feminism: Sex, Gender And The End of Normal* (Boston, MA: Beacon, 2012).
61. Neil McCormick, 'Lady Gaga: "I've Always Been Famous, You Just Didn't Know It"', *The Daily Telegraph* (16 February 2010) (online at: http://www.telegraph.co.uk/culture/music/rockandpopfeatures/7221051/Lady-Gaga-Ive-always-been-famous-you-just-didnt-know-it.html) <accessed: 6 May 2012>.
62. See, for example, Butler, *Gender Trouble*, and Halberstam, *Gaga Feminism*, but also Jack Babuscio, 'Camp and the Gay Sensibility', and David Bergman, 'Strategic Camp: The Art of Gay Rhetoric', both in David Bergman (ed.), *Camp Grounds: Style and Homosexuality* (Amherst, MA: University of Massachusets Press, 1993), 19–38 and 92–109; Harry Brod, 'Masculinity as Masquerade', in *The Masculine Masquerade: Masculinity and Representation*, eds. Andrew Perchuk and Helaine Posner (Cambridge, MA: MIT Press, 1995), 13–19; Pamela Robertson, *Guilty Pleasures: Feminist Camp from Mae West to Madonna* (Durham, NC: Duke University Press, 1996).

63. Jonathan Dollimore (1996) *Sexual Dissidence Augustine to Wilde, Freud to Foucault* (Oxford: Clarendon Press, 1996), 310–311.

64. Lady Gaga, quoted in Lizzy Goodman, *Lady Gaga Extreme Style*, (London, Harper Collins, 2010), 19. The original quotation reads: "When the truth is, me and my big fucking dick are all out there for you." (Sylvia Patterson, 'She's the man', *Q Magazine* (April 2010), 52).

65. *Ibid.*, 30.

66. Steven Avalos, 'Lady Gaga's Wild, Nearly Naked Crowd Surf At Lolla-palooza', *Pop Eater* (09 August 2010) (online at: http://www.popeater.com/2010/08/09/lady-gaga-lollapalooza-crowd-surf-stage-dive/) <accessed: May 6 2012>.

67. Interestingly, Camille Paglia claims, as a criticism, that Gaga lacks sex appeal (see Camille Paglia, 'Lady Gaga and the Death of Sex', *The Sunday Times* (12 September 2010) (online at: http://www.thesundaytimes.co.uk/sto/public/magazine/article389697.ece) <accessed: 6 May 2012>).

68. Miranda Purves, 'New York Doll', *Elle* (US edition) (January 2010) (online at: http://www.elle.com/Pop-Culture/Cover-Shoots/Lady-Gaga) <accessed: 6 May 2012>.

69. Hadley Freeman, 'Is Lady Gaga a Feminist Icon?', *G2: The Guardian* (17 September 2010), 9 (online at: http://www.guardian.co.uk/music/2010/sep/17/lady-gaga-feminist-icon) <accessed: 6 May 2012>.

70. Pastorek, 'Lady GaGa: Bonus quotes'.

71. Sontag, 'Notes on "Camp"', 286.

72. Freeman, 'Is Lady Gaga a Feminist Icon?'

73. Paglia, 'Lady Gaga and the Death of Sex'.

74. Andreas Kokkino, 'Fashion Déjà Vu | Lady GaGa Strikes Again', *T: The New York Times Style Magazine* (19 March 2009) (online at: http://tmagazine.blogs.nytimes.com/2009/03/19/fashion-deja-vu-lady-gaga-strikes-again/) <accessed: 6 May 2012>.

75. Jocelyn Vena, 'Lady Gaga Arrives At Grammys In An Egg', *MTV.com* (13 February 2011) (online at: http://www.mtv.com/news/articles/1657833/lady-gaga-grammy-arrival-egg.jhtml) <accessed: 6 May 2012>.

76. Jocelyn Vena, 'Lady Gaga Shoots "Judas" Video', *MTV.com*, (4 April 2011) (online at: http://www.mtv.com/news/articles/1661221/lady-gaga-judas-video.jhtml) <accessed: 6 May 2012>.

77. Lady Gaga, quoted in Dodai Stewart, 'Lady Gaga Reveals The *Only* Controversial Thing About "Judas" Video' (online at: http://jezebel.com/5799284/lady-gaga-reveals-the-only-controversial-thing-about-judas-video) <accessed: 6 May 2012>.

78. Gil Kaufman, 'Lady Gaga Says She Raised $500,000 For Haiti Relief', *MTV.com* (27 January 2010) (online at: http://www.mtv.com/news/articles/1630614/lady-gaga-raised-500000-haiti-relief.jhtml) <accessed: 6 May 2012>.

79. Cover, *i-D* magazine, no. 308 (pre-Fall 2010).

80. Chris Harris and Kim Stolz, 'Lady GaGa Brings Her Artistic Vision Of Pop Music To New Album—and A New Kids Song', *MTV.com* (9 June 2008) (online at: http://www.mtv.com/news/articles/1589013/lady-gaga-revives-art-pop-music.jhtml) <accessed: 6 May 2012>.

81. Adrian Henri, *Total Art: Environments, Happenings, and Performance* (London: Thames and Hudson, 1974).

82. 'In Camera: Lady Gaga', SHOWstudio. Lady Gaga performed with Yoko Ono at the Orpheum, Los Angeles, in 2010 (see Halberstam, *Gaga Feminism*, 138).

83. Halberstam, *Gaga Feminism*.

84. 'In Camera: Lady Gaga', SHOWstudio.
85. Lady Gaga, 'V MAGAZINE MEMORANDUM No. 1'.
86. Jocelyn Vena, 'Lady Gaga On Success: "The Turning Point For Me Was The Gay Community"', *MTV.com* (7 May 2009) (online at: http://www.mtv.com/news/articles/1610781/lady-gaga-on-success-turning-point-me-was-gay-community.jhtml) <accessed: 6 May 2012>.
87. Gil Kaufman, 'Lady Gaga Talks VMA Meat Suit With Ellen DeGeneres', *MTV.com*, (13 September 2010) (online at: http://www.mtv.com/news/articles/1647701/lady-gaga-talks-vma-meat-suit-with-ellen-degeneres.jhtml) <accessed: 6 May 2012>.
88. Mark Turner, *Backward Glances: Cruising the Queer Streets of New York and London* (London: Reaktion, 2003), 45.
89. *Ibid.*
90. Lady Gaga, 'V MAGAZINE MEMORANDUM No. 4', *V Magazine* (November 2011) (online at: http://www.vmagazine.com/2011/10/v-magazine-gaga-memorandum-no-4/) <accessed 6 May 2012>.
91. Butler, *Gender Trouble*, 136–137.
92. Lady Gaga, 'V MAGAZINE MEMORANDUM No. 4'.
93. Andi Teran, 'Lady Gaga Opens the 2011 VMAs In Menswear As Alter Ego "Jo Calderone"', *MTV.com* (28 August 2011) (Online at: http://style.mtv.com/2011/08/28/lady-gaga-jo-calderone-vma/) <accessed 6 May 2012>.
94. Lady Gaga's video for *Marry the Night* video includes 'next season's Calvin Klein' (online at: http://www.youtube.com/watch?v=cggNqDAtJYU) <accessed 6 May 2012>.
95. Denise Winterman and Jon Kelly, 'Five Interpretations of Lady Gaga's Meat Dress', *BBC News Magazine* (14 September 2010) (online at: http://www.bbc.co.uk/news/magazine-11297832) <accessed: 18 March 2013>.
96. Jodi Jill, 'Cher Talks about Lady Gaga Meat Dress on Twitter: Calls It "Art"', *examiner.com* (13 September 2010), (Online at: http://www.examiner.com/article/cher-talks-about-lady-gaga-meat-dress-on-twitter-calls-it-art) <accessed: 6 May 2012>.
97. Nicola Formichetti, 'LADY GAGA FOR VOGUE HOMMES JAPAN 5' (n.d.) (online at: http://www.nicolaformichetti.com/2010/09/06/lady-gaga-for-vogue-homems-japan-5/) <accessed: 6 May 2012>.
98. Sharon Clott, 'Everything You Wanted To Know About Lady Gaga's VMA Meat Dress!', *MTV.com* (13 September 2010) (online at: http://style.mtv.com/2010/09/13/2010-vmas-lady-gaga-meat-dress-real/) <accessed: 10 May 2012>.
99. 'A Conversation with Franc Fernandez', *Art Guide Miami* (n.d.) (online at: http://www.artguidemiami.com/interviews/franc-fernandez) <accessed: 10 May 2012>.
100. Christopher Knight, 'Lady Gaga, Meat Jana Sterbak', *Los Angeles Times* (13 September 2010) (online at: http://latimesblogs.latimes.com/culturemonster/2010/09/lady-gaga-meat-dress-recycled.html) <accessed: 6 May 2012>.
101. Eleanor Heartney, 'Zhang Huan: Becoming the Body' (originally published in *Zhang Huan: Altered States*, ed. Melissa Chiu (Milan: Charta, 2007) (online at: http://www.zhanghuan.com/ShowText.asp?id=30&sClassID=1) <accessed: 19 March 2013>.

4 Who's Calling?

Telephone Songs, Female Vocal Empowerment and Signification

Lisa Colton

Among technologies of the past century, the telephone is surely one of the most ubiquitous, even within its constantly developing packaging.[1] It has functioned as a transporter of voice for over a hundred years, and has also featured prominently in popular song. Songs featuring women on the telephone provide paradoxical, performative examples of female vocal empowerment and entrapment: their voices contained within the technology, their bodies primed to pick up the call, their utterances and inner desires amplified and directed through the mouthpiece. Other songs present male singers but use the telephone as a gateway to women and their bodies. This chapter examines the corpus of telephone songs, looking especially at the ways in which fictional romantic relationships are governed by, or heightened by, telephone technology. Lady Gaga's 'Telephone' (2009, *The Fame Monster*) serves as a stimulus to explore the history of telephone songs and their relationship with the discourse of female empowerment within popular music. Going beyond the words spoken, I will demonstrate how the presentation of women's telephone voices, in song and in music, affects the significance of the singer's gestures through the musical presentation of these words.

GENDER AND THE TELEPHONE

There are well over one hundred popular songs that feature telephone technology. What is it about the telephone that has attracted so many commentators in the musical world? The social history and function of the telephone are fundamental to understanding the reasons why performers have returned to telephones in their songs; the telephone is tied to a history that is strongly inflected by issues of sex, gender, and ethnicity. Developed and initially marketed as a technology to facilitate business transactions between men, a stage in its history in which the advantages of the invention were not immediately embraced as one might have expected, the telephone was emblematic of a culture in which technological mastery was associated with masculinity and the public domain. The gender split here was typical of nineteenth-century culture, in which women's place on the social spectrum was distant from logic and the industrial trappings of civilized society, located instead as part of the innocent, natural world.[2] However, simply because the telephone was marketed for a particular type of user did not prevent its increasing adoption elsewhere: by the 1920s, telephones had become a more prominent part of domestic life. Although the telephone was now marketed as something to enable women to work within their domestic space more efficiently and safely (ordering deliveries instead of needing to leave the home, for example) women quickly appropriated the telephone for their own purposes, which were focused on sociability. The telephone may have been invented by Scotsman Alexander Graham Bell in the US, but in the transition from manual to automatic switching systems America lagged behind the rest of the world. In place of the automation enjoyed in the United Kingdom and elsewhere, American Telephone and Telegraph—by far the largest of such companies—continued to rely upon 'hundreds of thousands of high-school educated, middle-class young women who served as human telephone switches'.[3] This manual work was in keeping with women's place in business and industry more generally, in which they occupied temporary, low-status, and repetitive jobs in production lines or in the office environment. In these scenarios, women were simply part of the technology, rather than being empowered by it; women's hands worked the mechanisms that produced a range of goods and services, but the economic and power structures that controlled the industry were governed by men. Switch operation was a low-paying activity, whose cultural image was primarily a white one, even though many black women were employed by the telecom industry.[4] At this stage in the telephone's history, musicians already used connection technology as the stimulus for new material: Glenn Miller's swing band number 'Pennsylvania 6–5000' (1940), for example, takes its name from the manually switch-operated number of the Hotel Pennsylvania, in which his band performed. The association between women as switchboard operators, sex and the body appeared increasingly in popular song; Nick Lowe's 'Switchboard Susan' (1979) is packed with fairly basic innuendos about Susan's 'number' (actually her bust, waist and hip measurement, as one might find in a personal advert: 38–27–38) and her ability to give the singer an 'extension'.

In the middle of the twentieth century, the telephone as a piece of technology was still explicitly gendered in Western culture.[5] In the 1950s and 1960s, the popular media frequently reflected on the tension between a father's control of the home as head of the family, and his wife and daughter's use of the telephone to organize social and even romantic engagements; the image of young women waiting for the phone to ring from a potential suitor was ubiquitous (it was considered improper or forward for her to make the first move). Women used the telephone differently, making longer, more frequent, social calls than men, or using the phone for contact with others if isolated in a rural community. As with other forms of technology developed in the nineteenth century, most notably the bicycle, social commentators lampooned women's embrace of new contraptions, revealing a fear that unchaperoned women would be unregulated in their movements, behaviors, thoughts, or interactions. They might also engage in frivolous activities and 'idle talk' or gossip. As Julie Wosk has explained, 'social critics fretted about opportunities for unsupervised romance. They worried, too, that women and men would take sexual liberties, a theme that occurred often in tales about technologies like the telephone and the telegraph, which offered new opportunities for courtship and flirtation'.[6] Wilson Pickett's 1966 hit '634–5789 (Soulsville U.S.A.)' demonstrates the perceived causal link between a woman calling her lover and a guaranteed sexual encounter to follow, underpinned by a chorus ending 'all you've got to do is pick up your phone and dial 634–5789'. By the late 1970s, attitudes had not really changed, so that when Blondie covered The Nerves's 'Hanging on the Telephone' (1976) in 1978, the effect was quite different in terms of its reception. With a male protagonist, as performed by The Nerves, 'Hanging on the Telephone' fitted alongside similar songs that used the notion of the girl answering the telephone as a signal to her suitor of his likely sexual conquest, and her ignoring of the call as sexually frustrating; the one left hanging and powerless in this song was the caller rather than the recipient. With Debbie Harry singing, it is difficult to avoid hearing the lyric as anything other than a woman waiting on a call, regardless of the actual text. The association of women's phone calls with gossip was also treated satirically in Lou Reed's 'New York Conversation' (on *Transformer*, 1972), in which his campy vocal delivery and Eastern melodic accompaniment aped Jewish women or gay men on the phone, before finally closing with a line that brings the song back to the core telephone song genre in referring to needing to speak to his lover.

New additions and adaptations to telephone technology in the later part of the twentieth century continued to affect the ways that women managed their relationships with men and with one another. The answering machine, intended to prevent important calls being missed if one was out of the home, was also 'misused' to screen calls, enabling the avoidance of certain callers or conversations; a woman's availability was now more in her control as she could pretend to be elsewhere. Facilities such as 'call interrupt' or 'caller display' (showing the number of origin) were appropriated in similar ways.[7] Although one might expect developments in technologies made during an age of increased emancipation of women to be free from the strictures of gender roles, in fact the weight of cultural history simply tends to translate previous power structures to the new version of each invention. Digital technologies—such as the smartphone—'thus have embedded within them histories of these "simple" technologies on which assumptions about masculinity and femininity have been formulated'.[8] As Frissen has explained, the mobile phone's use by men and women is perceived very differently: for men, mobile technology has extended their public sphere work activity into their private, domestic space; for women, the technology has allowed them to 'take their personal lives with them wherever they go', for example in staying in contact with young family when at work.[9]

The perpetual embedding of previous constructions of gender within new versions of the telephone can be demonstrated readily in the corpus of 'telephone songs', which for the purpose of this chapter I define as any song in which the telephone features as a significant component of lyric. Such songs are, almost without exception, related in some way to romantic relationships, usually explicitly from a boy to a girl or—less frequently—the other way round. Songs featuring calls between men are rare, arguably because of the combined implication of a popular song, commonly about romance, and the trope of the telephone song that tends to emphasize the dynamic of separated lovers. Exceptions include Steely Dan's 1974 hit 'Rikki Don't Lose That Number', a song believed by some to relate to a man running away from a potential same-sex relationship, and Rufus Wainwright's typically ambiguously sexed 'Vibrate' (released on *Want One*, 2003), in which Wainwright weaves a yearning melody over a simple, ringtone-like, bass line, with the lyric 'My phone's on vibrate for you' and emphasizing the vocal/telephonic vibrations by extending the syllable '*vi*-brate'. Some telephone songs discuss the technology itself, or are based on a telephone number (often that of a girl's home); others may contain lyrics that recreate a telephone conversation, and some songs have music that contains samples of ringtones, automated voicemail, or musical transcriptions of these sounds.

Since the advent of the music video, artists have additionally had the scope to enhance the listener's/viewer's understanding of the song's meaning and context by showing the telephone in use. Occasionally a live performance will offer the opportunity to position the song in relation to communications technology. Although a significant proportion of social interaction in the digital age takes place online—through social media sites, texting, and instant messaging—the telephone remains unrivalled in terms of the number of songs that focus on, for example, email or social media. Arguably, this is because the cultural associations of such communications are more strongly related to written rather than spoken communication, and although there is also a corpus of 'letter' songs, fewer examples of songs about written forms of communication have been produced in recent decades. Exceptions to this are usually rather clunky. For example, Britney Spears' 'Email My Heart', a ballad from her 1999 release . . . *One More Time*, seems to chime with the 'look but don't touch' attitude of the overall album, in which Spears (and her musical persona) were successfully marketed to Bush's conservative America as safely at arms length of any real sexual contact. Incidentally, her second release from that album, 'Oops, I Did It Again' features an interjection of a conversation between Spears and her unnamed romantic interest, at odds with the song's central knowing flirtation, describing a naïve and fantasy story in which the boy has retrieved a piece of jewelry from the bottom of the ocean, previously lost by an 'old lady'. This song shows that conversation can be dangerous if direct and unmediated; rather, the songwriters have emphasized the distance between Spears and her lover(s) in both songs. By contrast, telephone conversations represent intimacy; as Glenna Matthews has commented: 'In the twentieth century the telephone has replaced personal correspondence as the most significant means of communicating those feelings [of emotional intimacy], aside from face-to-face contact'.[10] The relationship between intimacy and song is attested by the majority of the history of Western music, dominated as it has been in various periods by secular, amorous song, from the troubadour *canso* to the nineteenth-century Lied. As such, songs that feature the telephone can be read as a metaphor for deep levels of intimacy between men and women in particular, and often hint at the promise of a sexual encounter.

CONSTRUCTIONS OF GENDER AND POWER IN TELEPHONE SONGS

If, as social historian Claude Fischer and others have argued, the telephone itself has been appropriated from its origins as a 'masculine technology for distinctively feminine ends', the transition has not resulted in an alternative, balanced relationship between gender and technology.[11] Instead, the telephone continues to act as a locus for anxiety about female empowerment. The telephone number itself, as a gateway between (usually) male caller and (usually) female recipient, is a common trope of telephone songs. A woman's phone number is her own property, hers to make available to a chosen male partner as an early part of courtship. As a result, the telephone number is a potent metaphor for the availability of the woman and her body to the sexual advances of her lover. Common perceptions about the power dynamics of women and the telephone can be demonstrated in three contrasting songs from the late 1970s/1980s: Meri Wilson's novelty hit 'Telephone Man' (1977), which reached No. 6 in the UK chart and No. 18 in the United States; Cyndi Lauper's 'Girls Just Wanna Have Fun' (1983) from the album *She's So Unusual*, a single that topped the charts in several countries; and Kraftwerk's 'The Telephone Call' ('Der Telefon-Anruf'), a single released from the 1986 album *Electric Café*, and which topped the Billboard Dance chart in 1987. These examples have been chosen in part because of the way in which each deals with the relationship between the telephone and women, and also because Lady Gaga's own work would appear to reference music from this era quite strongly, not least in terms of the synthesized pop sound embraced by the latter two.

Meri Wilson's 'Telephone Man' narrates the story of a lone, purportedly innocent female in a home that requires a new telephone to be wired. Inviting the engineer to the property, she squeals melodically with joy on the information that s/he can 'have it' (the phone, but in a not-so-subtle innuendo, also sexual gratification and her body) on the landing, in the hall, in the bedroom or against the wall. This song is exceptional in Wilson's double 'voicing': the engineer's vocal is lower in register and clearly an impersonation of a sexually experienced, older man ready to take advantage.[12] The engineer's voice forms the chorus, privileging his position of control of the song and of the situation. By contrast, the 'female' vocal is declaimed in a childish squeak, interjected by nonsense words that one might expect of a very young girl, or at least someone pretending to be a virgin. Furthermore, the jazzy accompaniment with limited scoring in the treble register emphasizes the bass line and creates a gulf in pitch that makes Wilson's girly squeaks seem even more pronounced. Meri's female character is portrayed as vulnerable, but also both naïve and willing to be corrupted, in a stereotype of femininity common to Western song from the Middle Ages.[13] In several ways, 'Telephone Man' plays up to traditional stereotypes about women and technology, as well as exemplifying prejudicial views of the 1970s about woman's role as sexually available and confined to the home; indeed, humor of the period frequently collapsed these aspects together.

By contrast, Cyndi Lauper uses the telephone to escape the traditional expectations for women in her recording of 'Girls Just Wanna Have Fun'. Originally written and recorded by Robert Hazard in 1979, Lauper had refused to perform it at first, believing it to be sexist.[14] However, she agreed to record the track with the proviso that its lyrics and style could be altered to give a more feminist perspective. The telephone features from verse two, opening '[t]he phone rings', with a melody that echoes the ringing of a telephone in its three, high repeated notes on the initial three words of the line. Lauper's image at this time was a rebellious, confident young woman (younger than her thirty years at the time of the song's release), and the video, which was put together shortly after the track was released, reflects this attitude. The nighttime phone call acts as a call to arms for Lauper and her group of friends (played by eight secretaries from the record label, Portrait/CBS), who gather and form a conga line through the city, leading back to a party at the house. The telephone call takes centre stage in the set-up, showing each of the friends talking on the phone in turn in a variety of domestic situations. The women, representing different ethnicities but all young, energetic and assured 1980s female role models, offer a generational contrast with Lauper's parents in the video, especially with her 'mother', to whom Lauper remarks that girls may not be as fortunate as men in society, but that they do want to enjoy themselves. Lauper's 'father' is stereotypically that of a working class male, whose identity is emasculated by his daughter in his own home. The song became something of an anthem of female empowerment in the early 1980s, affirming the importance of social networking between young women, and was assisted in no small measure by an iconic video that was well played on the relatively new music television channels.

Kraftwerk's 'The Telephone Call' is crafted largely from sampled sounds from a telephone; this sampling and manipulation is obvious to the listener, and includes a pretend automated female voice announcing that the number dialed has been disconnected, as well as the sound of automatic redialing.[15] As an album, *Electric Café* (rereleased in 2009 under its original title, *Techno Pop*) was the first Kraftwerk LP to be largely crafted from digital technologies. In line with Kraftwerk's aesthetic in which technology and the human are closely intertwined, the telephone functions both as a piece of technology and as a mechanism whose *raison d'être*—namely the communication between human beings—is rendered impotent by both the lack of interest shown by the recipient of the call (perhaps Kraftwerk are calling an automated message deliberately?) and by the lack of engagement in conversation of the caller. Lyrically, the song is one-sided, and this is emphasized by the accompanying video that shows members of Kraftwerk making calls to hear a voice, but then remaining silent. This sinister set-up reflects the standard social dynamics of phone calls since the early 1900s, where men were active callers of women in setting up romantic liaisons, and women waited by the phone passively expecting it to ring. It also explores the power relationship of nuisance callers in which women feel vulnerable when unwanted and unsolicited calls are made by a man who knows her home number, and who often remains silent on the line. The musicians occupy an ambiguous social space, as their use of telephones, phone directories, and eventually a typewriter evoke a one-sided sexual pursuit that is also attractive to callers of sex chat-lines. By cutting off the recorded voice at the close of the song, Kraftwerk retain the upper hand.

In these three examples, it is possible to see a range of ways in which the telephone is positioned between women and other callers, either men pursuing them romantically or other women in a social capacity. The dynamics of the male-female calls are strongly one-sided, with the balance of power weighted firmly to the man, who controls the technology and the relationship that is formed by it. Telephone songs are relatively less common in the past 20 years than they were in the period 1950–1990; however, more recent examples tend to explore the same trope of negotiating power within a relationship. For example, Tracy Chapman's Grammy-winning blues number 'Give Me One Reason' (1995) depicts an ultimatum, where the power imbalance is illustrated by the fact that she has called her lover 'too many times' but (s)he has not called back, even though (s)he has her number. Evanescence's song 'Call Me When You're Sober' (2006) has been described by its writer and performer, Amy Lee, as a 'chick anthem' for women who are only called by their boyfriends when the men have been drinking.[16] In this way, telephone songs present a remarkably coherent corpus, offering women the opportunity to assert themselves against the grain of standard stereotypes or (as in the case of Wilson) to play along with cultural expectations for women and their passive gender role in society.

TELEPHONES, VOICES, AND THE BODY

Popular music and performance commonly fall within traditional frameworks of the male gaze. In terms of the use of technology, this is more commonly associated with masculinity: the strong numerical bias of men employed in the music industry is an important reason for the perpetuation of this particular dynamic. Bosma has argued within the field of electronic music, 'the world of technology seems to be a man's world', in which women composers are still a rarity, but in which the (electronically manipulated) female voice has become one of its central pillars.[17] In both art and popular music, women are typically cast as 'performer' (especially vocalist), the object of a male gaze. The contribution made by those who take an active role in the production of their music (such as Björk or Kate Bush) is frequently overlooked or dismissed. Bradby's work on gender and sexuality in popular music has further explored the significance of women who actively manipulate or distort their own voices using technology such as the vocoder, eliding such transformed female voices with those of robots and casting an 'ever-youthful-body as the "fembots" of male sci-fi fantasy', in the case of Cher.[18] For Bradby, within dance music, the gaze is still male, but is 'that of the active, gay male dancer', a position that still expects a female central performer but enjoys the ambiguity and fluidity of sexuality that a technologically mediated voice can offer.[19] The meeting place of the body and technology has been effectively explored in the music and performances of Kraftwerk and Björk (who acknowledges a debt to the German band). Where Kraftwerk have mimicked machines in image, musical style and vocal delivery, Björk's work, such as her multimedia app-album and associated live performance *Biophilia* (2011), explores the blending of the technological and natural worlds. These performers have problematized the human-technological axis, to the effect that a richer expressive potential is available to performers such as Lady Gaga who are playful in their self-representation within multimedia performance.

Manipulated voices, either through sampling or digital distortion, are especially ripe with potential signification. For Loza, '[w]hen human vocals are denatured, mechanized or otherwise tainted by technology, sonic cyborgs, fembots and posthumans are conjured into existence', through techniques such as looping, the use of vocoders, altering parameters such as speed, or extending the peak of female vocals into an exaggerated 'ultrafeminized orgasmic cry'.[20] The manipulated voice, and the boundaries between nature and technology, are both explored in Lady Gaga and Beyoncé's song 'Telephone'.[21] But we might also see a parallel between the symbolism of the telephone (a device into which one speaks one's private thoughts to a friend or lover) and the microphone (a device through which one speaks or sings one's thoughts to a wider public). In telephone songs, the microphone represents the communication technology of the telephone, while also acting to transmit the sound of that conversation to the audience.

The intimacy of a telephone conversation can therefore be read from the intimacy of the recorded mix. Philip Tagg has explained that in popular music, the singer is recorded in such a way that the audience hears the voice prominently in the mix, and is thus the implied primary locus for how the listener expects to engage with a song's meaning. This central mixing 'creates an actual or imagined distance between two persons (the singer and the listener) which is that of an intimate and confidential monologue'.[22] The mix also contributes to notions of a close connection with the audience, through the singer's ability to project a sense of emotional authenticity in the virtual space of the recording.[23] It is as if the singer is talking, whispering, or singing directly into the listener's ear, in a personal one-to-one relationship. The effect is powerful, adding to a sense of involvement from the listener with the vocalist and what s/he is expressing in terms of lyric and emotion. In a sense, the listener occupies a double subjectivity: both an observer of a song 'about' a relationship, and as the individual receiver of the call, a direct line from the singer. If, as Dibben has argued, 'popular music reception and production is marked by cultural anxieties about the relationship between humans and technology', then in telephone songs this dynamic is also overlaid with constructions of gender and sexuality.[24]

FREEDOM AND THE VOICING OF TECHNOLOGY IN 'TELEPHONE'

The theme of freedom—physical, emotional, and sexual—is fundamental to 'Telephone', and is immediately signposted in the opening shots of the extended video release (directed by Jonas Åkerland), which show the upper part of a barbed wire security fence, itself part of a prison compound. The 'Telephone' video was designed as a sequel to 'Paparazzi', in which Gaga's character took murderous revenge on her violent lover who had pushed her from a balcony. In 'Paparazzi', the fall caused Gaga to be encased in layers of stylish, metallic medical correctional clothing, which at first forms a kind of fetishized bodycast, and then is gradually removed to allow Gaga to dance, albeit with crutches. 'Telephone' picks up the story from Gaga's incarceration, as she is led into the prison to be greeted with enthusiasm by fellow (sexy) female prisoners. After being thrown into a cell by a pair of butch prison officers, the scene cuts to a prison yard in which Gaga enters wearing sunglasses covered in lit cigarettes, signifying her power through the common use of cigarettes as currency within the prison system. Sitting down, she is immediately joined by a further butch lesbian, dressed in black leather, who kisses her seductively; an announcement that Gaga has a phone call to answer is ignored. After a fight between two other inmates inside the prison, Gaga is again called to the phone, which rings as the musical intro is finally heard. The depiction of the phone call is initially diegetic, as the call is to indicate that Beyoncé has posted her bail. Yet it is also unsettling, as the lyrics, which refer to Gaga ignoring her lover because she is busy socializing in a club, do not match the film's setting. Furthermore, there is a further dissonance between the lyric implying the lover's signal is breaking up and the use of distortion and manipulation of Gaga's *own* voice to create a shuddering effect on the words '[w]hat, what did you say?' as the line apparently fails. Indeed, the repetition and 'failing' of individual syllables or words is a feature of the song, and its chorus, in which the word 'me' is extended with short, punctuated repeated syllables. Beyoncé's lines are also delivered on the same pitch. The vocal stuttering mimics the ringing of a telephone, a feature emphasized by the underpinning of the chorus (whose melody is largely delivered on one note, with a rapid delivery of lyrics) with sounds sampled from telephones themselves, notably a 'caller busy' sound and a dial tone.

'Telephone' explores a queer space, not only through the song but also in its collaboration with co-writer Beyoncé and through the video's various references to empowering road-movie *Thelma and Louise* and its pervading lesbian subtext.[25] The metaphor of the prison or other enclosed space is not unusual in media that explore the queer female body within the male gaze of visual media, and the first scenes of 'Telephone' recall the barbed wire fencing trapping the pseudo-lesbian Russian singers t.A.T.u from their voyeurs in their 2002 hit 'All the Things She Said'. The lyric threesome of Gaga, Beyoncé, and unnamed lover destabilizes the usual binary dynamic of the telephone song, as well as providing a further disruption in the traditional mono-ethnicity of coupling in pop song and video. The arguably queer space occupied by Gaga, Beyoncé, and their lover(s) is not an isolated example in popular song, though it is a prominent one. For an additional example, ex-Spice Girl Melanie Chisholm's most successful solo release, 'Never Be The Same Again' (UK No. 1 in 2000) employs sexually ambiguous or veiled references to a platonic relationship that has progressed to a sexual one now that the (metaphorical closet) door has been opened by a spontaneous sexual gesture or encounter. The object of Melanie C's affections is not named, or sexed, but in a central, contrasting rap, Lisa 'Left-Eye' Lopes provides a complementary subject position, leaving the listener wondering if she might be the friend/lover in question. The accompanying video for 'Never Be the Same Again' (dir. Francis Lawrence) is set in Iceland, and features the two vocalists performing Tai-chi, united in wearing white clothing, while Lopes reflects that they have 'intertwined' their 'life forces'. Significantly for this interpretation, the song opens with the line 'I call you up whenever things go wrong', a social use of the telephone associated more fully with women's use of the technology for the best part of the past century.

If Gaga and Beyoncé can be seen as a queer pairing in narrative terms, this is compounded by their visually contrasting ethnic identity, and aurally by merging their usually highly distinctive styles. While Gaga's image betrays her Italian/European heritage, Beyoncé's ethnicity—essentially African-

American and African-European through her parentage—has been the focus of frequent critique by the media and her fans, who have queried the extent of her 'blackness'. So how are the singers presented aurally? Within the single release of 'Telephone', a song whose musical and lyrical content is attributed to a collaborative team that includes both lead singers, Beyoncé's contribution arrives relatively unexpectedly (1:34 into the song). There are some commonalities between the musical material assigned to each of the women, notably the relentless and limited harmonic palette that comprises just three chords (F minor, A flat major, B flat major). Both singers also concentrate their melodies around repeated notes, giving the whole song a commanding, declamatory style that is forthright, even rigid; syncopation is almost entirely eschewed in favor of a combined melodic, harmonic and rhythmic character perhaps more readily associated with the reciting tone of simple plainchant. Lady Gaga's melody is dominated by paired quavers on one note, with the pitch changing mechanically on the crotchet beat; a stuttering effect on the word 'what' is mapped musically by a repeated F. Beyoncé's contribution opens as a pitched rap on the tonic, but then departs briefly for an arpeggiated gesture before rising stepwise to the dominant (as the singer recalls how she should have left her phone at home). The melodic shape for both singers is very much focused on the tonic, and the pitch does not escape the octave from the C below to that above the tonic on any occasion. Melodically and rhythmically, the character of the song has the feel of a simple ringtone, with its restricted musical gestures acting as a nagging reminder of the incoming call that Gaga and Beyoncé are trying so hard to ignore. In terms of the musical texture, there are some strong contrasts between Gaga, whose opening verse is accompanied by only a resonant, folk-style harp before the main electronic dance track enters, and Beyoncé, whose solo section is limited to active, fiery beats and a warm electronic bass line. In the final verse, both singers share the main melody evenly. The singers are locked together with music that, albeit with some stylistic differences (mainly in delivery and accompaniment), is remarkably uniform.

Apart from the melodic contour evoking telephone technology, the telephone is also referenced in two other ways within the track, both of which might be seen as referential of previous artists. The most obvious reference comes by way of sampled telephone sounds, first appearing in the chorus, in which a variety of ring tones and dial tones are featured. At the song's outro, the music is overlaid with a sample of a telephone operator, stating that the number reached is not in service, and apparently featuring both male and female voices. The use of sampled phone sounds is not unusual in telephone songs in general, the main exemplar being Kraftwerk's 'The Telephone Call', which features a range of sounds. Beyond direct samples, the voices of Gaga and Beyoncé are treated to electronic manipulations that make them stutter, akin to the buzzing and ringing of telephones; this happens throughout the song, and is also mirrored in the video by synching the film to the music to give a visual stammer in several places, as well as some telephone-related poses and dance moves. The bridge, with its repeated, monotonous patterns on the syllable 'eh', mirrors this effect. In this way, the singers almost become part of the technology, their bodies subjected to shuddering as if they are controlled by the vibrations of their phones. The vocal imitation of technology in the stuttering effect within 'Telephone' can be seen as playing with similar ideas to Rufus Wainwright's 'Vibrate'. A merging of the technological and the natural recalls the aesthetic of Björk, whose unification of these worlds underpins much of her output, not least in her video 'All is Full of Love' (dir. Chris Cunningham, 1999) in which robot Björks are seen in a seductive coupling.[26]

Gaga's use of telephone technology is iconic rather than aiming at realism. The chief evidence for this is the dated telephone technologies used in the video, which hark back to far more basic examples than the smartphones of the twenty-first century. The only mobile phone to appear is in the initial prison scene, in which a handset powered by Virgin Media is symptomatic of product placement. By contrast, the bedroom scene for Beyoncé's solo interjection features red, white, and green domestic telephones with curled wires; she seems trapped within the four walls, wrestling with the technology while surrounded by colors of the Italian flag, perhaps symbolic of Gaga's heritage and perhaps dominance. The overall effect is therefore nostalgic, recalling phones with old-fashioned dials and buttons. Gaga's telephone hat, for example, which she wears during the *Pulp Fiction* section of the video, includes a dial with retro information in its center advising the numbers of UK emergency services and operator. A similar shape is created by her hairstyle immediately afterwards, in which her hair is curled to represent the twisting wire of the domestic telephone. Again, one might consider this to be an allusion to Kraftwerk, who featured 1930s telephone technology in 'The Telephone Call', in a stylistic reference that their audience would have recognized from earlier releases such as *Radio-Activity* (1976), in which a 1930s radio was placed on their LP artwork. Against the iconic imagery of old telephone technology, the lyrics in 'Telephone' create tension with the video. Gaga's phone is clearly mobile and interactive; she can choose to ignore it, even though escaping from home does not mean that she is free from being pestered. The lyrics also show a woman who is not only physically in control of her environment, but also economically; her leisure time is spent dancing in clubs and drinking champagne rather than in the domestic space. However, the telephone that is depicted in the lyrics works within the video to signal that Gaga's freedom is also constrained—as if at home—by her availability though being contactable on the phone.[27] This can be seen as a metaphor for twenty-first-century lifestyle, in which mobile phone technology—like the technologies developed in the nineteenth century—does not necessarily emancipate women from their traditional obligations and social roles.

CONCLUSION

Through situating 'Telephone' in a cultural history of women's vocality in relation to technology and gender, it is possible to see the song as both typifying tropes of the genre and acting to destabilize some of those features. 'Telephone' problematizes the concept of passive/willing female recipient of male attention, instead offering a characterization in which Gaga constantly ignores the technology to engage in social activities within the public domain, such as dancing (lyrics) or spending time with marginalized female companions who include criminals, black women and lesbians (video). The very technology that enslaved women as human switches in the early part of the twentieth century, or as passive 'hangers on the telephone' in the mid- to late twentieth century, is represented as blocking those lines of communication through both poor reception and Gaga's manipulation of it (we only have her word that the signal is poor). Stuttering distortions of Gaga and Beyoncé's voices elide their bodies with the technology itself. By the final section of the 'Telephone' video, it is clear that the women are united through their gestures, music and all-American costumes, though they have resorted to violence to gain control over their personal space in a male-dominated, technologically driven world. Cultural expectations for women, and white women and non-white/black women in relation to each other, are thereby disrupted. Gaga's and Beyoncé's 'voices' are delivered to an absent, unlistening object, rather than being forced to respond through the mobile telephone technology available to them. Paradoxically, the listener becomes that object through the mapping of telephone onto microphone/sound recording technology that arguably occurs during telephone songs. In a number of ways, 'Telephone' therefore offers a surprisingly rich exemplar of Gaga's embracing of the politics of diversity, equality, and empowerment.

NOTES

1. I am grateful to Catherine Haworth for reading an earlier draft of this chapter, and making several pertinent suggestions.
2. Jennifer Terry and Melodie Calvert, 'Introduction', in *eaedem*, *Processed Lives: Gender and Technology in Everyday Life* (London: Routledge, 1997), 2–3.
3. Kenneth Lipartito, 'When Women Were Switches: Technology, Work, and Gender in the Telephone Industry, 1890–1920', *The American History Review*, vol. 99, no. 4 (1994), 1075.
4. Venus Green, 'Race, Gender, and National Identity in the American and British Telephone Industries', *International Review of Social History*, vol. 46, no. 2 (2001), 185–205.
5. A good overview of the relationship between gender and telephone technology is Valerie Frissen, 'Gender is Calling: Some Reflections on Past, Present and Future Uses of the Telephone', in *The Gender-Technology Relation: Contemporary Theory and Research*, ed. Keith Grint and Rosalind Gill (London: Taylor & Francis, 1995), 79–94.

6. Julie Wosk, *Women and the Machine: Representations from the Spinning Wheel to the Electronic Age* (Baltimore, MD: The Johns Hopkins University Press, 2001), 7–8.
7. Terry and Calvert, 'Introduction', 5.
8. *Ibid.*, 6.
9. Frissen, 'Gender is Calling', 93. See also Lana F. Rakow and Vija Navarro, 'Remote Mothering and the Parallel Shift: Women Meet the Cellular Telephone', *Critical Studies in Mass Communication*, vol. 10, no. 2 (1993), 144–157.
10. Glenna Matthews, Review of Lana F. Rakow, *Gender on the Line: Women, the Telephone, and Community Life* (Urbana: University of Illinois Press, 1992), in *The Journal of American History*, vol. 80, no. 2 (1993), 756.
11. Claude S. Fischer, 'Gender and the Residential Telephone, 1890–1940: Technologies of Sociability', *Sociological Forum*, vol. 3, no.2 (1988), 212.
12. Vocal impersonation is more prevalent within the comedy or novelty song than in serious forms, in a history linked to music hall and vaudeville traditions which frequently included cross-dressing or characterization.
13. For medieval examples of fictional, willingly corruptible virgins, see Lisa Colton, 'The Articulation of Virginity in the Medieval *Chanson de nonne*', *Journal of the Royal Musical Association*, vol. 133, no. 2 (2008), 159–188.
14. Gaby Alter, 'Cyndi Lauper's "Girls Just Wanna Have Fun"', *MIX* (April 2004), 134.
15. 'The Telephone Call' features a recorded voice of Walter Sneider's girlfriend Sandhya Whaley claiming that the number reached had been disconnected.
16. Amy Lee interviewed in Camille Dodero, 'Tough Questions for Evanescence's Amy Lee,' *Spin* (4 October 2011) (online at: http://www.spin.com/articles/tough-questions-evanescences-amy-lee) <accessed 19 July 2012>.
17. Hannah Bosma, 'The Death of the Singer: Authorship and Female Voices in Electronic Music', *Contact*, vol. 1, no. 3 (1998) (online at http://cec.sonus.ca/econtact/Voice/Bosma.html).
18. Barbara Bradby and Dave Laing, 'Introduction to "Gender and Sexuality" Special Issue', *Popular Music*, vol. 20, no. 3 (October 2001), 296.
19. *Ibid.*, 297.
20. Susana Loza, 'Sampling (hetero)sexuality: Diva-ness and Discipline in Electronic Dance Music', *Popular Music*, vol. 20, no. 3 (2001), 349–350.
21. 'Telephone' has words and music attributed to Stephani Germanotta, Rodney Jerkins, LaShawn Daniels, Lazonate Franklin, and Beyoncé Knowles. Although the song was originally written by Lady Gaga for performance by Britney Spears, this was not officially released, so the level of input from the various contributors to the song cannot be reliable unpacked. For the purpose of this chapter, 'Telephone' will be understood as primarily Lady Gaga's creation, with some co-writing from Beyoncé.
22. Philip Tagg, *Fernando the Flute* (Liverpool: Mass Media Music Scholars' Press, 1991), 60.
23. Nicola Dibben, 'Vocal Performance and the Projection of Emotional Authenticity', in *The Ashgate Research Companion to Popular Musicology*, ed. Derek B. Scott (Aldershot: Ashgate, 2009), 319.
24. Nicola Dibben, *Björk* (Bloomington, IN: Indiana University Press, 2009), 73.
25. The video is cluttered with intertextual references, especially to films directed by Quentin Tarantino such as *Pulp Fiction* and *Kill Bill Vol. 1*. The film *Reservoir Dogs* acted as the stimulus for another, less successful, Beyoncé-Gaga collaboration, 'Video Phone' (2008, remixed as a duet with video in 2009), in which the male gaze is made literal when male dancers are shown with

video camera lenses for faces. It is beyond the scope of this chapter to discuss these references in detail, as they have little bearing on the central points being made here.

26. Dibben, *Björk*, especially Chapter 4, 'Technology', 72–99. Incidentally, Björk's song 'Possibly Maybe' used a sample of a telephone that itself had been taken, initially without credit, from Scanner, a British musician whose untitled track had featured on his album *Mass Observation*.

27. A number of songs from the twentieth century focus on unavailability, notably Curiosity Killed the Cat's 'Name and Number' (1989), which was later parodied by De La Soul in 'Ring Ring Ring (Ha Ha Hey)', a song that protested against the deluge of demo tapes received by the band. Female punk track 'Your Phone's Off the Hook but You're Not' by X (1980) represents a further song where the freedom and power of the (male) receiver is dismissed through a telephone-related metaphor.

5   Lady Gaga and the Drop
Eroticism High and Low

Paul Hegarty

When Georges Bataille looks at the big toe, he sees the join between human and animal, a join that is also a separation, something we hide, shy away from, and cover. 'The big toe is the most *human* part of the body', he writes, as it marks how humans left the trees and stood upright.[1] In this short essay, first published in the para-surrealist journal *Documents*, in 1929, Bataille lifts the human up, only to replant it squarely in the animal, the natural, the muddy. Maintaining the upright position is made possible by the big toe, shaping the foot for 'giving a firm foundation to the erection of which man is so proud'.[2] Uprightness is the beginning of the path to greatness, to enlightenment, but Bataille questions the attainment of humanity. The rising above is illusory in many ways. First, in order to gaze upon ever-higher sights without climbing, human feet must be steadfastly planted in the earth. The one does not happen with the other, so the heights are only ever achieved in concert with not just a persistence of the animal, but a new emphasis on it. This is not an end to the compromised nature of human ambition to be human, to be more than animal. When Bataille used the word 'erection', he meant it: that sanctimonious superiority, whether moral, biological, logical, religious is actually a form of tumescence, the high in the low, to paraphrase Hermes Trismegistus. All life is essentially a process of fucking, in his own early hermetic text, 'The Solar Anus'.[3] All life is also about death, waste, excretion, loss, and this thought will permeate the entirety of his writings. In terms of the compromised nature of humanity and the relation of high and low, there is a further part, also signaled in 'The Solar Anus', where 'the erection and the Sun scandalize'.[4] For all the striving for elevation, it is too much for us when revealed, and so the high rejoins the low yet again.

The foot might scandalize a Freudian, just as they might spill their ideas about fetishism and the absence of a penis into a shoe, but it is not the foot that troubles, it is its recalling of a border condition that has been hidden rather than overcome that shocks. Or excites. A further crossover occurs for foot fetishists, who whether they like clean or dirty feet, are working from the starting position that 'the foot' is unclean, not proper,[5] and they therefore re-iterate uprightness's reliance on upright balance on the earth along with the fundamentally erotic nature of the animal, and of leaving the animal behind.

The shoe fetishist notwithstanding, the foot is to be hidden for decency's sake. The greater the elaboration, the safer any witness could be in the presence of the foot, and its lynchpin, the big toe. This too would have unforeseen and ironic consequences, such as when foot binding in the name of beauty would actually mangle and crush the foot, moving it further from the human order it was bound to please. To elevate the foot is to increase all the tendencies noted above, ostensibly to raise the human into being more human, but also reminding us of eroticism precisely as it moves away from it: 'heels of greater or lesser height, depending on the sex, distract from the foot's low and flat character'.[6] The wearing of high heels is not so much one of sex, but of changing historical norms, just as with leg-revealing tights, heels have been a male province at some points, and at others, such as contemporary Western culture, firmly part of female attire.[7]

In this chapter, I will be looking first at those heels, as shown primarily in the videos for 'Paparazzi' and 'Bad Romance' to provoke thought about how heels position Gaga with regard to all the borders of the human: erotic, mortal, animal, machine. From there, I will develop a more extended idea about the importance of height, of the raised and lowered Gaga body, as a more complex theorization that she develops on erotic limits. These two videos are of particular interest because unlike, say, 'Telephone', the lyrics and visuals map onto one another fairly closely. In 'Paparazzi', the photographer Guy Bourdin is taken as a guide for modeling Gaga dead. In 'Bad Romance' we veer explicitly between the highs of tragic love and the willed degradation of violent eroticism.

Arthur Kroker has questioned whether Bataille's 'Big Toe' can still serve us the same way as it did for him, given we now inhabit a very differently-mediated universe of simulations, parodies, hyper-realistic reality TV (including news). In an era of highly modifiable bodies, Bataille's purposeful intellectual *fetishizing* of one part of a body is redundant: now everything can signal the borders, while at the same time the idea of a border is lost.[8] To some extent, this is true, and we can imagine that Gaga is precisely a hyper-Bataillean, who exudes border points and liminal moves. In another way, the idea that the big toe's work is over is not really right. If anything, it lives on as the trace of itself, buried further, denied not by prohibitions but by excessive re-workings of the human/nature or human/animal line. In the case of Gaga, the foot, metamorphosed into the heel, changing shape incessantly, opens up the space of reflection on human existence as a perpetually threshing deconstruction of high and low impulses and outcomes.

'Paparazzi' very clearly connects violence, sexuality, and the question of living in public, living as public object. It refuses none of these, instead exploring them, particularly in the video for the song, as a confluence of conditions that sets up a peculiar border condition. Lady Gaga is a performer and writer who focuses intently on sex, sexual identity, the body, and even death. But it is not just a use of those, it is more of a theorization, a playing out of possibilities that largely exceeds psychoanalytic or gender-based readings of sexuality in these videos. Gaga does not represent these things, but operates them, trying to act on them as she cites. The same applies to the use of Guy Bourdin's style in 'Paparazzi'. Controversially, he introduced a high-sheen morbidity to fashion photography, girls as artfully lost and damaged as in the work of photographer Francesca Woodman. Notwithstanding Elisabeth Bronfen's reading of the problematic nature of using the image of a dead woman as the content for art,[9] Bourdin was pushing fashion photography to an extreme position, just as designers such as Vivienne Westwood, Jean-Paul Gaultier, Alexander McQueen and John Galliano would do. At a certain point objectification can only be parodic, and hence Gaga's use of that photography, in parallel to her choice of clothes, designers, accouterments. Those dressings form part of the construction of a troubled sexual identity, a shifting persona. Beyond that, the introduction of death and sexual violence is where identity and the limits of the human come in to play.

Again, there is hardly any mystery in Gaga's explicit use of sexuality and the sexual, and its purpose is to indicate freedom through letting go, as well as 'being yourself': 'I want women—and men—to feel empowered by a deeper and more psychotic part of themselves'.[10] There are competing theoretical readings of such a liberationist perspective, from Michel Foucault's suspicion as to how precisely human truth came to be defined through sexual identity, to Judith Butler's post-Foucauldian sense that identities can be played with, if they are constructions, through those who imagine that Deleuze and Guattari or French feminism of the 1970s can set us free through sex. So, let's not take Gaga at her word. Let's see how liberation is not easy, and how it involves constraint and a transgression that always risks (or courts) failure and comedy. Goodman notes that Lady Gaga 'wants to be a sex object—but only on her own terms'.[11] This is a more interesting idea than it at first seems: it is much more than using the idea of being a sex object in order to challenge exactly what that would be. That is part of what is going on in these videos and her performances, but not as much as the centrally violent rethinking of sex that is presumably affecting the tens of millions who have watched those videos on streaming sites. In Bataillean terms, sex, in the form of the erotic, rather than reproductive, functional, and therefore a merely biological activity, is about breaking down the limits of the individual, the subject. Human subjects are insulated, enclosed, argues Bataille. Death, eroticism, and other kinds of wasteful activity can break down those barriers where individuals can lose themselves in the true nature of the universe which is based on the principle of excess.

Well, maybe. To expand, we need to note that Bataille views death itself as a 'luxury', a wasteful activity. Eroticism is profoundly human because it taps into that greater death, and lets you come back. Waste, failure, and abjection are, in a way, the highest forms of activity a human can aspire to. But like heels, you can't live permanently in them. Instead you reach toward them, approaching, fingertip-touching. Death might be there to be embraced, but you cannot dwell there. In 'Paparazzi', Gaga herself does not die, but instead kills, while a long sequence of dead female house staff lie artistically broken around the grounds of the big house the video occurs in. The story of the song is itself a mixed one, with the narrator both referring to the perils of fame and putting herself in the position of celebrity stalker. The visual story begins with Gaga's boyfriend throwing her off a roof, having already 'fed' her to the paparazzi. She does not die, and ultimately poisons him, pausing to shiver excitedly as she sips a small amount of poison from a spoon.

It is a long way into the video before Gaga's heels touch the ground, and when they do, it is to the accompaniment of crutches. She starts, fully dressed, in the bed with the boyfriend, and is carried waist-high on him, to the ledge, her heels at his knees. The heels here are even more exaggeratedly functionless as shoes than usual.[12] Instead they have some new sex function, an indication that Gaga is not interested in simple sex. As she tumbles, first she goes into a 1970s-style time vortex, then we cut back to her twisted body on the pavement. As she does not die, but emerges from a car to first be placed in a wheelchair then walking in metal (gold?) 'medical support' armor with crutches, death goes elsewhere, radiating out to hit the female staff (or maybe they have been transported from a parallel Bourdin world to decorate the place and drive Gaga's revenge mission).

I do not think that the dead women littered so crisply around the demesne are a critique of fashion, fame or overzealous fascination with celebrity. Oddly, these are almost faceless women, mostly suicides, it would seem. These could be those who seek to follow too intently, without resorting to personal pursuit of a star. They specifically echo, with variation, the broken star of Gaga's dropped body early in the video, as she fractalizes through the video. The last dead woman we see does not actually have her face directly revealed. Instead, we go from a shot of the generic and perfectly made up face to a shot of legs gently swinging from the ceiling (maybe a chandelier). This is part of a sequence of height depictions that direct a narrative of erotic death (*i.e.* not making death erotic, but taking both as what lie at the borders of the human). Although it is not Gaga here, it ambiguously suggests it might be her, and in her performance of the song at the 2009 MTV video music awards (VMA), she ends up hanging from a rope, drenched in fake blood, at the close of the song. She hangs from her hand, but glassy-eyed, she is raised like a body in an abattoir—in this performance there is no winning outcome for Gaga, but even in the video, vengeance is incidental, some sort of added frisson to the core deadly eroticism, because the moment of the boyfriend's death is marked by him slumping, dropping the glass, next to a shot of Gaga's shoes—the high, the human, is defined by lowering literally and figuratively (in death, crime, pleasureful murder).

The same applies in 'Bad Romance', a multi-layered descent into the exploitation and diminishing of Gaga that ends in ecstatic immolation of the man who buys Gaga in some sort of slave auction. Before getting into how the video structures a narrative, let us remember that the lyrics tell us throughout how Gaga seeks the 'bad romance', fosters it and thrives while involved in it. So the first layer established by the video, is, like 'Paparazzi', about treating people as commodities, and how fame drives this to extreme and highly monetized levels, only a means to an end. The opening shot shows Gaga seated on a throne, surrounded by the cast of the auction section, one knee on the ground, the other poised at a right angle over its raised heel. This pose re-occurs in a short interlude where Gaga is dressed in black, admiring herself in a mirror, touching herself as fetish, and once more at the dénouement. The posture indicates both the move of shoe from utility to aesthetic value, and also to become a means of bodily alteration. The raised knee indicates this is not a helpless position, rather it is one poised to act (while also ensuring the legs are a long way apart . . .).

The first segment takes place in the 'Bath Haus of Gaga', where a latex-clad Gaga leads a group of dancers from sleek white pods. They could be manufactured, alien travelers, or voluntary prisoners of the pods. Gaga is the only one whose body completely covered by white latex, and only her mouth area is visible. The others, conversely, have full-face masks, but their eyes are exposed. The power to speak from within the material enclosure ensures we get a sense of Gaga as in control of her restriction at this point, a sense that falls away as the others drag her to the slave auction, and she dances, then crawls, in a costume which is mostly jewels, pants, heels. Interspersed with this narrative line is a parallel Gaga, with unnaturally large eyes, and this one spends most of her time in and around a bath in what could be an asylum, but is more likely the Bath Haus of Gaga. This figure, as well as the glimpses of a more or less straight Gaga shown in close-up being sad, crying and so on, seem to indicate there is a sequence, that the sadness and/or madness comes later, after the 'bad' romance. Wide-eyed Gaga initially joins in with the song, and also dances and smiles, but she will soon be forcibly tossed about by two women (nurses? Fellow slaves?) and force-fed what could be medicine but is just as likely to be the Nemiroff vodka on product placement in earlier and later shots. Again, the suffering of wide-eyed Gaga might be much more consensual than we first imagine, the aggressive handling part of some contractual physical arrangement, given that it occurs precisely as the first chorus begins 'I want your loving . . . '

Pod Gaga, now mostly undressed, apparently vulnerable, crawls toward a group of stock 'futuristic' oligarch types, and bidding begins. The man with an echo of Gaga's therapeutic 'Paparazzi' on his chin wins. The objectification here is both a critique of the treatment of women as sexual means to ends and the assumption of that role as a positively erotically charged submission. I am not suggesting Gaga adopts the victim position allocated to the public figure or women in more general terms. No, it is more than that, as I think the video builds a sequence of scenarios entirely for the gratification of the various Gagas in the video (backed up strongly by the yearning for 'wrongness', 'freakiness' in the lyrics). The visual moment this becomes clear is the slowing, the dwelling in a premonition/anticipation of ecstasy that is the curtain of suspended crystal drops that surrounds her in the midst of the auction (3:02–3:22). She is the one who can summon up material, events, and even herself from parallel timelines. There are three sequences which show Gaga alone, the first, in black, mentioned above; the second is her in a non-functioning shower, wearing only the heels, and almost meditatively scheming about the 'bad romance' in prospect (or in the past); the third shows Gaga in Alexander McQueen's armadillo shoes, and matching costume. It cuts between the return of the half-kneel position, and her walking in these very difficult shoes. They are shaped like a claw, the front platform very minimal in terms of support, and the heel is ten inches high. In fact, walking in them almost betrays their submissive purpose to restrict movement. In choosing to walk in them Gaga shows how submission and dominance combine, and makes that explicit, literal: the shoes have been mastered, but are also continually modifying pace and posture. Returning us to Bataille, the armadillo shoe distorts the real foot, and refigures it visually as a claw, extending Bataille's theory of the high heel's relation to the foot, the big toe, and the repression of eroticism that marks the crossing of the border from animal to human. It is this Gaga, in the half-kneel posture, one foot submissive, the other in anticipation of action, the legs spread wide, that makes the shape of a gun shooting with her fingers.

Slave Gaga has already at this point begun walking into stock oligarch's room, where he waits on the bed. As Armadillo Gaga cocks her fingers, the bed explodes into flame (we watch from behind Slave Gaga). After a series of brief shots of various Gaga aspects/avatars, we end with a shot of her lying on the bed, a burnt-out corpse next to her. She smokes a cigarette, while her flamethrower bra fizzles out, and one leg is flung out toward camera, a ridged heel almost as high as the armadillo, leading the viewer into and then out of the scene. Although this last scene breaks free of the voluntary and complex submissions already seen, it does not suggest vengeance for mistreatment. In fact, it is also possible that stock oligarch has paid for his immolation at the hands, well, breasts, of Gaga.

But we can look at this all a different way: let's go back and take in the elevations, drops, highs and lows. Pod Gaga edges out at first of her pod, in spiderly fashion, and meanwhile wide-eyed Gaga is in her bath, a single gnarled white heel raised high above her head as she sings along. The two Gagas track each other, as Pod version arises tentatively, and then we cut back to wide-eyes, dancing this time. As the latter returns to the bath, her left hand clenches, gnarling in a way that not only connects to the shoe, but also to the reptilian back of latex-covered Pod Gaga, crouching, emphasizing spine and ribs. As this Gaga starts dancing more assertively, the other one in the bath swings through rapid mood changes, and as she declares she wants 'your bad romance', is dragged from the bath. As Pod version will soon be led into the auction, wide-eyed version seems to pre-empt a decline, a loss of control that has brought about an oppressive reaction (by minders for one, by purchasers for the other). But just before wide-eyed Gaga is 'force-fed' the clear liquid, we see her (from behind, perched on the lip of the bath) raise her hands, in something like ecstatic supplication, to her two female warders. Subsequently, this Gaga flails in the bath, as the other is led into the bidding room, also struggling. This struggling is an immediate shrugging off of actually being dominated, not a last-ditch attempt to prevent being controlled, as later events (and lyrics) demonstrate vividly.

For the following section, it is nude Gaga (except for heels) in the shower who alternates with 'slave' Gaga. Nude shower Gaga holds her hands in front of her, speculatively, turning them over, as she shifts position, almost hunched over she is raised so high. At this point, Gaga who was Pod Gaga and now up-for-sale Gaga, is flung to the floor, a position she embraces by crawling rapidly toward the potential buyers. Both wide-eyed and nude shower Gaga seem to direct from afar as they make abrupt finger-wagging gestures. At 2:38, Gaga jumps into the lap of the stock oligarch who will buy her, as the lyrics tell us 'you know that I want you/And you know that I need you', while behind, and in between those lines, another Gaga declares 'cos' I'm a freak bitch baby'. As the three Gagas (Pod, Nude, Wide-eyed) alternate, and offer different postures on what is transpiring as 'bad romance', the slave section has its own bifurcation, between the Gaga who is for sale and crawls aggressively, and the one who dances with a group behind her, upright, controlling her proximate space with sharp hand gestures, body turns, quasi-marching moves. All these diverging paths are held together for a moment, in the shot of the suspended crystal droplets. This Gaga is only the illusion of stasis, instead this is all times at once, happening forever, as if fixed, like Nietzsche's eternal return. That this is Gaga stepping into the current of those parallel lines and recurring moments is clear (in hindsight) from the presence of the monstrous mouth-fronted black platforms she stands on amid the droplets, one of which will stretch from her to us in the closing shot of the film. These crystals are all the drops in one, all the Gagas in brief stasis, a quantum stasis at that, because as we are not permitted to see them move, they are both rising and falling. If there is an observer it is the briefly glimpsed Gaga amid metal circles, turning with them, holding out the left hand, palm out, to prevent access to the moment of observing transition.[13]

Instead, we move to armadillo-shod Gaga, whose role is to focus deathly eroticism into the fiery conclusion. As noted above, this Gaga connects us to the other arrayed Gagas, one knee on the floor, another bent at right angles, the legs much wider apart than before, while moving us toward a hard-won height. As this Gaga splits into two, both inspect the palms of their hands, briefly accessing the position of observer Gaga, and shots of wide-eyed Gaga return, singing along, then strangling herself, then reminding us 'I'm a freak bitch baby'. This is all from her bath, but now she faces us, both more and less than the observer, and this Gaga is the one who addresses us, addresses the actions of other Gagas. As white-clad 'slave' Gaga advances to immolate stock oligarch, another Gaga lies with her troupe of dancers at what seems to be the back of the same room at the same time (most of what happens in the parallel lines of the video can be identified as a parallel for occurring in more or less the same space, but something has broken through here, as the supine and advancing Gagas combine). This red-clad dancing Gaga seems be 'Gaga from previous songs', signaled by the gesture of the fingers around the eye, featured in several other of her videos, taking us beyond the world of the song to muse on the multiplicity of Gagas propagating beyond the video. Meanwhile, sad, close-up Gaga features in cuts in this sequence, parodying the simple idea of a romance that went wrong.

At 4:42, immolating Gaga (erstwhile 'slave' Gaga) poses in front of the burning bed (complete, we will soon discover, with toasted oligarch), slightly wobbling on her heels. This rocking cannot be about nerves, as she is holding a heroic posture; so, it shows us the fallacy, or even fragility, of heroism, and that crossing the line to eroticism and death is not just being strong and triumphing, but about giving in. Or, at least, it is about the balancing of those, and the proto-orgasmic fear of escaping constraint, while being constrained. At the close, Gaga has ostensibly taken her revenge, and as I have claimed earlier, taken her pleasure, in a way that suggests this scenario is something she has been in charge of all along. Better still, she has put herself in danger of not being in charge, only to better assert her control. But there is still more, as along the way, the idea of identity as stuck in one timeline or persona, the idea of a sequential narrative life, moving simply forward along the only possible timetrack, have been ruthlessly theorized out of existence. The concluding scene tells us more about the nature of Bataillean eroticism as failure, waste, and excess. The moment of destruction is missing, the moment of orgasm/jouissance likewise. As the perfect moment, outside of the constraints of rational, moral time, it is not something 'I' can be there for. This filters back into the multiplicity of Gagas: not one will ever be 'there' or present at the moment Bataille would identify as the highest possibility of humanity.

Why should Bataille's view hold so much sway here? For me, it is the only way to make sense of the interplay of personae, lyrics, events and fractured erotic narrative of the two videos. He, like Gaga, used explicit, painfully literal ways to get at something much more obscure and troubling about humanness as being defined by the moments the human is lost. Not only do these two Gaga videos theorize beyond Bataille, but they take a specific pressure point, the high heel and how it connects the high with the soil, and then ultimately with death, to use height as a means of addressing the constant fall that is the human attempt to rise away from eroticism.

If the positioning of Lady Gaga in 'Bad Romance' and 'Paparazzi' recalls, and even re-theorizes, Bataille in terms of the high and low, there is a further play on the space of the sacred (for Bataille, the sacred is not connected to religions as such, but to loss of the self).[14] The sacred cannot be present in space, it is always separated away, for fear of contagion. Even Christianity, which for Bataille is more or less a profanation of the sacred, knows this, in keeping the prospective bodies of Christ away from view (behind the altar, locked away). A sequence of rites, taboos both spatial and personal (*i.e.* who can access the sacred) separations is the essence of organized religion.[15] Even a completely profane sacred, as proposed by Bataille, maintains this: the sacred is other, or it is nothing. And it is nothing, a very particular kind of nothing, as that which must be kept away. In 'Paparazzi', the moment of Gaga's death is withheld, more than simply not happening, to be replaced by a swirly dream moment Gaga spins in. In 'Bad Romance', the culmination of submissive and fatal sex play is absent, the immolation something we are not present for, and there is no sign that any Gaga is there either. The Gagas are actually not present for it either: the visual absence of the moment for us is the representation of loss of self in that moment. The transgression is very directly spatial (in an extension of the height play of the two videos), a stepping outside of space. This stepping is always a stepping over a line which requires a falling back. There is no escape in ultimate transgressions, only the drawing back in of the line-crosser.[16]

Crossing, then, as well as rising and falling. The impossible and withheld crossings (into death or orgasm) show space as permeable, but also not something 'there' within which Gaga moves. Instead she constructs space around her, or better still is part of a construction of space that takes her as its moving epicenter. The sacred is the threat of sacred space and action coming to be, the potential for its disruption as well as its actually occurring. Sacred space deconstructs the idea of spaces being separated, but without destroying the separation on which it feeds. Another way of looking at this, or another thought that Gaga re-theorizes, comes in the shape of Deleuze and Guattari's distinction between smooth and striated space, and how the movement between them can be thought of as de- and re-territorializations (*i.e.* the occupation of space becomes a process, not a fact, event or definable situation).[17] This seemingly convoluted conceptualization actually clarifies how Bataille's more obviously deconstructive model works, and also respects the visual rendering of it in Gaga's videos.

All of the moves outlined above illustrate a negotiation of smooth and striated spaces, with the most explicit statement of this the moment in

'Bad Romance' where Gaga is surrounded by suspended pearl drops. For Deleuze and Guattari, these terms indicate a profound but not insurmountable division between ordered and free space: 'in striated space, one closes off a surface and "allocates" it according to determinate intervals, assigned breaks; in the smooth, one "distributes" one's crossings (*logos* and *nomos*)'.[18] The erotic and mortal play that emanates from the heel, from the border between human and animal, is more or less in free, smooth space, but the movement between controlled and smooth space is itself a smoothing.[19] It is the movement in space (high to low and vice-versa) that sets up a movement between spaces. We can take for example the group dancing elements in both songs. These are highly regimented, even if they display a Gaga in control. They use formulaic expectations of 'dance' videos, highlighting the main performer through an offset and subservient group. The particular quirks and signature gestures of Gaga stand out more against a group of dancers moving in unison. They occur in moments where the song hits a chorus, so there is a double grounding of the song, almost separate from the rest of the visual narrative that is unfolding (especially in 'Bad Romance'). The group dance structures space into order; this is not a pack or a swarm, but a regimented unit. The structuring of perverse, shifting space occurs outside, against and under these moments, with the occasional direct collision (of ordered striation and smoothness), as in 'Paparazzi', when Gaga is 'dancing' on crutches, accompanied by her troupe of servant dancers (3:14–3:53). This follows on from her being brought into her mansion in a wheelchair by a group of male, suited dancers, so the moves on crutches are a direct expression of leaving striated (ordered, limiting, oppressive) space behind. With the ensemble dancing in 'Bad Romance' the move is in the opposite direction—with lizard-like Pod Gaga and her cohorts disjointed, individually and as a group (beginning at 0:37), and gradually becoming more organized by the time the full lights flick on and we arrive at the first chorus (1:26). From 2:14 on, the chorus of dancers acts as a controlling frame for Slave Gaga at the auction, guarding her. She moves in and out of their orbit, as she moves in and out of striated space (and this is the main, longest section of the video, with the suspension of movement achieved in its midst. The troupe themselves are not exclusively about control—they retain the potential for breakdown, as seen in the traces of disjointed movement (3:12–3:15). The last group dance is interspersed with the entire final scene (3:48–4:57), leading up to the closing bed shot. Dressed in red, they begin supine, and rise, echoing the opening dance that followed the emergence from the pods, but this time, the dance is much more organized, and for most of the time, Gaga is performing the same actions as the group (let's note in passing that this is not a very precise dance group, even in moments of symmetrical dancing). The controlled space has now been taken by Gaga, and the fickle mass of dancers has rejoined her, in time for the lights to go out on the 'Bath Haus'.

Both songs and videos attack the myriad forms of control that are tolerated, suffered, and even desired by many. 'Bad Romance' in particular looks at complicity with controls as a way of surmounting them, and it is in this light that we return to the heels. High heels, as noted above, became female property in the twentieth century, cemented by the arrival of the stiletto, and for all their awkwardness, were a way of eluding the mundane, the functional, and to extricate the body from drudgery. But clearly, they are a constraint, too, and Gaga pushes the constraint to its furthest with McQueen's armadillo shoe, but also with other towering platforms. These are shoes that defy gravity, and gravity, according to Deleuze and Guattari, is a determinant in striated space, as gravity determines lines of movement, where weight is and how it acts.[20] Gravity itself is all about falling, constant falling in curves, as well as the notional, parochial form we encounter as tiny dwellers on a big object's surface, which seems to work in terms of downwardness, specifically. So you can rise within gravity—it will be another gravity (mass) that draws you—in the case of these videos, the draw of the loss in eroticism and death. The drop in these videos is not the succumbing to mundane gravity, but an exaggerated, ironic acceptance of its working. The high heel is the same: ostensibly, it seems to act against the most obvious effects of gravity as the wearer is raised to the point of almost floating above tiny points of connection to the ground. But the engineering of shoes requires a sense of where weight will fall. The ultra-high heel becomes a distortion of gravity, a body designed by evolution to match the constraints of Earth conditions steps on to the heels in order to deliver a set of massive needles into the ground. The big toe acts as a new focus of a return of energy to the earth. Now balanced by the (body's) heel, the big toe is in a position to penetrate the ground itself, and yet it still stays above, while the body distorts and restructures its contours, as gravity's effect works upward. Rather than being a contingent biological product of forces, the Gaga body is a vector of forces that structure and delineate space, and from the height of the heel, this is a newly eroticized space, returning us to where we began, Bataille's perverse cosmology outlined in 'Solar Anus'. Instead of gravity as a weight-inducing force, rotation (movement creative of and due to gravity) and sexual arousal drive the universe, when in operation together.[21] All beings, all mineral objects are caught in a mighty whirl where death, sex, life, motion, and every incidental detail informs another. The example of the tree makes clear how this is a rise and fall, forever: 'the trees that forcefully soar end up burned by lightning, chopped down, or uprooted. Returned to the ground, they come up in another form'.[22] The form, the attitude (style and spatial position) of the various video Gagas are only waystations, temporary accretions in a wider theorization she makes, one where sex, death are brought into the almost-absent space where the heel touches the ground, penetrating only to the point of repulsion. Balance attained through the constant play of the irregular, the chaotic, the punishing erotic.

NOTES

1. Georges Bataille, 'The Big Toe', *Visions of Excess: Selected Writings, 1927–1939*, ed. Allan Stoekl, tr. Allan Stoekl, Carl R. Lovitt, and Donald M. Leslie, Jr. (Minneapolis, MN: University of Minnesota Press, 1985 [1929]), 20.
2. *Ibid.*
3. 'The Solar Anus', *Visions of Excess: Selected Writings, 1927–1939*, ed. Allan Stoekl, tr. Allan Stoekl, Carl R. Lovitt, and Donald M. Leslie, Jr. (Minneapolis, MN: University of Minnesota Press, 1985 [1927], 5–9.
4. *Ibid.*, 8.
5. Bataille, 'The Big Toe', 23.
6. *Ibid.*, 21.
7. Just how little any separation on gender grounds can occur will be seen as we look closely at Lady Gaga's heels, and not in the literal sense of men wearing high heels in the video for 'Alejandro', but in the sense of the shoes themselves performing erotic roles beyond ready male and female characterizations.
8. See Arthur Kroker, *Spasm: Virtual Reality/Android Music/Electric Flesh* (New York, NY: New World Perspectives/St Martin's Press, 1993), 136.
9. Elisabeth Bronfen, *Over Her Dead Body: Death, Femininity and the Aesthetic* (Manchester: Manchester University Press, 1992).
10. Lady Gaga, cited by Lizzy Goodman, in *Lady Gaga: Extreme Style* (London: HarperCollins, 2010), 44.
11. *Ibid.*, 31
12. Lee Wright writes of this being the way in which the stiletto was initially sold, playing on the idea of liberation from domesticity in 'Objectifying Gender: The Stiletto Heel', in *Fashion Theory: A Reader*, ed. Malcolm Barnard (Oxford and New York: Routledge, 2007), 200.
13. This Gaga is different from all the others in that the height of her position and posture never alter from the upright.
14. How this might be done is a question Bataille poses throughout the length of his oeuvre, and the answer can be sexual (*Eroticism*, tr. Mary Dalwood (London: Penguin, 2001 [1957])), or be an emptying of the self through contemplation of all that is taboo (*Inner Experience*, tr. Leslie Anne Boldt (New York, NY: State University of New York Press, 1988 [1954]); *Guilty*, tr. Stuart Kendall (New York, NY: State University of New York Press, 2011 [1944])) or extreme waste and actual sacrifice (*The Accursed Share*, vol. I, tr. Robert Hurley (New York: Zone, 1991 [1949]).
15. See Georges Bataille, 'Attraction and Repulsion II: Social Structure' in Denis Hollier (ed.), *The College of Sociology, 1937–39* (Minneapolis: University of Minnesota Press, 1988), 113–124.
16. See Michel Foucault, 'A Preface to Transgression', tr. Donald F. Bouchard and Sherry Simon, in *Language, Counter-memory and Practice* (New York: Cornell University Press, 1977), 29–52 (35).
17. Gilles Deleuze and Félix Guattari, *A Thousand Plateaus*, tr. Brian Massumi (London: Athlone, 1988 [1980]).
18. *Ibid.*, 481.
19. The term 'smooth' [*lisse*] is somewhat misleading, as it could apply to a highly homogenized space. However, Deleuze and Guattari envisage it as something like the desert, or fractal space: it is not devoid of features, but it is open, flexible, and complex.
20. Deleuze and Guattari, *A Thousand Plateaus*, 489.
21. Bataille, 'The Solar Anus', 6.
22. *Ibid.*, 7.

6 Celebrity without Organs

Craig N. Owens

The Lady Gaga under examination here is not a person; she is what Gilles Deleuze and Felix Guattari call, in *A Thousand Plateaus*, an assemblage. According to Deleuze and Guattari, an assemblage, which is different from a mere machine, is a collection of decentralized dynamic functions and processes that produces various effects and phenomena. They explain that,

> as in all things, there are lines of articulation, segmentarity, strata, and territories; but also lines of flight, movement, deterritorialization, and destratification. Comparative rates of flow on these lines produce phenomena of relative slowness and viscosity, or, on the contrary, of acceleration and rupture. All this, lines and measurable speeds, constitutes an *assemblage*.[1]

Salient to an examination of Gaga is the way this description of the assemblage emphasizes movement, both organized along lines and into strata, on the one hand, and liable to changes in speed and rupture, on the other. Because the assemblage is a dynamic system, not every change in one part of the assemblage results in a concomitant change in another. Some 'rates of flow' may become 'relative[ly] slow' while others may undergo 'acceleration'. And because this system is at least partially 'deterritorialized'—that is, not under the control of some central consciousness or processor—we can expect the assemblage to produce some effects and phenomena at odds with others it may produce.[2] We cannot, in other words, expect everything the assemblage makes possible to point back to a single organizing principle or set of uncontradictory operating precepts. Indeed, we cannot even assume that there is any intentionality at all behind any one of the effects the assemblage produces; many may be accidental, ancillary, or epiphenomenal.

We see these features clearly in Gaga's work: in the multiple and incommensurable roles she assumes, often in the course of a single song or video; in the radical eclecticism her music evinces, quoting such bands as Queen, Aerosmith, and Eurythmics and such performers as David Bowie, Donna Summer, Michael Jackson and Madonna; in the resistance to establishing a signature sound, style, or thematic concern; in the often contradictory effects produced by her celebrity persona and her public behavior; in the bizarre combination of politically correct, leftist orthodoxy, on the one hand, with the espousal of a manifestly commodified, consumerist ethos of neo-capitalism, on the other; and, not least, in the tension that emerges between the idea of Lady Gaga as an embodied individual with a personal history, predilections, beliefs, and tastes, on the one hand, and of Lady Gaga as a brand name, an industry, a culture-machine: a radically collaborative enterprise, on the other.

And so, along with the stipulation that Gaga is an assemblage comes something like a celebrity theory of radical incompleteness:[3] one can never make a claim about Gaga that is both always true and comprehensive at the same time. Any comprehensive claim about Gaga must account for exceptions, and any claim without exceptions must necessarily bracket certain aspects of the Gaga Assemblage. We must take this as a caveat: even when an interpretation or analysis of the Gaga Assemblage makes totalizing claims, we must expect exceptions. If the totalizing claim is a convention of academic analytic discourse, the Gaga Assemblage exceeds that discourse's ability to contain it.

With Gaga, then, we can only remark on tendencies, patterns, structures of meaning and of feeling, always aware that in many cases the opposite, or nearly opposite remarks can also be made, and that there may be much to be said that has no connection to our analysis. We can only begin to map territories that, from the outset, we know will shift, will connect themselves with territories now distant and non-contiguous, or will turn out later to be something other than territories. After all, the Gaga canon is not closed; the body of work continues to grow and shift, and it bears within it the potential to continue to shift in relation to whatever comes after it and gets added to it. We can only speak of Gaga as a field of effects and potentials, and never as a single individual: If *Gaga* is sometimes the antecedent to personal pronouns in this chapter—'she' and 'her' and 'hers'—it is, to quote Deleuze and Guattari, '[o]ut of habit, purely out of habit. [. . .] Also, because it's nice to talk like everybody else, to say the sun rises, when everybody knows it's only a manner of speaking. To reach, not the point where one no longer says [she], but the point where it is no longer of any importance whether one says [she]'.[4] The simplest of reasons makes it necessary to keep this multiplicity in mind as we disport with the proper name and the singular pronoun. The liner notes to her album *Born This Way*, for instance, make the collaborative nature of her music manifest in the credits for the title track by listing the many individual collaborators and corporate investors and directors who made the album possible.[5] And, just as the liner notes credit the multitudes who/which have contributed to the production of her music, so, too, do they offer gratitude to yet more multiple multitudes. On the final page of text, the liner notes inform us that someone calling itself 'I' 'would like to thank' a number of entities, ideas, people, and sources of inspiration, including 'The Road, The Highway, and the wind,' 'little monsters,' several supporters and collaborators who committed 'bravery to [her] artistry.' This 'bravery' manifests itself in a 'labor of love and blood fight' they 'put into every moment and sound of this music.' The speaker also thanks 'The Banditos' and others for 'believing in [her] and protecting [her] vision.' These supporters are characterized as 'warriors' whose attributes include 'wisdom,' 'magic,' 'chemistry,' and 'true friend[ship]'.

The progression of these acknowledgments is significant. They go from thanking inanimate objects, to which they attribute human qualities and express gratitude in quite personal terms, to listing individuals by name after name, to naming corporate entities, before thanking 'everyone', leaving no one at all out of the list of contributors. And, in addition to acknowledging those who have invested time, energy, and money into the album and its 'artistry', the liner notes declare that 'This album is for Ü'. The album is also a tribute '[t]o Mom, Dad, and Natali' and 'Grandpa Germanotta, who passed The Edge into his Glory'.[6] And so the multiplicities reconnect: everyone has put something into the album, and it is given, in turn, to everyone.

I'd like to offer a couple of observations. The first is that all recording artists of wide reputation are similarly multiple. They depend on many inputs—from individuals to corporations, from labor to capital—even to 'be' who he or she 'is' as a celebrity—and they offer the result to the widest possible audience. What strikes me as unique about Gaga is that she makes this multiplicity manifest. That is, the multiplicity of her celebrity persona is not just in the background, animating a public identity that masquerades as singular and unified; quite the contrary, the personas Gaga assumes are manifestly fragmented, self-contradictory, multiple and dynamic, producing the spectacle of celebrity commodity production, rather than the spectacle of celebrity individuality.

Second, because the contributors to the album and its beneficiaries—its honorees, dedicatees, and recipients—are the same, virtually 'everyone', Gaga becomes a regulatory node in an economy of appetite. Desire circulates from those whose 'loyalty, commitment, and bravery' make it possible for them to 'believe in' Gaga, through the Gaga assemblage, and returns to 'Mom', 'Dad', 'Natali', 'Grandpa', 'Ü', and 'everyone else' in the form of a studio album. Gaga, in other words, emerges as a conduit, a valve through which emotional energy passes and by means of which it gets transformed, accruing surplus value in the practice, before it returns to those from whom it originally came.

In theorizing the assemblage and its multiple operations and connections, its many inputs and outputs, Deleuze and Guattari offer us a vocabulary for describing the way the Gaga assemblage, in particular, works. Apart from being a 'multiplicity', the assemblage has two distinct 'sides': 'One side [. . .] faces the strata, which doubtless make it a kind of organism or signifying totality, or determination attributable to the subject.'[7] In the case of Gaga, this would suggest that in some ways the Gaga phenomenon organizes and presents itself according to the logic of a single, unifying intention, a subjectivity or identity that stands above its creation, conceiving it, making it, and distributing it. This is the Gaga who speaks as 'I', who claims to 'love' and 'thank' individual other people who have made her the unique and distinct individual she 'believes' herself to be. The Gaga assemblage, then, depends on Strata inputs and produces Strata outputs, according to the logic of liberal human subjectivity and commercial capitalism (Figure 6.1).

The Strata—the layers upon layers of systematically, hierarchically, and completely regimented logic that make Stefani Germanotta the subject of contracts, that guarantee her certain intellectual property rights, and that recognize in her artistic authority—manifest themselves in the fine print of the liner notes. On the side of the Strata, Stefani Germanotta is a fiduciary subject, engaging with the institutions and apparatuses of the capitalist system that makes the recording industry itself a fact of modern culture. In Figure 6.1, I have indicated the flow of inputs and outputs on the Strata-side of the Gaga assemblage. The inputs include the apparatus of consumer capitalism, and the outputs are represented by the commodities and cultural phenomenon produced by and in response the Gaga assemblage.

But there is another side to the Gaga assemblage, too: the 'side facing a *body without organs*, which is continually dismantling the organism, causing asignifying particles or pure intensities to pass or circulate, and attributing to itself subjects that it leaves with nothing more than a name as a trace of an intensity.'[8] The organs in question here are, for Deleuze

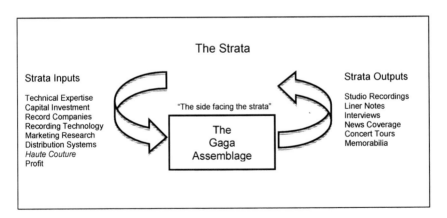

Figure 6.1 The Strata.

and Guattari, metaphors for inflexible organizational structures arranged in a hierarchical relationship to an organizing principle. The 'body without organs' is shorthand, then, for dynamic systems whose components are constantly in flux, reconstituting and deconstituting themselves and rearranging themselves both in relation to one another and in relation to the inputs and outputs of the system as a whole. As we examine Gaga, we see the Body without Organs manifesting itself in moments of excess: emotional outpouring, spurious identifications, and sentimental exchange. Additionally, the ersatz umlaut over the 'Ü' to whom *Born This Way* is dedicated is an 'asignifying particle' that emerges on the side of the Body without Organs: decorative, but finally meaningless.[9] The same umlaut appears atop the *u* of the song title 'Yoü and I', a quasi country-and-western song with no apparent connection to German phonetics. The umlaut, in both cases, may point to something like authorial intention, since for some time Gaga dated musician Lüc Carl, whose use of the umlaut is equally inexplicable.[10] So, in trying to make meaning out of the asignifying particle, we are simply directed to its prior appearance in the chain of asignification: an excess of absence. Gaga also presents herself as a Body without Organs when sudden shifts in point of view, vocal technique, song styling, and even thematic content, both from song to song and within a single song, trouble any attempt to identify who is the source of the utterance we hear.

Once again, the liner notes for *Born This Way* are instructive regarding the way the Gaga Assemblage engages on 'the side facing the body without organs.' Whereas the writing, recording, mixing, and production credits for each song testify to the stratified, territorialized operations of the Gaga Assemblage, the general acknowledgements and dedication quoted above manifest a much more deterritorialized entanglement of emotional and personal intensities. They enact a kind of breathless, Molly-Bloom stream-of-consciousness; grammar, syntax, and punctuation are stretched to their limits here. Distinct from the corporate formulations of the album's credits, which record the official, material investments that have been made in the recordings, these acknowledgements disport with the mystical and emotional investments: loyalty, commitment, bravery, brilliance, epic kindness, genius, protection, nurturing, wisdom, magic, chemistry, inspiration, and belief. As opposed to the professional labor many of these individuals provided, these acknowledgments draw our attention to the 'labor of love' and the 'blood fight' that Gaga's supporters have invested in her. In return, she offers her love and gratitude. After all, the acknowledgements suggest, this isn't a business arrangement: It's a family, and that family includes not just her literal family or the individuals named, but 'everyone.' And one is given to understand that these relationships to friends, family, fans, and everyone are marked by an emotional reciprocity: Gaga is as devoted to her fans and supporters as they are to her.

Let me schematize the Gaga Assemblage's inputs and outputs on the side of the Body without Organs thus:

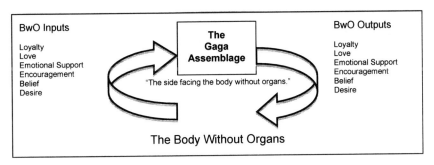

Figure 6.2 The Body without Organs.

On the left-hand side of the scheme appear the personal investments that Gaga's fans and supporters have made; on the right hand side, we see the same list, only this time figured as what Gaga offers everyone. And this, in my view, is the major distinction between the Body-without-Organs side of the Gaga Assemblage and the Strata side: On the side of the Strata, the inputs get processed by the Gaga assemblage, transformed into materially altered outputs. Money, infrastructure, logistics, and the like are turned into albums, commodities, and cultural productions, which then get monetized and either reinvested into maintaining the Gaga Assemblage or distributed among those with stake in it. But, on the side with the Body without Organs, there is no apparent processing: raw emotional energy, 'magic' and 'brilliance' are put in, and raw emotional energy, 'love' and 'gratitude', pour out. Figure 6.3 is a composite of the first two, showing inputs and outputs on both sides of the assemblage. Given that the 'organs', as Deleuze and Guattari figure them, are those structures that support and perpetuate hierarchical and sequential functioning, we should not be surprised that on the Body-without-Organs side of the Gaga assemblage we find minimal processing of inputs into outputs.

As if in anticipation of a Deleuzo-Guattarian analysis of her work, Gaga seems simultaneously to quote and mock Deleuze and Guattari, and to deny the theory its analytical purchase, by literalizing the attenuation, removal, and erasure of bodily organs time and time again in her songs, which frequently deploy organs as sites of contested meaning. 'Love Game', featured on her first album, *The Fame* (2008), begins with this pair of lines, repeated continually throughout the song: 'Let's have some fun, this beat is sick / I wanna take a ride on your disco stick'. Gaga acknowledged that 'it's another of my very thoughtful metaphors for a cock.'[11] Apart from the use of the term *metaphor* to mean *euphemism*, Gaga's reading of her own lyrics seems to state the obvious, and it also provides the word missing from the lyric later in the song: namely, *cock*, suggested by the rhyme with *block* and the anatomical parallel with *mouth*: 'I can see you standing there from across the block / with a smile on your mouth and your hands on your *huh*!' In the recording of the song, the 'huh' that concludes this couplet is uttered

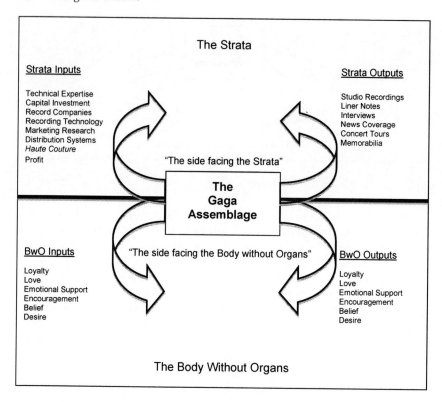

Figure 6.3   The Strata and The Body without Organs.

as a chesty, fist-pumping, guttural bark, suggesting in its phatic rawness a thrust or punch to the mid-section.

If the penis finds itself the object of lyrical evasion in 'Love Game', in 'Poker Face', it's the vagina and its environs. The song, which uses poker playing—with its bluffs, delays, mind-games, and secrecy—as a conceit for teasing a potential lover, features this passage, chanted, rather than sung:

> I won't tell you that I love you
> Kiss or hug you
> 'Cause I'm bluffin' with my muffin
> I'm not lying
> I'm just stunning with my love-glue-gunning.

In these lines, remarkable for the way in which their enjambment and lack of punctuation make possible a range of mutually exclusive interpretations, 'muffin' seems to euphemize female genitalia, echoing Aerosmith's use of the same word in the first stanza of their 1975 song 'Walk This Way'. The 'Poker Face' video features Gaga, clad in an off-the-shoulder black latex body suit and boots, pointing at her crotch at the moment she sings the word 'muffin', thus making explicit the song's barely veiled emphasis on sex.

Coupled with the use of euphemism to avoid explicitly naming genitalia, the dramatization of organ removal and the substitution of objects for body parts lay still heavier significance on the attenuated body. In the opening shots of her 'Alejandro' video, Gaga is discovered walking at the head of a funeral procession, as if she is the bereaved. On a pillow, she carries an oversized, jeweled heart, entwined with barbed wire and pierced with what appears to be a large decking nail. This image fades as that of a bronzed, oiled, buff young man appears wearing only black briefs and a silver-studded black helmet. He is seated on the edge of a bed, situated among ruins, gazing out, as if awaiting the arrival of a lover. This soldier-lover conceals his crotch with a high-caliber golden semi-automatic pistol, pointed downward, which he holds by the grip. The gun both symbolizes the penis it conceals and suggests its displacement onto the upward-pointed finial atop the black helmet on the soldier's head. And so, within the first couple minutes of the 'Alejandro' video, we have the suggestion of two organs displaced: the heart and the penis.

If the men in the early part of the 'Alejandro' video are subject to the literal and figurative removal of vital organs—heart and genitals in this case—Gaga is the subject of organ substitution at the video's end. The misty, mysterious, and bombed-out military setting gives way to a sleek, minimalist, ultra-modern song-and-dance sequence during the song's final chorus. In this sequence, Gaga first appears dancing alone, wearing a sleek black pantsuit. Soon, though, she is joined by a chorus-line of male dancers, and the top of her suit is transformed into a black brassiere sporting two machine-gun barrels that take aim according to the disposition of Gaga's breasts. At times she intentionally aims them; at other times, she dances as if they weren't there, leaving them to sway and bob in an ungainly but vaguely menacing way.

The addition of weaponry to the female breasts in these closing sequences of the 'Alejandro' video recall a similar breast enhancement revealed at the end of the 'Bad Romance' video (2009). In the closing sequence of the video, we find Gaga walking seductively toward a black-clad man who sits on the edge of a satin bed, gazing randily at her as she approaches. At once, the bed and the wall behind it erupt into flames, while the man remains in place, and, in the very final shot of the video, we find a bizarre visual *dénouement*. Gaga, her hair fried, her body and lingerie smeared and stained with soot, lies on the smoldering bed, smoking a cigarette, next to the charred, barely recognizable corpse of her would-be lover. In place of bra-cups, her breasts sport two flame throwers, still sparking and smoking from the exertion of having, apparently, burned her lover in bed.

These sequences thematize two tendencies of the Gaga oeuvre with regard to bodily organs: substitution/displacement, on the one hand, and surfacing. When the expectant soldier-lover in 'Alejandro' conceals his crotch with his downward-facing gun, when 'huh' and 'muffin' stand in as lyrics for the names of male and female genitals, respectively, and when the title character of her song 'Monster' eats the female singer's heart and brain, as we shall see, we are confronted with organs that get moved, removed, or displaced by something else. At the same time, when we see a jeweled heart upon a pillow, a gleaming phallic helmet atop a glowing, bronze, statuesque young man, and breasts augmented with gun barrels or flame throwers, we are witnessing the surfacing of the organ: the functioning organ, retooled, moves to the surfaces of the body, and in doing so calls attention to that surface *as surface* (rather than, say, as that which conceals the 'real' person or the 'real' workings of the human body).

Indeed, our attention is frequently drawn to Gaga's surfaces and those of her surroundings. Of course we see only surfaces, since that's how human sight works; but these surfaces continually appear as significant for being surfaces. Alexander McQueen's couture, which appears in 'Bad Romance', is both visually and texturally complex, inviting us to imagine touching them. The video version of 'Paparazzi' commences with an extended narrative prelude. Finding herself entangled in a dangerous and mutually manipulative affair with a celebrity (or celebrity wannabe), played by Alexander Skarsgård, she resists his attempts to use her to solidify his own fame. He, in turn, throws her from the parapet of the mansion in which they have been carrying on their tryst. Immediately, we see newspaper headlines spinning toward us à la *Citizen Kane*, with headlines like 'Lady Ga Ga Hits Rock Bottom' or 'Lady Gaga Over'. Then, when the song commences, we see Gaga emerge from a limousine, returning to the mansion where she will take revenge on her lover. When she arrives, she is clad, head-to-toe, in a brazen body cast, reminiscent of the droid C3PO from *Star Wars*. As she begins to dance, the cast falls away, and the Gaga is revealed whole and unscathed, surgically reconstructed after her fall. Here, again, our attention is drawn to the surface of the body, its smooth metallic contours producing an intensity that goes beyond the suggestion of prosthesis or medical apparatus alone as they invite a tactile longing.

These surfaces, emphasized as such, exaggerated and tactile, are both over-determined and underdetermined at the same time. Rich in their suggestion of immediate sensory effects, these surfaces announce themselves as immensely significant, symbolic, and suggestive. At the same time, they are also carapaces, protective coatings that ward off the penetrating analytic gaze. And so, although they seem to invite interpretation, these surface coatings also frustrate the interpretive enterprise. In other words, when the body manifests itself as entirely surface, literally eviscerating itself to achieve a kind of depthlessness, we are challenged to find other ways of understanding the relationship of body to identity and meaning.

The literalization of a Body without Organs and the emphasis on surface phenomena and effects is the physical and visual manifestation of a more general literalization that pervades Gaga's work. After all, literalization is the flattening out of metaphor; it renders meaning in two dimensions, so that an utterance's or enactment's manifest content exhausts interpretation, denying that there's any more to it than what appears up front. In 'Speechless', from her first studio album, *The Fame* (2008), Gaga sings of a man whose rejection has left her 'speechless'. In common usage, to be 'speechless' is to be so surprised as to not know what to say. It is a very common figure of speech, but a figure of speech nonetheless. Not so in the song: Gaga avows that she'll literally 'never talk again' because something she has literally said has precipitated his rejection of her. Like the flames of desire that literally burn her would-be lover in the 'Bad Romance' video and the newspaper headlines that literalize otherwise metaphorical expressions, the literalization of speechlessness and the gesture indicating that her 'muffin' is, in fact, her genital region ensures that meaning remain a surface phenomenon, and not one that emerges from a deep reading through surface.

The literal, I should mention, falls on the side of the Body without Organs. The metaphor is a process, converting literal into figurative meaning, and thereby producing a surplus aesthetic value: poetry. Whatever Gaga's songs are, they are not poetry; they are almost defiantly, aggressively self-apparent, in fact. So, let me offer yet another version of the scheme that I have been developing over the course of this essay:

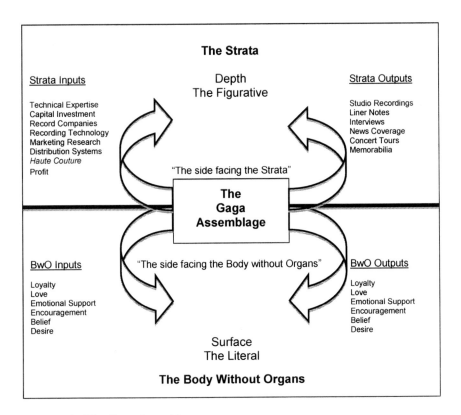

Figure 6.4   The Gaga Assemblage.

In this figure, I have added the terms 'Depth' and 'The Figurative' to the side of the assemblage facing the Strata, and 'Surface' and 'The Literal' to the side facing the Body without Organs. Figuration—whether visual or linguistic—always implies a depth, an intentionality beyond the merely visual. Poetic language, including metaphor and simile, conceit, and plays on words, demands that the reader or listener perceive a meaning beyond the literal or surface meaning. The meaning has been processed, re-ordered, *organ*-ized in such a way that it must be interpreted. The opposite is true of surface and literal meanings: they are just what they appear to be, requiring no processing; there is nothing going on behind the scenes.

The most persistently literalized figure in the Gaga canon is that of the monster. The monster pervades Gaga's work and thematizes her celebrity persona, as is well known to her fans, collectively to whom she refers as 'little monsters', and even '*my* little monsters'. This repeated use of 'monster' encompasses a broad and vaguely defined field of meanings that swirl around the idea of the misfit: homosexuals, high-school outsiders, freaks, transgendered and transsexual people, people of color, and even (as emerges in the title song of her album, *Born This Way*) people of faith. The Gaga monster is akin to the eighteenth- and nineteenth-century western European conception of the monster, which Michel Foucault examines in his 1974–1975 lectures to the Collége de France, collected under the title *The Abnormal*. According to Foucault, as late as the eighteenth century, civil and ecclesiastical authority identified as monsters those people whose bodies manifested a degree of deformity or hybridity that challenged conceptions of nature's laws: hermaphroditism, in particular, seems to have been a deeply troubling phenomenon.[12]

Such a conception of monstrosity focuses on externally visible proofs to determine who is a monster and who is not. Monstrosity is marked on and expressed through the bodily form, and these markings exhaust this kind of monstrosity. As the modes of social control became increasingly medicalized, psychologized, and science-based, however, conceptions of what constituted monstrosity began to change, so that, by the middle of the nineteenth century, the site of monstrosity had shifted from the body to the moral constitution. Whereas the monster of the eighteenth century and before had been the abnormal body, a century later, it had become the morally corrupt and socially maladjusted. The locus of this maladjustment and corruption was no longer the body, though bodily features could sometimes symptomize them; rather, monstrosity was a condition of one's interior personhood.

This shift from the monster on the surface to the monster in the depths provides an analog for the distinction between the literal and the figurative I discussed earlier. In calling her fans monsters, and in identifying with them, Gaga seems to want to celebrate the moral and psychological outsider: the person whose desires or internal self-conception runs counter to the social dominant. One is valuable, her song 'Born This Way' insists, 'no matter gay, straight, or bi, transgendered, [or] lesbian', because 'it doesn't matter if you love him, or capital H-I-M'. In 'Bad Kids', Gaga speaks for and on behalf of socially maladjusted young people. The lesbian persona of 'Americano' and the codependent lover who imagines herself unable to resist her love for 'Judas' are two examples of Gaga inhabiting roles whose monstrosity inheres in the moral constitution. 'Bad Romance', the lead single from her second album, *The Fame Monster*, similarly celebrates deviant desires.

But, as if unable to resist the resurfacing of the monster through the reinscription of monstrosity on the body, Gaga's music and videos much more frequently represent monstrosity as physical deformity or bodily abnormality. The visual and verbal discourses often disport with that older conception of the monster: the deformed, unnatural, or hybrid body that confronts nature with its own limits. *The Fame Monster* features the song 'Monster', in which the singer reports on an unexpectedly savage erotic encounter that begins with a meeting in a dance club:

> He licked his lips, said to me,
> '[. . .] you look good enough to eat.'
> Put his arms around me.
> [I] said, 'Boy, [. . .] get your paws right off of me.'

The eponymous 'monster' of the song is attributed with 'paws' not only because it's a common figure of speech, but also because, as we have already learned earlier in the song, he is characterized as 'a wolf in disguise', and a particularly voracious one who 'ate [her] heart / instead' of whatever it was she expected him to eat. Indeed, this monster 'ate [her] heart out', invoking the transitive phrasal verb 'to eat out', which commonly means to perform cunnilingus. This wolf/lover hybrid is monstrous in the pre-nineteenth-century sense, as Foucault theorizes it, because it manifests itself as an unnatural bodily hybridity: the evil eyes, the paws, the lupine attributes, and the carnal acts. Likewise, the rock anthem 'Hair', featured on *Born This Way*, starts by figuring the high-school-aged singer-persona's hair as a sign of her resistance to convention. But, by the end of the song, the lyrics proclaim 'I am my hair' over and over again. What began as a sign of a deeper spirit of resistance has become the locus of identity, literally on the surface of the body.

But Gaga's music video 'Bad Romance' performs this kind of monstrosity most starkly, even as it already gestures toward the moral corruption characteristic of a later cultural conception of the monster. We are introduced to the 'Bath Haus of Gaga', a sterile, glass-and-tile series of rooms that recall mid-twentieth-century sanitoria and institutional shower rooms. In the first room we see a row of seven white, coffin-like pods, each with the word 'Monster' inscribed in red, sans-serif capitals and underscored by a red cross. As the signature 'ohhh's that open the song tower over the soundtrack, the 'monsters' emerge from their pods and begin to dance somewhat awkwardly, more or less in unison. They all bear classic female forms—buxom with slim waists and curved hips—except for the central monster, who, though apparently female, is more willowy in stature than the three monsters on either side of her. Whether or not it is Stephani Germanotta's body that takes center stage, we are to identify it as Gaga herself. The doubt this account expresses comes from the fact that the central monster's body is clad, head-to-toe, in tight white latex, a body suit that leaves only the mouth and nose exposed. Other monsters are less fully enwrapped, but all show very little of their faces: sometimes the eyes, sometimes the mouth, but never enough of the face to be identifiable.

The figure of the monster early in the 'Bad Romance' offers an especially rich line of inquiry, and so I want to maintain my focus on the opening sequence of the dance, what I'll call the 'monster dance'. Two observations suggest their salience to my inquiry. First, the dancers in this sequence cannot be individually identified: whatever kind of monster has emerged from the pods, their monstrosity has somehow erased or occluded or prevented the development of recognizable human identity. Second, the dance they engage in includes a precise quotation of the monster dance in Michael Jackson's 'Thriller' video. In both Gaga's video and Jackson's, the monsters present themselves in profile, and, with elbows bent, raise their two hands in front of them, one slightly higher than the other, the fingers crimped into the shape of outward-facing claws. The movement suggests both ferocity and clumsiness. In 'Thriller', the clumsiness is visually emphasized by the fact that the monsters are dancing in grave clothes: dusty, rotting, and tattered versions of everyday street clothes, costumes that do not conduce to balletic elegance. In 'Bad Romance', this clumsiness is heightened by the extremely high stiletto heels that force the dancers to move in mincing, ungainly steps, as if always about to lose their balance.[13]

The timing of these two versions of the same dance further invites comparison between them. Both videos begin with a kind of curtain-raiser, a brief scene before the song begins. But it is exactly one minute into the performance of the songs that each one's respective monster dance takes place. This line of flight, which leads us out of Gaga, into Jackson, and back to Gaga, helps us identify just what kind of monsters we're dealing with in 'Bad Romance'. For, though the white pods from which the Gaga monsters emerge may or may not stand in for coffins, in 'Thriller', we see the monsters claw their way out of their graves: they're zombies.

And the zombie is the quintessential monster without organs. The zombie horrifies us not because of its ability to cause pain, but because it confronts us with the possibility of an appetite without intention, desire without a subject; in its mindless, directionless wandering it embodies—but only barely—the disorganized, and even chaotic flow of intensities, recognizable as somehow formerly human in traces of behavior we recognize in ourselves. It's not that they literally have no organs, even though literality figures as a kind of organlessness in the most recent schematic I've offered. In fact, in zombiedom, there is a superabundance of organs, both those of their victims, which they ingest, and their own heightened senses of vision and smell, their greater strength, and their improved ingestive and digestive apparatuses. But the disorder they threaten and embody reminds us that the 'BwO is not at all the opposite of the organs. The organs are not its enemies. The enemy is the organism. The BwO is opposed not to the organs but to the organization of the organs called the organism'.[14] This 'organization of the organs' into an 'organism' is precisely what distinguishes humans, who recognize themselves as such and, in all zombie films, possess the ability to organize as a group, from zombies, whose group identity resembles that of the ant colony, one of Deleuze and Guattari's favored models of rhizomic behavior.

When one watches George A. Romero's *Dawn of the Dead* (1978), the second in his *Dead* trilogy, one notices an interplay among three modalities germane to our considerations. The first, that of the human, comprises order, intention, and goal-oriented behavior as when, trapped in an eerily deserted mall, the four humans striving to survive take measures appropriate to doing so. Their attempts to impose order upon the chaotic, unpredictable, and harrowing world of the zombies who will also flock to the mall represents the film's first modality, and the one with which we, as viewers, are asked to identify.

The second modality is that of the zombie in chase, and is characterized by intense scenes of pursuit and getaway, narrow escape and carnage. In later zombie films, the intensity is heightened by filmmakers' decision to endow zombies with the ability to move very fast when they chase their prey. But these are not truly scenes of chaos, because they organize the narrative and provide the film's very structure, the fundamental action.

The truly harrowing, rather than merely frightening, scenes of the film are those in which the zombies engage in uncannily recognizable, but meaningless, behaviors. Their congregation at the mall that serves as the setting for most of the film is inexplicable in terms of zombie intentionality. They go there not because they have somehow run their human prey to ground or deduced their likely whereabouts; they're certainly not there to pick up a new pair of khakis. Rather, they gather at the mall because some remainder of their human behavior, now unmoored from intention and rational decision-making, compels them to walk to the mall. This shell of human-like behavior, emptied of its capitalist imperative to purchase and the subject's intention to do so, strikes us as uncanny because it confronts our Cartesian self-conceptions with the threat of a completely deterritorialized non-subject.

A more recent version of *Dawn of the Dead* (2004) includes a storyline that rewards scrutiny in this regard. In it, the band of would-be survivors, like their filmic forebears, have taken refuge in a shopping mall toward which the zombies migrate *en masse*. From the safety of the mall's rooftop, the human refugees take stock of the siege, and there form a relationship with the owner of a gun shop, visible to them on the rooftop of his shop, where he has hidden out. They communicate with him, and he with them, by means of dry-erase boards and binoculars. But soon enough, we—and the observers on the roof of the mall—see a zombie infiltrate the gun shop, and we experience the mall-bound characters' tension as they watch this breach.

A few minutes later, the owner appears on his roof, takes up his whiteboard, and, to our relief begins once more to write a message. But when he holds the whiteboard up, we see his transformed features and a whiteboard smeared with blood, a message of quite a different kind than we were expecting. This scene strikes me, above all the others in the film, as the most deeply harrowing and depressing, because of the revelation that his behavior—scrawling on the whiteboard—which we believe is a testament both to his continued survival and his ongoing integration into a symbolic universe and a community is, in fact, the very sign of his having been zombified. This very powerful image of the blood-smeared whiteboard confronts us at once with the possibility of a world of gestures and marks emptied of meaning and intention.

I have spent so much time reflecting on the peculiar way in which zombie behavior deterritorializes human behaviors by means of grotesque parody, because it seems that Gaga's lyrics and videos frequently engage in zombie deterritorialization. The pure phonemes—often nonsense lyrics and imitations of other sounds—collapse the signifier/signified relationship that structures human language, once again forcing us to attend to the phatic surface, the mere sounds of the voice, rather than the depth: what they mean. The bizarre intonations that begin 'Government Hooker', on *Born this Way*, are perhaps the best example of this linguistic deterritorialization, which occurs throughout her music. And the frequently ungainly or workmanlike dancing, not just in the opening sequences of 'Bad Romance', but throughout it, as well as in 'Alejandro', 'Poker Face', and 'Paparazzi', also suggests the halting, death-stiffened movements of zombies. But, in my view, the significance of the zombie/Gaga connection is in the way these two phenomena manage flows, particularly of bodies and of desires.

Having been deprived of the individualizing rationality that would make them human, zombies are more in touch with instinctual, animal drives common to their type (and presumably, to humans, as well). Among the effects of this deprivation is blockage. Because zombies in a mass will go to the same places, pursue the same prey, and react the same way to various stimuli, the crisis of zombie films is almost always precipitated by the concentration of zombies in a confined area—a mall, the city of Philadelphia, a farmhouse in the country, a church—that forces the humans in that area to hole up and stay put. The impact of mass zombification is precisely impaction, and the goal of the humans in zombie films is less often to destroy the zombies than simply to escape them, to find 'a way out' or a 'line of flight', as Deleuze and Guattari would have it.

In comparison, consider two descriptions of Gaga's fans from recent interviews. The first comes from her interview with Lisa Robinson, published in the September 2010 issue of *Vanity Fair*, on whose cover Gaga appears. Gaga describes an encounter with her fans, in Australia, that made her realize what a huge pop phenomenon she had become:

> 'I don't remember what city it was,' she says, 'but [. . .] after the show there were 5,000 people standing on stairways and platforms leading to a train station—I couldn't even see how far back. The car drove out, and I said, "Stop the car," and I got out and walked out, and the scream was so loud, it was a *roar*. I went over to the fence and signed as many autographs as I could without them pulling me through. More fans than ever had been waiting for me outside after the show [. . .]—5,000 of them. It was *insane*.'[15]

The second comes from the November, 2010, issue of *Vogue* in an interview with Jonathan Van Meter, who reports standing 'in the wings and watch[ing] as at least a dozen women were pulled out of the crush in front of the barricades and taken away on stretchers because they were overcome and near collapse.'[16] Later, embedded with Gaga and her entourage, Van Meter recounts another of Gaga's encounters with her fans, after she has instructed her driver to stop so she can greet them outside a concert venue:

> The doors swing open, and Gaga, surrounded by security, plunges in. '*Gaga! Gaga! Gaga!*' [. . .] The crowd surges forward. A security guy yells, 'One at a time! Take it easy!' There are girls with tears streaming down their faces. I almost get knocked over. Morris pulls me out of the maw and shoves me into the van, and the doors close behind us. But the fans do not give up. They are banging on the windows, pressing their faces against the glass.[17]

If Gaga's fans resemble zombies in their relentless crush and voracity, she, too, at times seems to have become zombified. Again, Van Meter offers a salient observation:

> After [. . .] her performance, [. . .] Gaga herself looked like a lunatic: Barefoot, still covered in fake blood, mascara running down her face, she was careening around the room [. . .] There were dancers running in and out, mixing and spilling drinks, and a peanut gallery of strangely bedazzled gay men [. . .].[18]

He also relates two meals the singer ordered: the first, a midday snack of sorts, consisted of 'enough filet mignon to feed twelve'; the second was a repast of 'escargot, steak tartare, and chicken' at Chez André. Added to the infamous 'meat dress', which the singer wore to the 2010 MTV Video Music Awards, and the polar-bear cape, complete with head, that she dons in 'Bad Romance', this animal-protein-heavy diet emphasizes the literalization of the body-without-organs Gaga enacts. Without her own organs, she must constantly ingest and wear the organs of other animals. The editorial introduction to Robinson's interview uncannily draws our attention to the circular economy of appetites that animates and is animated by the Gaga Assemblage, noting her 'total identification with the millions of "Little Monsters" who feed her hunger with their own'.

As is probably clear at this point, I'm inclined to include the zombie on the BwO side of the Gaga Assemblage: the monstrous appetite and the unprocessed circulation of hungers, as well as the emphasis on literal organs—those of the animals she wears and eats—makes it easy to think of the Gaga-Zombie as another figure through which the celebrity-without-organs manifests itself. And yet, doing so forces us to contend with the role the morally corrupt monster, the monster whose appetites and desires are less bodily and more psychologically or constitutionally construed: the misfit, the sexual deviant, the monsters of the interior. So, what strikes me

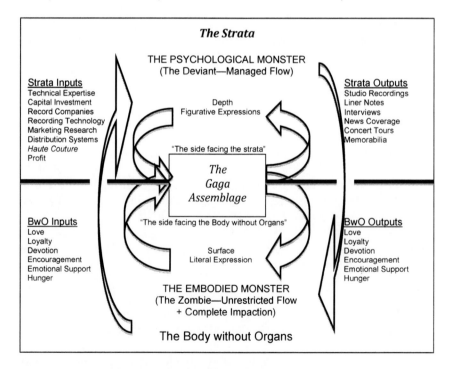

Figure 6.5   The Gaga Assemblage and its Monsters.

as the more nuanced understanding of the way the monster functions in and around the Gaga assemblage is as the figure that troubles the Strata/BwO binary in the first place: the boundary crosser and shape-shifter who moves between the two registers. If the assemblage has two sides, one facing the plane of consistency, and the other facing the Strata, the monster is on both sides.

In this regard, the monsters are the boundary breakers, the figures that circulate through schemata, troubling their alluring and satisfying rigor. The *and* is the term of the monster: dead *and* alive; voracious *and* anorexic; active *and* without intention.[19] The monster is a figure of a troubling both-ness that allows it not only to exist on either side of the assemblage, but to move from one side to another according to a logic that does not respect binarity.

This observation leads me to two conclusions. First, the zombie enacts the integration of the stratic into the plane of consistency, such that the stratic emerges as a high-viscosity consistency distinct from, but flowing through, the other consistencies that characterize that plane. For, in effecting blockages, in penning in the humans whose most urgent need is to escape, they act as agents of the Strata, constricting flows (of people, food, supplies, and information). And yet, they do so only by virtue of a consistency of behavior across the horde that emerges from the deterritorialization of the individual human subject that defines the zombie in the first place.

The second, and related claim I wish to make is that, as object lessons in the interplay between de-individualization and the management of flows, there is little to distinguish between the zombie and the celebrity of the Gaga type. Beyond the explicit ways in which Gaga deploys zombie tropes—spastic monster dancing, repeated invocations of and identitification with 'the monster', the frequent phatic howls and intonations that occur throughout her songs, and her reportedly voracious appetite—Gaga strikes me as a zombie for other reasons. For one, she manages flows of consumer desire and cultural capital. One the one hand, she is a conduit for these flows: desire flows through her, not just toward her, so that the emotional intensity that her fans express toward her gets expressed back at them. The same can be said for the flow of capital: the millions upon millions of dollars that pour into Gaga, minus her own 'take', gets reinvested in the apparatus that makes her possible, from the discrete units of labor and studio time to more nebulous, but no less material, cultural shifts her capital outlay makes possible. On the other hand, her presence, whether as a distraction from a baseball game or as the occasion for fanatic mobs, impacts movement, brings events and traffic to a halt, and impedes the flow of bodies, objects, and information.

As I have been arguing, the Gaga phenomenon is the celebrity body-without-organs; it should not surprise us, then, that these 'two poles'—the 'strata' and 'the plane of consistency'—are observable in it. The susceptibility of Gaga's oeuvre to interpretation and explication mark the stratified pole, and the invitation to read out of the manifest content of her lyrics and videos some kind of latent message or further significance is indicative of the degree to which the Gaga assemblage engages with established herme-neutics. At the same time, her work's resistance to such analysis pulls it back toward the 'plane of consistency', that patchwork surface of flows and intensities, asignifying images and particles, phonemic play, the dissonances between word and image, and the continual literalizations that characterize many of her videos. Indeed, in mapping these two poles vis-à-vis Gaga, we can list, on the side of the plane of consistency, Gaga's performances, her public misbehavior (at Yankee Stadium, for example), the nonsense words that populate her lyrics, and her outlandish couture (including, of course, the aforementioned 'meat dress'). On the side of the Strata, by contrast, we have the whole mass of celebrity interviews and profiles (*Rolling Stone, Vanity Fair, Larry King Live*, and many more), criticism and interpreta-tion (including the emerging corpus of professional academic responses to Gaga's work, such as the one in which this essay appears), the manifest produced-ness of her albums, and public apologies and self-explanations (such as the one she delivered to Ellen Degeneres the day after she wore the meat dress). But the apparent binarity of the 'two poles' model of the Body without Organs does not fully account for the way in which these so-called 'poles' really form a more reticulated, mosaic surface. They are not on opposite 'ends' of a 'spectrum', but rather, they are mixed together, monstrous in their hybridity, more tabby cat than tiger. Gaga teaches us this, shows us how the two sides of the assemblage erupt into one another, through the figure of the celebrity-monster.

And this is the point at which I want to close this essay by noting that Gaga, as the Celebrity Without Organs, also anatomizes a mode of female pop-celebrity which, though not new, is newly dominant: the celebrity who one no longer is able to think of as a Cartesian subject whose deep individu-ality somehow finds expression in her utterances and performances. While it seems to me that in some confessional modes of music, for example, a kind of authenticity still abides—Taylor Swift and Adele come to mind as quintessential examples of this kind of celebrity identity—the female pop-musician is increasingly becoming monstrous in her ability to shift shape, inhabit temporary identities, and to go with the flow.

NOTES

1. Gilles Deleuze and Félix Guattari, *A Thousand Plateaus*, tr. Brian Massumi (London: Athlone, 1988 [1980]), 3–4.
2. *Ibid.*, 4.
3. I borrow this term from Kurt Gödel's mathematical theory of radical incom-pleteness, which holds that no formal symbolic system can be both complete and consistent with its own principles. This, I would argue, is the position we find ourselves in as we try to analyze the Gaga assemblage.
4. Deleuze and Guattari, *A Thousand Plateaus*, 3.

5. Lady Gaga et al. *Born This Way*. Liner Notes (Interscope, 2011). The complete album booklet, including the liner notes excerpted here, are (as of this writing) available at http://ladygaga.wikia.com/wiki/Born_This_Way_%28album%29?file=BTW-Booklet-18.png.

6. *Ibid.*

7. Deleuze and Guattari, *A Thousand Plateaus*, 4.

8. *Ibid.*

9. *Ibid.*

10. Carlos Greer, 'Lady Gaga Rekindles Romance with Ex-Boyfriend', *People* (6 July 2010) (online at: http://www.people.com/people/article/0,,20399834,00. html) <accessed: 13 July 2012>.

11. Austin Scaggs, 'Lady Gaga Worships Queen and Refuses to Wear Pants', *Rolling Stone* (19 February 2009) (online at: http://www.rollingstone. com/music/news/lady-gaga-worships-queen-and-refuses-to-wear-pants-20090219) <accessed: 27 March 2013>.

12. Michel Foucault, '22 January 1975', *The Abnormal: Lectures to the College de France 1974–1975*, eds. Valerio Marchetti and Antonella Solomoni, trans. Graham Burchell (Brooklyn, NY: Verso, 2003 [1975]), 55–80

13. See Paul Hegarty's chapter in this volume.

14. Deleuze and Guattari, *A Thousand Plateaus*, 158.

15. Lisa Robinson, 'Lady Gaga's Cultural Revolution', *Vanity Fair* (September 2010) (Robinson's emphasis) (online at: http://www.vanityfair.com/hollywood/features/2010/09/lady-gaga-201009?currentPage=2) <accessed: 27 March 2013>.

16. Jonathan Van Meter, 'Our Lady of Pop', *Vogue* (November 2011) (online at: http://www.vogue.com/magazine/article/lady-gaga-our-lady-of-pop/) <accessed: 27 March 2013>.

17. *Ibid.*

18. *Ibid.*

19. I'm using the term *anorexic* here in its etymologically literal sense: 'without desire'.

Part II
Gaga and Representation

7 Celebrity, Spectacle, and Surveillance

Understanding Lady Gaga's 'Paparazzi' and 'Telephone' through Music, Image, and Movement[1]

Lori Burns and Marc Lafrance

INTRODUCTION

For Lady Gaga, writing songs and making videos are part of the same creative process. Gaga does not, as she puts it, 'write records and then decide what the video will look like.' Instead, song writing and video making are part of what she calls a 'complete vision' in and through which 'the song and the visual [. . .] all come [. . .] at once.'[2] Far from mere promotional materials for her songs, Gaga's videos are an integral part of her artistic production. This is especially true of her cinematically inspired videos 'Paparazzi' (2009) and 'Telephone' (2010). Conceived as short films complete with title cards and end credits, these ground-breaking videos bring to life the human drama and the collateral damage associated with present-day celebrity culture.[3]

When viewed alongside one another, 'Paparazzi' and 'Telephone' are linked on a number of levels. Characterized by a wide range of common themes, the links between the two videos suggest that a broader narrative is at work across them. We explore this broader narrative while thinking critically about the themes that make it both creatively effective and culturally evocative. In the first part of the chapter, we present a general reflection on the thematic relationship between the two videos. In doing so, we formulate a conceptual framework for making sense of this relationship and how it both shapes and is shaped by the broader narrative at work across the two videos. In the second part of the chapter, we move the analysis from the general to the particular. That is, having identified the themes that link the two videos, and having established a framework for making sense of them, we focus on the dance sequences in 'Paparazzi' and 'Telephone' in order to explore how they can be seen to crystallize our more general reflections on the two videos. In other words, we take the dance sequences in 'Paparazzi' and 'Telephone' as the key moments in and through which the common themes and central narrative problems of the videos come into view. With their choreographed movements, their distinct forms of performance expression and their provocative image styling, the dance sequences offer us creatively charged points of entry into the videos and their narrative themes.

Given the 'orgy of signification'—as Jean Baudrillard might put it—that characterizes 'Paparazzi' and 'Telephone,' analysts have little choice but to choose a particular point of entry into these videos and organize their approach to them around a specific set of questions.[4] Our questions grow out of an interest in the culturally driven themes at work in the videos and our hypothesis that these themes are crystallized in the coming together of sound, word, and image in the dance sequences of 'Paparazzi' and 'Telephone.' In fact, director Jonas Åkerlund filmed these sequences while paying close attention to the timing and editing of musical, lyrical and visual gestures. Similarly, B. Åkerlund and the production team attended to the minute details of the costuming, stylistic staging and presentation of materials.[5] Under Åkerlund's creative direction, music, image and movement are woven into a highly compelling and powerful communicative form.

Lady Gaga makes clear that the primary theme of 'Paparazzi' relates to the extraordinary lengths to which artists will go to achieve and maintain celebrity status.[6] With this primary theme in view, we have developed an analytic model that permits us to identify the themes that characterize the two videos and interpret how they are connected to one another. We call this model a thematic network. Our model is grounded in two separate but related assumptions: first, that the themes we identify and interpret are made meaningful in and through their relationship to one another; and second, that these themes are only fully understood when we consider how they are bound up with the mutually constitutive and reinforcing categories of sexuality, race and ability. Informed by an intersectional approach, we examine how the coming together of music, image, and movement in 'Paparazzi' and 'Telephone' allows Lady Gaga to create an intricate and incisive cultural commentary on what it means to be a popular cultural icon in what Guy Debord calls the 'society of the spectacle'.[7]

RELATIONAL AND INTERSECTIONAL ANALYSES OF 'PAPARAZZI' AND 'TELEPHONE'

Directed by Jonas Åkerlund, costumed by B. Åkerlund and choreographed by Laurieann Gibson, Lady Gaga's film-like videos 'Paparazzi' and 'Telephone' are at their most meaningful when viewed alongside one another. Above and beyond the fact that both videos are strewn with product placements, popular cultural references, and the artifacts of a highly commercial Americana, viewers are given a variety of visual cues that connect the two videos. To mention just a few, Gaga's arrest at the end of 'Paparazzi' (Figure 7.1a) leads to her arrival in prison in the opening scene of 'Telephone'; the mug shot taken of Gaga at the end of the 'Paparazzi' is used by the media to help locate and incarcerate her at the end of 'Telephone' (Figure 7.1b); and the dead fashion models in 'Paparazzi' are paralleled by the dead diner customers in 'Telephone' (Figures 7.1c-d). Similarly, Gaga wears a cartoon-like yellow outfit and Mickey-Mouse glasses when poisoning her boyfriend in 'Paparazzi,' as does Beyoncé in 'Telephone' (Figures 7.1e-f); both Gaga's facial expressions and Beyoncé's are inert and immobile as the poisoning is carried out; and both poisoning sequences see Gaga and Beyoncé performing an ironic hand-to-mouth gesture (Figures 7.1g-h).

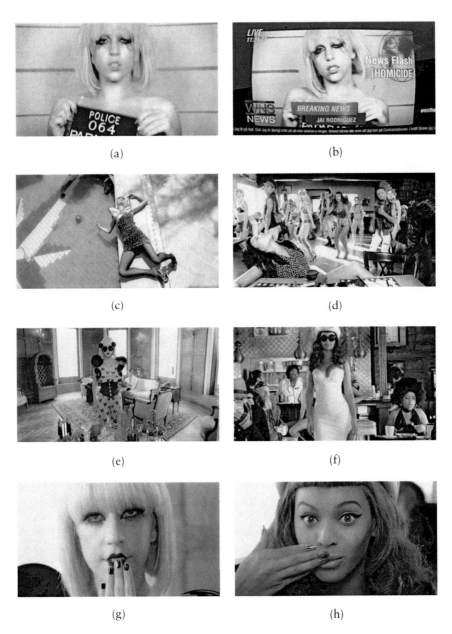

(a)

(b)

(c)

(d)

(e)

(f)

(g)

(h)

Figure 7.1   Similar Visual Cues in 'Paparazzi' and 'Telephone'.

Like the visual cues, the musical cues encourage viewers to link the two videos. More specifically, the opening sequence of 'Paparazzi' features soft piano music while the opening sequence of 'Telephone' features stylistically comparable harp music; the 911 call in the first video prefigures the strong presence of telephones in the second; and both videos feature the diegetic sounds of technology, pointing to their shared emphasis on telecommunication and its tendency to give rise to increasingly widespread forms of spectacle and, by extension, surveillance.

Relational Analysis

The themes in 'Paparazzi' and 'Telephone' are relational; that is, they gain their full meaning in and through their relationship to one another. In what follows, we show that this relationship is structured by binary oppositions that are brought into being through contrasting cultural references. Indeed, it is only when we understand how these oppositions are played out that we are able fully to account for the themes that make the two videos intelligible and meaningful.

'Paparazzi' is set in a palatial mansion and characterized by all the trappings of affluence and success (Figure 7.2a). The mansion boasts seaside panoramas, mountaintop vistas, marble fountains, and vast courtyards. Airy, luminous and lush, the video's setting points to a kind of hyperbolic wealth defined by an ostentatious display of financial fortune, an overt fascination with artifice and the artificial and an over-the-top desire to imitate the aesthetics of high culture. The scattering of 100-dollar bills embossed with Lady Gaga's image (at 00:37 and 04:20) drives this point home, as do the repeated references to jewelry makers like Swarovski and fashion designers like Chanel, Dior, Dolce and Gabbana, Mugler, and Boudicca. With its ongoing emphasis on pecuniary excess, the video's setting suggests that Gaga has reached the height of star status. And though it is not without its macabre moments, this setting can be seen to set up an equation between the realization of Gaga's star status on the one hand and the realization of the American dream on the other.

Unlike 'Paparazzi,' 'Telephone' is a gritty video that is less about the American dream than it is about a kind of abject Americana (Figure 7.2b). Far from trading in the bright and the dreamy, 'Telephone' trades in the dirty, the deviant, and the disgusting. Characterized by crime and violence, the world we see in 'Telephone' is the dark underbelly of the world we see in 'Paparazzi.' While the cultural references in 'Paparazzi' are linked to glamour and prestige, those in 'Telephone' are linked to mainstream consumer culture (*e.g.* cigarettes, Diet Coke, Duchess Honey Buns, Wonder Bread, Miracle Whip, Virgin Mobile and Polaroid), popular media culture (*e.g.* *Kill Bill*, *Pulp Fiction*, *Thelma and Louise* and *Wonder Woman*) and porn culture (*e.g.* Jessica Drake and Alektra Blue).[8] The contrast between glamour and prestige on the one hand, and mainstream consumer culture on the other, is made especially clear when we consider how Gaga is costumed in the two videos: in 'Paparazzi,' she is seen in nothing but designer threads while, in 'Telephone,' she is shown to wear Coke can hair rollers and a pair of DIY glasses made of burning cigarettes.[9] Here the distinction between the high culture of 'Paparazzi' and the low culture of 'Telephone' could not be clearer.

As in 'Paparazzi,' the settings in 'Telephone' say a great deal about the network of themes at work in and through it. The settings for 'Telephone' include a female prison (00:30) featuring scantily clad inmates reminiscent of the 'women in prison' subgenre of exploitation films, a stereotypical highway diner (5:51) where customers eat cheap greasy food, and the 'Pussy Wagon' (4:38) where Gaga and Beyoncé speak in sexualized terms to one another while tearing through town in a hotwheels-inspired getaway car. Indeed, if the lavish setting that characterizes 'Paparazzi' points to elitism and exclusivity, then the commonplace setting that characterizes 'Telephone' emphasizes bawdiness, coarseness, and vulgarity.

The contrast between the settings of the two videos goes beyond their spatial-temporal locations and their material components. In fact, the chromatic elements of 'Paparazzi' and 'Telephone' are also opposed to one another on a range of fronts. The colors used in 'Paparazzi' are dominated by white, gold, and purple while those used in 'Telephone' are defined by black, blue, red, and yellow. In the case of the first video, the color scheme communicates opulence, refinement, and sophistication while, in the case of the second, it corresponds with cartoons, comic books, and pop art (*i.e.* Roy Lichtenstein and Andy Warhol). Viewed together, the chromatic elements express one of the more important thematic oppositions at work in the two videos: that is, the neutral colors characteristic of 'Paparazzi' point to a world of privilege and nouveau riche rarefaction while the primary colors characteristic of 'Telephone' gesture at a mundane universe of everyday consumption.

The themes at work in 'Paparazzi' and 'Telephone' function in and through contrasting cultural references to affluence and decadence, privilege and marginalization, and wealth and poverty. These themes are, however, tied together by Gaga's broader creative concern with celebrity culture and its relationship to spectacle and surveillance. In fact, spectacle is at the heart of both videos. In 'Paparazzi', it is the spectacle of stardom that is at issue. This spectacle is driven by a dramatization of the demands of life as a celebrity, particularly as they relate to the tension between the unrelenting need to be looked at and the unavoidable pressure caused by this looking. Through its emphasis on looking and being looked at, the spectacle of stardom as it is represented in 'Paparazzi' is inextricably linked to surveillance. In the second video, 'Telephone', it is the spectacle of crime and violence that takes center stage. And again, this spectacle is closely connected to surveillance: that is, the surveillance directed not only at the inmates of the 'prison for bitches' but also at Gaga and Beyoncé as they attempt to avoid arrest after having poisoned those they encountered in the diner. In both videos, then, spectacle and surveillance are shown to be tightly tied to one another.

In keeping with the contradictory nature of the themes at work in the two videos, 'Paparazzi' and 'Telephone' are characterized by dichotomous depictions of the relationship between fandom and stardom. While, in both cases, this relationship is linked to some form of harm, the harm in question is played out in an oppositional manner. In 'Paparazzi,' the star is harmed by the force of the media interest directed at her. What is more, the scattering of beautifully styled female corpses throughout the video intensifies its symbolic statement about the collateral damage caused by the media's intrusive and, indeed, insatiable appetite for celebrity skin. In 'Telephone', however, it is the stars who do the harming. The mass murders committed by Gaga and Beyoncé can, therefore, be seen to function as a metaphor for a revenge fantasy driven by the desire to escape the exigencies of fame and fortune. Put slightly differently, the diner deaths can be seen as the star's solution to the problem of being 'eaten alive' by her fans. Unlike 'Paparazzi,' then, 'Telephone' sees its stars reversing the relationship between those who consume and those who are consumed by the culture of celebrity.

Intersectional Analysis

Having established the relational nature of the themes at work in the two videos, we now consider how these themes are bound up with the intersections of sexuality, race, and ability. In the same way that the themes of the videos are structured in and through a binary logic, so too is our intersectional analysis. Insofar as the creative materials with which we work demand it, we approach our analysis using the dichotomous categories of heteronormativity/queerness, whiteness/blackness and ability/disability.

Heteronormativity/Queerness. Over the course of recent decades, scholars in the field of sexuality studies have shown that the mainstream media tends to represent heterosexuality as the normative standard and queer sexuality as a pathological deviation.[10] More specifically, these representations have tended to link heterosexuality with health, prosperity, and success and queer sexuality with disease, deviance and failure. This has been especially true of Hollywood movies, which have a long history of associating heterosexuality with social order and queer sexuality with social dysfunction.[11] That said, however, both 'Paparazzi' and 'Telephone' are prime examples of an increasingly wide range of representations that work against the mainstream media's tendency to construct heterosexual sex in positive terms and queer sex in negative terms.[12] Insofar as they connect heternormative sexualities with danger and death and queer sexualities with agency, autonomy and freedom, Lady Gaga's videos can be seen to complicate conventional understandings of pleasure and desire.

In both videos, heterosexual relationships are seen to have catastrophic consequences. In 'Paparazzi', they lead to the threat of imprisonment while in 'Telephone' they appear to result in an abusive relationship. Heteronormativity is, therefore, shown to be a problem that needs to be solved. In both videos, the solution is murder. In 'Paparazzi', the boyfriend implicated in Gaga's disability-causing accident dies from poison put in his drink. And, in 'Telephone', Beyoncé's menacing male lover chokes to his death from poisoned bacon and eggs. In both cases, getting rid of men is presented as necessary for women's self-realization. In contrast, queer female sexualities are celebrated, particularly as they are expressed in and through Gaga's erotic play with the female inmates and her sexualized relationship with Beyoncé in 'Telephone'. Both videos present female sexuality as a positive choice, enabling Gaga to break free of her metaphorically disabling relationship in 'Paparazzi', and enabling Beyoncé to break free from a domineering boyfriend in 'Telephone'. It is, moreover, worth noting that the queer sexualities celebrated in the video are not restricted to readily identifiable lesbian relationships. For instance, in 'Paparazzi', we see an ambiguous sexual scene between Gaga and a trio of blonde rock stars. Though the rock stars are male, their long hair and thin builds give them an androgynous look and, in doing so, cause viewers to question whether they are witnessing heterosexual or homosexual activity.

Ultimately, the themes at work in 'Paparazzi' and 'Telephone' tend to represent queer sexualities as linked to emancipation and self-determination while representing heteronormative sexualities as linked to confinement, disability, and death. In this way, Gaga's videos can be seen to celebrate—rather than denigrate—non-normative sexual experiences.

Whiteness/Blackness. In his landmark work on racial stereotypes in Hollywood movies, film theorist James Snead formulates a framework for thinking critically about the cinematic uses and, indeed, abuses of the colors white and black.[13] This framework consists of two key concepts: marking and mythification. Snead defines marking as a representational strategy that 'repeatedly overdetermines' and 'redundantly marks' the color black, 'almost as if to force the viewer to register the image's difference from white images'.[14] For Snead, this strategy involves using the color white to convey goodness, moral purity, and social order and using the color black to express evil, moral decay and social dysfunction. Marking, as Snead understands it, is very much in evidence in both of the videos we consider.

In 'Paparazzi', the setting, lighting, and styling of the video's opening scene make a clear connection between whiteness and symbols of upward mobility. Behind the white tone-on-tone title credits, we see a light and luxurious setting: a sprawling white mansion, white roses, a jet of clear water from a white fountain, a crystal chandelier and white statuary. Like the setting, the props of the video are evidently and exaggeratedly white: white Beats by Dr. Dre headphones, white dollar bills, off-white bedroom décor and clear crystal. Not surprisingly, Gaga and her male lover—played by the Swedish actor Alexander Skarsgård—are also wrapped in white: their clothes are white and both their skin and their hair have been lightened. When the lovers move to the ornate white balcony overlooking the ocean, we see them through the telephoto lenses of the paparazzi and this too has the effect of whitening the setting, the props, and the characters. In all of these ways, then, the video uses the color white to communicate personal achievement and success.

Like Snead, black feminist theorist bell hooks discusses how mainstream media forms like music videos use white to connote status and black to connote stigma. For hooks, 'blackness remains a primary sign of transgression'.[15] It is, therefore, not surprising that as the video's emphasis shifts from status and prestige to crime and violence, its color scheme shifts from whites and off-whites to greys and blacks. No longer bathed in lightness, the video soon becomes drenched in darkness: Gaga's fetish-style clothing is black as she has a sexual encounter with three androgynous rock stars, her lipstick and Mickey-Mouse glasses are black as she poisons her boyfriend, and her clothing is black as she is arrested and photographed for her incarceration.

'Telephone' begins where 'Paparazzi' leaves off, with an emphasis on greys and blacks. From the outset, the video establishes an industrial setting characterized by dark wires, train tracks and concrete prison walls. In and through this setting, blackness becomes symbolically linked to the prison, the ghetto and, as previously mentioned, non-normative female sexualities. After the lead characters are introduced, Beyoncé's blackness is made to contrast with Gaga's whiteness in a variety of ways. This is especially the case in the Pussy Wagon scenes, where Beyoncé wears black lipstick, a shiny black wig, and black clothing while Gaga wears very red lipstick and light facial powder, yellow hair, and a dress with a pristine white front. In keeping with the oppositional nature of the themes at work in the two videos, the pristine whiteness of 'Paparazzi' is set against the gritty darkness of 'Telephone'. In fact, the only instance in which white is emphasized in 'Telephone' occurs during the infomercial scene at the diner. Here Gaga and her sous-chef team dance around in a white room, wear white clothing and make sandwiches with white ingredients such as Wonderbread and Miracle Whip. That said, however, the whiteness that characterizes the sequence in 'Telephone' is not comparable to that which characterizes the sequences in 'Paparazzi'. With its emphasis on everyday consumption as opposed to elite consumerism, the whiteness seen in 'Telephone' stands at a distance from the whiteness seen in 'Paparazzi'.

Like his concept of marking, Snead's concept of mythification is also relevant here.[16] For Snead, this concept allows us to understand how black people are repeatedly represented in mythic terms: that is, as criminals, as monsters and as marginalized members of the working classes. For Snead, as for critics like Angela Davis and Toni Morrison, black people are represented in and through these terms in order to perpetuate racist relations of ruling.[17] In this way, the white self relies on the oppressed black other for its sense of individual and collective superiority. Mythification is, in our view, at work in both 'Paparazzi' and 'Telephone'.

In 'Paparazzi', the black people who feature in the video are butlers and chauffeurs: that is, stereotypical black characters whose only purpose is to serve the white character at the center of the video's narrative. In 'Telephone', black people figure more prominently but no less problematically:

they are tough female inmates in the prison or brutish and overbearing boyfriends at the diner. The binary opposition set up between Gaga's boyfriend in 'Paparazzi' and Beyoncé's boyfriend in 'Telephone' is a telling one: where the fine-featured fair-skinned Alexander Skarsgård (Figure 7.2c) is represented as charming and clever, the brawny dark-skinned Tyrese Gibson is represented as mean, menacing and rude (Figure 7.2d). Here, then, the videos draw on stereotypical codes and conventions where race is concerned insofar as whiteness is associated with bourgeois respectability and blackness with a transgressive stigma.

Ability/Disability. Over the course of the last two decades, disability theorists have criticized the tendency to treat disability as metaphor for something other than what it is.[18] In particular, David Mitchell and Sharon Snyder have argued against the 'the pervasive use of disability as a device of characterization in literature and film'.[19] For Mitchell and Snyder, treating disability as a kind of 'narrative prosthesis' rather than as an embodied experience with serious social consequences has the effect of evacuating the complexities of living with a disability while, at the same time, representing it in 'dehumanizing terms (monster, freak, madman, suffering innocent, beggar)'.[20] In some respects, 'Paparazzi' can be seen to mobilize and deploy the disabled body in precisely these terms.

In 'Paparazzi', Gaga goes from being able-bodied, to disabled, to able-bodied. In the opening scene of the video, her male lover carries her to the balcony before pushing her over the ledge. This push results in Gaga being rushed to hospital. She returns home temporarily disabled and is greeted by a team of black male servants who carry her to her wheelchair and support her while she walks with her new crutches. Above and beyond its regressive representations of race and class, this scene is problematic insofar as it depicts disability not as a bodily state or a medical condition but as a metaphor for the ill-fated consequences of the celebrity lifestyle. Put differently, Gaga's disability functions as what Mitchell and Snyder would call a 'narrative prosthesis' for what happens to a star's life when she surrenders her privacy to the paparazzi and, by extension, allows herself to be devoured by her own appetite for fame and fortune. Disability is, therefore, presented as that which happens to those who fly too close to the celebrity sun. And this, according to critical disability theorists, is a clear example of how the disabled body gets metaphorically exploited in a variety of mass media forms.[21]

Gaga's disability is, at its core, portrayed as temporary. It is the result of an injury, and she is shown to fully recover. The tone of the media attention appears to shift along with the state of Gaga's physical ability: when she falls, she falls from media grace and is seen to be out of favor with the public (Figure 7.2e). However, when she recovers, she once again becomes a successful artist and a fully able-bodied dancer. Interestingly, however, her success and able-bodiedness are then mapped onto crime as she murders her male lover. In this way, she becomes not only able-bodied again, but so able-bodied that she is able to gain power over the bodies of others as well.

Like those in 'Paparazzi,' the representations that characterize 'Telephone' suggest a linear progression from an absence of power to an abundance of it. At the beginning of the video, Gaga's body is depicted as physically confined in her jail cell, especially when she is covered in the crime scene tape (Figure 7.2f). Shortly thereafter, however, Gaga goes from powerless to super-powered. This is clear to see when the cyborg-like Gaga performs in the sandwich-making infomercial. Here Gaga appears to have a highly rhythmic and, above all, robotic command of her body as she prepares the poisonous lunch for the customers of the diner. After the poisoning takes place, the infomercial ends with a dance sequence that sees Gaga and Beyoncé dressed in Wonder Woman costumes as they celebrate their super-powers and their predatory kill.

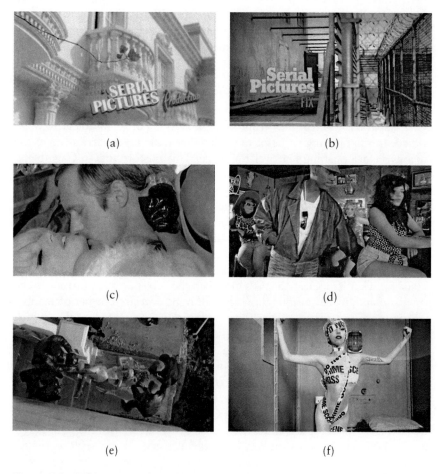

(a)

(b)

(c)

(d)

(e)

(f)

Figure 7.2 Whiteness and 'High' Culture in 'Paparazzi' vs. Blackness and 'Low' Culture in 'Telephone'.

MUSIC-IMAGE-MOVEMENT ANALYSES OF 'PAPARAZZI' AND 'TELEPHONE'

'Paparazzi'

(*The Fame*: August 2008, single: July 2009, video: June 2009)

> The song is about a few different things—it's about my struggles, do I want fame or do I want love? It's also about wooing the paparazzi to fall in love with me. It's about the media whoring, if you will, watching ersatzes make fools of themselves to their station. It's a love song for the cameras, but it's also a love song about fame or love—can you have both, or can you only have one?—Lady Gaga[22]

> I'm very proud of [the video] [. . .] It has a real, genuine, powerful message about fame-whoring and death and the demise of the celebrity, and what that does to young people. The video explores ideas about sort of hyperbolic situations that people will go to in order to be famous. Most specifically, pornography and murder.—Lady Gaga[23]

For Lady Gaga, the video 'Paparazzi' is characterized by a number of themes relating to the vicissitudes of life and death in celebrity culture. While the lyrics suggest that the song's protagonist is chasing and declaring devotion to a celebrity, the video inverts this relationship and, in doing so, portrays the protagonist as the recipient of the paparazzi's attention. This inversion brings into relief the star-seeking behavior of the fan and the media-mongering behavior of the star. Ultimately, it is the extreme and excessive media mongering of the star that becomes the video's central concern. The effects of this behavior are represented by newspaper headlines that track the trends associated with the protagonist's career reception. For example, when her body is photographed after she is thrown off the ledge of her balcony, her attempts to attract attention pay off. And while the media headlines that follow ('Lady Gaga Hits Rock Bottom') are ostensibly negative in nature, they are nevertheless shown to revive the protagonist's career and propel her back into the spotlight.

Wheelchair Scene (Intro and Verse 1; 2:57–3:38)

<u>Music</u>: Against the austere backdrop of a jarring syncopated kick drum beat and backbeat claps, Gaga's vocals are placed in the center of the mix and processed with a simple reverb. The vocals are characterized by a unique nasal quality that she achieves even in the low chest range. In keeping with the video's emphasis on status and prestige, this nasal quality makes the vocals sound more refined and sophisticated than if they had come from a

more full-bodied chest range. Although the vocal phrase of verse 1 begins with a straight rhythmic delivery and angular descending fifth motive (G–C), the melody becomes more fluid in the middle of the phrase as Gaga sings about desiring a picture of the star. A high theremin-like synth line picks up the melodic gesture from the vocal line, momentarily extending the instrumental spectrum.

In response to her vocal phrase, edgy and syncopated synthesizer gestures feature octave leaps on C. These leaps are sometimes mediated by the dissonant interval of the diminished fifth (C–G flat), alternating from bar to bar between hard-panned left and right stereophonic channels to create a disorienting 'ping-pong' effect. The angular synth gesture is elongated to accompany the more fluid vocal line at 'magical'. As the verse continues, the pattern of left-to-right panning for the synth gestures is reversed, contributing to a sense of aural disorientation.

The harmony of the verse suggests an anxious holding pattern, followed by directed movement into the ensuing chorus: that is, in its first iteration, the verse phrase maintains harmonic stasis (on C minor), with change (to A flat) happening only at the fluid lyrical turn ('magical'), however in its second iteration, this moment of change is extended as the harmony descends further (to F minor) in preparation for the chorus.

The musical story in the verse is the contrast between the functions of hold and release, as well as angularity and lyricism.[24] Moreover, the stark musical setting creates a hollow space that calls out to be filled.

Images: The song intro and verse 1 coincide with the visual representation of Gaga's arrival home following her disability-causing accident. The purple carpet has been rolled out to greet her and a team of doting white-gloved black butlers moves her stiff body into an adorned wheelchair (Figure 7.3a).[25] Gaga's stiffness is reinforced in two ways: first, by the fact that she is wearing tight and rigid clothing; and second, by the squared and frontal camera shots that capture her arrival at the door. These shots are edited to switch abruptly between medium, close and long shots and this, in turn, creates a sense of visual disorientation that parallels the aural disorientation in the music. The wheelchair scene is intercut with images of Gaga (Figure 7.3b) singing the song on a gold couch, wearing a shiny black dress and gloves.

Movement: The movements of the butlers are sharp and square, delivered in a manner that appears to mimic 'vogueing'.[26] Their movements are accentuated by hand flourishes and spins. The butlers arrange themselves around Gaga's wheelchair and do so in a ceremonious and supportive style. Gaga's body is for the most part immobile, though when she arrives at the doorway to the lavish hallway, she effects a series of hand gestures that are synchronized with the angular synthesizer gestures. As the verse closes, the butlers shield her while she appears to change her clothing.

The intercut scenes of Gaga on the couch feature her in either seated or supine poses that are choreographically consistent with her immobility in the wheelchair scene.

Dance with Crutches (Chorus; 3:39–4:20)

Music: The chorus features an immediate contrast to the verse: Gaga's vocals, now in the mid to higher register, are instrumentally enhanced as atmospheric string pads provide harmonic changes on the downbeat of each bar. The vocals are treated with a lush reverb and are overdubbed with vocal harmonies that spread to the left and right, creating a broader spectrum of vocal texture. Her use of falsetto creates a lighter, more feminine vocal sound that complements suggestive statements like 'love me', 'Paparazzi', 'promise I'll be kind' and 'until that boy is mine'. Similarly, the synth background is more layered as the centered low register string chords (A flat–E flat–F minor 7–D flat) drive the harmonic motion to a deeper level. At the same time, popping synth effects to the left and right produce a playful texture while a filtered vocal 'ah-ha' is placed at the back of the mix at the close of the first three of four vocal phrases.

The musical story of the chorus is one of sound saturation, with every possible space in the arrangement filled with rich textural effects. Compared with the hollow sound and harmonic stasis of the verse, we are now immersed in a more robust sonic experience that builds harmonic momentum.

Images and movement: The abundant sound of the chorus is complemented in the visual field by the expansion of the supporting dance troupe, as four female dancers join the four butlers. The female dancers wear elegant dark suits and long gloves accentuated with extravagant dark fringe that creates a visual match to the resonant string pad harmonies. While the dancers continue to surround, support and showcase her, Gaga rises from the wheelchair in a metallic robot costume designed by Thierry Mugler and crutches.[27] The camera shots emphasize the otherness of her disabled body by fragmenting her image, showing only her legs or her body (Figure 7.3c). Even her eye and her face seem to be 'injured' as her left eyelid droops beneath the metal of the head cap (Figure 7.3d).

In juxtaposition with this scene, the movements of Gaga on the couch, accented in time with the music, appear to become more and more masturbatory in nature. Additional image inserts feature the bodies of staged female victims (as in Figure 7.1c), and these shots are edited according to an aggressive visual rhythm that corresponds to the musical timing.[28]

The visual and musical opulence of the scene is counteracted by Gaga's awkward, angular physical gestures as she rises from the wheelchair and walks with the crutches wearing high heels. As she moves forward, her entire body appears to lurch and strain with effort. The butlers and maids

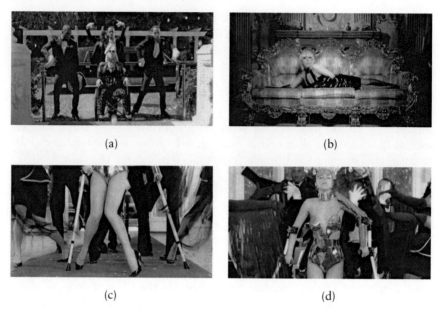

(a)   (b)

(c)   (d)

Figure 7.3   'Paparazzi' images: Intro, Verse 1, Chorus.

swirl around her, creating an aisle for her to walk along the purple carpet, mimicking the effect of a red-carpet moment.

<u>Intersectional Analysis of the Wheelchair and Crutches Scenes</u>: These two scenes represent the categories of sexuality, race and ability in a variety of ways. First, the sexual dynamics are non-normative insofar as they feature female masturbatory pleasure; here the emphasis is on the protagonist pleasuring herself rather than in engaging in heteronormative sexual acts. Second, the racial dynamics that characterize these scenes correspond with the concepts of marking and mythification: the butlers are marked as black insofar as they are the only black people in the scenes in question and, at the same time, they are mythified as black given that they are relegated to stereotypical working-class black characters whose primary function is to reinforce the central importance of the white protagonist. Third, the ability-related dynamics that define these scenes are once again consistent with prevailing representations of disability in popular culture. In 'Paparazzi', disability is portrayed as a metaphor for both her fall from grace and her insatiable appetite for adoration and attention. The protagonist's body is crippled, as it were, by her near fatal quest for fame. What is more, the video sets up an equation between disability and the quest for fame by representing the protagonist's wheelchair and crutches as encrusted in glitz and glam. Perhaps most importantly, the video undermines the agency of those with disabilities while perpetuating the stereotype that they require

constant assistance. For example, the protagonist's movement is shown to be reliant on the help of her butlers and this, in turn, creates a contrast between ability and disability. We see the same contrast once again when the disabled protagonist is surrounded by an able-bodied group of dancers. Ultimately, these scenes suggest that the disabled body requires ongoing protection and yet, ironically, they also suggest that disability—much more than ability—is what allows the protagonist to catapult herself back into celebrity culture. Disability, then, is shown to be both disabling and enabling at the very same time.

Couch Scene (Verse 2; 4:20–4:51)

<u>Music</u>: Verse 2 returns to the sparse texture, the refined chest voice and disjointed left/right synth gestures from verse 1. The more fluid melodic line now sets the lyrics, 'Cause you're my rock star in between the sets', intensifying the fan's desire to develop an intimate relationship with her object of attention.

<u>Images and Movement</u>: The increasingly masturbatory movements of the protagonist as she writhes on the couch are juxtaposed with inserted stills of female corpses. These stills are characterized by abrupt image changes and striking camera angles in a visual rhythm that corresponds with the syncopated patterns of the synthesizer. Three men appear on the couch in rock-style clothing (Figure 7.4a), with long blonde hair, heavy eye makeup and features that are, at first glance, feminine.[29] The protagonist is seen to be in intimate contact with all three men at the same time. As intercut images of the couch scene continue over the course of the subsequent Pierrot dance scene, the sexual contact between the protagonist and the three men escalates. Insofar as the protagonist appears to be looking back at an audience (Figure 7.4b), a link is established between the spectacle of her sexual play with the three rockers and the surveillance of the paparazzi.

<u>Thematic Analysis of the Couch Scene</u>: Taking an intersectional approach to sexuality, race, and ability, the themes that drive the couch scene are for the most part in keeping with those discussed in the first part of the chapter. First, non-normative sexuality is celebrated insofar as three of the four participants in the scene are gender-ambiguous men engaged in what appears to be a playful group sex experience. In this way, the scene stands in stark contrast to the dark, dyadically-organized and, of course, death-defying heterosexual relationship presented at the beginning of the video. Second, whiteness is emphasized throughout the couch scene. Like 'Paparazzi' in general, this scene in particular profiles four pale, blond, Caucasian characters whose whiteness is marked by rapid-fire cut-away

shots of their white skin, white teeth and, perhaps most impressively, the whites of their eyes. And finally, all the characters in the scene appear to be able-bodied. The group sex scene represents the moment at which the protagonist regains full functionality in her legs and, by extension, complete able-bodiedness. Here non-normative sexual practices appear to be linked to heightened autonomy and increased freedom. It is, moreover, only with the gender-ambiguous rockers that the protagonist appears to want to be watched by an audience. That is, if at the beginning of the video she refuses to pose for the paparazzi while sharing an embrace with her lover on the balcony, then over the course of her sexual relationship with three effeminate men she actively encourages audience attention. Again, non-normative sexuality seems to be linked to opening the protagonist onto the world rather than shutting her off from it.

At least one other key theme is made manifest in the couch scene; namely, the mutually constitutive and reinforcing relationship between fandom and stardom. Here the scene encourages us to ask: who is the fan and who is the star? The lyrics tell us that the protagonist is the fan who wishes to get close to the star, but the video tells us that the protagonist is the star who both runs towards and away from the fan (or, rather, the fan's most important representative: the paparazzi). In this way, the couch scene causes us to question the distinction between fan and star and, in doing so, points to their inextricable entanglement.

Pierrot Dance (Chorus; 4:51–5:26)

<u>Music, Images and Movement</u>: Set to the musical return of the robustly arranged chorus, this scene, more than any other one in 'Paparazzi', aligns with standard music video representations of dance performance. The dance takes place in a large space, framed by white and gold classical columns and a crystal chandelier. Over the course of the movement sequence, Gaga sings, dances, and is choreographed with five back-up dancers in Pierrot-inspired costumes (that is, white body suits, ruffled accents and white caps). Gaga's costume features an enormous midnight and white shoulder frill and layered half-skirt, with ruffles wound around her legs (Figure 7.4c).[30] Her reference to Pierrot—the stock character of the *Commedia dell'Arte*—suggests that the scene is driven by the themes of artistry, alienation, and fame. Of course, Pierrot represents an archetypal melancholy subject: one who is estranged from himself, his artistic practice, and society at large.[31] The power of the dance scene, then, comes from the fact that it combines the sad whimsy associated with Pierrot with the hyperbolic high-energy performances associated with Lady Gaga. The scene is, moreover, brought very vividly to life by Åkerlund's editing of the sequence which brings the movements of the dancers into crisp alignment with the rhythmic features of the lyrics and music, creating the illusion of precise music-to-dance coordination and control.

Thematic Analysis of the Pierrot Scene: Pierrot has long been associated with artistic personas or alter-egos. In 'Paparazzi,' this association could not be more appropriate; the Pierrot dance scene can be seen to link celebrity culture with a number of themes that run through the video such as inauthenticity and isolation. These themes are articulated by and through contradictory representations of the protagonist's sexuality. Indeed, these representations are divided between those that emphasize her innocence and naïveté (as evidenced by the Pierrot motif) and those that emphasize her knowingness and willingness (as evidenced by the intercut scenes of the group sex on the couch). Here the protagonist's sexual disingenuousness in particular can be seen to serve as a metaphor for the disingenuousness of star subjectivity in general.

The themes that drive the Pierrot dance scene are also brought into relief by the whitened setting and costuming choices. More specifically, the room in which the dance scene takes place is white from top to bottom: the ceiling, chandeliers, columns, and floor are all bathed in bright whites and off-whites. And, like Pierrot, the costumes are almost entirely white; even the dancers of color are wearing white head caps, which make them blend in with the whiteness that characterizes the rest of the scene. Like much of the rest of the video, the dance sequence involves few signs of chromatic difference and, as a result, makes a strong connection between whiteness and the hallowed heights of star status.

The Pierrot dance scene also marks the point at which the protagonist goes from being newly able-bodied to hyper-able-bodied. The hyper-ability of the protagonist's body is, however, complicated by the fact that it comes into being through a Pierrot-inspired dance. There is, therefore, a contradiction at work here. On the one hand, the protagonist appears to be able to perform superhuman dance moves in lockstep with a square meter. On the other hand, however, these dance moves are carried out while the protagonist imitates a character who has, throughout history, been defined by frailty and weakness rather than by power and strength.

Strobe-light Posing Sequence (Bridge; 5:27–5:44)

Music: The elemental statement of the verse was contrasted by the rich expanse of the chorus, and now the bridge establishes an alternative sonic environment which comprises the darkest moment—musically, lyrically and visually—of the song. Against the background of a sparse, dry synth texture featuring truncated sounds and stabs, Gaga's low-pitched vocal is split to the left and right and is slightly time-delayed to create the effect of two voices in the stereophonic field. A harsh, guttural, impersonal sound masks the core of her voice as she asserts both her autonomy and intention to have fun in the dance studio ('Don't stop for anyone'). The vocal line takes material from the instrumental content of the verse, outlining the falling fifths and dissonant leaps (G flat–C) that were heard in the syncopated synth patterns. At the end of the section, her vocals tend toward a pitched yelling sound ('but we still have fun').

Images and Movement: The protagonist's costume in the strobe-light scene is created from discarded film stock, folded to create a ribbon flounce on her right shoulder and wrapped around her body to yield a revealing body suit (Figure 7.4d). This costume picks up many features from the Pierrot outfit (the black and white ruffles, the ribbon wrapping her body, the shoulder frill and the cap which now features a feather Mohawk). That said, however, the binding of the film around her body to create minimal coverage points to a fetish style (which suggests sexual experience) that was not in evidence in the Pierrot scene (which suggests existential innocence).

In contrast to the bright and bourgeois space of the ballroom, the protagonist is now seen against a wood-tiled wall and appears to be posing for a photo shoot. The strobe lighting creates a fast pace of pornified body shots, with an emphasis on the protagonist's mouth.

Thematic Analysis of the Strobe-Light Scene: The theme of 'fame-whoring', as Gaga herself puts it, is evident here as Gaga participates in a highly sexualized photo shoot. In contrast to the white aesthetics of the Pierrot scene, the strobe-light scene 'repeatedly over-determines' and 'redundantly marks' the color black. Similarly, the brightened designer costumes of the earlier scenes are replaced by a darkened fetish-style dress made of film stock. Taken together, the setting, the lighting and the celluloid-inspired

(a)

(b)

(c)

(d)

Figure 7.4 'Paparazzi' images: Verse 2, Chorus, Bridge.

costuming that characterize this scene point to the dark side of stardom. In fact, the strobe-light scene immediately precedes the scene in which Gaga poisons her boyfriend, ultimately leading her to the path of criminal behavior and revenge that becomes the focus of 'Telephone.'

'Telephone'

(*The Fame Monster*: November 2009; Single: February 2010; Video: March 2010)

> There was this really amazing quality in 'Paparazzi', where it kind of had this pure pop music quality but at the same time it was a little bit of commentary on fame culture, [. . .] I wanted to do the same thing with this video—take a decidedly pop song, which on the surface has a quite shallow meaning, and turn it into something deeper—the idea that America is full of young people that are inundated with information and technology—and turn it into something that is more of a commentary on the kind of country that we are.—Lady Gaga[32]

The most obvious story of the song is the protagonist's frustration with her boyfriend's phone calls, which interrupt her dancing and drinking at a club.[33] As the song is transformed into the video, however, the theme of technologically driven surveillance is developed in such a way that it takes the story to a deeper level of cultural critique. This critique is, moreover, made clear by the fact that 'Telephone' is linked to 'Paparazzi' in a range of ways; these links—be they musical or visual in nature—reveal the former to be every bit as bound up in issues of fandom and stardom as the latter. The video's opening scene—which is set in a prison—might seem to be at odds with the song's simple lyrics about being annoyed by telephone calls in a club. We argue, however, that this scene sets up an equation between the club mentioned in the lyrics and the prison seen in the video. Since clubs are hubs of celebrity culture, the opening scene of 'Telephone' can be seen to link this culture with a prison-like environment. Ultimately, the theme of resisted phone surveillance in the song's lyrics becomes a tale of resisted criminal surveillance in the video. Here the two protagonists—Gaga and Beyoncé—become fugitives after they kill those who invaded their privacy and, by extension, pushed them to the point of mass murder.

Phone Call Scene (Verse 1 and Verse Extension; 2:54–3:18)

Music: Several features of the structure and recording of verse 1 take us into the sonic world of a phone call: (1) The recording of Gaga's voice is filtered to limit the high frequencies and create a masked and deadened quality; (2) The common transmission problems or glitches associated with cellphones are integrated into the musical structure itself, as the vocal melody includes a repetition of the first syllable in 'What did you say?' and this is enhanced with a mechanical sound stutter; (3) The vocal melody is accompanied by the gentle strains of the harp, suggestive of the kind of non-intrusive background music that can be heard when a phone call is put on hold; and (4) In the verse extension, the closing words 'I'm kinda busy' are treated to insistent repetition that features a mid-range and somewhat snide operator's voice.

The overall impact of these phone effects is the dehumanization of Gaga's voice: the production values mask the complexity and emotional potential of the human voice. Having positioned the listener inside the phone call in verse 1, the verse extension introduces the sound environment of the dance club: the gentle harp arpeggiation gives way to a strong electro-pop beat, featuring synthesizer octave jumps on each beat, a heavy saw-tooth distorted bass sound on every second eighth, and an aggressive backbeat handclap on beats 2 and 4 (with a double clap every second bar on beat 4).[34]

Images: Gaga's costuming for the phone call sequence (Figure 7.5a) makes references to several iconic images of the late 1960s and early 1970s. The Coke can curlers in her hair serve as both a product placement and a potential homage to Andy Warhol's use of Coca-Cola products in his art.[35] Similarly, her exaggerated eye make-up and lipstick are reminiscent of Lichtenstein's cartoon images.[36] The hand holding the phone is adorned with a skull ring that showcases Mickey Mouse ears—which, as we have already mentioned, is a clear reference to the murder sequences in both 'Paparazzi' and 'Telephone'—that was designed by The Great Frog (an iconic designer of punk rock jewelry).[37] Her studded jacket is another nod to punk aesthetics, confirming her symbolic identification with the anti-establishment values of the punk movement.

Movement: Gaga divides her attention between the caller on the phone and the camera as she makes eye contact with the viewer. Her increasing resistance to the phone call culminates when she throws down the phone, adjusts her jacket, and begins to thrust both arms forward in punch-like gestures. Director Jonas Åkerlund edits the images and increases the speed to create aggressive, rhythmically precise movements in tight synchronization with the driving music of the Extension.

Thematic Analysis of the Phone Call Scene: The unwanted attention the protagonist is receiving from the phone caller can be seen as a metaphor for the ongoing attention of the paparazzi and her growing resistance to the intrusiveness the attention entails. Here, then, the themes of spectacle and surveillance are clearly connected to one another. What is more, the collateral damage caused by these two separate but related phenomena is brought into relief by the protagonist's reflection on who she was before she became famous. More specifically, when her phone call is announced over the prison intercom system, Gaga is seen gazing into the eyes of a video extra who is, in fact, her younger sister in real life. In this way, Gaga's visual exchange with the extra conveys her concerns over the constraints placed on her by celebrity culture.

Over the course of this scene, the themes of spectacle and surveillance are brought to life in and through a homosocial prison environment. This environment is shown to be both pleasurable (as evidenced by the erotic exchanges the inmates have with one another) and dangerous (as evidenced by the physical fights between inmates as well as between inmates and guards). Despite the mix of pleasure and danger that characterizes the confines of the prison environment, the protagonist is represented as more agential than she was in her mansion in 'Paparazzi'. Where, in 'Paparazzi', the protagonist lives in seclusion and speaks a foreign language (which, of course, further reinforces her separation from mainstream American society), in 'Telephone' the protagonist is surrounded by others at all times and speaks English in an assertive manner. Here again, then, same-sex relationships become linked to self-determination and self-realization.

Prison Dance (Verse 2, Chorus and After-Chorus; 3:18–4:04)

Music: Following the heavier sounds of the verse extension, verse 2 features a lighter texture and dance groove. The saw-tooth bass accents only the downbeat of each bar, and the upper octaves 'pop' lightly to create an energetic upbeat. Gaga's voice is enhanced with a warm and rich reverb and this resonant quality is heightened when the last word of line 1 ('play') is treated with a delay that pans very quickly from left to right. The darker, muted vocal quality of verse 1 returns abruptly at the end of verse 2 when she repeats the line 'I'm kinda busy' (3:32).

During the chorus sequence, Gaga's vocal is centered for the antecedent phrase ('Stop calling, I don't want to think anymore') and split to the left and right for the consequent phrase ('I left my heart and my head on the dance floor'). The melodic span requires her to straddle head and chest voice placement in a passage of vocal gymnastics that is technically challenging. This, in turn, adds a sense of excited tension to the sound.

An after-chorus section reiterates the sentiment 'stop telephoning me', once again engaging the resistant and rebellious voice that was heard in the verse extension. A pitch-modulated low voice responds to each of the primary vocal phrases in a distorted descending gesture. The subject's resistance and anxiety reach a fevered pitch, propelled by the insistent repeated vocal 'eh, eh, eh, eh' and the intensified textural layering.

In sum, while the music of verse 2 communicates excitement and abandon, the chorus conveys the protagonist's mounting frustration with the telephone surveillance, her anger culminating in the frenzied after-chorus.

<u>Images</u>: Gaga's short blonde hairstyle (Figure 7.5b) is reminiscent of Madonna's look in her video 'Vogue' (Figure 7.5c). It is, moreover, tempting to draw a connection between Gaga's hairstyle and make-up in 'Telephone' and Andy Warhol's iconic *Marilyn* portraits.[38] Gaga and her four back-up dancers wear studded swimsuits and black booties (Figure 7.5d). Throughout the prison hallway sequence, the camera follows Gaga with a variety of medium close-up shots, long shots and side-angled shots that capture all of the dancers. During the after-chorus, the video shifts to grainy black and white footage, with a time stamp and recording label on the screen (3:49), invoking the perspective of the surveillance camera.

<u>Movement</u>: During verse 2, Gaga walks seductively down the prison hallway toward the camera, while her back-up dancers move quickly into visually disruptive positions on both the floor and the bars of the prison cells. For the statement, 'I'm kinda busy', her gestures intensify as she aggressively and assertively tosses her hands over her shoulders. The chorus initiates a sequence of unison gestures with the back-up dancers, the movements once again carefully edited by Åkerlund to create crisp synchronization of sound and image. This is especially noticeable during the after-chorus, as the increased anxiety ('stop telephoning me') is enhanced by accelerated gestures and blurred images (4:02).

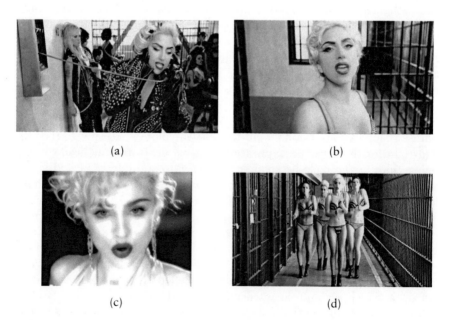

(a)   (b)

(c)   (d)

Figure 7.5 'Telephone' images: Verse/Chorus 1 and 2 (with Gaga's image compared to Madonna in 'Vogue').

<u>Thematic Analysis of the Prison Dance Scene</u>: Over the course of this scene, the group of five female inmates are marked, not only by their whiteness but also by a broad range of physical similarities: that is, they have similar slim builds, similar heights and three out of the five of them have similar bleach-blond hair. Indeed, the only markers of difference are to be found in the darker hair colors of the two dancers positioned on the outer left and right edges of the group. Interestingly, then, the racial diversity that characterizes the video's earlier scenes—particularly those that featured the inmates in the prison yard and the collective cell—disappears completely when it comes time for the protagonist to make a spectacle of herself in the prison hallways. And, as always, this spectacle is closely connected to multiple levels of surveillance: the surveillance of the other prisoners, the surveillance of the guards and the surveillance of the security cameras

'Crime Scene' Posing (Bridge; 4:05–4:22)

<u>Music</u>: The bridge functions as the musical equivalent of a telephone's busy signal, conjuring up the feeling of frustration that an unsuccessful phone call can generate. The repeated mid-range notes in a spoken and mechanical vocal style can be read as a resistant gesture ('you can call if you want, but there's no one home'), with Gaga's vocal layered and panned to the left and right. A stripped-down arrangement brings the backbeat claps into sharp relief, with a ringing signal (split left and right) on beats 1 and 3 of each bar. During the second phrase, in response to the ringing pattern, a busy signal rings continuously on the subdivided beat of the song.

<u>Images and Movement</u>: Inside a jail cell, Gaga poses in a costume created from yellow crime scene tape (Figure 7.2f). The tape wrapping is similar to the film stock wrapping in 'Paparazzi' (Figure 7.4d). Here the color yellow is once again connected to crime, picking up on the yellow paint lines in the prison hallway, the outfit Gaga wears to poison her boyfriend in 'Paparazzi', the yellow dress Beyoncé wears when she poisons her boyfriend in 'Telephone' and the yellow 'Pussy Wagon' that serves as the getaway car.[39] Gaga's body, shown in a variety of poses in the cell and on the bed, is treated with post-production distortion that makes her look extraordinarily elongated and thin while the movements of her head, particularly when she leans back over the edge of the bed, are sped up to the point where they appear unnatural.

<u>Thematic Analysis of the Crime Scene Posing</u>: In this scene, the protagonist's female body is quite literally represented as a crime scene. The collateral damage of fame and fortune, symbolized by the female corpses in 'Paparazzi,' is now symbolized by the protagonist's imprisoned body in 'Telephone.' While it is no longer hyper-able-bodied as it was in the prison dance scene, the post-production distortion used in the crime scene posing scene make this imprisoned body appear hyper-real. Indeed, with its

extreme thinness and its rapid movements, the protagonist's body functions as a metaphor for celebrity embodiment.

Polaroid Posing in the 'Pussy Wagon' (Verse 3 featuring Beyoncé; 5:34–5:50)

<u>Music</u>: Beyoncé's verse delivers hip-hop phrasing characterized by a deeper, heavy and full-bodied vocal quality. Her vocal styling is reminiscent of 'Video Phone', featuring Lady Gaga, (released in November 2009), in which Beyoncé's vocal is characterized by the sung/spoken gestures on repeated notes, accented by leaps to the upper fifth. The 'ticky' sixteenths on the high hat that characterize the 'Video Phone' chorus appear for this featured moment of 'Telephone', creating a cleverly devised intertextual reference and emphasizing—in a manner not unlike product placement—their earlier collaborative project.[40]

<u>Images and Movement</u>: Inside the Pussy Wagon, Gaga and Beyoncé are styled with cartoon-inspired colors and contrasts (Figure 7.6a). Gaga's bright yellow hair and very white skin, accentuated by red lipstick, function as a foil to Beyoncé's dark skin, black lipstick, shiny black 'Bettie Page' wig and Mickey Mouse headpiece. [41] As Beyoncé drives the Pussy Wagon, Gaga takes photos with a Polaroid camera.[42] Throughout her verse delivery, Beyoncé poses for the camera at the same time that she operates the vehicle. Here the images of the video mimic the photography, complete with moments that light up from the flash (Figure 7.6b).

<u>Thematic Analysis of the Polaroid Scene</u>: The surveillance that has been thematized throughout the two videos is now shown to be carried out by one star against the other, as Gaga takes photos of Beyoncé driving the Pussy Wagon. The intertextual references to Quentin Tarantino's *Kill Bill* and *Pulp Fiction*, reinforced by the honey bun product placement in the scene that leads up to the verse, link the Pussy Wagon to misogynistic violence. Yet in this scene, as in *Thelma and Louise*, misogynistic violence is replaced by female solidarity and triumph. Here again, then, same-sex relationships between women are tightly tied to emancipation and freedom. However, as we mentioned earlier, the politically progressive parts of this scene are made problematic by the range of ways in which it relies on a whitening of Gaga and a blackening of Beyoncé in order to make its themes intelligible and meaningful.

Sandwich 'infomercial' (Verse Extension and Chorus; 6:34–6:59)

<u>Music</u>: Following a shared verse (6:18–6:32), which features minimal background instrumentation and highly reverberant vocal effects for Gaga on

phrase 1 and Beyoncé on phrase 2, the verse extension features a heavy backbeat with both artists singing in a defiant manner that they are not taking calls because they are dancing. Vocal layering showcases the interactions of the two artists and builds intensity for the return of the chorus.

Images: This scene is cleverly framed as an infomercial, complete with title captions ('Let's Make a Sandwich') and an audience laugh track. Gaga wears an elaborate blue headpiece incorporating a rotary dial piece and handset and a silicone rubber dress with white apron. Her exaggerated make-up points to artifice and is matched by the make-up on her five supporting male dancers. Of course, the infomercial features Gaga making a sandwich with Wonder Bread and Miracle Whip, both of which are artificial food products (Figure 7.6c).

Movement: The stylized dance sequence consists of hand gestures that imitate slapping pieces of bread together and dramatic music-image editing that emphasizes the artificial nature of the gestures in question. Gaga's biting gestures (6:53 and 6:55) are spliced in such a way that they suggest cyborg-like movements and inhuman appetites. Gaga is featured in a series of five frozen poses (6:55–57), which also connect her and her body to the inhuman, while her dancers continue to move around her. The infomercial is briefly interrupted by an image of Beyoncé's boyfriend coughing on his bacon and eggs (6:58–7:02). When the infomercial returns, the subject matter of the infomercial has changed to 'Poison TV' featuring 'Cook 'n' Kill Recipes' (Figure 7.6d) while Gaga taints the breakfasts she is preparing with poison. The boundaries blur between the artificial world of the television infomercial and the real world of the public diner when Gaga—still in her infomercial costume—enters the diner to serve her poisonous food to Beyoncé's boyfriend. Here her posed movements, her straw-yellow telephone-styled hair and her ultra-high heels point to artifice and the artificial.

Thematic Analysis of the Sandwich Advertisement: In contrast to the posh poisoning sequence in 'Paparazzi', the infomercial sequence in 'Telephone' sets mass murder against a synthetic landscape of monstrous appetites, fake food and cyborg bodies. Over the course of the sandwich scene, the artifice of advertising is combined with the dregs of consumer culture to create a setting that we refer to as abject Americana. It is in and through this setting that celebrity culture is cast as the 'ground zero' or, perhaps more appropriately, the 'lowest common denominator' of present-day US society. Through its graphic allusions to the alimentary, the fans who hound the stars and the stars who whore for the fans are shown to constitute a decadent and dysfunctional dyad. Both necessary for and a threat to one another's survival, the scene reveals this dyad as driven first and foremost by an all-consuming desire to be the one who eats rather than the one who is eaten.

Americana Diner Dance (Chorus; 7:42–8:29)

<u>Music, Images and Movement</u>: The culminating musical chorus and dance sequence of the video takes place in the center of the diner, featuring Gaga and Beyoncé in red, white and blue costumes reminiscent of Wonder Woman and surrounded by a cast of outlaw dancers, wearing torn jeans, bandanas and vests (Figure 7.6e). The energetic choreography is intercut with images of the poisoned diner customers who have collapsed as a result of the contaminated food they have consumed (Figure 7.6f).

<u>Thematic Analysis of the Americana Diner Dance</u>: Like the sandwich scene, this scene emphasizes the iconography associated with Americana. Gaga and Beyoncé dance in Wonder Woman outfits covered in stars and stripes while the dancers who surround them are dressed in jeans, cowboy boots

(a)   (b)

(c)   (d)

(e)   (f)

Figure 7.6 'Telephone' images: Verse 3 (feat. Beyoncé), Chorus and Final Chorus.

and other items of clothing reminiscent of the American frontier aesthetic. Once again, the female protagonists are represented as hyper-able-bodied and this is further reinforced by the fact that they are dressed in superhero costumes. The hyper-ability of Gaga and Beyoncé is set against the dozens of dead bodies that surround them. In an ironic juxtaposition, Gaga and Beyoncé are depicted as larger-than-life superheroes while the ravages of their vengeful acts are everywhere in evidence. By representing Gaga and Beyoncé as superheroes even as they dance around the dead bodies in the diner, this scene suggests that the two protagonists have been a force for good in society; that they have, in other words, saved America from an out-of-control celebrity culture and the perverse practices of fandom and stardom with which it is associated.

CONCLUSION

In an attempt to interpret the 'complete vision' of Lady Gaga's artistic commentary on celebrity, spectacle, and surveillance, we explore the network of themes that characterizes the videos 'Paparazzi' and 'Telephone'. By adopting a systematic approach to music, image and movement, we show that these themes are more fully understood when they are seen as both relational in nature and bound up with the categories of sexuality, race and ability. We argue that Lady Gaga and director Jonas Åkerlund present their viewers with a complex critique of fandom and stardom in contemporary American culture. That said, we also show that this critique is both progressive on some levels and regressive on others. As our intersectional analysis makes clear, the representations of sexuality in the two videos are progressive insofar as they link non-normative bodies and identities with agency, autonomy and freedom. At the same time, however, the representations of whiteness/blackness and ability/disability in these same videos are regressive insofar as they connect whiteness to status and blackness to stigma while connecting ability to emancipation and disability to constraint and confinement. Yet, regardless of their problematic propensities, 'Paparazzi' and 'Telephone' ask important questions about celebrity culture and the entertainment industry that has come to constitute it. Having illuminated some of these questions, we hope that both our methods and our findings will contribute to an enhanced appreciation of Lady Gaga's creative production and a deeper understanding of her cultural impact.

NOTES

1. The authors' names are listed in alphabetical order. The authors wish to thank graduate students Keri Ferencz (Concordia University), Megan Johnson (University of Ottawa), and Courtney Constable (Carleton University) for their thoughtful contributions to the research of this chapter. We are also

grateful to Carol Vernallis for her collegial exchange of ideas about these two videos.

2. Ron Slomowicz, 'Lady Gaga Interview—Interview with Lady Gaga' (online at: http://dancemusic.about.com/od/artistshomepages/a/LadyGagaInt.htm) <accessed: 21 November 2012>.

3. Keri Ferencz, '"I'm Your Biggest Fan, I'll Follow You . . . ": Lady Gaga, Little Monsters, and the Religious Dimension of Fandom in Pop Music', (unpublished MA Thesis, Brock University, 2011).

4. Jean Baudrillard, 'The Precession of Simulacra', *Simulacra and Simulation*, tr. Sheila Faria Glaser (Ann Arbor, MI: University of Michigan Press, 1994 [1981]), 1–42.

5. B. Åkerlund describes her work on the videos in an interview with Kee Chang, 'Q&A with B. Åkerlund', *AnthemMagazine.com* (09 June 2009) (online at: http://anthemmagazine.com/b-Åkerlund/) <accessed: 21 November 2012>.

6. We cite Lady Gaga's comments on the meaning of the video 'Paparazzi' at the beginning of the analysis section of this chapter.

7. Guy Debord, *The Society of the Spectacle*, tr. Donald Nicholson-Smith, trans. (New York, NY: Zone, 1994 [1967]).

8. Two of the inmates are well-known porn stars Jessica Drake (http://jessicadrake. com, featured at 00:50) and Alektra Blue (http://www.clubalektrablue.com, featured at 00:45) and much of the clothing in the prison sequence is designed as fetish clothing.

9. In popular culture representations of prisons, cigarettes often work as a form of currency. Here, then, Gaga is effectively burning money. The cigarette glasses can, therefore, be taken as another sign of conspicuous consumption but one more appropriate to the new environment.

10. In this regard, see Stephen Tropiano, *The Prime Time Closet: A History of Gays and Lesbians on TV* (New York: Applause Theater and Books, 2002); Simon Watney, 'The Spectacle of AIDS', in David Crimp (ed), *AIDS: Cultural analysis, cultural activism* (Cambridge, MA: Massachusetts Institute of Technology, 1989 [1987]), 71–86; Suzanne D. Walters, *All the Rage: The Story of Gay Visibility in America* (Chicago: University of Chicago Press, 2001); and Lauren Berlant and Michael Warner, 'Sex in Public', *Critical Inquiry*, vol. 24, no. 2 (Winter 1998), 547–566.

11. In this regard, see Vito Russo, *The Celluloid Closet: Homosexuality in the Movies*, revised ed. (New York, NY: Harper & Row, 1987 [1981]) and the documentary film *Common Threads: Stories from the Quilt*, dir. Jeffrey Friedman and Rob Epstein (New Yorker Films, 1989).

12. See Larry Gross, *Up From Invisibility: Lesbians, Gay men, and the Media in America* (New York, NY: Columbia University Press, 2001).

13. James Snead, *White Screens, Black Images: Hollywood From the Dark Side*, ed. Colin MacCabe and Cornel West (New York, NY: Routledge, 1994).

14. *Ibid.*, 5.

15. bell hooks, *Cultural Criticism and Transformation*, dir. Sut Jhally (Media Education Foundation, 1997). Her comments about blackness and transgression can be heard at 56:07.

16. Snead, *White Screens, Black Images*, 4.

17. See Angela Davis, *Women, Race and Class* (New York, NY: Random House, 1983) and Toni Morrison, *Playing in the Dark: Whiteness and the Literary Imagination* (Cambridge, MA: Harvard University Press, 1992).

18. See Lennard J. Davis, *Enforcing Normality: Disability, Deafness and the Body* (London: Verso, 1995); Rosemary Garland Thompson, *Extraordinary Bodies: Figuring Physical Disability in American Culture and Literature*

(New York: Columbia University Press, 1997), and Tobin Siebers, *Disability Theory* (Ann Arbor: University of Michigan Press, 2008).

19. David Mitchell and Sharon Snyder, *Narrative Prosthesis: Disability and the Dependencies of Discourse* (Ann Arbor, MI: University of Michigan Press, 2000), 5.
20. *Ibid.*, 15.
21. See Apolloni in this volume.
22. Slomowicz, 'Lady Gaga Interview'.
23. Nick Patch, 'Lady Gaga Announced as performer at MuchMusic Video Awards in June', *The Canadian Press* (26 May 2009) (online at: http://www. cp24.com/lady-gaga-announced-as-performer-at-muchmusic-video-awards-in-june-1.401896) <accessed 21 November 2012>.
24. We are indebted to Carol Vernallis for this concept of hold and release, which she observed in the video images.
25. Costume designer for the video, B. Åkerlund, describes the wheelchair and many of the costumes and props for the video in Chang, 'Q&A With B. Åkerlund'.
26. The intertextual reference to Madonna's 'Vogue' is quite evident here, as the black dancers offer arm flourishes and strike sharp poses.
27. The vintage robot outfit was designed by Thierry Mugler for his 1991 Spring/Summer *Haute Couture* collection. The collection can be viewed on YouTube at: http://www.youtube.com/watch?v=RU26Olqrs70 <accessed: 21 November 2012>. Mugler's robot costume was featured in the *Superheroes: Fashion and Fantasy Exhibition*, Metropolitan Museum of Arts, 7 May–1 September 2008. A review video of the exhibition can be viewed at the *New York Magazine* web site: http://videos.nymag.com/video/Superheroes-Fash-ion-and-Fantasy;Costume-Institute-Gala#c=65DY6SVJQN8KKBP5&t=Sup erheroes: Fashion and Fantasy <accessed: 21 November 2012>. The Thierry Mugler robot costume appears at 00:58 and the Dolce & Gabanna dress that Gaga wears at the end of 'Paparazzi' appears at 1:09. Helmut Newton created a fashion photo spread for *Vogue* magazine in 1995 that featured fashion models in wheelchairs and with crutches. The photo spread was reviewed in Teresa Wiltz, 'February Issue of Vogue is Way Off the Mark', *Chicago Tribune* (2 February 1995) (online at: http://articles.chicagotri-bune.com/1995–02–02/features/9502020321_1_michael-kors-vogue-faces) <accessed: 21 November 2012>.
28. The staged victims' bodies are stylistically and aesthetically similar to the photographic work of David LaChapelle and Helmut Newton, who both photographed women, dressed and styled in high fashion, in positions that suggest victimization and vulnerability. LaChapelle's 'Couture Story: Collapse in a Garden' (1995) is an example of a frail woman, collapsed in an artful pose and setting. This photograph can be seen at David LaChapelle's web site: http://www.davidlachapelle.com/series/couture-story/ <accessed: 21 November 2012>.
29. The three men are from the Swedish band Snakes of Eden. This aspect of the video is discussed in 'Lady Gaga shares passionate embrace with trio of brothers in steamy new video', *Daily Mail Online* (2 June 2009) (online at: http://www.dailymail.co.uk/tvshowbiz/article-1189680/Lady-GaGa-shares-passionate-embrace-trio-brothers-steamy-new-video.html) <accessed: 21 November 2012>.
30. Gaga's Pierrot costume was designed by London-based Boudicca, whose design aesthetic embraces punk and the avant-garde. The fashion label is reviewed by Sandra Backlund, 'Fashioning the Object: Bless Boudicca', *The Art Institute of Chicago* (2011) (online at: http://www.artic.edu/aic/

collections/exhibitions/Fashioning-Object/Boudicca) <accessed: 21 November 2012>. It is worth noting here that the perfume produced by this design house, Wode (released in 2008), is distinguished by a purple color and advertised with an image of a woman who appears to be a murder victim with her neck marked by the purple splash of liquid. Not insignificantly, one of the posed victims in the 'Paparazzi' video features a smear of purple finger marks on her neck. For a review of the perfume, see Hilary Alexander, 'Boudicca's Blue blooded perfume', *Daily Telegraph* (11 November 2008), (online at: http://fashion.telegraph.co.uk/article/TMG3441778/Boudiccas-Blue-blooded-perfume.html) <accessed: 21 November 2012>. Gaga's own perfume, Fame (released in 2012), is black in the bottle, but sprays clear in the air so as not to stain clothing. At the release of this perfume, Gaga staged a performance art piece in which she was housed in a dome-shaped chamber for two days at the Guggenheim Museum, while fans touched her and observed her in sleep. The event was reviewed by Colleen Nika, 'Lady Gaga Gets Wild at 'Fame' Masquerade Ball in New York', *Rolling Stone* (14 September 2012) (online at: http://www.rollingstone.com/music/blogs/thread-count/lady-gaga-gets-inked-at-fame-masquerade-ball-in-new-york-20120914) <accessed: 21 November 2012>.

31. Two of Gaga's self-declared inspirations, David Bowie and Michael Jackson, were featured in Pierrot costumes on album covers: Bowie's *Ashes to Ashes* (1980) and Jackson's *Mega Box* collection (2009). The significance of Pierrot for David Bowie is examined by Alexander Carpenter, 'Give a man a mask and he'll tell the truth: Arnold Schoenberg, David Bowie, and the Mask of Pierrot', *Intersections*, vol. 30, no. 2, 5–24. Carpenter explores Bowie's development of artifice and the mask in rock performance and traces the historical development of the character Pierrot as the 'melancholy artist-prototype' (7).

32. Gil Kaufman, 'Lady Gaga Talks Hidden Meanings in Epic "Telephone" Clip', *MTV.com* (12 March 2010) (online at: http://www.mtv.com/news/articles/1633776/lady-gaga-talks-hidden-meanings-epic-telephone-clip.jhtml) <accessed: 12 November 2012>.

33. We understand the lyrics to imply a boyfriend, especially in Beyoncé's verse, where she resists the nagging phone calls: '*Boy*, the way you blowin' up my phone/Won't make me leave no faster/Put my coat on faster/Leave my girls no faster.'

34. There is a similarity of stylistic sound here with Gwen Stefani's 'What You Waiting For' (2004) and Ladytron's 'Destroy Everything You Touch' (2008), and further back, The Eurythmics' 'Sweet Dreams Are Made of This' (1991), but there is also an edgy electrorock sound as in Nine Inch Nails' 'The Hand That Feeds' (2005).

35. Several of Warhol's 1962 iconic Coca-Cola paintings can be accessed at Adbranch, 'Andy Warhol's Coca-Cola paintings', *adbranch.com* (17 November 2010) (online at: http://www.adbranch.com/andy-warhols-coca-cola-paintings/) <accessed: Nov. 21, 2012>.

36. For example, Lichtenstein's 1964 pop art painting 'Oh Jeff . . . I love you, too . . . but . . . ' features a woman on a telephone with characteristic yellow hair, strong eyebrows, and red lipstick. This painting can be accessed at: http://www.leninimports.com/roy_lichtenstein_gallery_7.html <accessed: 21 November 2012>. In *Roy Lichtenstein* (New York, NY: Guggenheim, 1993, 113), Diane Waldman writes about Lichtenstein's representations of women in love affairs with domineering men, in which the artist tracks the anxiety of the woman in the controlling relationship. This painting captures the emotion of the woman as she talks to the man on the phone.

37. The Great Frog (http://www.thegreatfroglondon.com) was established in 1972 in London, and catered to rock and punk artists and fans with uniquely designed bespoke pieces and hand-carved jewelry.

38. Madonna's 'Vogue' video (1990) adopted Hollywood and Art Deco styling of the 1930s and 1940s in black and white film, with Madonna's look paying homage to stars such as Marilyn Monroe and Marlene Dietrich. Andy Warhol's *Marilyn Diptych* (1962) features an image of the star with her distinctive short blonde hair and red lipstick based on her photograph to publicize the film *Niagara* (1953). The acrylic painting was purchased by the Tate (online at: http://www.tate.org.uk/art/artworks/warhol-marilyn-diptych-t03093 <accessed: 21 November 2012>) in 1980. It is also worth noting here that the CD cover for Madonna's album *Celebration* (released September 2009) featured the artist in a re-creation of Warhol's *Marilyn* image.

39. Atsuko Kudo, designer of latex feminine fetish fashions, designed the yellow dress and hat for Beyoncé, as described at their blog, 'Beyoncé in Atsuko Kudo', *AtsukoKudo.com* (12 March 2010) (online at: http://www. atsukokudo.com/blog/2010/03/beyonce-in-atsuko-kudo/) <accessed: 21 November 2012>.

40. Beyoncé's 'Video Phone' (featuring Lady Gaga) was released as a video on 16 November 2009. The genre Snap, a forerunner to Crunk, is a southern Hip-Hop style that emerged in the clubs in the late 1990s and was made popular with Billboard hits such as D4L's 'Laffy Taffy,' T-Pain's 'Buy You a Drank' and Soulja Boy's 'Crank That.' The genre is characterized by hypnotic drum loops and synthesizer ostinatos produced by the Roland TR808 drum machine.

41. Bettie Page's career as a pinup model is outlined on her website (http://www. bettiepage.com) <accessed: 21 November 2012>. Beyoncé wears the same style of wig (long black straight hair with bangs) in 'Video Phone'.

42. Polaroid did not pay for this inclusion, but Gaga did have a partnership with Polaroid, making this a mutually beneficial reference. See: 'Lady Gaga Named Creative Director for Specialty Line of Polaroid Imaging Products', *Polaroid.com* (5 May 2010) (online at: http://www.polaroid.com/news/2010/ lady-gaga-named-creative-director-specialty-line-e) <accessed: 21 November 2012>.

8 Storytelling on the Ledge
'Telephone' and 'Paparazzi'

Carol Vernallis

What can music video do, and what are its limits? Much has changed since MTV's first broadcast—platforms, technologies, social configurations, and economic structures, as well as the genre's ripening and (possible) maturation. Makers' and viewers' shared knowledge about forms and conventions has also caused shifts. Most strikingly the arrival of YouTube, prosumer work, and the end of censorship—more sex, drugs, and product placement—seem to make it all so different.

My *Experiencing Music Video* makes claims about the limits of music video's ability to narrate.[1] To some extent these arguments still hold: music video is a short form that tends to draw attention to the song's features. It has limited resources—just lyrics, no dialogue—and it bears a responsibility to foreground the star. But in recent months my students and I have gone back and forth on music video's narrativity. Only one music video director's work *really* confounds us—Jonas Åkerlund's—but his clips may be enough to call for new models. Åkerlund's and Lady Gaga's 'Paparazzi' and 'Telephone' suggest something about the features and possibilities of the genre. In this opening section, I'll argue for and against music video's ability to present a narrative, taking these clips as case studies. Next I'll show the ways 'Paparazzi' and 'Telephone' mobilize both traditional Hollywood narrative and musical form. I'll close with the claim that the style that emerges produces transgressive images of personhood that allow Gaga's persona to hover uncomfortably between murderer and victim. These rapid shifts of valence are something that Gaga's well suited for, but they may produce an ambivalence in the viewer that neither song nor plot can resolve. Through overlapping, and often conflicting patterns, 'Paparazzi''s and 'Telephone''s, song, image, and audiovisual relations encourage me to support revenge killings. In these new videos, understanding narrative structure is important, but attending to musical form and local audiovisual flourishes is essential as well.

A SCUFFLE

What do I actually know about the more traditional, Hollywood-like narrative plots of 'Paparazzi' and 'Telephone'? In 'Paparazzi', Lady Gaga becomes disabled after a fall off a balcony (though I don't learn whether her lover intentionally pushed her off, or, if, in the struggle, she was accidentally shoved). Toward the video's end, she poisons her boyfriend. But even then this poisoner may not *really* be the same Gaga—this is an *evil* Gaga, who's been overcome by some sort of Mickey Mouse-Avatar. 'Telephone' shares similar narrative conceits. Gaga's released from prison, and at the clip's end she poisons a fleet of customers at a diner (here, however, I'm more certain I'm following a consistent character—a recidivist jailbird, her wardrobe hangs together more). These two clips share much funny stuff in the middle, such as Gaga's dressing up in a half-tutu in 'Paparazzi,' or wearing a phone on her head in 'Telephone.' And why is Beyoncé dressed up like she's a member of the Beatles' *Sergeant Pepper's*? Or why do the bandits' closing costumes look like Beardsley-wear in 'Telephone?' Beats me. It's all up for grabs. So maybe I'm not watching a narrative. Actions I understand as sensible or coherent begin well before the song's opening, or the first substantial break before leading into the song proper. The closing incidents occur as I'm heading into the out chorus. In the middle I'm somewhere else. I might claim instead that I'm watching something like a musical, with one non-narrative music-video-like number embedded in it.

Readers may say I've overstated the case. Admittedly I'm starting with a definition of narrative that has tight constraints, though it's applicable to almost all feature films. This characterization of narrative derives from David Bordwell's *Classical Hollywood Cinema*, which requires the following elements for a story: that all of the events we see and hear, plus those we infer or assume to have occurred, can be arranged according to their presumed causal relations, chronological order, duration, frequency, and spatial locations. Bordwell draws upon an Aristotelian understanding of narrative—it ought to contain characters with defined personality traits, goals and a sense of agency who encounter obstacles and are changed by them.[2] I'd claim Åkerlund's characters are too unfathomable and unreliable and the ways they encounter and respond to obstacles too mysterious for me to get a bead on things.

One counter-argument is that I *can* impose a narrative on these videos. A five-act structure for 'Paparazzi' and 'Telephone' might look like this (see Figure 8.1a-b). I can move through these five turning points while tracing emotional rises and falls. But, playing devil's advocate again, I may find a plot here only because this is the kind of narrative I am most familiar with—not because of patterns inherent to the music video itself. The music video remains agnostic and offers many trajectories. *I* force an understanding on the clip; I adopt this trajectory but I could just as easily take another (see, again, Figure 8.1a-b).

So let's chart a more narrative-driven path first through 'Paparazzi' and then 'Telephone.' The first task of a Hollywood film's narrative is to elicit the viewer's support for the protagonist, through either a display of the protagonist's admirable qualities or deft handling of a hurdle. 'Paparazzi' opens on a manicured lawn, and then in the bedroom, of a grand villa. A powerful Gaga, engaged in foreplay with her boyfriend, commands him to kiss her and declare his love. He carries her from the bed sheets to the balcony's ledge,

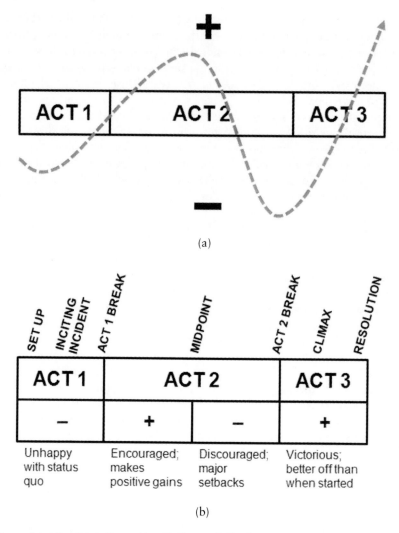

Figure 8.1   Traditional narrative Hollywood film form.

where I assume a furtive photographer captures celebrity pics. It's unclear whether Gaga panics and the lover, reacting too quickly, throws her over, or, intent on financial gain (either for the pics or her death), deliberately shoves her over. Having nearly died, Gaga returns home in a limo. With much pomp—and vogueing—her wait-staff carry her into a wheelchair and then push her forward; she, with their continued encouragement, stumbles down her foyer's carpet on silvery crutches. The video draws here on familiar tropes of the fighter's great rehabilitation: nursing old wounds, she pushes her body forward against nearly intractable odds. Intercut are sexual activities among Gaga and three young, androgynous characters on the couch (dressed like *Blade Runner*'s Pris or rag-dolls with mop heads and suspenders) who too seem to bestow health and vigor on her. (Gaga becomes increasingly more sexual and mobile through their embraces.) Also intercut are a number of murdered dead women, presumably her staff—in the bushes, the bathtub, by the pool. Since Gaga is recouping and has gained my sympathy, I don't implicate her in these deaths, even though her hand forms a cocked gun that points at these women out of frame.

In the second chorus, Gaga delicately and nimbly runs out into the villa's main hallway with back-up dancers (supporters?), in tow. I interpret her costume—tights, half-skirt, half-collar, earrings made up of upside-down crosses—as a sign that she's partially recovered from her injuries; her background dancers' Pierrot-like headgear (that she had worn previously when she was in crutches) and her tightly cinched, high-heeled shoes (linking to the concerted close-ups on feet in the previous scene), reminds me of her history of severe impairment. Unlike the previous scenes focused on striving, Gaga's Pierrot-dance has a melancholy, vulnerable feel to it.

And now she hits a nadir at the song's bridge, though I suspect Gaga's low point is due only to my projection as a viewer; such a turn fits snuggly within a narrative curve, and when a darkest hour in a music video *might* come. The video offers few immediate signs to help me read it this way. The section opens with another dead female staff person, limbs unnaturally twisted, but this time on the bed. So, as any female viewer might suspect, punishment, sexual behavior and women are linked. There's another dead woman in ivy and one who had possibly hung herself, feet dangling with (again) dainty shoes. The music sounds dark, and color has been drained to black and white. Gaga wears spools of film in an odd headdress (the death of celluloid and the new reign of the digital?). There's one lone Dalmatian and a simple (cheap?) wooden wall. Gaga sings of libertine behavior: too much partying. There's also one crotch shot (like with the lovers on the couch). But still the scene is so under sketched (a medium close-up against a bare wall) that this section may only suggest waiting, emptiness, and passage. The rest are my viewer's contributions.

I cut now to the final chorus. Once again there's a conjugal scene with Gaga and boyfriend, now both seated on a living room couch, while her maid, in the foreground, prepares drinks. The maid resembles a woman who has been murdered, causing confusion about the video's earlier deaths. Gaga and the maid seem to be in the know; as Mary Ann Doane has pointed out, a woman wearing glasses (as this maid does) can suggest both vision and power, especially in women's melodramas.[3] A dropped newspaper telegraphs Gaga's ascendance: 'The New It Girl.' Perhaps Gaga's maid conspires with Gaga and helps prep her poison. Tasting the toxin in her black Mickey Mouse outfit, with her heavy black makeup, and black glasses, Gaga seems like someone from the underworld. She seats herself upon the couch, as her boyfriend drinks her concoction, stages a moment of recognition of the evil deed, and slumps dead. Here the music video truly moves out of joint, though I don't yet realize it. I've invested in the protagonist, and I support her vengeance. I want her to succeed but she seems to be enjoying the payback too much. I'm surprised by the flatness of her 911 call: 'I've just killed my boyfriend.' After Gaga's exoneration, as her limo travels through public space with her fans visible outside her car window, she seems spacy. And when she poses for a mug shot, she looks so white-trashy, she might indeed have been the perpetrator of the crimes. This new counter evidence almost, but not quite, shakes my support for the star (see Figure 8.2a-q).

(a)

(b)

(c)

(d)

(e)

(f)

(g)

(h)

(i)

(j)

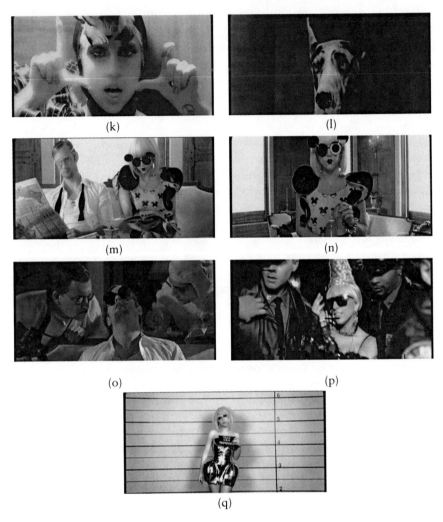

Figure 8.2 'Paparazzi''s Hollywood-like narrative form.

I might feel tempted to call 'Paparazzi' an aberrant, lucky discovery, a one-off, but Åkerlund may have created something new and repeatable. 'Telephone' and 'Paparazzi' make similar attempts to elicit viewer identification through narrative structure and emotional arcs. As in 'Paparazzi,' 'Telephone' begins with Gaga winning our loyalty and respect. Brought into a woman's prison as an inmate, she conveys a liberatory sense of style. Look at that striped black and white dress! Those curlers made out of coke cans and cigarette butts! Mega-DIY! She also possesses more access to both media and terrain than do other inmates. She calls in a helicopter on the phone; she can glide past catfights, and lead other prisoners toward freedom. Only a few cellmates possess anything like this reach. One shines a mirror through the bars of her cell. Another has black-and-white boots (for walking! but is still immobile). In the prison courtyard, overweight African-American women rim Gaga's outer circle, much like the black butlers who swirl in the background in 'Paparazzi.' For better or worse these stereotyped images support the video: they accentuate Gaga's and Beyoncé's power and beauty, giving the sense that no one compares with them. Like 'Telephone,' 'Paparazzi' solicits my admiration for the heroine: Gaga gains my admiration through aggressive lovemaking in the grand villa, and effusive newspaper headlines.

Like 'Paparazzi,' 'Telephone' gains my sympathies by next placing Gaga in an abject position. Tossed into a cell and bound with yellow tape (as opposed to a broken body strewn on the couch in 'Paparazzi'), Gaga must surmount difficult odds. As in 'Paparazzi,' background characters seem to bestow her with power. She and a phalanx head down a corridor. After she's sprung from the clink, she gains additional resources. Beyoncé picks her up in a trademark car, the 'pussy wagon' *à la* Tarantino's *Kill Bill*. Then, much as in 'Paparazzi', there's a vulnerable moment. In 'Telephone,' Beyoncé hand feeds Gaga and they both have the sad talk about—it must be—men. 'To make a burger you gotta kill the cow' and 'The crack in the mother fucking mirror.' ('Paparazzi''s similar moment was the Pierrot dance.) And like with 'Paparazzi,' the role of secondary characters is uncertain. Is Beyoncé Gaga's lover? Does she empower her in the same way as do the three lovers on the couch in 'Paparazzi'? Other secondary ambiguous characters in 'Telephone' will soon appear—why does Beyoncé wear the Sergeant Pepper outfit? Who are all those people in the diner? Why are so many of them overweight? And that dog again? And much as disability shadows Gaga in 'Paparazzi,' jail-time follows her in 'Telephone.' As the two women travel the lonely desert, the same gay-identified voice calls out 'This is radio KUK. This is Lady Gaga featuring Beyoncé in "Telephone"'.

Now a low point at the song's bridge. Why? As I suggested in connection with 'Paparazzi': it's time. Transporting Gaga from prison, Beyoncé sings low bluesy material, and Gaga tips her hat back and forth, repeatedly filling the frame with blackness. Gaga also takes pics from a Polaroid camera: digital mournings for the end of celluloid.

The scene in a diner brings me toward the end of the song. As in 'Paparazzi,' Gaga has an obscene appetite. She's become one of the cooks for the diner, with a consort of gay sous-chefs. She eats what looks like a bad sandwich, gnashes her teeth, and hops up and down as she sprinkles poison on the foodstuffs. She becomes a kind of phoenix-robot. As a waitress bringing food and the check, she freezes into a cardboard cutout and presents the American flag. This time not only her boyfriend but everyone in the diner keels over. And again, as in 'Paparazzi,' the murder's aftermath is completely confusing. Why is Gaga in that leopard-colored limousine driver's uniform? Why are Gaga and Beyoncé dancing around in nineteenth-century outfits? Does it seem touching that the credits run too quickly against the harp?

Still, 'Telephone''s tale could be read as a strong departure from traditional narrative. In both 'Paparazzi' and 'Telephone' Gaga might seem unstable and incoherent, perhaps even post-human. More than Michael Jackson's 'Thriller,' 'Paparazzi' and 'Telephone' present a protagonist who's equal parts lovable and hostile, and 'Paparazzi' goes further, by pushing this ambiguity farther forward in the clip, and it doesn't trade in zombies or werewolves. Jonas Åkerlund's radical presentation of identity is in sync with understandings drawn from contemporary cultural studies and psychoanalysis of people as composed of multiple forces that are shaped and constrained by social frameworks. Such depictions of persons, however, can be threatening and hard to assimilate; the myth of complete identities can be reassuring, providing a surer sense of self and others, as well as a sense of control. If people are multiple, I will be unable to predict behavior. Everyone, under the right circumstances, may be floozies, murderous, vain, vulnerable, sexually precocious, frozen, communally-directed, melancholic, romantic, desolate, striving, endearing, frightened. The myth of complete identities gives me a surer sense of myself and others, as well as a sense of control. In 'Paparazzi' and 'Telephone' the characters' dark sides emerge suddenly, but in a way that feels right. In these fictions I am able to support Gaga as a killer. Perhaps I cheer her on because her character has experienced great wrongs. She's able to gather power by aligning with the destructive proclivities of large institutions (Disney, the U.S.). Her supporters, cooks, fellow dancers, and friends accept her behavior. Subtle signs suggest she's a special kind of human, a demigod. She has an inhuman appetite. She's immune to poison. She gnashes her teeth. She makes eye-signals showing she has special communicative powers. And she becomes increasingly robotic, frozen, allegorical.

To achieve such transgressive depictions, Åkerlund draws support from visually-based narratives, musical and audiovisual forms. All of these structures depart from the ways life normally works: life may rarely follow the traditional five-act narrative structure, nor the logic of musical or audiovisual forms. Typical pop song structures can suggest telling a tale (verse), reflecting on it (chorus), and finding a moment outside it (bridge), but their rhythms only sometimes map onto lived experience. Audiovisual moments can unpredictably break from the texture, connecting to others farther away. A music video that interweaves narrative, musical and audiovisual teleologies may be able to achieve something quite radical. Thus far, I've shown how 'Paparazzi' and 'Telephone' reflect narrative forms, and, in what follows, I'll illustrate the ways they overlay and showcase musical and audiovisual ones. What's remarkable about music, as Nicholas Cook and Levi Strauss have argued, is that more than any other art form, it's better able to resolve difference or myth.[4] A musical composition can present one element, attribute, or state, embodied as musical material, and another that goes a different way, and make them meld, mingle or resolve. If images are tied to musical elements and follow the music's trajectories, all sorts of differences can be worked out. Visual materials and audiovisual moments bound to the music of a pop song might drive us toward conclusions we might otherwise not accept.

So let's return to my initial question. For me, Gaga seems like a good woman who's been treated badly by her boyfriend and fights to make a comeback. How does she turn murderous, while at the same time garnering my support? I've trusted Gaga and I've invested myself in her project. When she kills her boyfriend I find myself thinking 'go girl!' But I don't understand how I've come to such a position. So shocking! Can looking closely at 'Paparazzi' help me understand myself and contemporary artmaking?

THE AUDIOVISUAL CONTRACT

I've argued that music videos show off features of songs so they can 'sell' them. The image teaches the viewer memorable aspects of the song so she'll wish to return to it. In music videos we can sometimes even sense the image reaching to forge a connection with the music. Conversely, Bernard Herrmann quipped that film music seeks out elements in the image.[5] This linking, exchanging, and imparting create a range of relations among image, music and text. But it's important to note also that music and image can be polygamous. One particular connection may be engaging, but many others will do. The music might work just as well with another set of images. It's helpful to consider what Jonas Åkerlund heard in 'Telephone' and 'Paparazzi' that might have encouraged him to choose particular images and it's useful to ask what we as viewers pick out in the relations between music, image and text. We should keep in mind that different viewers will make different connections. Still: what in 'Paparazzi' makes song and image seem to belong to one another? A fine skein of connections leads the listener (and viewer) to the boyfriend's death. These overlapping patterns suture us into the video and lead toward an outcome that feels increasingly inexorable as the video unfolds.

ARRANGEMENT AND SONG SECTIONS

The song-sections and musical arrangement of 'Paparazzi' are the two most forceful structuring elements in service of its story. The song's high-register synthesizer sounds a bit like a theremin. The theremin has been associated with Gothic and horror films and can set the stage for multiple killings in the mansion, and more broadly the clip's more macabre tones. When this synth-sound breaks away from the voice and hovers in the musical texture, it might also relate to aspects of the setting: the villa's high ceilings, for example. The song proper begins with a tonic minor seventh chord, but the root immediately drops out, leaving a major chord built on the third scale-degree: this unsettles any sense of harmonic centerdness, and this uncertainty may open up space for seeing Lady Gaga as damaged goods. Simultaneously, the song's opening 'da-da' rhythm suggests a big arrival, hence the limo, glam clothing, and waiting staff. A dirty sounding synth in the middle register sounds a bit 80s, perhaps just enough to suggest high shoulder pads and the rhinestone-studded retro look. A second, soon appearing squeaky-squishy synth timbre might correspond to the vinyl strips Gaga wears. Overall the verse is reiterative and spare, with much empty space around each carefully produced sound element: percussive hits, especially, are finely crafted. This might suggest why Lady Gaga doesn't go far in the verses; she remains in her foyer, or on the couch. Her voice is dissonant with the synths underneath her, and this too might encourage the video's sense of trauma as Gaga stumbles. Sounds are ping-ponged in the stereo field, which creates a sense of enclosed spaces. The men hover around Lady Gaga tightly. She's irised in the couch. She's hemmed in by bandages or her metal outfit. Her hands make bounded, circular shapes in front of her face.

The choruses are more luscious than the verses: they are where we as viewers want to be. The chorus is the good object. Its harmonic rhythm speeds up to one chord per measure, and gains a cycling quality. (This differs from the verse, which stays primarily on the tonic.) The voices are multitracked with reverb, creating a rich wash of sound. While the verse's percussion are brittle and harsh, the chorus's percussion become progressively warmer, taking on increasingly human-like qualities, to eventually sound like domesticated hand claps. This is partly why the choruses feel hospitable, like home.

Gaga's straight and gradually raised arm at the close of the verse also conveys us into the chorus. 'Paparazzi''s first chorus departs from traditional forms of music video, because it stays rooted in the same environment as the verse. Nevertheless, the two sections are different. In the first verse, Lady Gaga hobbles on her crutches, but the chorus adds a sense of movement and flow through the appearance of her waiting staff, who, in two lines, encourage her onward with flowing fringe. After much lying on the couch in verse two, in the second chorus, Gaga runs into the large hallway and dances with broad frontal gestures with her supporting performers. And in the third chorus she comes forward off the couch and heads for murder. All this movement from the back to the front of the frame suggests greater mobility and freedom than in the verses, and I applaud her progress in the third chorus.

The contrast between the sparsely arranged verses and the thickly orchestrated chorus may be enough to align me with Gaga as she commits murder. The breaks, however, solidify these relations. They are even sparser and more repetitive than the verses—they're stripped down to almost nothing. In the first break, Gaga's waiting staff strut off, almost as if they might leave her. In the second, she's backed into a corner, and she's dressed in black and white with celluloid spooled on her head. The flash-frames make it difficult to see, but she seems to be in bondage. At one point her head seems turned away from her body, like a possessed Regan in *The Exorcist*, with her hands spread like talons. It's a frightening image. Gaga drops in the frame against an adjacent shot of the dog's foot with its sharp nails; the dogs might attack Gaga. All this moves too fast to take in, except subliminally. But I may experience palpable fear that Gaga may become one of the dead women. In addition, the music foregrounds the sound effect of a fuse being lit, and Gaga's wrapped in celluloid. If a match is struck she'll go up in flames. In the third chorus, as the flashing light transfers its rhythmic pattern to the repetitive synth in the conjugal scene with the boyfriend, I may feel a sense of relief. Gaga's out of danger. She's not like the dead women. I can trust the music to carry me out of a dangerous situation. I align myself with it. I support Gaga's mixing of the poison. Better him dead than my heroine.

The chorus's flow, with its rejuvenating possibilities, supports Gaga in what may first look like a loyal act of mixing a drink for her partner. It's only at the sprinkling of the powder that we see there's been a turn. The choruses have brought us here. The first two possess harpsichord-like sounds that oscillate quickly and are reminiscent of Baroque music. Since the location is a grand villa from the Baroque period, the orchestrational touches might suggest that Gaga and her dancers possess both a knowledge and history tied to this place. Its moneyed surfaces and high style belong to her, not the maids or the men. In the third chorus, the arrangement drops out, and all that's left is the women's voices and a reiterating synth figure, which I hear as, 'This is your moment!,' 'Do it now!,' 'Take the stage!' (See Figure 8.3a-i).

PERFORMERS

My description thus far might sound grim or dour, but the video isn't. It stays cheery by capitalizing on the nature of performers in music video. The dead women are models who function as mannequins. Mannequins are meant to be more an absence than a presence: they should display clothes. So these high-fashion dead women's business is to trade in absence and stillness. Music videos are not very good at dealing with real death, or even stillness, however. Nor do they have true villains. No musical or

Figure 8.3 'Paparazzi''s imagery tells its story through the song's sections. (8.3a, verse 1; 8.3b, chorus 1; 8.3c, break; 8.3d, verse 2; 8.3e, chorus 2; 8.3f, bridge; 8.3g, chorus 3; 8.3h-i, out chorus).

audiovisual element can ever be completely vanquished or extinguished in a pop song or music video. In music video, music washes over the whole surface, animating everything. Almost nothing is really inanimate.

In music video clips, supporting characters often function as odd, mute, inanimate, symbols, and they appear only in interstitial sections. They possess a blankness that's almost deathly. Such depictions started early: the second clip screened on MTV's first broadcast, Ph.D's 'Little Susie's on the Up,' contains a background figure lurking around like a silent executioner. Jonas Åkerlund extends the depictions of the background character much further than their initial and historical uses, suggesting something new and uncanny. The functions of 'Paparazzi''s and 'Telephone''s mannequin-like characters are impossible to determine. 'Paparazzi''s inability to suggest cessation or death is revealed by the music's pause after the poisoning. Two uncanny doctors are needed, both with glasses, one with blue skulls and another with green, to keep the body down. Real, depicted death, tends to be rare in music videos. Sometimes in a hip-hop video a member of the posse might toss a handkerchief at a camera, whose lens peers skyward from the bottom of a grave. A body in a casket might appear, as in Jay-Z's '99 Problems,' but the corpses tend to like to open their eyes. Even Guns N' Roses's 'November Rain' was unable to bury its corpse. The success of 'Telephone''s odd deaths can be explained as well.[6]

So perhaps 'Paparazzi' is cheerier and more life affirming. The clip exploits the ambiguity between one real death and many supplementary ones, or one real death and many who are just ornamental symbols of something else, like the death drive of fandom. It's unclear. The video is also chipper because, though some of the material in the verses might be bleak, the choruses are opulent. Gaga's singing here is prettiest, when she hits the highest pitches on 'until that boy is mine.' Here, the voice is colored with a bit of sadomasochistic teasing. Gaga is able to suggest something vulnerable and lethal at the same time: perhaps she's offering death through orgasm. And even if this video suggests death, attractive, beautiful materials of gold, fur, marble, diamonds, orchids, and glitter gild the video. Vibrant pinks, purples, greens, reds, blues, and oranges also brighten it. The model's bodies are also strewn like Easter eggs. They seem more like clues or hieroglyphs, text to be read, than real dead bodies. The video hovers between the real and the unreal.

But the most surprising depiction of performers occurs in the third chorus. Here, as mentioned, the thick arrangement of the first two choruses fails to appear. Only a pulsing synthesizer fills its place. This encouraging synth along with a bevy of multitracked voices feels trustworthy, like home. Lady Gaga rides this wave and struts forward to commit murder. I, too, come forward, and am implicated in this gesture. When her glasses are removed, I see her face. She's an Olympia, a puppet doll! She's become like the mannequins, and perhaps even more so. Is she the queen of the dead? (See Figure 8.4a–1)

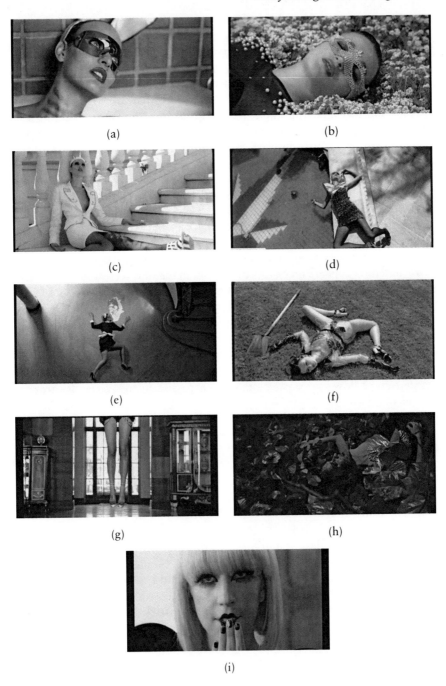

Figure 8.4 Lady Gaga is queen of the mannequins.

FLOW

Many subtle sonic and visual features work together to suture the viewer into the video and lead her, as an active witness, to the third chorus's murder. Visual motifs, for example, reappear in tandem with other processes like shifts in color or rhythmic patterns to form wavelike builds that carry the viewer into the third chorus. The mop-like straight hair of Gaga in chorus two (the sad Pierrot section) initially appeared less prominent (when Gaga is in her wheelchair and her lovers are on the couch). Flounce adorns the edges of the skirts of women's dresses as the women form two supportive lines ushering in Gaga's rolling wheelchair and then her march down the foyer. Gaga also wears a short flounce on her couch in the first two verses and choruses, and then her clothes become extremely flouncy by chorus two. The line of the waiting staff in the first chorus also showcase long strips that ripple, and then a single strip trails the female maid's dress as she turns to mix the poison, almost like a path, or something unspooled (Gaga had spools of celluloid on her head in the bridge). Cross-hatching appears on Gaga's dress both in the first verse and the chorus. In the bridge, where she's stripped down, in black and white, in an S&M scenario, the cross-hatching becomes more extreme. These shapes: flounce, coil, ribbons, crosshatching appear and reappear based on song section, gathering greater intensity, and, as decorative patterns, flow. Every image also possesses a spiral and something that juts out. Consider Gaga falling through space, hands and arms at odd angles, before the twirling 'vertigo' wheel. A larger alternating pattern of flow and stasis established across shots also extends through the video.

COLOR

Color takes on form and meaning in 'Paparazzi'. In the final chorus, when Gaga poisons her boyfriend, her bright yellow jumpsuit appears as an eruption. The pinks, purples, and greens also return from the opening; nature has been brought back in an orchid-like environment. Notice, too, the green from the cobra candelabras and phone, as well as the purple of the candlesticks, teacup, and boyfriend's socks. In the clip's center, the blue of the sky seems to flow down to the dancers in the second chorus, and to the pool with the dead girl at its edge, as well as the blue plastic tarp (a second pool?) on which a dead mannequin model rests. Red lipstick and pink mouths and tongue and red and blue jewelry erupt almost as moments of unleashed sexuality. The dark green and black of the Dalmatian and dead woman with ivy, and the fiery puddle of gold, pooling from the maid's mouth, are nadirs. Several functions: patterns of color, costume, lyrics, and gesture provide enough momentum to carry me like a wave into the murderous chorus. Each alone is sparse, perhaps inconsequential, but as an additive effect they get me there.

LYRICS

As in most music videos, the lyrics establish a range of connections between the music and the image, from direct to remote.[7] One obvious connection is Gaga saying 'got my lashes' followed by a cut to the eyes of a stunning, green-eyed woman. The 'ta-da' of the song's opening suggests a big arrival, hence such heavy makeup. Mascara is worked overtime in the video! Colors are strongly suggested in the lyrics: 'yellow dance,' 'purple teardrops,' 'cherry pie.' Similar big splashes of color pop out against a white, blue and gold background. The lyrics 'cigarettes / shadow is burnt' may be the most interesting use of underscoring. A flayed-out, dead maid sprawls at the bottom of a spiral staircase, with a vomitous puddle of fiery goo pooling from around her mouth. Earlier, on the couch, Gaga had made rapid-fire gestures as if she were puffing. In the bridge, there's the sound of a fuse being lit, or the flicker of a lighter. These establish the sense of smoking (and the bloodshot Great Danes seem to corroborate this). As is often with music video (as I've claimed elsewhere) lyrics head off in another direction from where the imagery suggests.[8] The line 'until that boy is mine' is opaque. Is it possible Gaga takes her boyfriend's life to make him hers? The ambiguity establishes a tantalizing distance between music, image and lyrics.

AMBITUS

The song's range from high to low extends from the Theremin-like synthesizer to the highly compressed bass drum. Åkerlund reflects this space visually with the clip's highest point: a woman's feet dangling from the ceiling as if she's hung herself with a rope. It's almost as if this is the point from which everything will descend downward. Height is sustained through Gaga's tall, punk-mohawk black-and-white headdress during the bridge, and her beehive extravaganza, post-murder, as she's driven through town. The video's lowest point is the dead maid in the ivy: Gaga seemingly drops toward that depth, almost falling off her couch in the second verse, and, in the bridge, sliding downward off frame in response to the threatening Great Danes.

GESTURE

Fundamental patterning in 'Paparazzi' might be elucidated through the metaphor of Gaga as a young bird breaking out of its shell. 'Paparazzi' overlaps actions, repeatedly returning to earlier stages in this process; across the clip, I seemingly find myself at various junctures of Gaga's attempt to break out of her confines. When Lady Gaga comes out of the limousine, she's encased in a neck and chest guard and her waiting staff angularly vogue around her, giving her no greater space than the narrow boundary of her wheelchair. On the couch, Gaga is enframed by a black iris, and she's dressed in crosshatched, black, shiny, veneer bands. She repeatedly makes pointed gestures with outstretched fingers as if to pierce a boundary and break out from the space. When kissing her lovers, Gaga's and their tongues meet, almost like hungry, young birds. The wait staff's fluttering fingers and flowing fringe seem an encouragement to propel oneself forward, even to fly (the waiting staff looked to me a bit like 1950s airline stewardesses). In the Pierrot section (second chorus) the dancers make full arching clock-like shapes with their arms, as if they were claiming a larger sphere. Their leotards are smooth, as if Gaga and her dancers had been newly born, and the ruffles on their costumes resemble remnants of a struggle to break loose, but their gestures ape the postures of the mannequin's dead bodies, suggesting the impossibility of departing from the past. In the bridge, Gaga's tall head-gear of piled up celluloid and feathers resembles a cockatoo's, and the two Great Danes adjacent to her lend her an animal-like quality. Gaga propels her head forward in aggressive bird-like gestures. All of this imagery of emergence, of an attempt to get out, encourages me to cheer her on as she walks forward to mix a poisonous elixir to kill her boyfriend.

CLOSE RELATIONS

As mentioned, song sections and musical arrangement are the clearest means by which the viewer becomes implicated. But many other functions contribute as well. One is simply sewing the moment-by-moment flow of the music and the image together in a way that naturalizes them. Åkerlund adopts a range of approaches to highlight local features in the music. Some of the gestures are so grand and obvious, they could be read as mickey-mousing. Near the opening of the first verse, Gaga's waiting staff ferry her from her limo to her wheelchair. One African-American chauffer pats Gaga's shoulder on the beat, and then two of the men freeze on a synthesizer hit. At the end of this first melodic phrase, a dirty sounding 80s synth comes forward, and Gaga and her waiting staff repetitively cross their palms straight out before them, as if to catch the funny quality of the timbre. Towards the end of the verse, there's a sudden harmonic shift, and Gaga's melodic line finally opens up into something more song-like. Here, she starts pulling off her long stocking-like gloves. Her movements, established across shots, suggest an opening out that responds to the harmonic movement. Gaga then stumbles forward on crutches, first on one knee and hip, and then on the other, emphasizing each downbeat measure, while her staff strut, passing her by.

There are other subtle touches. At melodic high-points, performers showcase the brighter features of the voice through raised arm gestures. Note the chauffer's hands high above his head directly behind Gaga's wheelchair at 'we'd be so fantastical'. Gaga also raises her arms above her at 'promise I'll be kind'. Also, through the thicket of gestures, the waiting staff trace shapes across edits. As Gaga is lifted out of the car, a sense of line is created by the waiting staff's demonstrative pat on Gaga's shoulder, followed by the waiting staff's swirling gestures around Gaga, to finally resolve on a shot of Gaga's feet. As Gaga is rolled down the carpet, a dancer traces a complicated swirling gesture against her left arm, as if to extend the melody's resonance. On beat four of each measure, a waitperson's hand makes a funny gesture, something fluttery, or suggestive of a 'halt'. The first times Gaga appears on the couch, there's a little more glistening post-production effects added to the fabric to make these phrases pop.

Verse two distinguishes itself from verse one through less moment-by-moment underscoring. Groups of images are phrased together to suggest melodic lines. Gaga swoons off her couch, and then the dead woman's torso and outstretched arms, revealed through rapid editing, form a larger pattern. One of the song's prominent rhythmic articulations is a triplet. The triplet-like shots of dead women, each slightly offset from the other, are punctuated as if the shots were recollecting this pattern. Gaga, too, just once, on her couch, bounces up and down, like a mechanical doll, three times, as if responding to the rhythm. Towards the end of verse two the sync becomes looser, providing a moment of respite or openness before a strong contrast: the crisp, demonstrative articulations of the dancers in the Pierrot section (chorus two).

THE DETAIL THAT JUTS OUT

'Paparazzi''s plethora of eccentric details supports the murder. Different visual marks or musical moments might stick out for different viewers. Those I find most prominent function similarly to what Žižek calls 'quilting points,' Hitchcockian details that poke a hole in the film's fabric.[9] In 'Paparazzi' these include the following: a sudden cross-hatch that appears on Lady Gaga's cheek in one shot of the first chorus. Blue, not black, finger marks, that are imprinted into the dead woman's neck at the bottom of a red-tiled bathtub. One of the women who's been killed wears an odd crown of spikes. The beautiful green-eyed woman's eye has a dot or a flaw. One of Lady Gaga's half shut eyes droops, and her eye-shadow seems to change from thick black to silver and black, and back again across the first verse. The Great Dane's eyes are dirty red. The camera's light that illuminates the mug shot's snaps at the video's end is as dirty as a mottled egg. The dead women's bodies are also twisted into odd shapes like thrown-down Barbie dolls; they're also wrapped in their original plastic (like the famous Rosenquist paintings). The sound of a fly's buzz pops in for only a moment against one pink rose at the video's opening. In the second chorus, Lady

Gaga wears fragments of clothing, as she runs out as a Pierrot figure, and her cross-shaped earrings, dangling upside down, sway.

In 'Paparazzi' these odd details become predictable. This sets the stage for the out-chorus's closing scene, in which Gaga commits murder. It takes place in a Victorian death room, unaccountably embedded with a wide array of odd protruding, disruptive details: the snake candle (which appeared as two long standing candle sticks in the first verse at the end of the foyer); a scary coffin-like hooded Victorian seat; a black jacket hanging on a chair; a weird chotchka perched on the table that looks like something belonging to one's great grandmother; a replacement of the photograph in the boyfriend's newspaper from Africa to two ominous figures, one draped in yellow, the other in black; last, an old rotary, pea-green phone hovering on a background table. Like the other green in the room, the phone's a sudden eruption of nature. (Green has been downplayed so far.) So, when Gaga steps forward in the last chorus, with her odd suit peppered with faces, her strange goggled glasses, and blackly etched faces on her fingernails, she is only one more odd detail against a larger scape of death. Her glasses, the faces on her outfit, and her fingernails with faces (a triple staring back!) all stare back at me without seeing me.

FINAL KILL

I may accept the scene in which Lady Gaga murders her boyfriend for two additional reasons. Åkerlund here draws together many elements I've previously seen, and their recapitulation gives a sense of closure and rightness to the act. I may also be so busy trying to track the connections among these elements that I don't properly attend to the murder Lady Gaga is about to commit.

Here are some of the strands that get taken up in the third, deadly chorus. The pink rose with its green leaves at the opening could be said to return, now fractured. The color of the green leafery suddenly appears in the cover art of the magazine that is thrown down, as stark text 'She's back!', and the cobra candles and pea green telephone. The pink of the rose suddenly reappears as the poison Lady Gaga mixes and pours into a pink flowery tea cup. There are also the red bottles that are reminiscent of the blood and lipstick of the previous murders. And, as with each chorus, Lady Gaga starts at the back of the frame and gradually brings herself forward. When I see her in this last chorus on the couch, as she steps forth, recapitulating material appears in proximity immediately around her. Her glasses suddenly have the same diamond studding she wore in the first verse. Her ring has spikes that recall the dead woman on the staircase with her crown of spikes, and the spiked gloves Gaga wore on the couch. The poison Gaga sprinkles from her ring glistens, much like the sparkles we saw on the couch's upholstery. (The powder also flows like the streaming detritus of the petals and dust from earlier sections.) These last items appear first, on the left side of the frame then on the right, then on the left, then on the right, pulling me back and forth, perhaps reminding me of the aural ping-ponging so predominant in the verses. I may also be primed for this moment by a transmedial exchange between the flash-frames of white light in the bridge and the synth pulse in this third chorus. Gaga brings a spoon to her mouth, that reminds me of her penitent, robo-android silver cap, bodysuit and crutches in the first verse, as she made her promenade down her foyer.

I've claimed that 'Paparazzi' superimposes classic Hollywood narrative structures on musical form. The music video's allure stems from the way that both forms unfold simultaneously. I can't get a fix on which one deserves preeminence, so I can't decide what's transpired. The narrative suggests a classic character arc in which Gaga starts out as a woman who's been wronged and who eventually decides to take revenge. But the music and audio-visual relations tell a different story. Pop songs often focus on recurring musical events, and they often possess an air of inevitability. Gaga moves between the abandonment of the breaks, the inhospitality of the verses, and the lush choruses, which seem connected with women's voices. She aligns with the chorus's multi-tracked voices, which we might decide belong to the women strewn around the villa. The melodramatic opening piano-accompaniment too might be associated with turn-of-the-century stage plays and old black-and-white films, both showcasing strong villains and victims. I surmise someone will be rescued and someone must pay. The music that accompanies Gaga as she lies injured on the sidewalk suggests she's aligned with strong forces. She is owed something. Even though the visual scapes of the choruses and the verses change, Gaga acts with determination, moving briskly or gazing fixedly as if on a mission. If I take these moments seriously, I might assume she was set to kill from the beginning. Psychologists have noted that when we interact with people, we experience two separate streams of information, visual and aural. People often dissimulate, cloaking their true intentions and desires. We are better interpreters of our interlocutors' intent when we attend to the voice than when we focus on visual gestures. A jury might not convict Gaga, seeing her as a victim of abuse, but I might, against my better judgment. The jury might vaguely sense that the song's bridge places Gaga at risk, and it's either her or the boyfriend. But I've been attending to the song and its relations with the image. Gaga's determined comportment at the openings of song-sections, and the siren song of the lush choruses, lure me to follow her as she prepares the poisonous drink. I bet Gaga will get off scot-free. For me Jonas Åkerlund and Gaga get away with murder.

NOTES

1. Carol Vernallis, *Experiencing Music Video: Aesthetics and Cultural Context* (New York: Columbia University Press, 2004), 5.

2. David Bordwell and Kristin Thompson, *Film Art: An Introduction* (New York, NY: McGraw-Hill, 1997), 482.

3. Mary Anne Doane, *The Desire to Desire: The Woman's Film of the 1940s*, 2nd edition (Bloomington, IN: Indiana University Press, 1987), 99–100.

4. Nicholas Cook, *Analysing Musical Multimedia* (Oxford: Oxford University Press, 1998), 3–24. Claude Levi-Strauss, *Myth and Meaning* (Toronto: University of Toronto Press, 1978), 20–25.

5. Michel Chion has called this 'added value' (that the sound melds with and becomes a property of the image). Michel Chion, *Audio-Vision: Sound on Screen* (New York, NY: Columbia University Press, 1994), 5. Claudia Gorbman (in 'Aesthetics and Rhetoric,' *American Music*, vol. 22, no. 1 (Spring 2004), 14–26), cites Bernard Herrmann's famous quote, drawing on Cook's *Analysing Musical Multimedia*, 104.

6. The song is broken up into many parts. The strewn bodies might relate to the held tones at end of lines in the lyrics—tele-phoh—-ne. New performers supplement the older ones and the new characters dance, in a kind of celebratory erasure and transcendence of what's gone before, while the ornamental others are strewn about the diner.

7. Vernallis, *Experiencing Music Video*, 140–143.

8. *Ibid.*, 146–147.

9. See Slavoj Žižek, *Looking Awry: An Introduction to Jacques Lacan through Popular Culture* (Boston, MA: MIT Press, 1992), 88. His examples include a knife cradled under the family table in *Shadow of Doubt*, and a windmill that turns the wrong way in *Saboteur*.

9 Television Gaga

Lady Gaga, *Glee*, and Popular Music's Place on the Small Screen

Simon Warner

INTRODUCTION[1]

Music television, as opposed to Music Television (MTV),[2] has been an intriguing, frequently dynamic, hybrid, its two components sharing an often fertile, sometimes tense, relationship over the last six decades. This extended association has witnessed two hyperactive fields of post-Second World War creative activity—the medium of small screen broadcasting and the project of popular music recording and production—often engage while playing out a complex power relation, the ascendancy of one or the other never fully established in an inter-weaving narrative. It has, in other words, been hard to assert which format has been driven by which, and the question whether popular music needs TV more than TV needs popular music has been intermittently raised but never satisfyingly resolved. Perhaps there has been an ideal symbiosis, each medium nourished by the other: TV benefitting from the abundant supply of new artistic content, popular music gaining critical advantage from a key promotional platform which has frequently displayed the ability to transcend traditional demographic communities. This chapter will attempt a concise summary of this cross-media history but principally endeavor to explore the connection through a particular contemporary lens and a focused case study: the contribution of an early twenty-first-century pop star, Lady Gaga, to this creative exchange, with specific reference to her links to a current and highly successful, teen-oriented television show, *Glee*. What occurs when a performer, who appears to straddle the two worlds of mass culture and the avant-garde, becomes entwined in the agenda of a mainstream television production? Is her art compromised or does her radicalism have impact on the more conservative foundations of the standard entertainment menu? What does television do to the pop star and what does the pop star bring to the medium? And do the middle-of-the-road protocols of the prime-time screen have the capability of containing the sometimes taboo-testing behaviors of a controversial artist who courts media headlines?[3]

TELEVISION AND POPULAR MUSIC:
A SHORT HISTORICAL SURVEY

First, though, what can be said about the unfolding relationship between the realm of television and that of popular music? Between the dizzying height of Hollywood in the 1930s and 1940s and the spectacular emergence of the internet at the end of the last century, we might reasonably claim that the two colossi of global mainstream entertainment business were TV and pop music. Their emergence was not precisely synchronous but they came to the fore in the similar, post-war, mid-century phase and they would each, ultimately, have a bearing on the progress of the other. For various social, cultural, and economic reasons, the US proved to be the key crucible, the most significant marketplace, for these developments to gain pace and take hold. In the US, television began to secure a serious foothold in the later 1940s; it would take until the mid-1950s for pop to erupt as a mass cultural force with the teen market—with adolescents enjoying the possibilities of disposable income and asserting their spending power, snapping up the new vinyl singles by the millions—at the heart of that eruption. Before TV, radio and the movies had been the principal draw for audiences, across wide age ranges. Television directed its product at a more narrow band of the population, its general appeal to youth restricted. Its limited attraction to that not-yet-adult, teenage group and its challenge to the long-standing tradition of regular and universal cinema-going produced interesting and influential effects. The phenomenon prompted film producers to tailor movies, from the early 1950s, at younger, adolescent crowds in a bid to rejuvenate box office returns at the time when many parents were quite content to take their entertainment via the small screen in their own homes.[4]

By the middle of the decade, the synergy between such late-teen-aimed film releases, like *The Wild One* (1953) and *Rebel Without a Cause* (1955), with their striking rebellious icons James Dean and Marlon Brando, and the novel musical sounds of the day—namely rock'n'roll, a highly-charged marriage of black blues and white country—flared, with Bill Haley and His Comets achieving national and international fame for their, only brief, contribution to the 1955 movie *The Blackboard Jungle*—Haley and his band contributed the song 'Rock Around the Clock' and quickly starred in a 1956 movie of the same title—and virtually launched the vogue for a revolutionary, upbeat song and dance form, one that hinted at creative miscegenation and, by extension, appeared to undermine long-protected racial divisions in US society.[5] It should be added that the establishment of TV would also trigger crucial shifts in US radio and the way in which popular music was projected and promoted. Assumptions that radio would soon disappear—who would want to merely listen when the new medium offered both sound *and* vision?—saw the Federal Communications Commission sell off hundreds of cheap broadcasting licences at the end of the

1940s.[6] Hungrily snapped up by independent entrepreneurs, these licenses enabled a new generation of broadcasters to gain a toe-hold, constructing ('niche-ing') their playlists around musical styles—most often linked to ethnic minorities and so-called 'race' music—that had not previously been adequately catered for by the national radio broadcasting outlets. This expansion in independent radio outlets would further the cause of marginalized genres—from R&B and blues to jazz, country to Latin—by providing shop windows for the booming independent label sector,[7] contributing to the presence of an increasing number of records from these sectors entering in the Top 40 by the later 1950s, and helping to foster an environment in which Elvis Presley, Jerry Lee Lewis and Carl Perkins, Little Richard, Chuck Berry and others could eventually prosper.

It was only when a seemingly irresistible force like the young Presley met the more inhibited mood of national American TV in September 1956, that the moral guardians of the Ed Sullivan-fronted show, *The Toast of the Town,* felt the need to draw the line. Booked for three appearances, when the singer gave the last of his trio of performances, his gyrating pelvis was censored, and the sexually suggestive lower half of his body did not appear on screen for that final transmission.[8] Such generational clashes between television and popular music would arise on a number of occasions in the years that followed: from Bob Dylan and the Rolling Stones facing restrictions on the songs they could sing or the words they could repeat on US television, to Jimi Hendrix's refusal to curtail a performance on live UK television and the Sex Pistols' profanity-peppered appearance on a London-aimed regional news show.[9] The association between a mainstream force like TV, particularly reliant in the US on the whims of the sponsorship of their advertisers, and a more testing medium like popular music—firmly aimed at adolescent audiences and frequently capable of pushing at the boundaries of conventional codes and tastes—was therefore almost certain, from time to time, to create tensions for the stations, program producers and the performing artists. Yet there were moments, too, when television and pop forged extraordinary alliances: for example, the Live Aid concert broadcasts, from the UK and the US, were shown around the world in July 1985, when around 1.9b viewers in 150 countries, the biggest-ever TV audience,[10] were able to watch on-stage performances as they occurred via the small screen.

To move forward, however, and consider the present setting, we should say that, since the start of the new millennium, television and popular music, once vastly profitable sectors, have faced the specter of uncertainty and gradual weakening of their powerbases. This may come as scant surprise to those who survey the volatile character of the entertainment business of the last hundred years or so: an ever-changing landscape in which the most ferociously effective of cash-generating carnivores tend to discover that there is almost inevitably a metaphorical Ice Age to negotiate—one premised not on temperature change but technological transformation or shifting social patterns—with the prospect of significant, even terminal, decline.[11] Pre-Hollywood, the nascent cinema (massively boosted by the rise of sound in 1927) and the live stage were principal commercial contestants; the inter-war years also saw the new form known as radio rub bristling shoulders with phonography or recorded music; [12] and both radio and records were threats to the performing and publishing circuits that had grown up in the large-scale urban expansions of the later nineteenth-century, in North America and Western Europe, particularly in musical foci like New York and London, Paris and Vienna.[13]

As in earlier days, format wars, fuelled by new innovations, have both undermined TV and popular music's long-running ascendancy in the leisure field and diluted the impact of those two mediums. This as a trend is nothing new; there have been few periods over the last century when there have not been technological clashes with eventual winners and losers, survivors and casualties: discs and cylinders in the 1890s; shellac and vinyl records in the late 1940s; 33⅓ rpm long players and 45 rpm singles in the 1950s; AM and FM radio in the 1960s; and VHS and Betamax video systems in the 1980s, to name only some important examples.[14] Today, the setting is more complicated still, as well-established formats, visual and aural, face threatening challenges from changing production outlets and shifting patterns of consumption, as both television and music's existing platforms of presentation—principally TV sets and Compact Discs, at the end of the twentieth-century at least—have come under attack from myriad rival broadcasting and downloading models and the core profitability of the two business areas come under intense threat.

New products and platforms have disturbed the largely stable and profitable environment that applied to television and popular music until the later 1990s. Among the innovations in this process of transformation have been the availability of Digital Video Recorders (DVR), cable and satellite broadcasting, complete series boxed sets on DVD or BluRay, Netflix and TiVo, subscription TV and internet radio, Napster and Spotify, iTunes and YouTube, computers and laptops to tablets and smartphones. While these new systems and visionary businesses have been a catalyst for fascinating market opportunities, they have also tested, compromised and even confused older, more secure and familiar systems in which mass audiences were reachable via a relatively small number of routes. The sale of TV advertising, for example, has been valued on the basis of the medium's ability to hit—even guarantee—vast audiences at peak times that comply with the demographic aspirations of a product.[15] If television cannot generate multi-million grade viewing figures, the value of the small screen ad slots dips dramatically and program makers' income slips proportionally.

If audiences have the technical ability to record program and skip advertisements,[16] this further cripples the old equation that unmissable TV content means huge viewing figures, an axiom on which program sponsors and advertisers have, in the past, built their rationale for massive investment. Instead, the audience has become dispersed and diverse to such an extent that older certainties of reaching particular viewers at a scheduled and specified moment have largely evaporated. This is to discount, too, the effect of piracy and other illegal practices—affecting music particularly, but television also—which have further eroded the once reliable income streams of the biggest players.[17]

One must also factor in that the biggest companies in these realms of production have interests across the board: Universal, the biggest music production company with 38% world market sales, has fingers in movie and internet pies, too; Sony is not just a creator of playback hardware, mobile telephony and computers but has vast stakes in music, films and TV via its Columbia property, acquired as long ago as 1988. At the end of 2011 an important act of consolidation occurred: Universal took over EMI's recorded music roster, while Sony acquired the UK label's publishing division. Universal and Sony's diverse portfolios have been helpful to those massive media corporations: the patterns of profit and loss have fluctuated across their various fields of interest and the largest businesses in the field have been able to compensate for those disparities. EMI's focus on music alone left it fatally ripe for take-over.[18]

In the period from the mid-1950s to the present day, however, amid ever-shifting technologies—from radio to albums, music cassettes to videocassettes, CDs to DVDs and the ever-growing, ever-tightening tendrils of the internet—the affair between the box in the corner and the sounds on the turntable has been frenetically played out. From Elvis Presley on *The Toast of the Town* to Simon Cowell on *The X Factor USA*, it has been difficult to fully appreciate the importance, the influential nature, of this trans-media marriage. The Beatles could hardly have become a worldwide phenomenon without the aid of the TV screen, reaching 70 million Americans on the night of their first Sunday evening appearance on *The Ed Sullivan Show* on 9 February 1964. By then, in the US, *American Bandstand* (1952–1989) had already made its mark on television and more genre-nuanced programs like *Soul Train* (1971–2006) would follow. In the UK, pop television has also been seen as a key player in the establishment of a high profile popular musical culture with weekly shows like *Top of the Pops* running for decades (1964–2006) and more short-lived ventures from *Thank Your Lucky Stars* (1961–66) and *Ready Steady Go* (1963–66) to *The Tube* (1982–87) maintaining television's interests in the changing pop and rock landscape.[19]

Prime-time TV could barely prosper today without a sequence of pop-centered reality shows exemplified by *American Idol* and *The Voice*, *The X Factor* and *The X Factor USA*, all of which have managed to engage and retain massive youth viewerships and also hold the attention of older audiences. *American Idol* may be in relative decline after years of dominating its mid-week slots, but even in Season 11 as the final loomed, voting numbers in excess of 130 million were revealed,[20] suggesting that there remains something compelling about young, unknown talent performing live before experienced judges and a vast television audience, with that public still keen to play an interactive (and indeed critical) role in deciding who proceeds and who drops out and adding to the coffers of the TV (and telecommunication) companies through their phone votes.[21]

GLEE AND LADY GAGA

I now want to focus on the modes and meanings of a very specific music television alliance, one that will be exemplified and illustrated by two episodes from the hit TV comedy drama *Glee* which, in each of its three US seasons to date, in 2009–10, 2010–11 and 2011–12, has paid attention to the work of the singer-songwriter, musician and dancer Lady Gaga, an artist whom we may consider one of the world's most high-profile popular musical performers, certainly a most significant generator of global music sales during a period when physical distribution has gone into free fall.[22] My emphasis will be on the impact of two editions in which Gaga's influence is particularly evident, with specific reference to their reception in the US, where the episodes in question were first aired.

I want to consider various questions. What does Lady Gaga's involvement with *Glee* invoke? How does her work fit the show's image? Why has the show *Glee* become associated with Lady Gaga? What does the gesture say about popular music on television currently? What questions does it raise about the outsider and particularly about issues of sexuality and gender? And what does it say about the broader relation between popular music and TV? How does Lady Gaga manage to spread her appeal between the worlds of left-field performance and fashion and the mainstream flow of popular musical fandom? How does an artist like Lady Gaga, with certain avant-garde affectations, become the biggest-selling global artist of the two years in question, and how does a show like *Glee* reconcile its high-school manners and conventional show-tune ordinariness with the mores of this unconventional singer-songwriter and performer?

Created and written by Ryan Murphy,[23] Brad Falchuk, and Ian Brennan and initially aired in 2009 by the Fox network in the US, *Glee* centers on life at a fictional Ohio high school, William McKinley in Lima, a genuine town located in that state. But the show focuses more pertinently on its glee club, New Directions, a singing group directed by popular teacher of Spanish, Will Schuester (Matthew Morrison), and comprising a talented gathering of outsiders, separated from their mainstream class mates by their ethnicity, sexuality, and disability but also distinguished by their outlook, personality, and their high levels of dedication and aspiration. For them, the musical stage and the show tune are their ultimate motivation. Despised by the jocks—members of the sporting fraternity—and regarded somewhat dubiously by the mainstream school constituency, they are marked as geeks and targets of ridicule and verbal, even physical, abuse. As in life though, there are contradictions: while there are clear examples in the singing group of the black, the gay, the disabled, the Asian, the Jew, the obese, the intellectually challenged, and so on, some members of New Directions also have divided identities, even loyalties. Thus three 'Cheerios', as the cheerleaders at the school are characterized, are part of the glee gang, as is a sometime football star, while a juvenile delinquent rumbles the notion that the group is made up only of the goody two-shoe pupils in this American educational community.

Glee has also become a transatlantic phenomenon, with its three seasons transferring to UK screens, at first on the terrestrial Channel 4 and, by the latest series in 2012, to the satellite channel Sky Atlantic, like Fox a Rupert Murdoch-owned subsidiary. Fans of the show dub themselves gleeks, echoing the show's title, of course, but also subverting the notion that to be a geek is something to hide. Hardly as politically disruptive as the reclaiming of more controversial, and culturally sensitive, terms—like nigger or queer or slut—the self-identifying with many of the show's characters and the notion that geekdom can have its own value, its own distinctive and separate worth, is a noteworthy challenge in itself to more conventional notions of cool and credibility. [24]

As for the show's critical reception, *Time*'s John Poniewozik saw the first season as one of the best shows of 2009, including it in his 'Top 10 TV Series' of the year. He commented:

> This musical-comedy-drama about a misfit high school show choir [...] succeeds where [...] other small-screen musicals have failed, but it also shows the genre's challenges. Some of its story lines (especially the fake pregnancy of the choir director's wife) are distractingly implausible. But when *Glee* works—which is often—it is transcendent, tear-jerking and thrilling like nothing else on TV. It takes a gay kid, minority kids, jocks and nerds and explodes their stereotypes, channelling high school's heightened emotions through joyous pop music. It can be a mess, but it's what great TV should be: reckless, ambitious, heart-on-its-sleeve and, thanks especially to Jane Lynch as drill-sergeant cheerleading coach Sue Sylvester, gaspingly funny. When it hits its high notes, nothing else matters.[25]

Nancy Franklin, writing in *The New Yorker*, had a broadly positive take on the production, as she considered the closing forays of the premiere season. Although she described the show's 'cartoonish feel', suggested that the young people at the heart of the drama were 'cluelessly wrapped up in themselves' and proposed that *Glee*'s positions in the schedules, following Tuesday's edition of *American Idol*, was to its distinct advantage, she still felt a general warmth to the melange of music and action. She remarked:

The real engine of the show isn't the machinations of its characters or its unfolding plot but its basic structure. Because *Glee* is actually about a group of singers, it doesn't seem artificial when the cast breaks into song; the music fits into the proceedings organically. The songs—which Murphy chooses—range from oldies to newies, so that there is, theoretically, something for everybody, from 'Sing Sing Sing' and 'Sweet Caroline' to 'Gives You Hell' and 'Single Ladies'. Still, it must be said, even people who love these songs may find something to hate in the style of singing sometimes showcased in *Glee*—the ear-splitting, maniacally melismatic car-alarm whine that Whitney Houston popularized—but, thankfully, there are quiet ballads to balance things out.[26]

Yet this essentially lightweight dramatic package, even if it is marked by some serious cultural/adolescent themes alongside its central, 'let's do the show right here' mentality, has not secured *Glee* a blame-free ride from the more mainstream press and some web commentators. If some reviewers could revel in the show's knockabout vim, Poniewonik's *Time* colleague Nancy Gibbs saw threads of moral ambiguity which tended to unravel the instructive fiber of the song-fest from her Christian standpoint, and she perceived more negative than positive vibrations being generated by the production. She admitted that she had perceived *Glee* as hilarious, if occasionally mockingly cruel, but she had begun to moderate this general thumbs-up when she 'heard a bright, earnest youth minister tell a group of high school kids that he thought *Glee* was "anti-Christian"'. She explained:

> It is easy to see his point, if you look at the specifics. In his view, *Glee* portrays Christians as phonies and hypocrites. He observed that the only self-identified Christian is the shiny blond Quinn, cheerleading president of the celibacy club, who is pregnant by one classmate but pretending the father is another. (To make matters more complicated, in a heartbreaking scene, she begs her parents' forgiveness; in righteous fury, they throw her out of the house.)[27]

Gibbs felt that the general manifesto of the show, framed by its sizeable cast of protagonists and its multiple storylines, was less than wholesome and, within a US television-viewing context at least, very likely to raise parental eyebrows if mothers and fathers bothered to dig below the glossy surface. However, she continued:

> It insults kids to suggest that simply watching Characters Behaving Badly onscreen means they'll take that as permission to do the same themselves. The fact that *Glee* is about a club full of misfits already

makes it ripe gospel ground; Jesus was not likely to be sitting at the cool kids' table in the cafeteria. And it's set in high school, meaning it's about a journey not just to college and career but to identity and conviction, the price of popularity, the compromises we must make between what we want and what we need.[28]

Gibbs' reservations about the TV production's unsettling sub-texts in respect of accepted religious teachings are not the only ones that have been raised. Matters of sexuality, more specifically homosexuality, have also been explored in the series and these have caused more conservative American commentators to express their ire and vociferously. Lady Gaga's own place in that debate has not been irrelevant. But to that detail I will return.

While there may be discernible connections to Gaga in some of *Glee*'s storylines, it should also be stressed that even though the artist's work has been featured in a small number of key episodes, the singer has made no actual appearance in the show herself.

That said, she has appeared more than willing to endorse this association and, through social networks like Twitter (she famously had over 10 million followers around this time),[29] has expressed her positive impressions of the show. She appears to be a fan of the piece and more than happy to share her creative catalogue and sartorial style with the show's producers in various set pieces.

So, when and how has Lady Gaga been a presence in the series? This chapter will concentrate on a pair of shows which have most significantly embraced the signs of the Gaga oeuvre and look. The initial example formed part of Season 1's Episode 20, entitled 'Theatricality' and originally aired in the US on 25 May 2010. The second, Episode 18 of Season 2, took its title from the Lady Gaga song 'Born This Way', and enjoyed its American screen premiere on 26 April 2011. However, for the record, we might also note, there are other occasions when Gaga's work makes an appearance in *Glee* shows. In Episode 1 of Season 2, entitled 'Audition' and premiered in the US on 21 September 2010, Rachel (Lea Michele) and Sunshine (Charice) share a duet on 'Telephone', Gaga's 2010 single featuring Beyoncé; in Episode 6 of Season 3, entitled 'Mash Off' and screened in the US on 15 November 2011, a mash-up of two songs both called 'You and I', the 2011 Gaga song and a 1982 Eddie Rabbitt & Crystal Gale piece, forms a duet for Will (Matthew Morrison) and Shelley Corcoran (Idina Menzel); while Gaga's 'Edge of Glory' (2011) is showcased in the closing section of Episode 22 of Season 3, shown in the US on 22 May 2012, which carries the title 'Goodbye' when a number of the students take part in a farewell graduation performance. But, to return to the pair of shows under closer consideration here, the shows 'Theatricality' (2010) and 'Born This Way' (2011) and examine the Gaga-linked ingredients in more detail.

'THEATRICALITY': QUESTIONS OF IDENTITY

In 'Theatricality', adolescent identity is under the microscope as Tina (Jenny Ushkowitz) faces censure for adopting goth garb in the school corridors and attempts to defend her right to express her unique personality through her dress to Principal Figgins (Iqbal Theba). But when New Directions discover that Vocal Adrenaline, another singing group and their keen rivals from a nearby school, are planning to draw on Lady Gaga (Rachel discovers that their local textile supplier is out of red Chantilly lace and thus comes to this conclusion),[30] their vocal director Will Schuester okays his own club to take a similar route and proposes that this may be a suitable device through which Tina establishes a fresh persona. The decision to 'do Gaga' is not universally fêted, particularly among some of the boys. Puckerman (Mark Salling) asks group members: 'What's up with this Gaga dude? He just like dresses weird like Bowie'. But gay Kurt (Chris Colfer) is plainly in the know and a huge fan, retorting: 'Lady Gaga is a woman. She's only the biggest pop act to come along in decades. She's boundary pushing, the most theatrical performer of our generation and she changes her look faster than [fellow member] Brittany changes sexual partners'.[31] Will is fully convinced the move is the right one, enthusing to star quarterback Finn (Cory Monteith) as he pores over the web: 'I'm looking at all this amazing stuff about Lady Gaga. She's got this thing called the Haus of Gaga which is like this collection of artists and designers who collaborate on her styles, stage sets and her music. I think it's an exciting model for what we could be doing in glee club'.[32] Despite this positive testimony, footballer Finn says he will not participate in the Lady Gaga venture, a hint that his own machismo will not allow him to traverse the cross-dressing line the project implies. But all the girls plus Kurt enthusiastically pursue their own 'Bad Romance' Gaga tribute and, in a lavish, energetic and highly physical homage, all adopt different costumes associated with the artist.

Creating the song and dance sequence that follows was one of the biggest challenges the makers of *Glee* had taken on, with a huge amount of time dedicated to the filming of a 2'20" segment. Ryan Murphy, who oversaw the section, said: 'I'm directing that episode and I did more coverage on that song then we've ever done in the history of the show. It's a big number. It's like, big and athletic and hard. And those girls and Chris, I think, did it for six hours straight'.[33] The show's costume director Lou Eyrich told *InStyle*: 'I have great respect for Lady Gaga. This episode is a tribute to her genius. The costumes are not replicas; we wanted it look like the kids made them'.[34] As such, the items the cast wear, while glamorous and convincing, also possess homemade details, like DIY stapling. Rachel wears two Gaga outfits: a Kermit the Frog version hung with stuffed animals, based on a dress the artist wore for a television interview in Germany, designed by Jean-Charles de Castelbajac,[35] and a piece based on mirrored triangles, witnessed in the singer's stage show. Of the dress worn by the expectant Quinn (Dianna

Agron), seen when Gaga attended the Fifty-second Grammy Awards in 2010, Eyrich comments: 'We built the Armani orbit dress around [her] pregnant belly'.[36] The look is accessorized by a stylized and heavily spiked stellar orb. Brittany (Heather Morris) reveals a Philip Treacy lobster hat, seen on the singer in London in March 2010,[37] while Tina (Jenna Ushkowitz) is clad in a version of the Haus of Gaga, Hussein Chalayan-inspired, bubble dress the performer unveiled on the cover of *Rolling Stone* on 13 June 2009. Mercedes (Amber Riley) appears in a silver, high-shouldered body suit that Gaga utilized in a performance at the 2010 Grammys topped off with a purple hair-bow, while Santana (Naya Rivera) wears a Jeffrey Bryant-style, black lace ensemble topped by a Charlie Le Mindu-like black rose hat both of which the singer displayed as she attended an Aids charity event in London on 1 March 2010.[38] Kurt employs a costume referencing the Georgian-style Alexander McQueen look which Gaga incorporates in the 'Bad Romance' video. Actor Colfer said it was 'like a George Washington meets an Oceanic whale disco ball type thing. And part of the outfit is 10-inch heels'.[39] Lou Eyrich had a problem when it came to replicating 'Armadillo' platforms, unavailable in the size 13 version required by the actor, so again the costume team had to construct copies.[40] While all seven outfits feature in the 'Bad Romance' dance sequence,[41] there is one further costume to be seen in the show. Finn, having resisted the overtures to participate in the Gaga celebration earlier in the episode, later shows solidarity with his gay colleague Kurt by wearing a full-length red vinyl dress while confronting those jocks who have been bullying his more effete friend. This outfit was based on the striking latex item Gaga wore to meet Queen Elizabeth II at the Royal Variety Show in Blackpool, UK, on 10 August 2009. Of the regal encounter, Chris Ryan blogged: 'Gaga kept fierce with this red Elizabethan-inspired Queen Of Hearts rubber dress by Atsuko Kudo and wild-style crystal eye accents'.[42] On a tall and muscular man, the camp impact is emphasized still further by the exaggerated scale of the design. There was one further notable Gaga ingredient in 'Theatricality': a musical number. The adopted Rachel discovers that the singing coach of Vocal Adrenaline is her long-lost birth mother, Shelby Corcoran. In a radically different arrangement, the pair take on 'Poker Face' as a stripped-down and intimate duet, the frenetic energy of the original contained within the framework of a dramatic Broadway ballad, intense but under-stated in an acoustic setting.

'Theatricality' asks questions about identity for adolescent students and drags up issues linked to subcultural and tribal, gender and sexuality, even racial and cultural choices, played out against the background of adult authoritarianism, as represented by the school principal, the more liberal tendencies of the choir director, and the menace posed by deeply conservative and fist-happy bullies who are keen to ensure that traditional order, represented by accepted male/female gender roles, is not challenged by the theatrical flamboyance of the glee club caucus. For Lady Gaga a number of the issues had relevance and resonance: here was a now successful artist who had kayaked the rapids of rejection and ridicule yet, by fiercely following a unique personal line, has managed to secure fame and acclaim as an original performer, dancer and songwriter. She remarked to the web version of *Entertainment Weekly*, shortly in advance of show's airing: 'I love *Glee*. I love the cast and the creativity of the writers. I went to a musical theatre school, and used to dream that someday the students would be singing my songs. Can't wait for "Bad Romance" and "Poker Face" in *Glee* fashion!'[43] For Gaga, the episode surely represented an extraordinary example of self-actualization, her output revered and replicated by a fictional cast but celebrated by a genuine TV audience of around 11.5 million on the night it was initially screened.[44]

Where though is the connection between *Glee* and Gaga? Clearly there is a powerful commercial imperative here: the synergy of a popular TV show consumed by a huge teenage demographic featuring material from a dominating world artist, in terms of sales and earnings, has a compelling power for both sides of the equation: television and popular music. The production was heavily trailed and widely reviewed. But what broader critical issues arise from this alliance? Where, for instance, was the social or aesthetic fit between these two factors? Does the broadly mainstream agenda of this small screen project dovetail comfortably with the more outrageous concepts that the artist frames in her own pop life?

Dressing up, as we have seen, is clearly a central inspiration to Lady Gaga. Some of the costumes she adopts fetishize material and textile, say rubber and lace; some obscure the face of the individual wearing the outfit, suggesting perhaps masquerade but possibly hinting at the darker recesses of S&M ritual. Gaga's songs, too, are played out in the adult zone: to watch the 'three-minute Hollywood' represented by her videos for 'Poker Face' and 'Bad Romance' is to enter an essentially alien territory.[45] Amid the kitsch glamour, harsh and cold, there is an potent air of decadence, even danger. The drama is mechanical and soul-less; the fantasy is visually impressive but emotionally hollow. The moves are tightly syncopated but the posturing belongs to dispassionate automata: robotic rather than visceral. Here there is no evident sweetness and lightness, no sense of anticipated joy, no proposal that these may be songs of innocence, of hope, of satisfying romantic resolution; there is no sense in these celluloid cameos that idealized notions of teen passion or young love or the naïve crush are privileged or even recognized. As the videos are an integral part in the Gaga myth, it is difficult to disconnect the visually compelling, yet bloodless, gestures of the short screen dramas from the compositions themselves. This is where the relationship between post-pubescent, pre-adult performer/singers in New Directions and the Gaga material becomes potentially problematic. If 'Poker Face' is played out in the louche setting of an upscale country club—the tawdry gloss of gambling furnishing its sub-text—with powerful suggestions of sexual preparation and probable engagement, even clues that an orgy is about to commence, then 'Bad Romance' (with low-grade women's literature as its prime metaphor) is premised on a more unnerving blend of dream and nightmare, with visual grotesquery, even the simmering presence of violence, among the unsettling features central to a disrupted, possibly cracked, narrative.[46] If the video for 'Poker Face' could imply that the Gaga character is a high-end sex worker in control, 'Bad Romance' constructs a mysterious and unsettling scenario in which Gaga's persona is the one under threat from forces not quite made flesh.

Whatever is read into these songs and accompanying films, the themes are hardly ones commonly associated with the hormone-drenched tensions and acne-tinged anxieties of mid-teen characters, temporarily traumatized by confused notions of self and sex. In short, the environments in which Gaga sets her two videos are quite dislocated from the gentler, more inno-cent confines in which *Glee*'s plots and sub-plots are enacted. While the TV storylines do possess certain moments of genuine intensity, they are ultimately quotidian classroom romps played out by emotional novices and resolved by dramatic devices that use the purifying power of a well-modulated pop anthem to rinse away the strains and pains of high school angst. It would appear that Gaga's creative constructs, her dramatic dilem-mas, are much more complex in character, much more mature in subject matter, riddled with ambivalence, far too convoluted and tangled to settle with a catchy hook and a memorable chorus. This is where there appears to be a serious misfit between the worlds of *Glee* and Gaga and the mix can be disconcerting. The signs and symbols, the meanings and mores of Gaga's vision, may well be considered less than suitable for young actors playing teenagers to manipulate and interpret, and for their predominantly adolescent viewership to digest whole. This is not a plea to censor Gaga's artistic practices but to perhaps propose that teen dramas may better look elsewhere for their models when this artist's work, with its predominantly adult perspectives, seems thematically detached from this particular field of youthful experience.

'BORN THIS WAY': ISSUES OF ACCEPTANCE

The second *Glee* show under scrutiny lifts the title of a Gaga track ver-batim. 'Born This Way' utilizes fully the name of the singer's 2011 hit and applies its core manifesto in a way that is still concerned with issues of identity, just like 'Theatricality', but spreads that concept beyond mere matters of teen uncertainty and issues of dress selection and raises signifi-cant points about the unique genetic information we possess that molds our development and may mean that we are exposed to mockery or suf-fer social marginalization as a result of our inherited characteristics. The fact—or curse—of DNA extends beyond just the young members of New Directions, with Will Schuester and obsessive-compulsive school counselor

Emma Pillsbury (Jayma Mays) among the adult characters who also attempt to confront their so-called impediments, physical or psychological. As Pillsbury comments: 'Most of the adults we know have trouble embracing their eccentricities, so how can we expect kids to?' Schuester responds: 'It should be our job to help them. I don't want my legacy as a teacher to be conjugated verbs and glee club trophies. I want to help them love themselves for who they are, warts and all—especially warts'. He continues: 'I know how I am going get the kids to accept what their differences are: by using their two favorite teachers—me and Gaga'. He later dubs Gaga 'the queen of self-love'.[47]

The plot sees the cast confessing openly to their innate foibles, trying to come to terms with them and also work to accept those perceived flaws in the individuals around them. Gaga's strident statement of intent in her global smash is then adapted as the closing sequence in which all participants trumpet their own identifying mark in a very public forum and, by doing so, hope to neutralize the stigma by accepting it as unavoidable fact rather than a point of shame.

The central storyline, however, concerns Kurt's homosexuality and it is this ingredient that caused most uproar and consternation among some American commentators, including widely read critics, who saw this *Glee* episode as a dangerous propaganda vehicle for the gay cause, a campaign that continues to divide the US even after more than forty years of organized activity by the homosexual community for recognition and rights. Concern over this was partly as a result of context: the worry that if a character in a teen drama might feel able to reveal his sexual orientation openly, this could perhaps imply that homosexuality and its practices are normalized by their inclusion in a mainstream production such as this. The fact that other characters in the drama, including Santana and Dave Karofsky (Max Adler), a football-playing jock who has terrorized Kurt in the past, are also revealed to be closet gays, adds extra layers to the tale.

Conservative media critic Dan Gainor wasted no time in launching an assault on the 'Born This Way' episode, even before the show was screened. He told ABC News: 'This is Ryan Murphy's latest depraved initiative to promote his gay agenda', dubbing the fictional William McKinley High School the 'gayest high school in the history of mankind'. Vice President for business and culture at the Media Research Center, Gainor added: 'This is clearly Ryan Murphy's vision of what growing up should be, not most of America's. It's a high school most parents would not want to send their kids to'. Another political conservative with an outspoken manner, one-time *Saturday Night Live* comedian Victoria Jackson also spouted vitriol, angry at Kurt's kiss with another gay character Blaine (Darren Criss) in the show as she reviewed it. She wrote, in her column for WorldNetDaily.com: 'Did you see *Glee* this week? Sickening! And, besides shoving the gay thing down our throats, they made a mockery of Christians—again![48] I wonder what their agenda is? Hey, producers of *Glee*—what's your agenda? One-way tolerance?'[49]

However, there was praise, too, for the 'Born This Way' screening. Perhaps not surprisingly, Gaga herself was quick to back the agendas explored in the episode. On Twitter she commented: 'I really loved *Glee*'s "Born This Way" episode. I admire the show for being brave and fighting for such modern social messaging. Never back down'.[50] Jarrett Barrios, the president of the Gay and Lesbian Alliance Against Defamation (GLAAD), also spoke out, defending the episode and the show in general. He stated: 'Fair minded Americans are tuning in by their millions to watch shows like *Glee* because they don't care if someone is straight or gay—what they care about is seeing characters and stories they can relate to'.[51]

'Born This Way' is about the stresses that the young homosexual faces but the concluding performance sees each of the New Directions crowd unveil their own distinctive feature, their own personal burden. As they present their version of Lady Gaga's title song on stage, all the members confess their apparent weaknesses on their T-shirts.[52] Kurt's states 'Likes Boys', wheelchair bound and bespectacled Artie's reads 'Four Eyes' and Brittany's 'Bicurious', while Will's carries the words 'Butt Chin' and Emma's, 'OCD'. The proposal of the scene appears to be that by announcing your imposition openly and publicly, in this cathartic setting, you can come to terms with it and, by doing so, persuade others to recognize, accept and accommodate it.

The pairing of *Glee* and Lady Gaga here seems to have a more powerful rationale, a more plausible context and greater substance, and, arguably, promotes a worthier agenda than the earlier 'Theatricality' construct, an edition concerned more with superficial issues of clothing and style rather than the characters' deep-seated vulnerabilities. An extended 90-minute episode, 'Born This Way' was clearly a venture which attracted a large-scale investment from the production team and the performing cast. Yet it proved to be the most poorly viewed of all episodes in Season 2, garnering an audience of just over 8.5 million, a statistic which can be blamed in part on the launched of a much-heralded new show on NBC, *The Voice*, on the same evening. Megan Angelo, writing for *Business Insider*, claimed that 'the incessantly hyped Lady Gaga episode of *Glee* turned out to be a serious flop'. She went on:

> A *Glee*-Gaga collaboration seemed unbeatable until it wasn't. And the episode's failure is an equally bad sign for both of them. Here's what it means for Gaga: her rise to hysterical, ubiquitous star status happened with incredible speed. Now, she's plateauing—or maybe even slipping. (If *Glee* fans won't tune in for her, who will?) Plus, the criticism long-hurled against the singer—that her fame comes from outfits and controversy, not musical innovation—is finally catching up with her.[53]

Perhaps Angelo's acerbic remarks on the Gaga phenomenon possessed some insight: the costume-heavy concerns of 'Theatricality' around a year before may have put off a certain segment of the standard *Glee* audience, though Christina Aguilera's arrival as a judge on the much-vaunted premiere of *The Voice* must have mopped up many gleeks and prompted them to switch to NBC for a new concept in TV and pop reality, where young singers' vocals were to be blindly judged first over physical appearance, content over style, an interesting juxtaposition on a evening when the glee club of William McKinley were up-profiling their failings in the spotlight as part of Fox's fictional showcase.

CONCLUSION

Notions that Lady Gaga may be in decline proved premature, however, and *Glee*'s third and now fourth season have followed in the wake of what seemed like a substantial setback to the show's fortunes in Spring 2011. Gaga remains one of the most interesting, engaging and inventive singer-performers and her associations with mainstream television via the key *Glee* episodes discussed above appeared to have no detrimental impact on her upward trajectory, nor did the show's associations with Gaga's unconventional ethos appear to damage *Glee*'s long-term health.

The collaborative pact between TV and popular music shows few signs of waning. Simon Cowell's defection to *The X Factor USA* in 2011 after ten years on *American Idol* has inevitably de-stabilized what seemed a winning formula: *Idol*'s numbers have reduced, while Cowell's new show has achieved viewing figures nowhere near the ones he predicted he could attain when he announced his fresh project. It seems that too many shows—*The Voice* included—may be seeking a similar, possibly even diminishing, body of viewers. Yet, the audience statistics are still strong enough to suggest that the concepts will continue to endure for some time, though I must stress the differences between reality driven projects, with the instantaneous spark of their live-ness, and drama filmed months in advance with unfolding fictional scenarios. Yet popular music is the fuel at the heart of both the many talent parades and *Glee*.

If the actual balance between television's muscle and popular music's power is still hard to call—who leads and who follows?—what I can assert is that the relationship between the two has never been so important. When technological developments, particularly in a period of digital transformation, have threatened the very production bases, distribution systems and anticipated audiences of both of these entertainment mediums, collaborations between the small screen and pop have proved to possess a reassuring longevity, capable of maintaining a high presence for each outlet in an increasingly competitive marketplace.

As for the specific examples under consideration here, Gaga, it seems, has been quite happy to draw on *Glee*'s popularity and *Glee* has been content to utilize Gaga's high recognizability, even valorize her more controversial strategies, even at the risk of upsetting more conservative blocs in US society. *Glee* producer Ryan Murphy, a committed gay activist, is clearly keen to see his show push at the doors in respect of social issues; Gaga's sexuality appears somewhat fluid, perhaps deliberately ambiguous, but she has been very happy to pin her colors to the cause of homosexual emancipation, backing, for instance, in vociferous style the campaign for the legalization of gay marriage in New York state in 2011.[54]

While Gaga has appeared as a live performer and on-screen mentor on US pop reality shows, perhaps her logical step will be eventually to bring her rhetorical skills and industry experience to the judging table in due course. As Mariah Carey secures a $17m fee to adjudicate the twelfth season of *American Idol* replacing Jennifer Lopez—whose alleged attempt to raise her $15m pay packet was resisted by the program's purse-holders—it appears that the financial potential for pop on television remains staggeringly high.[55] *Glee*'s dalliance with Gaga, without proving a copper-bottomed success, has certainly not put a stop to that alchemic process by which popular music and the small screen can prosper in harness, even as the vultures of a digital age circle above the TV and recording studios.

NOTES

1. The author would like to thank Ella Brown, his niece and Lady Gaga fan, for her advice on some of the costume details.
2. '[T]he first true global television network. Since going on air in August of 1981 [MTV] had transformed the music, television and film industries'. See Tom McGrath, *MTV: The Making of a Revolution*. (Philadelphia, PA: Running, 1996), 7–8.
3. Says Ann Powers, chief pop critic of the *LA Times*, of Lady Gaga: 'She is tapping into the curiousness of the moment, in that we're fascinated by extremes [. . .] We're really having a moment in which the freak is the central figure'. Quoted in Maureen Callahan, *Poker Face: The Rise and Rise of Lady Gaga* (New York, NY: Hyperion, 2010), 205.
4. Simon Warner, 'Sifting the Shifting Sands: "Howl" and the American Landscape in the 1950s', *Howl for Now: A Celebration of Allen Ginsberg's Epic Protest Poem*, ed. Simon Warner (Pontefract Route, 2005), 36.
5. A white Cleveland DJ Alan Freed claimed to be the first to use the term 'rock and roll', long-time black slang for the sex act, for the new musical form on his early 1950s radio show *The Moondog House*, which had no racial bounds on the records it played (see James Miller, *Flowers in the Dustbin: The Rise of Rock and Roll, 1947–1977* (New York: Simon & Schuster, 1999), 84). A little later Bill Haley took songs from the black catalogue—like Big Joe Turner's 'Shake, Rattle and Roll'—changing the words and thus reducing the level of sexual innuendo (see Charlie Gillett, *The Sound of the City* (London: Souvenir, 1987), 20–21).
6. Richard A. Peterson, 'Why 1955? Explaining the advent of rock music', *Popular Music*, vol. 9, no. 1 (January 1990), 102.
7. Gillett, *The Sound of the City*, 67–118.
8. Ed Ward, Geoffrey Stokes and Ken Tucker, *Rock of Ages: The Rolling Stone History of Rock and Roll* (London: Penguin, 1987), 131.

9. Dylan was denied the chance to perform the politically inflected 'Talkin' John Birch Paranoid Blues' on *The Ed Sullivan Show* on 12 May 1963, while The Rolling Stones were forced to amend the lyric of their song 'Let's Spend the Night Together' to 'Let's spend some time together' when they appeared on *The Ed Sullivan Show* on 15 January 1967. On the BBC's *The Lulu Show* on 4 January 1969, Jimi Hendrix took advantage of the live broadcast to pursue an extended jam on 'Sunshine of Your Love', a tribute to Cream who had just announced their dissolution (see: http://www.youtube.com/watch?v=elqJBWU4dOc) <accessed: 30 July 2012>, and on 1 December 1977, the Sex Pistols were interviewed on *Tonight* by host Bill Grundy. The band and their entourage employed a number of expletives in the live item (see Caroline Coon, *1988: The New Wave Punk Rock Explosion* [London: Omnibus, 1977], 60).

10. Graham Jones, 'Live Aid 1985: A day of magic', *CNN International* (6 July 2005) (online at: http://edition.cnn.com/2005/SHOWBIZ/Music/07/01/liveaid.memories/index.html) <accessed: 10 December 2012>.

11. Variety and music hall, the silent cinema, dance halls, and picture houses, for example, have all fallen prey to changing times and demands since the later nineteenth-century, while once-established playback formats from vinyl to 8-track, video to cassette, have become virtually obsolete.

12. Hollywood in California became a film-making center after 1912 (see Susan Hayward, *Cinema Studies: The Key Concepts*, Second Edition [London: Routldge, 2000], 363), though the cinema had emerged as a commercial proposition as early as the mid-1890s (Hayward, *Cinema Studies*, 433). It is perhaps no coincidence that popular music was at the heart of the talkies' launch with *The Jazz Singer*. Spoken dialogue was, of course, crucial in the shaping of a new cinema but music was almost as important. The 1930s saw an impressive combination of Broadway-sourced song and dance theatre shows transferring to the big screen of Hollywood.

13. See Derek Scott, *Sounds of the Metropolis: The 19th-Century Popular Music Revolution (in London, New York, Paris, and Vienna)* (New York, NY: Oxford University Press, 2008).

14. See Simon Frith, 'The industrialization of music', in *idem, Music for Pleasure: Essays in the Sociology of Pop* (Cambridge: Polity, 1998 [1987]), 11–23.

15. The particular relationship between television, advertising and popular music is explored by Bethany Klein in *As Heard on TV: Popular Music in Advertising* (Farnham: Ashgate, 2010).

16. Kenneth C. Wilbur states: 'The Digital Video Recorder [...] allows a television viewer to easily skip past television adverts [...]. The fundamental effect of DVR proliferation is a shift in control, from television networks and advertisers, to viewers' (Kenneth C. Wilbur, 'How the Digital Video Recorder changes traditional television advertising', *The Journal of Advertising*, vol. 37, no. 1 (Spring 2008), 143).

17. According to Ian Paul, '[o]nline piracy costs the US economy $58 billion in losses each year, including 373,000 jobs, the entertainment industry argues'. (Ian Paul, 'ISPs fight piracy: Meet the six strikes', *PC World* [8 July 2011] (online at: http://www.pcworld.com/article/235261/isps_fight_piracy_meet_the_six_strikes.html <accessed: 10 December 2012>).

18. Mark Sweney and Dan Sabbagh, 'Universal and Sony reach deal to buy EMI for £2.5bn', *The Guardian* (11 November 2011) (online at: http://www.guardian.co.uk/business/2011/nov/11/emi-sold-to-universal-and-sony <accessed: 12 December 2012>.

19. Note that *Soul Train* creator Don Cornelius and *American Bandstand* stalwart Dick Clarke both died within weeks of each other in 2012: Cornelius on 1 February, Clarke on 18 April.

20. Laura Prudom, '*American Idol* winner: Phillip Phillips crowned Season 11 champion', *Huffington Post* (23 May 2012) (online at: http://www.huffingtonpost.com/laura-prudom/american-idol-winner-phillip-phillips_b_1541110.html) <accessed: 12 December 2012>.

21. *American Idol* became the most-watched TV show in the world in its early seasons, with Season 2's finale attracting an audience of 38m. By Season 11, viewing figures for the show had fallen to just under 20m but it still remained America's biggest draw after *Sunday Night Football* (see Bill Gorman, 'TV ratings: *Idol, Glee* tops; *NCIS: LA, Good Wife* hit lows', *TV by the Numbers* (26 May 2010) (online at: http://tvbythenumbers.zap2it.com/2010/05/26/tv-ratings-idol-glee-tops-nciss-good-wife-fall/52437/) <accessed: 12 December 2012). Simon Cowell's rival project, *The X-Factor USA*, attracted 12.5m viewers to its debut in September 2011.

22. Lady Gaga's *The Fame Monster* was the world's biggest-selling album in 2010, with sales of 5.9m copies. See Media Traffic, 'United world chart: Albums countdown 2010' (online at: http://www.mediatraffic.de/albums-2010.htm)<accessed: 12 December 2012>.

23. Ryan Murphy was also the creator of *Nip/Tuck*, a drama set in a plastic surgery practice, which ran in the US from 2003–2010.

24. It should be stressed that African-Americans have not only subverted the term by re-adopting it but they have also re-conceived it as 'nigga', best exemplified, perhaps, in the name of the late-1980s rap group NWA, otherwise Niggaz With Attitude. Carmen Gillespie's essay, 'The N-Word, the F-word and All that Jazz: Race, Sex and Transgressive Language in Contemporary American Literature and Popular Culture', explores some of the broader issues, in Susan J, Behrens and Judith A. Parker (eds.), *Language in the Real World: An Introduction to Linguistics* (Abingdon: Routledge, 2010), 123–135.

25. James Poniewozik, 'Top 10 TV Series: 8. *Glee*', *Time* (8 December 2009) (online at: http://www.time.com/time/specials/packages/article/0,28804,1945379_1944142_1944160,00.html) <accessed: 12 December 2012>.

26. Nancy Franklin, 'Teen Spirit: The Joyful Noise of *Glee*,' *The New Yorker* (10 May 2010) (online at: http://www.newyorker.com/arts/critics/television/2010/05/10/100510crte_television_franklin#ixzz21dCm0Ayq) <accessed: 12 December 2012>.

27. Nancy Gibbs, 'The Gospel of *Glee*: Is it Anti-Christian?', *Time* (7 December 2009) (online at: http://www.time.com/time/magazine/article/0,9171,1942957,00.html#ixzz21YTOKg8Z) <accessed: 12 December 2012>.

28. *Ibid.*

29. It was reported on 6 March 2012 that Lady Gaga had become the first person to pass the 20m followers mark. Justin Bieber was in second place with 18m, while Katy Perry was third with over 15m. President Barack Obama was listed in eighth place with close to 13m (see Alexandra Topping, 'Lady Gaga racks up 20 million Twitter followers', *The Guardian* (6 March 2012) (online at: http://www.guardian.co.uk/music/2012/mar/06/lady-gag-20-million-twitter-followers) <accessed: 27 March 2013>). Questions have been raised, however, about the actual scale of Gaga's following (see, for instance, Conal Urquart, 'How many Twitter followers to they really have?', *The Observer* (26 August 26 2012) (online at: http://www.guardian.co.uk/technology/2012/aug/26/how-many-twitter-followers-do-they-really-have) <accessed: 12 December 2012>.

30. Lady Gaga wore a dress, inspired by Alexander McQueen's 1998 Autumn collection, made of this material when she received the Best New Artist prize

at the 2009 MTV Video Music Awards. When members of New Directions secretly infiltrate a Vocal Adrenaline rehearsal, they see all members of the group clad in similar outfits as they appear to practice dance moves for a performance of Gaga's 'Bad Romance'.

31. Dialogue from 'Theatricality', *Glee*, DVD, 2010.
32. *Ibid.*
33. Kristin Dos Santos, 'Ga-gouch! *Glee*'s Lea Michele injured during Lady Gaga dance number', *E!* (13 April 2010) (online at: http://uk.eonline.com/news/176162/ga-gouch-glee-s-lea-michele-injured-during-lady-gaga-dance-number) <accessed: 12 December 2012>.
34. Joyann King, '*Glee*'s costumer dishes on Gaga looks', *InStyle* (24 May 2010) (online at: http://news.instyle.com/2010/05/24/glees-costumer-dishes-on-gaga-looks/) <accessed: 12 December 2012>.
35. Shawna Flavell, 'Lady Gaga wears coat made of Kermits', *peta.org* (5 August 2009) (online at: http://www.peta.org/b/thepetafiles/archive/2009/08/05/lady-gaga-wears-coat-made-of-kermits.aspx. <accessed: 12 December 2012>.
36. King, '*Glee*'s costumer dishes on Gaga looks'.
37. Dan Martin, 'Lady Gaga: "My tour is a religious experience"', *The Guardian* (13 May 2011) (online at: http://www.guardian.co.uk/music/2011/may/13/lady-gaga-exclusive-guardian-interview) <accessed: 12 December 2012>.
38. The hair-bow can be seen in Lady Gaga's video 'Poker Face' (2008) while the Jeffrey Bryant/Charlie Le Mindu combo is visible at 'Charlie Le Mag', *Charlie Le Mindu* (2 March 2010) (online at: http://www.charlielemindu.com/mag/?p=1534) <accessed: 12 December 2012>.
39. Korbi Ghosh, '*Glee*'s Chris Colfer on the Lady Gaga Episode: Get Ready to Cry', *Zap2it* (25 May 2010) (online at: http://blog.zap2it.com/frominsidethebox/2010/05/glees-chris-colfer-on-the-lady-gaga-episode-get-ready-to-cry.html) <accessed: 12 December 2102>.
40. Eyrich, quoted in King, '*Glee*'s Costumer Dishes on Gaga Looks'.
41. Note that Rachel discards the Kermit dress and is clad, instead, in the mirrored triangle outfit when she joins the dance troupe.
42. Chris Ryan, 'Lady Gaga Meets the Queen of England', *MTV* (12 August 2009) (online at http://buzzworthy.mtv.com/2009/12/08/lady-gaga-meets-the-queen-of-england/) <accessed: 12 December 2012>.
43. Michael Ausiello, 'Lady Gaga Calls *Glee* Tribute a "Dream" Come True', *Entertainment Weekly* (25 May 2010) (online at: http://insidetv.ew.com/2010/05/25/lady-gaga-glee/) <accessed: 12 December 2012>.
44. Bill Gorman, 'TV ratings'.
45. UK singer Adam Ant once described the new video format thus in the early 1980s. See '25 Years of MTV', *Broadcast* (25 July 2006) (online at: http://www.broadcastnow.co.uk/25-years-of-mtv/165204.article) <accessed: 12 December 2012>.
46. As I have observed previously, '[t]he drama that unfurls to the strains of the newest 45, "Bad Romance", is a strange burlesque, recalling, quite bizarrely, Boney M's "Rasputin", hinting at the menace of *Clockwork Orange*, suggesting the masqued ball of *Eyes Wide Shut*, bathed in the dazzling fluorescence of the *2001* flight deck and riddled with a multitude of other fleeting symbols: fetishistic white vinyl, cleft-chinned Russian gangsters, and a Leigh Bowery-like interlude'. (see Simon Warner, 'Video GaGa: The Lady and the Vamp', *Words of Warner* (1 January 2010) (online at: http://simonwarner.wordpress.com/2010/01/01/video-gaga-the-lady-and-the-vamp/) <accessed: 27 March 2013>.
47. Dialogue from 'Born This Way', *Glee*, iTunes, 2011.

48. I assume that the experience of the practicing Christian Quinn, who faces humiliating revelations in the episode, is the main trigger for Jackson's ire.

49. Luchina Fisher, '*Glee*: "Born This Way" Episode Has Sparks Flying', *ABC News* (26 April 2011) (online at: http://abcnews.go.com/Entertainment/glee-lady-gagas-born-episode/story?id=13451313#.UBVd6kRCunV) < accessed: 12 December 2012>.

50. 'Lady Gaga praises her Glee episode', *MTV* (2 May 2011) (online at: http://www.mtv.co.uk/news/lady-gaga/268577-lady-gaga-glee-born-this-way <accessed: 12 December 2012>.

51. 'Lady Gaga Praises Her Glee Episode'.

52. The T-shirts, white with black lettering, are reminiscent of the garments used by UK group Frankie Goes to Hollywood to promote their single, 'Relax', in 1982. Their original version stated, 'Frankie says Relax'.

53. Megan Angelo, 'What This Season's Worst-rated Episode of *Glee* Means for the Show, NBC and Lady Gaga', *Business Insider* (27 April 2011) (online at: http://articles.businessinsider.com/2011–04–27/entertainment/30074432_1_glee-lea-michele-first-episode#ixzz20tVt24kY) <accessed: 12 December 2012>.

54. Glenn Blain and Kenneth Lovett, 'Lady Gaga Pushes for Gay Marriage in New York, Asks "Little Monsters"to Contact Undecided Senators', *New York Daily News* (17 June 2011) (online at: http://articles.nydailynews.com/2011–06–17/news/29687552_1_gay-marriage-senate-republicans-lady-gaga) <accessed: 12 December 2012>.

55. See Sean Michaels, 'Mariah Carey Joins *American Idol* Judging Panel', *The Guardian* (24 July 2012) (online at: http://www.guardian.co.uk/music/2012/jul/24/mariah-carey-american-idol-judge) <accessed: 12 December 2012> and Iona Kirby and Eleanor Gower, '"Jennifer Lopez and Steven Tyler Dumped from *American Idol*" According to Reports Alleging J-Lo "wanted $2 million pay rise"', *Daily Mail* (15 July 2012) (online at: http://www.dailymail.co.uk/tvshowbiz/article-2173772/American-Idol-Jennifer-Lopez-Steven-Tyler-dumped-according-new-reports-alleging-J-Lo-wanted-raise.html#ixzz22OpbYGZP) <accessed: 12 December 2012>.

10 Starstruck
On Gaga, Voice, and Disability

Alexandra Apolloni

Lady Gaga opened her performance at the 2009 MTV video awards with an operatic incantation: 'Amidst all of these flashing lights, I pray the fame won't take my life,' she sang, evoking the danger and violent potential of fame, a theme that underscores much of her work to date. The performance continued with Gaga alternately prostrate on the ground, clawing her way towards her audience, or dancing in an aggressive and confrontational manner. Halfway through the number, Gaga began walking with a crutch, while an erratically moving dancer was wheeled onstage in a wheelchair, and was spun around several times before being whisked away almost as quickly as she appeared. By the end of the performance, Gaga was bleeding from her midsection, strung up from the ceiling, incapacitated, possibly dead. This macabre mise-en-scene, rife with representations of disability, was a surreal setting for a performance of Gaga's 2009 single 'Paparazzi'. It came in the wake of her video for the same song, which offered a similar narrative of bodily compromise; and of a set of promotional photos by photographer David LaChapelle, featuring Gaga thrown from a wheelchair, hooked up to an electroshock therapy treatment device, and presiding over a post-apocalyptic cityscape, knees askew and on crutches.[1] These visual references to disability peppered Gaga's work in late 2009, in ways that construct fame/celebrity as a disabling force.

Blogger Wheelchair Dancer, a performer who writes about issues of disability in dance, rightfully critiques these representations, focusing in particular on the MTV Video Awards performance. In reference to Gaga's wheeled-on background dancer, she says,

> I suppose that this was some hyper ableist imagination of spasticity and paralysis, but suppose for a moment that she is disabled. Imagine that this movement is what her body does as she dances. Why didn't they stop and explore it? Why not choreograph it so that we can see a disabled body move? [...] But no. As usual, the (fake?) disabled person is merely a body wheeled on for display in a piece of gaudy pop art that passes for a wheelchair.[2]

This chapter takes these kinds of critiques of Lady Gaga's use of disability as a starting point. While I admire Gaga's work, some aspects of it trouble me, and I am even more troubled by the critical conversation that surrounds it: comments of the nature of those that I cited above are frequently dismissed under the pretext that Gaga is edgy, is avant garde, and that she pushes boundaries in ways that those who criticize her don't understand. A commenter on the blog entry cited above, for instance, says 'the art is being taken out of context. Perhaps the woman was scenery—that doesn't mean Ms. Gaga is a hater of the disabled, it means it was used as a symbol',[3] completely missing the point of Wheelchair Dancer's critique, which takes issue with the very fact of the image of a disabled woman as symbol and scenery. Because of such discourses, Gaga effectively occupies a musical, cultural state of exception, to borrow from Giorgio Agamben,[4] and is given free rein to deploy imagery that other artists, perhaps those seen as less avant garde than Gaga, might be more readily censured for using. However, her use of disability has a function beyond simply shocking audiences: it is both a manifestation of and a reaction to discourses of bodily and psychic compromise and damage that are associated with the performances of female musicians. This chapter explores the way Lady Gaga is represented as having a disabled body both visually, through costume and choreography, and sonically, through a use of recording technology and musical gestures that mimic vocal damage and trouble the line between the human and the robotic. I am interested in how Gaga's representations of disability connect to a broader context of musical manifestations of vocal, physical, and emotional damage; and to the question of how women's bodies, and the bodies of celebrities, are put on display. I want to emphasize that my use of the word 'damage' throughout this chapter, in reference to voices and, in some cases, to bodies, is self-conscious and is intended to be critical: the question of what constitutes vocal damage is slippery and ambiguous, and cannot be divorced from performance practices. Likewise, the question of whether or not certain bodies are damaged is highly contestable. People with disabilities also have a long history of pushing back against the idea that a body with disabilities is somehow damaged or incomplete. When I use the word damage, then, I do so with an acute awareness of how a discourse of damage has been used to marginalize people with disabilities, and I use the word reference to how certain bodies or voices are discursively or performatively constructed as being damaged.

While I will begin with a discussion of Gaga's visual representations of disability, I am even more interested in what I hear as her vocal representations of disablement. Lady Gaga, like many popular musicians, uses technologies like vocoders and autotune to alter her voice. Such technologies were originally intended as tools for repairing the sounds of voices, to correct pitch and intonation, implying an inadequacy in both the voice and in the singer's bodily ability to control the voice and shape it to meet the musical standards of a given genre. At the same time, however, the use of vocoders, autotune, and other forms of digital manipulation are seen as threats to the authenticity and integrity of singing voices. In her discussion of vocoders and the construction of authenticity, Kay Dickinson argues that their use is seen as a threat to the fleshly authenticity and attributed to unedited vocal sounds, and describes the perceived threat of the vocoder in terms that evoke vocal damage. 'The vocoder effect', she says, 'impairs the "naturalism" of the female voice not by ignoring it, but by creating the illusion of rummaging around inside it with an inorganic probe, confusing its listener as to its origin, its interior and its surface.'[5] As I will discuss below, the increasing use of digital editing technologies as, essentially, pop instruments, heightens the tension between discourses of vocal 'naturalism,' as invoked by Dickinson, discourses of authenticity, and discourses of vocal perfection and damage. In several of Gaga's recordings, I argue, her voice is digitally altered in ways that deliberately perform the kinds of damage that the use of technology is sometimes assumed to enact on a voice. A combination of bodily and technological performance choices render Gaga's voice unintelligible, ugly-sounding, and sometimes stuttering: technologies intended to improve voices are thus used to create the opposite effect: to create ugliness. I will position this use of vocal manipulation within discourses of voices that are heard as damaged—that is to say, the voices of singers who are heard as having harmed the physical apparatus of the voice, either intentionally or not, in the quest for particular vocal sounds or as a result of other factors such as illness, age, smoking, *etc*. As Laurie Stras points out, vocal damage communicates particular affects and is a convention of certain genres, and as such, can be simulated, learned, and performed.[6]

When I discuss voice in this paper, I refer to the sound of a voice as listeners perceive it. Vocal sounds are originally produced through the work of a singer's body, but pass through layers of mediation before reaching a listener. For instance, imagine that somewhere, in a studio, Lady Gaga sings. Her recorded voice is tweaked, enhanced, and edited by a producer. It is mixed with other voices, with instruments, and becomes part of a song. Somewhere, someone listens to that song, on television or online, through a sound system or through headphones, another use of technology that shapes what Gaga's voice sounds like. The end product of this process is a voice that isn't possible without technology, a voice that is no longer the same voice that once came out of Gaga's mouth. The voice, however, is still considered her voice, and, in videos and performances, is shown coming out of her body. This body is, itself, a representation of Lady Gaga's body, that, like her voice, is created through technology and performance. While the highly theatrical nature of Gaga's performances draw attention to the artifice of these practices, no voice is ever heard without some process of mediation.

Despite these processes of mediation, voices are nonetheless understood in ways that construct how singers' bodies are perceived. Certain vocal timbres are mapped onto particular genders, certain vocal accents on to particular social classes and ethnicities, and, while these associations are performative and constructed, they nonetheless contribute to the meanings that listeners ascribe to a vocal sound. Nina Eidsheim argues that, prior, even, to technological mediation of voices, singers perform conventions of vocal timbre both consciously and unconsciously, using what she calls 'inner choreographies': the manipulation of the internal parts of the body that produce the voice to shape the sound in particular ways. Eidsheim argues that some singers

> become skilled at producing a particular vocal timbre through conscious efforts such as voice lessons [. . .] or listening to recordings and imitating their vocal mannerisms. When a singer deliberately learns a vocal style and timbre, the creation of that timbre becomes transparent. [. . .] In contrast, when the vocal style is adopted gradually through everyday vocalizing and music making, the singer and the audience may be less aware of the physical parameters of the style.[7]

Regardless of whether the adoption of particular vocal timbres is intentional or not, it always responds to timbral conventions associate with both musical genres and social categories.

A singer's ability to execute the kinds of inner choreographies and consequently constructed timbres that Eidsheim describes, depends on the state of her body. The specifics of each singer's physiological make-up are, of course, different, and can change over time due to any number of causes, including aging, overuse, underuse, the strengthening or weakening of certain muscles, etc., all of which have an impact on the sound of a voice and on a singer's ability to shape her voice. Once a singer has produced a vocal sound, it can be changed further, both intentionally and unintentionally. The space in which a voice is heard, and the resonances and echoes caused by that space will have a profound effect on the sound of a voice. Amplifying voices will change their quality, as will the listening equipment used to hear a voice, in the case of recorded performances. While the intentional manipulation of voices using digital technology is an increasingly prevalent phenomenon in popular and avant-garde musics—from the amplified screams of Diamanda Galas to the auto-tuned choruses of the television program, *Glee*—this use of technology for affective purposes is by no means new or exclusive to contemporary Western genres. The expressive properties of technology have long been manipulated in music-making, from the strategic use of acoustical spaces, to the use of various kinds of amplification. As I argued above, no voice is ever heard without mediation.

When I discuss Lady Gaga's vocal sound, then, I refer to a sound produced and mediated both by her body and by technology. My interest, is in how this voice works with visual representations of her body to construct her in a way that connects discourses of fame with discourses of disability. This is accomplished, I argue, through the use of technology that mediates her vocal timbre in ways that both enhance it and make it sound ugly, drawing on existing affects and aesthetics of vocal damage. The resulting damaged, robotic, vocal quality points to a relationship between technology, vocal affect, disability, and fame. I am not arguing that the use of technology damages voices, nor do I think that such technology renders vocal performances somehow inauthentic. Rather, I argue that the use of recording technology can be understood as affective gestures that, like the physical affectations used by singers, construct our perceptions of performing bodies. I emphasize, too, that this is not meant to be a totalizing argument: rather, my reading of Gaga's voice in this paper is one that relies on the context of her visual representations of disability, and is but one possible listening perspective. Throughout this chapter, I want to trouble the ambiguous line between audible physical damage to the voice, as might occur through injury to the vocal folds, and damage as a performed affectation, interrogating the role of voice-altering technology in these processes of pop artificiality.

FAME, CELEBRITY, AND DISABILITY

In Gaga's 2008 release *The Fame*, and in its sequel, 2009's *The Fame Monster*, questions of celebrity, excess, and the grotesque are foregrounded. Gaga says that '*The Fame* is about how anyone can feel famous. "Paparazzi" might come off as a love song to cameras, and in all honesty, on one level it is about wooing the paparazzi and wanting fame. [. . .] It's about everyone's obsession with that idea'.[8] In other interviews, she has spoken about *The Fame Monster* as an attempt to deal with fear, darkness, and the monstrous side effects of fame.[9] Fame, I would argue, renders the bodies of individuals abject, even while it glorifies them. The technologies of display—like film, television, the internet, and the news media—commodify the bodies of stars, while audiences might project their own fears and desires onto those bodies. Richard Dyer argues that stars are 'embodiments of the social categories in which people are placed and through which they have to make sense of their lives, and indeed, through which we make our lives.'[10] People thus have an investment in celebrities. When celebrities fulfill the expectations of social categories they affirm those categories. When they fail, they serve as examples of the consequences of not upholding cultural expectations. However, such failures may also draw attention to the shortcomings of the social roles that govern people's lives. The voyeuristic impulse that seems to be an integral part of celebrity culture doubtlessly stems, in part, from these factors. There seems to be an almost perverse cultural desire to bear witness to failure, in particular, the failure of female stars, who are objects of both desire and loathing. Disintegration as public spectacle is, of course, not only the purview of women but it plays into discourses of gendered performance and control. There is a particular impulse to document the downfall of female celebrities, one that connects to discourses of the female body that figure it as both an object to be seen and looked at, and to be ashamed of and hidden. The culture of celebrity is fundamentally about the tensions between that which is hidden, and that which is displayed, and the circulation of desire between those poles.

Lady Gaga's performance project takes these abstractions about desire and visibility and makes them tangible through display of her body. Her performances both celebrate and critique celebrity and the narrative of excess that is imbricated in it, deploying images and sounds that represent disability as a means of critiquing discourses of celebrity. However, the images that she creates rely on commonly held ableist stereotypes of the bodies of individuals with disabilities, figuring those bodies as grotesque, as damaged, as traumatized, and as abnormal, constructions of the body that scholars and activists have worked hard to redress. These kinds of representations exoticize, and commodify disabilities, dehumanizing persons with disabilities, while trading on their bodies to construct an illusion of a normative ideal body. Bitch magazine blogger Annaham points out that, in the 'Paparazzi' video, Gaga's disability is always figured as temporary and somehow chic failing to reflect the reality of disability that many people face.[11]

Annaham points out that in the video for 'Paparazzi', Gaga is only shown in a wheelchair on a set that depicts in the private spaces of the home. She says that the 'split between public and private is yet again reinforced in the guise of disability-as-chic representation. The overall message: Disability can be "cool," but only if it is temporary, not shown to the public, and that your eventual recovery from it can be portrayed through the timeless medium of dance!' Her critique draws on the work of feminist disability scholar Susan Wendell, who argues that bodies with disabilities, and their connections to illness, rest, recovery, and death, are almost always considered part of the private sphere. I want to take Annaham's argument one step further: while 'Paparazzi' does focus on a representation of disability that is bound to private spaces, Gaga's narrative of fame alters this private space, and transforms it into a public performance space. In the 'Paparazzi' video, the camera invites audiences into the spaces of the home. Film, television, and music videos have, for a long time, invited the public eye into traditionally private spaces, and this instance is no different. What is interesting, however, is the way in which music videos, in particular, are able to exhibit self-awareness of this phenomenon: the players wear elaborate costumes, their movements are stylized and choreographed as though on a stage, and the rules of reality and the social order are suspended for the time of the song. In the context of Gaga's tendency towards self-aware uses of media tropes, this instance of public/private breakdown reads as a performance of performance that speaks to how celebrity precludes private spaces, while drawing attention to her damaged body.

Similarly, a context of hyper-visibility and display has played a significant role in representations of disability and the construction of 'abnormal' bodies. Scholars including Petra Kuppers and Rosemarie Garland-Thomson both address the cultural cachet of the bodies with disabilities as sources of fascination and wonder, but a wonder that is made illicit through its connection to physical non-normativity. Kuppers discusses the freakshows and medical theatres of the nineteenth century as sites where the bodies of persons with disabilities were displayed because of their 'freakishness,' a context that Gaga plays into, through the display of her own body as freakish through the use of fashion (which will be discussed shortly).[12] Garland-Thomson argues that these kinds of bodily displays respond to the desire to see, to marvel at, and to self-identify against 'different' bodies. She says that people both want to look and are averse to looking, arguing that:

> Because staring at disability is considered illicit looking, the body is at once the to-be-looked-at and not-to-be-looked-at, further dramatizing the staring encounter by making viewers furtive and the viewed defensive. Staring thus creates disability as a state of absolute difference rather than simply one more variation in human form.[13]

Garland-Thomson argues that staring has a complex position in power relations: on one hand, it regulates, it surveys, it stigmatizes; on the other hand, there is power for the staree in staring back, in inviting the stare in some situations while denying it in others.[14] The mechanisms of celebrity and display further complicate these power relationships. The delight in watching a disintegrating pop stars is in part a result of the desire to watch someone lose power. When Gaga uses representations of disability, she is creating a different power relationship, destabilizing the connection between herself, as a person on display, and audience members by inviting the stare to her body, in ways that draw attention to the hypervisibility of female celebrities. The ambiguity between public and private spaces in 'Paparazzi' manipulates the relationship between staring and staring back.

'PAPARAZZI': DANCE, FASHION, AND THE VISUALIZATION OF DISABILITY

In the video for 'Paparazzi', Gaga's injured, disabled body becomes a locus of hypervisibility. Her body is physically limited and constrained as a result of technologies of fame: near the opening of the video, she is pushed off a balcony as photographers capture her image. She falls downwards, backed by a Vertigo-like spiral, while voices in the background call on her to strike a pose, as though she is at a fashion shoot. Photographers surround her while she lies prostrate on the ground, and a montage of newspaper headlines proclaim that Gaga has 'hit rock bottom', and that she is 'over', reproducing the commonly used media tropes that occur over and over again in descriptions of the downfall of stars. Her name in headlines, her body in stark relief against the twirling black and white spiral during her fall, her strangely bent form on the ground, and the voices of photographers calling out to her all call the eye and the ear to Gaga, who is represented as a casualty of her own celebrity.

Gaga, however, is not kept knocked down for long. The scene shifts to her returning home and emerging from a limousine in a wheelchair, entering the foyer of a mansion which becomes the public space of celebrity discussed above. In this space, her now-disabled body becomes hypervisible, fetishized, and idealized. Her dance movements as she stands up from her wheelchair and accepts a proffered pair of crutches, incorporate stereotypically spastic gestures associated with disability. Disability is not merely represented through costuming, but becomes part of Gaga's choreography and gestural vocabulary, and, as mentioned earlier, transforming the private space of the home into a public, theatrical space. The movements of her dancers, meanwhile, both mimic her stilted gestures but demonstrate more freedom of motion, constantly framing and drawing attention to her broken body.

Her dancers are mostly people of color. A group of four black and Latino male dancers escort her from the car to the doorway, constantly outlining her body with their hands, guiding the eye towards it. Once inside, four women dancers—two black and two white—emerge, flaking Gaga like an honor guard, their movements, again, drawing the eye to Gaga. In this visual context, Gaga's whiteness is striking, and cannot be divorced from the representation of her body as disabled. Her whiteness assists in constructing the particular narrative of disability that the 'Paparazzi' conveys. Paul Smith argues that people of color are at greater risk of 'acquiring disability labels and losing ability capacities', often as a result of poverty and social inequality that result from racism and prohibit access to needed social services. Eugenicist scientific approaches, he argues, conflate race and disability, using theories of genetics to tie disability to race, and resulting in social and historical context in disability-based discrimination has overwhelmingly affected people of color.[15] Meanwhile, scholars in disability studies have been calling for increased attention to the ways in which disability is raced, as much of the current scholarship, while extremely valuable, has silently assumed a white disabled subject as its focus.[16] Gaga's whiteness, then, which is heightened by the people of color she surrounds herself with, is a key element in how her disabled body is glamorized in the 'Paparazzi' video. The video portrays her as white and extremely wealthy, able to fill a mansion with her non-white staff, and, as Annaham remarks, able to overcome her disability, likely because she has access to resources that allow her to do so. Her disability becomes part of a romanticized narrative of a star's triumph over hardship, but this narrative is only available to her because her disabled body is of a particular race, and of a particular wealthy social class.

Figure 10.1   Still from 'Paparazzi'.

Furthermore, Gaga's body in the 'Paparazzi' video is supported by crutches and by wheelchairs and is encased in metal, making her seem almost robotic (see Figure 10.1). In the scene where she staggers out of her wheelchair, she is dressed in a metal body suit, with a skullcap and gauntlets, looking as much mechanical as she does human. This imagery evokes Donna Haraway's cyborg metaphor, which envisions the cyborg as capable of challenging binaristic and reductive was of conceiving of identity. Haraway's conception of the cyborg draws heavily on discourses of disability, figuring the use of technological prosthetics as means of supplementing bodies and forging disruptive new identities. She says that, 'for the cyborg, in imagination and in other practice, machines can be prosthetic devices, intimate components, friendly selves. We don't need organic holism to give impermeable wholeness'.[17] The cyborg body, according to Haraway, is a body made whole through technology, and a body that uses technology as a vehicle for transcendence. Sharon Betcher, however, critiques Haraway's insistence on transcendence. She argues that, while cyborg metaphors have made certain scholarly discourses on disability possible, they have precluded others. People with disabilities, she argues, 'have typically been made figuratively to speak for a cyborgian existence without being allowed to speak up, or, in Haraway's terms, to "witness"'.[18] Betcher's chief concern is with Haraway's insistence on technology as a vehicle for transcendence and holism, a construction, she argues, that figures disabled bodies as incomplete and assumes a compulsory quest for holism, while overestimating the transcendent capabilities of technology.[19] While technology can enable in some respects, it has not succeeded in effacing the social structures that continually marginalize people with disabilities. Transcending the body, then, remains an impossibility.

In 'Paparazzi', however, Gaga's robotic body is part of a transcendent narrative of triumph over and through fame. Throughout the video, she uses technology like any good cyborg would, manipulating the media's technology—specifically, their cameras—to facilitate her character's eventual triumph. At the end of the video, victorious over her abusive boyfriend, whom she has poisoned, her face flashes a robotic smile that looks like a computer glitch, suggesting that she is not entirely human, and that her in- or post-humanity enabled her success. Likewise, in an image from the LaChapelle shoot, she is shown in metal body suit from the 'Paparazzi' video, towering over a post-apocalyptic city, with bodies at her feet.[20] She is portrayed as a victor, as a shining Messianic figure. This kind of transcendence and victory over the flesh represents Gaga as both disabled and enabled by fame and by her post-human body. While the drive for transcendence is problematic and ignores the material realities of disability, the fantasy that Gaga presents is compelling, and gestures towards aspirational and utopic ways of conceiving of the relationship between technology and bodies.

While 'Paparazzi' represents Gaga's most literal use of disability imagery to date, her subsequent videos continue to connect disability and technology in more subtle ways that have particular gendered implications. Her videos for 'Bad Romance' and 'Telephone' continue to use very stilted, spastic choreography, of the kind seen in 'Paparazzi', and although it is tied less literally to disability, Gaga is still tapping into a context of how bodies with disabilities are understood. In the 'Bad Romance' video, for instance, Gaga and her retinue of dancers emerge from plastic, coffin-like cases labeled 'MONSTER', and move, zombie-like, across the set, connecting alterity, via Gaga's oft-employed trope of monstrousness, to the same kind of physical movements that signified disability in Gaga's 'Paparazzi' video and MTV video award performance. And even in the absence of disability masquerade in other videos, her use of fashion frequently impairs her body. Gaga wears clothes in ways that control her body to the point of impairing it: in the 'Bad Romance' video, she teeters around on uncomfortably high, constrictive Alexander McQueen heels that visually transform her feet into lobster-like claws; in later scenes in the 'Paparazzi' video, her dance moves are hampered by the sheer size of the ruffles of her dress; in live performances she often has to push her costume out of the way and adjust it so that she can dance or sit at the piano; and she has appeared in public wearing clothes that cover part or all of her face, conceivably limiting the use of her senses.

Gaga's sometimes outlandish style seems to be a deliberate attempt to construct herself as that freakish object to be looked at, but also has gendered implications. Fashion functions as a technology of the self and of the body, enhancing the body, extending its visibility, and providing individuals with a means of articulating and developing identities. Fashion is also, however, connected with policing the body, and, for women in particular, with disciplining and controlling the body. Gaga's extreme use of fashion is an exaggeration of the modes of self-discipline that many women undergo in their day to day lives, demonstrating that the overexposure engendered by celebrity is an amplification of the kinds of mechanisms of exposure and surveillance that even the non-famous face. Furthermore, Garland-Thomson argues that, through such practices, the bodies of non-disabled women become coded as disabled. She says that the practices of femininity have configured female bodies as disabled, citing foot binding, scarification, clitoridectomy, and corseting as examples of 'socially accepted, encouraged, even compulsory forms of female disablement that, ironically, are socially enabling, increasing a woman's value and status.'[21]

The practices of beauty can thus function as practices of disablement. They are heightened in the culture of celebrity, and Gaga's use of fashion speaks to the double edged sword of fame: even while it grants social mobility, it nonetheless impairs and controls by subjecting stars to a normalizing cultural gaze. However, any apparent critique by Gaga is undermined by her continued construction of disability as abnormal. Garland-Thomson argues that 'even while the normative female body is the negative term opposing the male body [. . .] it is also simultaneously the privileged term opposing the abnormalized female body.'[22] Gaga's narrative of fame is, again, invested in an ableist understanding of disability that relies on the normativity of non-disabled bodies.

VOICE, DAMAGE, AND AUTHENTICITY

While the implications of Gaga's visual references to physical disability are, I might venture, somewhat evident, her vocal allusions to bodily compromise are more elusive. However, Garland-Thomson's assertion that the female body is always already a disabled, lacking entity in opposition to the male body derives from a historical context in which the voice has played a key role in defining feminine physical and mental alterity.

The phenomenon of hysteria provides a particularly salient example of how women's bodily functions are discursively linked to failures of the mind and excess emotion, and, in turn, disordered vocalization. Rachel P. Maines documents how various illnesses and bodily disorders have been historically termed hysteric, arguing that these instances of physical excess are fundamentally tied to psychological states. She documents the range of symptoms that have been associated with hysteria at various points in history, including 'anxiety, sleeplessness, irritability, nervousness, erotic fantasy, sensations of heaviness in the abdomen, lower pelvic edema, and vaginal lubrication', as well as loss of consciousness, and spells of loss of control over the body, and, most importantly for our purposes, aphasia and loss of language.[23]

Despite, and, in fact, because of this loss of language and loss of vocal expressivity, Janet L. Bezier argues that the figure of the hysteric, of the woman who has lost control over her voice, provides a somewhat ironic vehicle for feminine narrativity. Bezier argues that in French literature of the nineteenth century, the hysteric emerges as a figure through whom women could ventriloquize experiences of bodily mobility. She says that at that moment in French culture, 'the body of the hysteric—mobile, capricious, convulsive—was both metaphor and myth, emblem of whirling chaos and cathartic channeling of it. Fashioned in the image of the times, the hysteric offers surface glitter and inner disarray.'[24] Attempting to see hysteria as more than a pathology, Bezier argues that hysteria offers important narrative possibilities:

> The silences and incoherences of hysteria were perceived as an invitation to narrate: it is precisely because they hysteric cannot tell her story that this story, in the form of a blank to be filled in, is so readily accessible as narrative matter. But also, it is because the hysteric's story is not only hers—it is a more inclusive cultural story that, repressed, can be spoken only in the Other's name—that the hysteric is so readily appropriated as narrative screen.[25]

While this may seem to be a mere appropriation of women's bodies to tell stories, Bezier argues that women writers used the figure of the hysteric in ways that, even while they upheld certain aspects of master narratives, also disrupted them, taking advantage of the liminal space occupied by the hysteric. These discourses of hysteria speak to an understanding of feminine psychological disorder as intrinsically embodied, and inexorably connected to the question of bodily, vocal expression. The conception of hysteria as an embodied state is further manifested through its purported remedies, which, as Maines documents, through the nineteenth and twentieth centuries, typically involved bringing women to orgasm through the use of various medical apparatuses that were the precursor to the modern vibrator, and thus make explicit a connection between bodily sensation and emotional and mental health.[26]

The use of vibrators and other such apparatuses represents an attempt to use technology to frame the excessive female body, a body pathologized and placed under the surveillance and supervision of doctors. These practices of medical surveillance connect to current practices of display and hypervisibility. In this context of display, the connection between hysteria and disordered vocalization informs how women's practices of music-making are experienced. Hysteria implies a connection between voice, mind, and body, and, as such suggests that singing responds to and creates both physical and mental feeling.[27]

Susan McClary has argued that, in opera, musical representations of feminine madness attempt to frame and constrain women, but that 'madwomen strain the semiotic codes from which they emerge, thereby throwing into high relief the assumptions concerning musical normativity and reason from which they must deviate.'[28] Displays of coloratura virtuosity, she argues, push against the formal framework of music, resisting containment. The excessive vocalizations of operatic madwomen translate mental and emotional states into vocal, and thus embodied, gestures.

Pop voices come up against different, albeit related frames. Depending on specific generic conventions, there is a cultural tendency to valorize voices that are perceived as somehow imperfect and damaged, voices in which bodily labor is audible. Stras argues that the so-called 'damaged', disrupted, or impaired voice holds a certain amount of cultural cachet, and is tied to discourses of authenticity. She argues that vocal disruption is heard as pathology, as suffering, disease, malfunction, abnormality, that it is connected to labor, authority, and authenticity, and that many singers have learned to simulate or manipulate damage in the voice, tapping into its affective power.[29] While this kind of stylistic choice is often naturalized and taken for granted, it is often very much a choice. Stras evocatively describes the painful practices she put her body through while training as a jazz singer, practices that involved causing harm to her vocal chords in order to produce the desired smoky, gravelly vocal sound.[30] These practices demonstrate that even voices heard as 'naturally' damaged are sometimes the result of deliberate labor and performance, that the 'authentic' qualities we hear in voices are quite often the result of affective practices that are taken for granted.

Following Stras then, I wonder what it means for a singer to self-consciously perform impairment, either when making a vocal sound with the body, or through technological means in post-production. Stras documents the ways in which singers use their bodies to manipulate and enhance, and create vocal damage for affective purposes, but Gaga's manipulation of her voice does not fit neatly into the discourses of affect and authenticity that Stras associates with the damaged voice. Rather, Gaga delights in inauthenticity and in artificiality. Her performances of vocal damage are so artificial that, like her use of faux-disabled choreography, there is no mistaking them for genuine impairment or disability. Instead, Gaga's vocal sound, mediated both by her body and by technology, becomes robotic and cyborg-like.

Gaga's music is constantly marked by a technologically-imposed vocal stutter. The opening 'Pa-pa-pa-pa-poker face' of 'Poker Face' is probably the most easily recognizable example, but it turns up again in songs including 'Starstruck', 'Paper Gangster', 'Telephone', and 'Dance in the Dark', among others. The use of stutter in American popular music, as documented by Daniel Goldmark has long functioned as a means of performing abnormality.[31] In 'Starstruck', the stutter occurs both in Gaga's vocal track and in that of her backing vocalists. The opening of vocal riff introduces us to a robotically bent version of Gaga's voice. 'Groove, slam, work it back, filter that, baby, bump that track', she chants, her voice quavering and robotic.

She wavers on ah vowels, an effect that sounds like a digital skip in the record. It sounds like her unnatural voice is incapable of achieving the vocal authority and authenticity of the flesh, and is always threatening to collapse. The line repeats three times, and on the third repeat, it sounds as though Gaga's voice is finally under control, a control that is belied by the next vocal line, in which her vocal quaver reemerges. In the verses, Gaga's voice seems almost normal, however, a sign of computerized vocal damage comes in at the end of each line. Lyrically, the song equates Gaga's body with the technology of dance music, of recording and mixing. 'Put your hands on my waist, pull the fader', she sings, 'Would you make me number one on your playlist?' This conflation makes it seem as though her body has become sound, as thought it has become the ultimate, technologically-mediated body of a celebrity, a body as a faltering sound object that you can own and put on your playlist.

The original usage of such technology, to repair or improve the voice, implies an ideological tension in popular music, a tension between the desire for an authentic, imperfect voice, as Stras describes, and the desire to manage and control a voice to the point of perfection. While the two poles in this dichotomy are associated with different genres of popular music, both communicate a system of aesthetic values that implies a fundamental dissatisfaction with the human voice as it is, and a need to change and modify it for affective purposes. I turn once again to Thomson, and her argument about the sense of to-be-looked-at-ness that she attributes to the bodies of people with disabilities. While such bodies demand the gaze and the stare, and in doing so, become object of wonder that controls that gaze, I would argue that the damaged voice creates a sense of what I would call to-be-heard-ness; one that draws attention to and insists upon the primacy of the voice as a function of the body, and, in Gaga's case, a damaged voice as a function of a damaged body, both resulting from the traumatic violence of fame.

If, as Stras contends, such vocal damage is already a performative affect, Gaga's deliberately artificial performance of damage is further artificializing the already-constructed sounds that are associated with vocal authenticity, drawing on the trickster-like technological affinity of the cyborg. Haraway refers to her cyborg's voice as 'powerful infidel heteroglossia', and 'an imagination of a feminist speaking in tongues'.[32] While Haraway refers to a metaphoric, discursive voice, rather than to a sounding voice, her use of 'heteroglossia' and 'speaking in tongues' refers to actual narratives of religious, ecstatic, irrational, and, consequently, feminized vocalization. Technology enables the cyborg to reframe and re-appropriate such tropes of feminine discursivity. Just as the hysteric is able to subvert master narratives, so too is the cyborg. Similarly, then, Gaga's cyborg voice reframes the way women's singing voices are understood by evoking and disrupting narratives of women's voices as disordered. Her performance of vocal disorder draws attention to the artificiality of such narratives, like a parodic gesture that signifies on discourses of vocal authenticity and authority.

Gaga's moments of technologically performed moments of vocal instability work in tandem with moments in which bodily vocal labor is audible. These are moments of when sounds of vocal damage appear to result from Gaga's physical manipulation of her own voice. Both 'Dance in the Dark' and 'Bad Romance', in particular, feature moments of what I would describe as vocal ugliness and abjection, in which sounds that can be heard as vocal expressions of pain and pleasure come through, evoking a 'real' (albeit totally performed) non-technological body. 'Dance in the Dark' opens with moans that alternate between sounding pleasured and pained, culminating in a deeply pained-sounding vocal outcry, all the while buttressed by loud, stuttering, masculine background vocals. As the song progresses, Gaga's recorded voice is multiplied and layered over the stuttering background vocals. Gaga's lead vocal becomes unintelligible and difficult to distinguish in the overall soundscape. This digital manipulation becomes intertwined with sounds of bodily disgust, pleasure, and pain that sound like Gaga is creating them with her body: she groans at the ends of phrases, and allows her voice to dwell in the very bottom of her vocal register where it sounds uncomfortably out of place.

Likewise, 'Bad Romance' includes several moments where Gaga gasps and moans in a way that sounds abject and both disgusted and disgusting. In addition, her vocal timbre in the verses of this song is in a much lower register than where she sings. The resulting sound is rough and unpolished, and when she spits out words like 'horror' in this low register, they sound somewhat dark and monstrous. I hear these moments as performances of vocal damage. They occur, not coincidentally, in songs that evoke violence and overexposure—in 'Dance in the Dark', for instance, she sings 'baby likes to dance in the dark, cause when he's looking she falls apart'—and allow an abject-sounding voice to emerge, signifying on the cultural valorization of feminine damage and self-impairment.

The song 'Speechless' from *The Fame Monster* is a clear tribute to the rock power ballad genre that Tavia Nyong'o compares specifically to Freddie Mercury's ballads, connecting 'Speechless' to a performer acknowledged as a master of camp and excess.[33] Gaga's vocal affectations in 'Speechless' border on the melodramatic: they are theatrical to the point of being over the top, which, I contend, emphasizes the performativity of her use of vocal damage.

The introduction to 'Speechless' opens with long, vocal 'ohs' outlining a wide-ranging, melody that immediately pulls the listener into a heightened emotional scape. As the song progresses, Gaga navigates the melody competently, managing extreme registererial shifts and extravagant sweeps with relative ease, however, moments of vocal ugliness break through and punctuate those lines. At key moments in the song, her vocal delivery seems sloppy; the shape of her notes inconsistent. She sings 'could we fix you if you broke? Is your punch line just a joke?' in a high chest voice, and she sounds like she is straining at the top of this vocal register, as her timbre becomes almost weepy. Likewise, she slurs her pitches when she sings 'I can't believe how you slurred at me', and again when she describes her antagonist's 'Johnny Walker eyes'. While these instances could be read as mere musical mimicry of the lyrics, the effect of these exaggerated vocal gestures is to highlight the affectation inherent in this performance. These gestures function as excessive, heightened appeals for emotional sympathy, and seem to the mirror instances of pain and damage audible in 'Bad Romance' and 'Dance in the Dark'. At the end of the final verse, Gaga sings 'I'll never write a song, won't even sing along, I'll never love again', a harshness and roughness dramatically entering her voice on those words. In 'Speechless', a song that is about vocal disruption, the sweeping vocal lines seem to carry and buttress these instances of vocal instability, their exaggerated, emotionality drawing attention to the art and artifice of the damaged voice.

When read alongside Gaga's visual representations of disability, these kinds of tactical deployments of vocal damage speak to the discourses of musical authenticity that Stras discusses, but also subvert how they typically work. The narrative used in performances like 'Paparazzi' construct Gaga as a romantic heroine who must overcome physical strife. The manipulation of her voice, meanwhile, both gestures to how the understanding of vocal damage is often seen as a consequence of living such a narrative, and thus as marker of authenticity, while her also demonstrating the artifice behind vocal authenticity. Through her cyborg body and robotic voice, Gaga denaturalizes practices of vocal affectation that are often unacknowledged. This performance strategy constructs celebrity itself as a disabling force, while concurrently figuring technology as an enabling force and a subversive tool.

The question remains, though, as to how Gaga's physical and vocal performances contribute to discourses of disability. Certainly, Gaga performs from a position of privilege: her social status and cultural capital give her the means to play with signifiers of disability for her own benefit. She uses such signifiers as part of a larger performance project that suggests that celebrity culture can be both a vehicle for transcendence, and a disabling source of strife. It is, of course, possible that Gaga has experienced or does experience a disability, and to automatically assume otherwise is a sign of the privileging of non-disabled viewpoints. However, audiences cannot know for certain whether or not she may experience an invisible disability and her deliberate construction of a pop persona depends on audiences not knowing too many truths about her (witness the way she coyly dealt with rumors that she was transsexual, embedding references to such gossip in her videos, while not addressing it outright). As such, regardless of whether it draws on her lived experience, Gaga's use of disability imagery is part of her self-construction: it surprises, it tantalizes, it creates mystique.

Gaga's songs and videos deftly navigate the theatricality that is so often a particularly salient feature of pop, calling into question the limits of artifice, while highlighting the ways in which identities are performed. Her fantastical enactments of disability may enable her audience members with or without disabilities to re-envision their identities and the social construction of their bodies. Ultimately, however, Gaga's self-aware performance of celebrity relies on dominant stereotypes and tropes of disability that risk romanticizing and misappropriating peoples experiences of disability, even while she challenges other norms. If, as Dyer argues, we make sense of our lives through celebrities, it's important to point to the implications of Gaga's performance of fame, not just for what it says about the lives of stars, but also for what it might be saying about the rest of us.

NOTES

1. These images can be viewed on LaChapelle's website: http://www.davidlachapelle.com/series/lady-gaga/.
2. Wheelchair Dancer, 'Lady Gaga And The Wheelchair', 16 September 2009 (online at: http://cripwheels.blogspot.co.uk/2009/09/lady-gaga-and-wheelchair.html). Kuppers offers a more extended critique of the use of wheelchair imagery by non-disabled performers. She says that 'when non-disabled people don disability paraphernalia or masquerade as disabled, the results rarely offer interesting insights to disability scholars looking for resistances to dominant images of disability [. . .]. Nondisabled people rarely work with the exciting sensual aspects of wheelchair use familiar to disabled performers, for instance the smooth and graceful curve that is impossible to achieve by bipedals, or the full-movement range of wheelchair athleticism.' (Petra Kuppers, 'The Wheelchair's Rhetoric: The Performance of Disability', *TDR: The Drama Review*, vol. 51, no. 4 [Winter 2007], 81). Similarly, Gaga's wheelchair dancer is not a subversive representation of disability that challenges dominant images, but rather, reproduces those images.
3. Comment from a trenchcoat on Wheelchair Dancer, 'Lady Gaga And The Wheelchair'.
4. Giorgio Agamben, *State of Exception*, tr. Kevin Attell (Chicago, IL: University of Chicago Press, 2005 [2003]), 1.
5. Kay Dickinson, '"Believe?": Vocoders, Digitalized Female Identity, and Camp', *Popular Music*, vol. 20, no. 3 (October 2001), 337.
6. Laurie Stras, 'The Organ of the Soul: Voice, Damage, and Affect', in *Sounding Off: Theorizing Disability in Music*, ed. Neil Lerner and Joseph Straus (New York, NY: Routledge, 2006), 173.
7. Nina Eidsheim, 'Synthesizing Race: Towards an Analysis of the Performativity of Vocal Timbre', *Revista Transcultural de Musica*, vol. 13 (2009), (online at: http://www.sibetrans.com/trans/a57/synthesizing-race-towards-an-analysis-of-the-performativity-of-vocal-timbre) <accessed: 28 September 2011>.
8. Lady Gaga, 'Biography', *Lady Gaga Official Site* (online at: http://www.ladygaga.com) <accessed 29 May 2010>.
9. See, for instance, Jocelyn Vena, 'Lady Gaga Says Decision to Cancel Kanye West Tour was "Mutual"', *MTV.com* (2 October 2009) (online at: http://www.mtv.com/news/articles/1622913/lady-gaga-decision-cancel-kanye-west-tour-was-mutual.jhtml) <accessed: 14 May 2011>.

10. Richard Dyer, *Heavenly Bodies: Film Stars and Society* (New York, NY: Routledge, 2004), 16.
11. Annaham, 'The Transcontinental Disability Choir: Disability Chic? (Temporary) Disability in Lady Gaga's "Paparazzi"', *Bitchmedia* (December 20, 2009) (online at: http://bitchmagazine.org/post/the-transcontinental-disability-choir-disabililty-chic-temporary-disability-in-lady-gagas-papar) <accessed: 3 April 2010>.
12. Petra Kuppers, *Disability and Contemporary Performance: Bodies on the Edge* (London: Routledge, 2003), 33.
13. Rosemarie Garland-Thompson, 'The Politics of Staring: Visual Rhetorics of Disability in Popular Photography', in *Disability Studies: Enabling the Humanities*, ed. Rosemarie Garland-Thomson *et al.* (New York, NY: Modern Languages Association, 2002), 57.
14. *Ibid.*, 53.
15. Paul Smith, 'Whiteness, Normal Theory, and Disability Studies', *Disability Studies Quarterly*, vol. 24, no. 2 (Spring 2004) (online at: http://dsq-sds.org/article/view/491/668) <accessed: 4 April 2013>.
16. See, for example, Chris Bell, 'Introducing White Disability Studies: A Modest Proposal,' in *The Disability Studies Reader*, ed. Lennard J. Davis (New York, NY: Routledge, 2006), 275–282, and Joanne Murray Ormandy, *Racing Critical Disability Discourse* (unpublished PhD dissertation, University of Toronto, 2008).
17. Donna Haraway, 'A Cyborg Manifesto: Science, Technology, and Socialist-Feminism in the Late Twentieth Century', in *Simians, Cyborgs, and Women: The Reinvention of Nature* (New York, NY: Routledge, 1991), 178.
18. Sharon Betcher, 'Putting My Foot (Prosthesis, Crutches, Phantom) Down: Considering Technology as Transcendence in the Writings of Donna Haraway', *Women's Studies Quarterly*, vol. 29, no. 3/4 (Fall/Winter 2001), 38.
19. *Ibid.*, 47.
20. As noted previously, this image can be seen on LaChapelle's website.
21. Rosemarie Garland-Thomson, *Extraordinary Bodies: Figuring Physical Disability in American Culture and Literature* (New York, NY: Columbia University Press, 1997), 27.
22. *Ibid.*, 28.
23. Rachel Maines, *The Technology of Orgasm: Hysteria, the Vibrator and Women's Sexual Satisfaction* (Baltimore, MD: Johns Hopkins University Press, 1999), 23.
24. Janet L. Bezier, *Ventriloquized Bodies: Narratives of Hysteria in 19th Century France.* (Ithaca, NY: Cornell University Press, 1994), 9.
25. *Ibid.*
26. Maines, *The Technology of Orgasm*, 11.
27. Singing as a feminized, embodied act predates nineteenth century conceptions of hysteria by several centuries. Examples abound, for instance, in discourses of both sacred and secular music of the Renaissance and Baroque periods. In *Monteverdi's Unruly Women*, Bonnie Gordon discusses, among numerous other examples of this discourse, the way women's mouths and sexual organs were conflated in early-modern medicine, often in ways that evoked the infernal abyss, connecting women's vocality to excessive bodily fluids and a lack of control (Bonnie Gordon, *Monteverdi's Unruly Women: The Power of Song in Early-Modern Italy* (Cambridge: Cambridge University Press, 2004), 79).
28. Susan McClary, *Feminine Endings: Music, Gender, and Sexuality*, (Minneapolis, MN: University of Minnesota Press, 1991), 86.
29. Stras, 'The Organ of the Soul', 173.

30. *Ibid.*, 175.
31. Daniel Goldmark, 'Stuttering in American Popular Song, 1890–1930', in *Sounding Off: Theorizing Disability in Music*, ed. Neil Lerner and Joseph N. Straus (New York, NY: Routledge, 2006), 97.
32. Haraway, 'A Cyborg Manifesto', 181.
33. Tavia Nyong'o, 'Freddy Mercury Deconstructed Roundtable', 2010 Pop Conference, EMP Museum, Seattle, WA, 16 April 2010.

11 Trans/Affect

Monstrous Masculinities and the Sublime Art of Lady Gaga

Theresa L. Geller

Gaga is a hypothetical form of feminism, one that lives in between the 'what' and the 'if': what if we gendered people according to their behavior? What if gender shifted over the course of a lifetime—what if someone began life as a boy but became a boygirl and then a boy/man? What if some males are ladies, some ladies are butch, some butches are women, some women are gay, some gays are feminine, some femmes are straight, and some straight people don't know what the hell is going on?[1]

Let's face it; Jo Calderone made all of us doubt our sexuality at one point.[2]

THE ART OF LADY GAGA

In *Gaga Feminism: Sex, Gender and the End of Normal*, J. Jack Halberstam presents a manifesto of, and for, millennial feminist and gender politics. In its wide-ranging and eclectic survey of popular culture and the social field it transects, shapes, and mediates, Lady Gaga is the figure and figuration to the ground of contemporary gender politics. Indeed, for Halberstam, Gaga is no longer a personal pronoun, but a noun—gaga—describing a set of oppositional, queer gender relations: 'the genius of gaga allows Lady Gaga to become the vehicle for performing the very particular arrangements of bodies, genders, desires, communication, race, affect, and flow that we might now want to call gaga feminism.'[3] Notably, for Halberstam, this 'genius' is exemplified by Gaga's performance at MTV's Video Music Awards in 2011, which 'Lady Gaga' did not attend; in her place, performing her hit song, 'Yoü and I', and accepting her awards, was Jo Calderone. No doubt, Lady Gaga has certainly pushed at the fault-lines of all sorts of social norms in her meteoric rise to status of fame monster. From meat dresses to egg yolks, her little monsters have stayed loyal throughout. However, at the 2011 VMAs, she took her subversive performance art to the next level, exploding the line between nature and artifice, authenticity and glamour, boy and girl, 'you and I' altogether, with the thoroughly committed incarnation of her alter, Calderone. Halberstam only briefly sketches this particular incarnation, taking it as a paragon of what one might call the cultural logic of gaga feminism, which stands, for the author, as 'a form of political expression that masquerades as naïve nonsense but that actually participates in big and meaningful forms of critique.'[4] Yet, to understand—and amplify—these forms of critique, I want to examine much more closely this exceptional moment in gaga feminism and contemporary popular culture generally.

In line with what Bill Nichols calls the 'contemporary moment of cultural study', we might begin to think of such moments in popular cultural history as loaded with both meaning and affect, that is, popular culture, and even Gaga herself, 'comes to be regarded as a socially constructed category serving socially significant ends.'[5] Lady Gaga is certainly an exemplar of this as a site of much cultural debate while using this position herself to effect political change (for example, fighting for gays in the military or bringing attention to the issue of young women's HIV risks). And this accrual of social significance has yet to wane, as is apparent in the ways Gaga becomes *gaga*—an adjectival modifier in Halberstam's new manifesto of millennial feminism. Yet, rather than explain Gaga's social significance, the argument that follows is shaped by the methodological stakes set out by this moment of cultural study, in which 'the goal of providing explanations for cultural forms and social practices loses its appeal in favor of an emphasis on the (preferably thick) interpretation of specific forms, practices and effects.'[6] While for Halberstam, 'gaga' signifies a kind of cognitive map of the larger state of contemporary feminism, with its concomitant play of genders and sexualities, what I will outline is a particular set of coordinates on that map, which I will chart via a thick description of Gaga's embodiment of Jo Calderone, one delineating a very particular arrangement of genders and their affects. Affect has a central role here, constituting the longitude in the conceptual grid I want to plot. If gaga is a form of feminism, as Halberstam defines it, 'that lives between the "what" and the "if"', then what emerges from this gap or interval is measured or recognized in terms of the affect it generates. 'Affect,' according to Gregory J. Seigworth and Melissa Gregg, 'arises in the midst of *in-between-ness*: in the capacities to act and be acted upon [. . .] affect is found in those intensities that pass body to body [. . .] in those resonances that circulate about, between, and sometimes stick to bodies and worlds.'[7] The intensities of affect that pass from body to body are all the more intensified when those bodies are unstable—are, in fact, transitive themselves. Jo Calderone, in this way, embodies a specific form of affect, identified here as 'trans/affect', a constellation of affects that refuse to solidify into a stable point but rather reside in the in- between, in the transitive, in the trans body, perpetually sliding between genders, ethnicities, classes, desires, and sexualities.

Although most of the American public was introduced to Jo Calderone at the 2011 VMAs, Calderone actually emerged as a conceptual project in

Vogue Hommes Japan (Autumn/Winter 2010).[8] As Gaga herself explains, in *V Magazine*, Gaga Memorandum #4, which she cc'd to 'intellectuals', 'Ms. Vreeland', 'art historians', 'the world', and 'Jo Calderone':

> My study of gender manipulation, though not a new endeavor in the fields of art and fashion, has been both revealing and terrifying—perhaps my most emotionally challenging performance to date. Beginning as an invention of my mind, Jo Calderone was created with Nick Knight as a mischievous experiment. [. . .] Given the nature of this *V Magazine* issue, an exploration of 'the model', I felt it appropriate to investigate, in diary form, how the past few months of my work have been a deliberate attack on the 'idea' of the 'modern model', or, in my case, the 'modern pop singer'. How can we remodel the model? In a culture that attempts to quantify beauty with a visual paradigm and almost mathematical standard, how can we fuck with the malleable minds of onlookers and shift the world's perspective on what's beautiful? I asked myself this question. And the answer? Drag. [9]

According to Gaga, she and Knight omitted gender references and shopped the images out, providing a backstory for Calderone as Gaga's former lover. This raised some questions in the popular press and the blogosphere, but nothing like Jo's appearance at the VMAs. Unlike other female performers who flirted with drag in their VMA performances but ultimately resumed their 'authentic' femme selves at some point in the performance—Madonna, Britney, and Annie Lennox being the most frequently cited examples—Gaga never appeared before the public. As Gaga describes it: '[I]n the fantasy of performance I imagined (or hoped) the world would weigh both individuals against one another as real people, not as one person playing two. Lady Gaga versus Jo Calderone, not Lady Gaga "as." That would be the intention of the process, to co-exist with an alternate version of myself—in the same universe.'[10] It was Calderone who was interviewed, Calderone who performed with Queen guitarist Brian May, and most pointedly, Calderone who accepted the award for best *female* performance, on behalf of Gaga, for the video, 'Born This Way'. Without the reassuring gesture to an authentic self—the very thing deconstructed in Calderone's monologue prelude to the performance of 'Yoü and I'—the audience appeared to grow increasingly uncomfortable, unsure what to make of Jo's appropriation of Gaga's 'spotlight'. The media response was equally befuddled; headlines followed which registered quizzical disapproval: 'Was it too much?', 'Brilliant or creepy?', or, 'Did Lady Gaga just end her career with this embarrassing Jo Calderone?' Even die-hard fans were perplexed, a few outright violent in their online postings. Yet, many followers—Gaga's 'little monsters'—were happy their Mother Monster now had a mate.

So, what about Jo Calderone was so disruptive? Notably, few could explain their reaction to the scenario, though reactions abounded; the cameras caught Britney Spears, mouth agape and furrowed brow of confusion, and then cut to other confused members of the audience, like Justin Bieber, frowning (possibly disdainful, possibly because he himself might be implicated in such a parodic gender citation).[11] A large factor in the response was that this was not just a character assumed for a song (as in the case of Annie Lennox in Elvis drag), it was the embodiment of an alter identity. While this is not unknown in the music industry, most notably, David Bowie as Ziggy Stardust and the Thin White Duke, Garth Brooks releasing an album as Chris Gaines, and the more recent Childish Gambino (Donald Glover), rarely have they assumed identities across gender lines (with the exception of Gaga's contemporary, Nicki Minaj, as Roman Zolanski). Jo Calderone came out on stage and gave a long monologue before performing. Dressed in a dirty t-shirt and suit, greased back pompadour, drinking a beer and smoking a cigarette, Calderone proceeded to open up to the audience about his relationship with Gaga. In a masculine voice and New Jersey accent, Calderone performed an act of public intimacy, sharing with the audience details of his and Gaga's sex life and ultimate break-up:

> Hey. My name is Jo Calderone. And I was an asshole. Gaga? Yeah her—Lady Gaga. She left me. She said it always starts out good. And then the guys (being me, I'm one of the guys), they get crazy. I did; I got crazy. But she's fucking crazy too right? I mean she is FUCKING CRAZY. For example, she gets out of the bed, puts on the heels, she goes into the bathroom, I hear the water go on, she comes out of the bathroom dripping wet and she still got the heels on. And what's with the hair? At first it was sexy but now I'm just confused . . . And I think its great ya know, I think its really fucking great that she's such a star. A big beautiful star in the sky. But how am I supposed to shine? I mean I think I'd be okay with it you know if I found out that she was really . . . And maybe she is, I'm starting to think that's just who she is, maybe that's just who she is. Cause when she gets on that stage she holds nothing back. That spotlight. That big, round, deep, spotlight follows her wherever she goes. . . . I gotta get in there. When she comes, it's like she covers her face cause she doesn't want me to see that she can't stand to have one honest moment when nobody's watching. I want her to be real. But she says 'Jo, I'm not real. I'm theater. And you and I—this is just the rehearsal.'

Calderone's monologue invited the audience into an intimacy with Gaga, one both utterly fictional and yet, on some level, authentic—and one that Gaga herself never allows. Gaga would later say that her embodiment of Calderone forced her 'to excavate what he didn't like about me, or rather, what I struggle with liking about myself. Concurrently, I felt it necessary to imagine what the public expects of me during a performance of this magnitude—the opening of the VMAs—and how I might destroy this expectation in a variety of ways.'[12] That Gaga succeeded with her destruction seems of little doubt, but how that destruction was wrought, and the affect generated by that destruction, requires both thick description and nuanced, intersecting interpretive frameworks.[13]

The destruction of the model of the modern pop singer that Jo Calderone signals turns on a constellation of discursive and affective regimes, including but not limited to gender, sexuality, glamour, intimacy, ethnicity, class and even musical genres. What are the conditions that make such destruction possible? I suggest that these conditions are immanent to Gaga's philosophy (and what, following Halberstam, one might call 'gaga philosophy'), that of monstrosity. Since her emergence, Gaga has taken the trope of the monster to define her art and her movement. Yet, this goes beyond a simple catch-all phrase identifying her fanbase: the little monsters she repeatedly references, encourages, and thanks. As Halberstam identifies, 'Gaga feminism, or the feminism of the phony, the unreal, and the speculative, is simultaneously a *monstrous* outgrowth of the unstable concept of "woman" in feminist theory, a celebration of the joining of femininity to artifice.'[14] In fact, this monstrous outgrowth comes not just out of feminist theory but is also essential to the discourses Gaga herself produces about her cultural practices and performances and those to whom these particular speech acts are addressed. As she herself insists: 'I refuse to draw a distinction between what's real and what is artifice.' From this refusal, all sorts of monstrosities arise.

What the little monsters celebrate about Gaga is the very thing that makes her monstrous, the repudiation of the divide separating nature from artifice. As Elaine Graham details in her discussion of the post/human,

> [o]ne of the ways in particular in which the boundaries between humans and almost-humans have been asserted is through the discourse of monstrosity. Monsters serve both to mark the faultlines but also, subversively, to signal the fragility of such boundaries. They are truly 'monstrous'—as in things shown and displayed—in their simultaneous demonstration and destabilization of the demarcations by which cultures have separated nature from artifice.[15]

And, even though Gaga has consistently highlighted the artifice of what she herself identifies as the 'modern pop performer', it was the embodiment of drag king or transman (depending on one's reading), Jo Calderone, that seemed to wreak such destruction. While meat slabs and Kermit the frog dresses point to the fragility of boundaries, Calderone teetered on the brink of destroying them altogether. The destruction of expectation of which Gaga speaks is key to the structures of feeling evident in the reception of Jo Calderone as *monster*. Lady Gaga's fashion, voice, persona, and other markers of feminine masquerade, even female drag, as many have surmised, have led to widespread speculation as to whether Gaga has a penis, a rumor both acknowledged and mocked in the opening of the 'Telephone' video, in which women bodybuilders, cast as prison guards, declare its absence as we see Gaga climbing the bars of her jail cell, crime scene tape forming an X to mark the spot of its (supposed) absence.[16] In other words, it is specifically the presence or absence of the penis that mark Gaga at the limits of the human—as monstrosity. So, when Gaga claims an altogether different relationship to the phallus, as Calderone, the line is drawn between artifice as fashion, artifice as speculative, and the monstrous—a line, as Julia Kristeva has theorized, that delineates me from not me, a delineation between the 'I' and the abject.[17]

Significantly, this is the line that, for many, divides the celebration of femininity as fashion, as artifice, from gender as pure masquerade. Certainly her audiences expect Gaga to fuck with fashion: 'when Lady Gaga wears a meat dress or five-inch heels, she does so to call attention to the whimsy of personhood [. . .] and confuse the relations between surface and depth.'[18] Yet, Calderone does something more monstrous by exposing the tenuous (anti-)foundation of gender that is something more than fashion. What audiences may have been expecting was Gaga's style but what they got in Calderone was stylization: 'the effect of gender is produced through the stylization of the body and, hence, must be understood as the mundane way in which bodily gestures, movements, and styles of various kinds constitute the illusion of an abiding gendered self.'[19] In Calderone's movements, voice, gestures, and general stylization of the body something else is signaled, something no longer in the realm of whimsy but rather in the realm of the monstrous, with all its destructive force. As Kaja Silverman argues, 'Dress is one of the most important cultural implements for articulating and territorializing corporeality—for mapping erotogenic zones and for affixing a sexual identity.'[20] Jo Calderone's realness, however, goes far beyond fashion. For instance, for an audience that did not seem to give a second thought to Katy Perry's cheese-cube hat, Jo Calderone was outside the range of even Gaga's avant-garde norm. This is because Jo Calderone, the Jersey-born, Sicilian stock, Jameson swilling, chain-smoking working guy cum rock star signals, in short, the *dis*articulation and *de*territorialization of corporeality, at least of feminine corporeality. As Calderone himself says as he accepts the award for 'Best Video with a Message': 'Gaga isn't here.'

GLAMOROUS FEMININITIES AND MONSTROUS MASCULINITIES

So who remains? What sort of embodiment or bodily map does Calderone inhabit? Implicit in Silverman's definition of fashion is the way fashion works to align sex, gender, bodies, and desire; she insists that 'clothing is a necessary condition of subjectivity—that in articulating the body, it simultaneously articulates the psyche.'[21] Yet, inherent in this alignment is a bifurcation between 'male' and 'female' dress that assumes which bodies wear what styles of fashion: 'Female dress [. . .] has undergone frequent and often dramatic changes [. . .] These abrupt libidinal displacements [. . .] make the female body far less stable and localized than its male counterpart.'[22] While Gaga's fans have come to expect dramatic, ironic, even parodic changes in fashion, Calderone signals a destruction of that very expectation by radically altering the relationship of figure (of fashion) to ground (of gender). It might be argued, in fact, that fashion, and its inherent division, are the very grounds of possibility for such as destruction to take place. In other words, not for nothing has drag been (mis)read and (mis)appropriated from Butler's *Gender Trouble* as *the* model of gender performativity. As Butler has pointed out, her goal was never to promote drag as some sort of ideal 'model for resistance', but rather 'to combat forms of essentialism which claimed that gender is a truth that is somehow there, interior to the body [. . .] something which, natural or not, is treated as given.'[23] To this extent, it is important to see beneath the work of drag a radical interrogation, indeed, the conditions of possibility for the deconstruction of gender (essentialism).

Jo Calderone, in other words, is not reducible to Gaga donning male garb.[24] Rather, as Twitter user Boygaga avows in the epigraph, Calderone makes us all doubt our sexuality—with the slippery, multiple meanings of this term very much in play. How Calderone throws sexuality into doubt is integrally connected with the function of drag, and the signifying practices that inextricably tie sexuality to gender. Both Butler and Gaga provide evocative, and related, responses to the question: 'Why drag?'[25] According to Gaga,

> [t]he performance of Jo is meant to manipulate the visualization of gender in as many ways as I possibly could. And in a completely different way, sort of do that by creating what seems to be a straight man—a straight and quite relatable American man. I wanted to see how I could take someone who is so approachable and so relatable and press a much more unrelatable issue [. . .] [I wanted to see] how I could put someone who is challenging all of those things in a very pop culture moment and force people to deal with it no matter how uncomfortable or exciting it may be.[26]

From the mainstream responses, one might surmise that discomfort was the overriding affective response to this trans incarnation sharing Gaga's fame, or as Jo puts it, 'that big, round, deep, spotlight.' For Butler, too, drag, and the gender trouble it indexes, generates a set of propositions that include: 'When one performance of gender is considered real and another false, or when one presentation of gender is considered authentic, and another fake, then we conclude that a certain ontology of gender is conditioning these judgments, an ontology (an account of what gender *is*) that is also put into crisis by the performance of gender in such a way that these judgments are undermined or become impossible to make.'[27] In other words, while all gender is a performance, a *subversive* gender performance is one that throws into crisis hegemonic gender norms and their very conditions of possibility. By putting the ontology of gender into crisis, drag (and transgender) confronts us with the *epistemological* foundations of gender, which reveal gender as a doing as opposed to a being.

Jo Calderone represents a subversive gender performance because of the way he presses on an 'unrelatable issue', indeed, presses on the unreal itself. Of course, Gaga's gender performance always pushes on the borders of the real, her hyperbolized femininity itself an insistent reminder of the contemporary pop singer as (always already) hyperreal spectacle. So what makes Jo Calderone different from Gaga's other personae (mermaid, cyborg, and such)? One especially salient reason turns on the question of the real, of authentic; or, as Gaga puts it, Jo is 'a straight and quite relatable American man.' Key to my analysis is Gaga's own insight about the affective response to her turning normative masculinity, a very specific sort of masculinity that MTV struck ratings pay-dirt with in its phenomenally successful *Jersey Shore*, into a drag king performance. Calderone signals a very familiar, assumedly *authentic,* masculinity within its particular moment of popular culture, and the context of MTV. In explicitly referencing a reality show version of masculinity—and a highly profitable one at that—Jo Calderone deploys drag as a critical intervention into the media's own investments in the discursive (and monetary) claims of the real. A crucial element that grounds this reality is the binary that poses Gaga's fashion as art/ifice and, say, The Situation as real. If, as Silverman argues, 'endless transformations within female clothing construct female sexuality and subjectivity in ways that are at least potentially disruptive, both of gender and of the symbolic order,' than fashion for men works, like the gender binary itself, 'by freezing the male body into phallic rigidity, the uniform of orthodox male dress makes it a rock against which the waves of female fashion crash in vain.'[28] In this way, Gaga's usual VMA drag might have been yet another wave, disruptive but expected; however, Jo Calderone thaws the phallic rigidity of *Jersey Shore* masculinity by drawing attention, via drag, to the 'three dimensions of significant corporeality: anatomical sex, gender identity, and gender performance.'[29]

Calderone drags into consciousness the profoundly performative nature of masculinity by making claims of authenticity while simultaneously foregrounding the significant intervals between these three dimensions of corporeality, in effect, deterritorializing this particular contemporary cultural norm of masculinity in its citation.[30] Notably, Calderone disturbs and, for many, is unreadable, because of the claims on and for the real he makes, claims that Gaga's own performative femininity disallow. This is due in no small part to what Gaga herself identifies as the 'model of the pop star' into which she is cast and casts herself. That this model is highly gendered goes without saying; however, it is this very divide that Jo Calderone exposes as a norm of expectation, one which produces, rather than reflects, the effects of gender. To parse the complex and complexly disruptive work of Calderone's intervention, and the affective responses it generated, a specific historically situated signifying economy must be traced that underscores—or, in effect, produces—the gender divisions drag seeks to reveal. In essence, the question is: what specific conditions make Calderone's citation of masculinity *in this context* radically defamiliarizing and critically parodic? Certainly, not all gender parody is disruptive, much less subversive. What makes Jo Calderone a subversive, indeed a *deconstructive,* gender performance is its context in which gender *and* performance takes it meaning. Tracing the influence of Jacques Derrida on Butler's understanding of gender performance, Jeffrey Nealon explains, 'if meaning and identity are always context-bound—if, as Derrida maintains, there is nothing outside of (con)text—then any particular meaning or identity carries with it the necessary, structural possibility of its own subversion by other recontextualizations or reinscriptions.'[31] It is within the context of reality television, with its particular truth claims, and within the genres of popular music— both the signifying economies that found the MTV VMAs—that Jo Calderone's gender performance becomes so bitingly parodic (in turn, biting the hand that feeds Gaga in the process).

What MTV and its audiences expected of Lady Gaga was an elaborate production number, lots of dancers, and her (un)usual elaborate (self) fashion(ing).[32] What they expected, in short, was glamour. This attribute associated with Lady Gaga must be key to any understanding of gaga feminism and its workings, in large part, to confront the knot of common sense that dismisses Lady Gaga as a pop phenomenon who simply steals from Madonna to line her bank account (despite the fact, as feminist critics Ramona Curry, Pamela Robertson and others have pointed out, that Madonna also stole from pop icons like Marilyn Monroe and Mae West). How glamour *works*, why it sells, demands analysis. Following from the insights of Gabriel Tarde, Nigel Thrift argues, 'economies must be engaging, they must generate or scoop up affects and then aggregate and amplify them in order to produce value, and that must involve producing various mechanisms of fascination. The economy is not, and never has been, a dismal science of simple profit and loss.'[33] That Lady Gaga is profitable, for herself and the transnational corporations with whom she is contracted, is often the very grounds on which the political work of gaga feminism is dismissed or disavowed, by the left and the right. Yet why and how she is profitable remains essentially unexamined. To understand Gaga's allure, indeed, her *seduction*, we might begin by recognizing Gaga's ability 'to generate a certain kind of secular magic that can act as a means of willing captivation [which in turn] becomes a key means of producing dividends.'[34] The frequent dismissals of Lady Gaga follow from this, ranging from cynical 'rip-off' accusations (almost always of Madonna, revealing a generational bias) and Frankfurt School-type criticisms of her collusion with capital to the expected denouncements of her by the right. Lady Gaga's 'kind of magical pleasure' is often regarded 'as a fraud and a trap'; I take Thrift's retort to be instructive: 'such an attitude, located somewhere between complex forms of suspicion and simple snobbishness, makes it impossible to understand why this magic has a grip on people's lives and both overestimates and underestimates capitalism's magical powers.'[35] Rather than dismiss Gaga's pleasurable performance out of hand, it is necessary to recognize that it is her glamour, a particularly gendered embodiment of glamour, which is the condition of possibility—the ground, if you will—for the subversive resignification that is figured in Jo Calderone. The context out of which the subversive gender performance that is Jo Calderone emerges involves the resignification of gender *qua* style. As Butler summarizes, 'gender is an identity tenuously constituted in time, instituted in an exterior space through a *stylized repetition of acts*'; however, Lady Gaga's stylization of the body is anything but 'mundane', always already troubling 'the illusion of an abiding gendered self.'[36] In some palpable way, Gaga's gender remains exterior, failing to signify as 'natural' or authentic in the ways gender norms usually come to be (mis)interpreted as the internal core or substance of the subject. It is in the emphasis on *style* in the stylization of Gaga's performance of gender that places the clear emphasis on performance rather than gender and this is due in no small part to a complex and, in the case of Gaga, antagonistic set of technologies—the technologies of gender, on one hand, and the technologies of glamour, on the other. Under the aegis of the technologies of glamour, the stylization of the body that is/does gender may be disarticulated from gender norms.

As Thrift suggests, the magical qualities that define glamour have to do with style as well: '*Style is a modification of being that produces captivation, in part through our own explorations of it.* [. . .] [C]apitalism captivates by addressing a specific style of allure, namely, *glamour*.'[37] Lady Gaga is famous (and profitable) for much more than her music; she is a glamorous celebrity with a huge following. Her glamour is intricately tied to her stylization, associated as it is with *haute couture* fashion (as a muse of the late Alexander McQueen, for example). Yet her particular incarnation of a glamorous persona is unique in its heightened interactions with the object world that constitutes it. 'What is important to understand about glamorous celebrity,' according to Thrift, 'is that is revolves around persons who are also things [. . .]. They become surrounded by an object world that confirms this model but also has its own existence.'[38] Unlike other celebrities, Gaga brings attention to this relation, using fashion to comment on the object world on which she draws to heighten her allure, often signifying fashion *as* objects, *e.g.* Kermit the frog dolls, slabs of meat, plastic bubbles, moving metal rings arranged like the rings of a planet. In themselves these objects do not necessarily register as glamorous; however, by attaching them to the body of a celebrity they are granted the allure of style. Yet they also, reciprocally, foreground Gaga as object among objects, denaturalizing the allure of celebrity. If 'glamorous celebrity is neither person nor thing but something in between, an unobtainable reality, an imaginary friend [. . .] something that is at issue in the world', then Gaga holds out this gap, this in-between longer than most to encourage an exploration of the model of the pop star *qua* object.[39] This is evident in the ways Gaga's style becomes art (meat dress, planetoid costume, frog dress, *etc.*) in order to present to her audiences an embodied commentary on the consumption of glamour (meat), on celebrity as object ('star'), and as toy or commodity (frog or plastic bubble).

This context is, of course, crucial as an interpretive grid through which to evaluate the cultural work of Jo Calderone. Calderone figures as an object of glamour in the ways he 'gets into that spotlight'. Yet, the spotlight into which he steps is actually a palimpsest, carrying the traces of these previous embodied commentaries (performed at previous VMAs no less). Gaga, through these many incarnations, troubles the glamour with which she is endowed while simultaneously adding to it. Specifically, she refuses to abide by the edict of glamour that its 'calculation must go unnoticed. It must appear effortless.'[40] Her performance of glamour refutes this founding quality precisely because of her rejection of the boundary between reality and artifice. In this way, Thrift's argument has specific ramifications about the gender of glamour, though he does not pursue this line of argument. His claim that 'glamour is selling. It is manipulation. It is seduction. It is a certain form of deception', cannot be understood apart from the discursive cultural formations that signify femininity. Woman as a figure of deception, manipulation, and seduction has a very long history in Western philosophy and religious discourses. And yet, to the extent that glamour does work in this way, Lady Gaga brings to the fore the machinery of selling and manipulation implicit in celebrity. Her public appearances, especially at the VMAs, pull 'performance always toward "impersonation" marked explicitly as such', and, to this extent, her transformation of glamour into performance art, 'constitute[s] the cultural field in which "the parodic" is situated in relation to "the authentic" [. . .] gender trouble [. . .] accrues from [the] uncertainty about the site of the authentic.'[41] Lady Gaga as star, as slab of meat, and her various other parodic outfits turns fashion away from authenticating gender as some truth about the subject, and instead opts for a mimicry of femininity to challenge its founding norms. Many have commented on the foregrounding of artifice and performance in Gaga's work, like Alexander Cho: 'Lady Gaga makes a very explicit attempt to shrewdly, purposefully—even politically—expose the nature of our fascination with pop icons by making it her mission to foreground the artifice *of her own performance*.'[42] Indeed, for many, this artifice or fakery clearly signals a critique of the very sorts of glamorous femininity associated with the model of the pop star generally. Such gender mimicry situates Gaga squarely within the domain of queer critique: 'in mimicry, as in camp, one "does" ideology in order to undo it, producing knowledge about it: that gender and the heterosexual orientation presumed to anchor it are unnatural and even oppressive.[43]

Still, this critical queerness sells, and propels Gaga's fame even further with each shocking, stylized performance. This is due in part to that constitutive feature of glamour: seduction. Lady Gaga seduces. The seductive qualities of glamour transcode the effects of Gaga's gender parody by reterritorializing them in terms of fascination. This is possible because, as a cis female performer, artifice is expected, as Jean Baudrillard insists: 'in the feminine the very distinction between authenticity and artifice is without foundation.'[44] Baudrillard finds femininity's dissimulation of the authentic to be its de(con)structive force. Lady Gaga's performative femininity is always already a seduction, because seduction refutes nature; as Baudrillard asserts, 'seduction never belongs to the order of nature, but that of artifice—never to the order of energy, but that of signs and rituals.'[45] In her insistence on artifice without a substantive ground (an authentic subject to anchor it), Gaga seduces (or disturbs those who refuse to be seduced) because her performances deny 'things their truth and turn it into a game, the pure play of appearances, and thereby foil all systems of power and meaning', by turning 'appearances in on themselves, [. . .] play[ing] on the body's appearances, rather than on the depths of desire'; indeed, many of Gaga's song lyrics directly celebrate this play, epitomized in 'Poker Face', in which she bluffs, and seduces, not just with her face but with her 'muffin'.[46]

I suggest it is Gaga's exceptional powers of seduction that spawn the rumors of her transexuality, that is, the suspicions that she might have a penis. This is because her excessive play on the body's appearances does more than blur the line between surface and depth (as other glamorous pop stars do), but rather shows a complete 'indifference to the authentic and artificial', and this indifference is at the heart of seduction because, as Baudrillard avows, '*seduction alone is radically opposed to anatomy as destiny*. Seduction alone breaks the distinctive sexualization of bodies and the inevitable phallic economy that results.'[47] Gaga's gender performance exposes femininity as hyperreality, undoing the surface of femininity from the supposed depth of anatomy. 'Seduction is more intelligent', according to Baudrillard, because 'it knows (this is its secret) that *there is no anatomy* [. . .] that all signs are reversible. Nothing belongs to it, except appearances.'[48] Lady Gaga's extreme gender parodies are anchored not on anatomy but on the technologies of glamour, and therefore are performed as seductions, taking their meaning from the infinite reversibility of signs. Because of this, she is associated with the signs and discourses of the drag queen. Gaga's '*transubstantiation of sex into signs*' aligns her with the transvestite because, like the transvestite, she appears 'obsessed with the games of sex, but obsessed, first of all, with play itself; and if [her life] appear[s] more sexually endowed than our own, it is because [she] make[s] sex into a total, gestural, sensual, and ritual game, an exalted but ironic invocation.'[49] And it is Jo Calderone that brings this to our consciousness in his monologue, directly addressing her sexual play (of signs), which only heightens the (mis)perception of Gaga as transvestite, something Calderone himself insinuates in his statement, 'I mean I think I'd be okay with it, you know, if I found out that she was really . . .', the ellipsis here implying, I think, 'a man'. If everything with the transvestite 'is makeup, theater, and seduction', isn't this exactly the point of Calderone's description of Gaga; or, as Gaga says to her lover, 'I'm theater'.[50]

Yet, it is Calderone, on the stage and in the spotlight, who narrates and reveals Gaga's seduction—who is, in fact, the assumed object of her seduction. Maybe this is why Gaga believes Calderone to be 'so approachable and so relatable' (though few seemed to experience him this way), because he can be a proxy for the audiences she aims to seduce. It is, however, in Gaga's masculine embodiment that her arguably most powerful transvestism is undertaken; in other words, what happens when Calderone is effecting the seduction of Gaga's audiences? As feminine transvestite, as drag *queen*, Lady Gaga's seduction is delimited by the supposed facticity of anatomy, by (the projection of) her 'real' sex. Like Baudrillard's assessment of Nico, we might say that Gaga emanates 'something more than beauty, something more sublime, a different seduction', but one undone in the same way, because, like Nico, she is 'a false drag queen, a real woman [. . .] It is easier for a non-female/female than for a real woman, already legitimated by her sex, to move among the signs and take seduction to its limit'.[51] In other words, as much as Gaga's parodic masquerade of gender pushes on the artifice of femininity, it is transvestism that 'play[s] with the indistinctness of the sexes [. . .] born of sexual vacillation'; it is only as drag *king* that the play of signs that is Gaga's glamorous seduction finally and irrevocably refuses to 'reduplicate biological being', because, as Jo, 'signs are separated from biology, and consequently the sexes no longer exist properly speaking.'[52] This is due to the fact that the signs are constitutively different: Calderone dissimulates the signs of masculinity as opposed to femininity. In an interview, a journalist asks Gaga if she is afraid the sexual content of her lyrics will somehow undercut the validity of her music; she grows irritated with his line of questioning, responding that if she were a man, he would not ask these questions, insinuating that sexuality is assumed to be somehow natural to the male rock star but a point of contention for the female pop star. Gaga insists in her retort to the journalist: 'You see, if I was a guy and I was sitting here with a cigarette in my hand, grabbing my crotch and talking about how I make music 'cause I love fast cars and fucking girls, you'd call me a rock star. But, when I do it in my music and my videos, because I'm a female, because I make pop music, you're judgmental, and you say it is distracting. I'm just a rock star.'[53] These are, of course, the very signs of masculinity with which Gaga plays as Jo.

Notably, the journalist's questions imply that a woman's having sexual desires, a woman as a desiring sexual subject, is inherently disruptive and incongruent with pop music, while Gaga's response exposes the (musical genre) norms that presume, and produce, the male rock star's particular performance of masculinity, one anchored the expression of sexual desire and activity, as authentic and, therefore, appropriate to the music (rock as opposed to pop). Such norms (of both gender and genre) go beyond the psychoanalytic claim that the libido is masculine—they turn on the ontological claim that masculinity alone has domain over the authentic, the true. If all signs are indeed reversible, as Baudrillard and Butler might agree, then Jo Calderone effectuates this sudden reversibility and, in doing so, throws into relief not just the model of the (female) pop star but also the model of the (male) rock star. Jo Calderone takes his meaning from the signs generated by *Jersey Shore*, that is, an ethnic, metrosexual masculinity that is often seen 'partying' in the form of drinking. On a synchronic level, Jo Calderone evokes these signs of masculinity celebrated by MTV's hit series, particularly on the ground of its claims to authentic 'identity': their Italian American ethnicity. Of course, Stefani Joanne Angelina Germanotta (Lady Gaga) is also Italian American, something the press is quick to point out. And, yet, the way Italian American-ness signifies for The Situation and the men of Jersey Shore as opposed to Lady Gaga is significant. Gaga's Italian American femininity is not a ground of authentic identity as much as a part of the constellation of performative signifiers she deploys. For example, her music video, 'Summerboy,' displays an abundancy of signs of Italian American-ness in the form of literal signs and iconography, from the opening shots of the 'Italia' flag followed by another close-up on an Italian flag hanging right next to an American flag to the Vespa scooters she rides through the Italian American neighborhood to the pizza place she frequents with her girlfriends. Beyond the clichéd stills of foods associated with the culture (pizza, parmesan, veal, 'olio d'oliva'), the video's saturated colors and pastiche 1950s nostalgia, with its caricatured 'guido' types gesturing and miming in the background, made all the more apparent by Gaga singing part of the song in front of 'Guido's Meat Market,' with her stereotyped male onlookers eyeing her like a piece of meat, foreground Italian American-ness as a cultural imaginary, a chronotope of a specific time (1950s–1960s) and place (the outer boroughs of New York City).

Jersey Shore—the name itself evoking a contemporary chronotope—also presents certain clichéd forms of masculinity; however, in this case, they are anchored in the reality of the reality show framework and iconography. It is these claims to authenticity that the embodiment of Jo Calderone radically challenges, exposing the authenticating grounds of masculinity the show forwards. Calderone's drag performance cuts both ways, revealing masculinity generally as a copy without origin, particularly East Coast Italian American masculinity (a fetishized masculinity in film and media, one Gaga cites and parodies in 'Summerboy') as a transferable set of attributes (as

Butler explains as the original insight about gender trouble). Yet, it simultaneously deconstructs (retroactively) the whiteness of Gaga's glamorous persona.[54] When Calderone asks his audience, '[a]nd what's with the hair', he
is asking about Gaga's blonde hair while Calderone's equally unreal black
pompadour both masks it and draws attention to it as a sign, a particularly
fetishized sign of glamorous femininity. Indeed, key technologies of glamour were the invention of hair dye and wigs.[55] Within film and popular culture, these techonologies were used frequently to mask cultural specificity
(for example, Rita Hayworth's red hair effaced her Mexican origins). Yet,
blondness specifically is associated with the figure of the seductress and/
or femme fatale, dating back to Jean Harlow, Barbara Stanwyk, and, later,
Rita Hayworth; these figures (and their blond epigones: Madonna, Sharon Stone, Gaga, *etc.*) suggest, according to Chris Holmlund, a fetishiza-
tion of '[f]emale whiteness': 'bleached, tinted, frosted, and dyed blondes
are everywhere, in the past as in the present [. . .] caught up with [. . .]
anxieties regarding racial origins and ethnic lacks.'[56] However, the excessive
spectacle of the bleached blondness of Gaga, particularly in the context of
the explicitly fake wigs she wears so often, and then called out as fake by
Calderone, asserts a critical relationship to racialized sexuality qua white
femininity through her exaggerated, denaturalized whiteness: a hyperbole
that highlights whiteness *as* performance, as yet another sort of stylization
of the body.

Yet, by invoking Gaga's regimes of appearance and seduction, Calderone
is undone by the relation, by being seduced. Recalling Baudrillard, 'it is the
feminine as appearance that thwarts masculine depth'; by calling up Gaga's
highly performative femininity (the hair, the phallic shoes, the obscured
visage as barred sign of *jouissance*), masculinity is troubled, unmoored.
'By idealizing feminine "masquerade"', Bristow points out, 'Baudrillard
observes how masculinity aggrandizes itself on the dangerous pretense that
it "possesses unfailing powers of discrimination and absolute criteria for
pronouncing the truth"'.[57] Yet, this is exactly the intervention that is staged
with the embodiment of Calderone. Taking the 2009 interview as a key to
the invention of the alter Calderone, it seems the drag of Calderone does
more than ironize the (un)reality of *Jersey Shore* masculinity. If Jo's origin
predates *Jersey Shore*, there is another Jersey masculinity evoked. The dia-
chronic analysis points to the contrast between Gaga as female pop star
(as artifice) and the male rock star (as authentic truth teller). Calderone
performs as a real rock star, singing 'Yoü and I', a song that explicitly
cites Bruce Springsteen's multi-platinum album, *Nebraska,* while parodying the authentic claims of masculine rock with lines like: 'I'm a New York
woman, born to run you down'. This is at odds with the rock idiom from
which it borrows: 'This rock idiom (often hailed as "pure" rock) uses a
basic rhythm and blues ensemble [. . .] to accompany lyrics that evoke
small (Midwestern) towns and working class perspectives, frustrations of
life and love, and escapism into drink, cars, or girls.'[58] While Calderone

appropriates the 'authentic' sounds of pure rock, down to the raspy, deep voice and screams of abjection of the rock gods, a critical irony is aimed at these very claims to authenticity and the truth of femininity they tend to describe in their lyrics.

As Judith Peraino makes clear, generally missing from rock ballads of these sorts 'is any sense of irony that might turn the surface of these melodramas into a camp critique of gender or sexuality'; rather, in songs such as 'Born to Run', 'Bruce Springsteen sings the bombastic lines: "just wrap your legs 'round these velvet rims, and strap your hands 'cross my engines."'[59] Yet, as Gaga made clear to her interlocutor, Springsteen would never be asked whether the sexual content of the lyrics would detract from the music, which is entirely the point of Gaga's own version of a rock ballad. In it, she sings, 'Muscle cars drove a truck right through my heart/On my birthday you sang me a heart of gold', mocking the cliché of the rock star's 'fetish for motor vehicles, and the conflation of engines with masculine (phallic) power', but, more significantly, she subverts their aggrandizing truth claims by critiquing the male rock star's 'projection of earnestness and [their] avoidance of irony [that] shores up the integrity of masculinity despite the theatrical display of emotion.'[60]

Indeed, Calderone's monologue foregrounds this theatrical display of emotion, but evokes it as an explicit citation of a gender (rock) norm, which is revealed to be a gender parody in the performance of 'Yoü and I', with its pointedly ironic lyrics: 'Something, something about this place, Something 'bout lonely nights and my lipstick on your face, Something, something about my cool Nebraska guy, Yeah something about, baby, you and I.' Gaga's Calderone, in this way, 'constitutes a subversive repetition within the signifying practices of gender' precisely because s/he reveals the supposedly authentic masculinity of the rock star to be an effect of his theatricality, that very thing for which she is so frequently condemned.[61] In effect, Calderone effects a gender parody of a double order by performing 'Yoü and I' as a direct citation of the male rock idiom of earnest vocals and melodramatic intonation, even spiked with the hypermasculine electric guitar solo, only to be undone by lyrics that expose the emptiness, the vacuous content of 'something, something about the chase.' This stark contrast, and the critical distance it evokes, prompts 'the subversive laughter in the pastiche-effect of parodic practices in which the original, the authentic, and the real are themselves constituted as effects', effects revealed, in this case, as a set of gender *and* musical genres norms that produces the illusion of authentic (geographical and classed) masculinity.[62] The question remains, however, *why* this specific form of gender parody? We have a clue in Calderone's acceptance speech: 'It doesn't matter who you are. Gay, straight, bi, lesbian, transgender—you were born this way.' Why do men, rock stars, or, as Gaga sums up—straight American men—get to claim any more right to an authentic self (and his experiences as rendered in song), and to those gender codes that humanize him while 'we regularly punish those who fail to do their gender right'?[63] The honest abjection of the male rock star (and the women who cite or emulate them) is founded on the authenticity derived from 'contrasting qualities of suffering and survival, vulnerability and strength, and even on authenticity and theatricality.'[64] Jo Calderone shows these to be, in fact, transferable attributes, and reclaims such qualities in the name of those who are systematically abjected out the social body in the name of the human, those who deal with 'suffering and survival' on a daily basis: her little monsters. In an interview with Larry King, Gaga clearly articulates her motives: 'I'm more interested in helping my fans to love who they are and helping them to reject prejudice and reject those things that they're taught from society to not like themselves. To be like freaks.'[65]

TRANS/AFFECT AND THE SUBLIME

It is important to remember when evaluating the cultural work of Jo Calderone, the 'point of drag is not simply to produce a pleasurable and subversive spectacle but to allegorize the spectacular and consequential ways in which reality is both reproduced and contested.'[66] While it is true that Jo Calderone certainly evokes a substantial amount of gender trouble, the key to this trouble are affects it produces, which, for many, had little to do with pleasure. For me, what is significant is that Gaga's pressing on the unrelatable issue of the violation of gender norms produces something between discomfort and excitement; this is what I identify as trans/affect. If Jo Calderone does Butlerian drag, the affect this gender performance generates can be explained by Jean-François Lyotard, who argues, in his reflections on popular culture, that 'the only line to follow is to produce in the viewer [. . .] an effect of uncertainty and trouble [. . .] the thing to aim at is a certain sort of feeling or sentiment. You can't introduce concepts, you can't produce argumentation [. . .] but you can produce a feeling of disturbance, in hope that this disturbance will be followed by reflection [. . .] and it's up to every artist how to create that disturbance.'[67] For Lyotard this represents the potential of postmodern aesthetics, which replaces the didactic forms of poetics and rhetoric with the analysis of the addressee's feelings. He says the question of aesthetics is, 'no longer "How does one make a work of art?", but "What is it to experience an affect proper to art?"'[68] For Lyotard, this affect, generated by aesthetic experimentation, is the result of the experience of the sublime—that experience which evokes a crisis in rationality and conceptualization.

The sublime identifies those aesthetic practices in excess of the viewer's cognitive capacity for reason; it remains obscure to our conceptual powers. In many ways, Gaga's monstrous aesthetics fit well within the category of the sublime, evident in her continual disruption of the boundaries between nature and artifice. Yet Jo Calderone stands apart because he evokes a very specific sort of sublime response. T. Benjamin Singer turns to the sublime, specifically Dick Hebdige's rereading of the Burkean sublime, in his analysis of photographic representations of non-standard bodies, including transgender and intersex bodies. He develops the concept of the transgender sublime to capture the unexpected nature of transgender complexity that induces disorienting encounters with the sublime, as demonstrated in the self-portraiture of transgender activist and artist, Del LaGrace Volcano, in *Sublime Mutations*. Because the category of the sublime 'surpasses bounded meaning and remains resistant to easy interpretation', Singer argues that it describes the affective encounter with transgender subjects.[69] Jo Calderone's performance of gender, sedimented with the paratext of Gaga's hyperreal fashioning of the female modern pop performer as artifice, indeed, as fashion, elicits the transgender sublime because it points to 'the non-binary range of bodies, genders and sexualities'.[70] Trans/affect names the complexity of affective responses evoked by transgender embodiment and therefore can be seen as an expression of the sublime, as it reveals the multiplicity and instability at the heart of gender. As Singer argues, transgender embodiments evoke the sublime because they 'confront us with a vision of potentially infinite specific possibilities for being human.'[71] One concept that has been used to efface these infinite ways of being human is the category of the monstrous; the sign of the monster may in fact work precisely to evoke these infinite ways of being human in its very act casting out that which does not abide by the norms of the human as we understand it *today*.

In this way, this analysis has aimed at expanding gaga feminism by undertaking a critical teratology, that is, of course, the study of monsters. The trans body has been and continues to be read as monstrous; as Susan Stryker powerfully sums up: 'I am a transsexual and therefore I am a monster.'[72] Stryker identifies this monstrosity as constituted from without, in the fears generated by the encounter, revealing the very grounds of trans/affect: 'To encounter the transsexual body, to apprehend a transgendered consciousness articulating itself, is to risk a revelation of the constructedness of the natural order.'[73] Jo Calderone evokes the transgender sublime by 'forcing people to confront' this very risk. So, what does it mean to have Lady Gaga (or Nicki Minaj, for that matter) occupy the space of transmen? Some feminist responses have been cynical (while, notably, many trans communities have lauded the performance in the name of trans visibility); yet, as Halberstam points out, this mistrust has a rather long history, dating back to the early twentieth century when 'female masculinity was cast by Otto Weininger and others, as simultaneously a sign of the collapse of gender distinctions and, by implication, of civilized society, and a marker of female genius.'[74] Maybe it is too much to suggest that Jo Calderone is the marker of Gaga's genius. Yet, in risking the trans/affect *and* trans *effect* of Jo Calderone, who throws all our sexuality into doubt, we also risk the encounter with the sublime. The sublime art of Lady Gaga incites a becoming of sorts, a temporal shift in subjectivity, edging those willing to take the risk a little closer to the monstrous. 'By remodeling the "model artist", "model citizen", or "supermodel"', Gaga theorizes, 'we can liberate the present. The transformation detaches the model from any universal paradigm and allows him or her to reinvent perspective in a pure, unattached moment.'[75] This Bergsonian insight from Mother Monster points towards the possibilities of the virtual, and these virtual selves emanate from the subversion of norms, or 'models'. The sublime art of Lady Gaga urges its viewer to 'use every ounce of potential you have, raise revolution against what people expect of you, and tell the world this is not a rehearsal. This is the real me. And listen up, 'cause it could be the most honest incarnation yet'. Jo Calderone may be the most honest incarnation Gaga has modeled to date precisely because he raises the revolutionary call for little monsters everywhere.

NOTES

1. J. Jack Halberstam, *Gaga Feminism* (Boston, MA: Beacon Press, 2012), 8.
2. BoyGaga, *Twitter* post, 18 July 2012, 3:15pm.
3. Halberstam, *Gaga Feminism*, xii. Throughout the book, Halberstam uses 'gaga' as an adjective, with a lower-case 'g'.
4. Halberstam, *Gaga Feminism*, xxi.
5. Bill Nichols, 'Film Theory and the Revolt Against Master Narratives', *Reinventing Film Studies*, eds. Christine Gledhill and Linda Williams (New York, NY: Oxford University Press, 2000), 36.
6. *Ibid.*
7. Melissa Gregg and Gregory J. Seigworth (eds.), *The Affect Theory Reader* (Durham, NC: Duke University Press, 2010), 1.
8. Heather Duerre Humann discusses the first appearances of Jo Calderone in her chapter, 'What a Drag: Lady Gaga, Jo Calderone and the Politics of Representation', in which she discusses the original photo layout and interview in Japan's *Vogue Hommes* (2010) and the subsequent media responses. However, Calderone's reappearance at the VMAs brought him into millions of living rooms, introducing him to a vastly larger audience than his first appearance in the media. See *The Performance Identities of Lady Gaga*, ed. Richard Gray II, (Jefferson, NC: McFarland, 2012), 74–84.
9. Lady Gaga, 'V MAGAZINE MEMORANDUM No. 4', *V Magazine* (November 2011) (online at: http://www.vmagazine.com/2011/10/v-magazine-gaga-memorandum-no-4/) <accessed 6 May 2012>.
10. *Ibid.*
11. For example, see http://lesbianswholooklikejustinbieber.tumblr.com/. A great deal of internet and media discourse circulating around Justin Bieber is dedicated to his particular gender embodiment as uncannily similar to a certain style of baby butch lesbianism.
12. Lady Gaga, 'V MAGAZINE MEMORANDUM No. 4'.
13. Destruction as anarchic feminist praxis has a long history, one in which I would situate Gaga's performance art. Halberstam argues for a more extensive lineage for Gaga beyond Madonna and Britney Spears. Halberstam names Yoko Ono, Valerie Solanas, while Gaga herself cites Grace Jones and Lady Starlight. However, within the context of Gaga as 'theater', her

foremothers include Yvonne Rainer, Carolee Schneemann, Valie Export, and many others; yet, here I am specifically reminded of *Destroy, She Said,* by Marguerite Duras.

14. Halberstam, *Gaga Feminism,* xii–xiii, emphasis mine.
15. Elaine L. Graham, *Representations of the Post/Human: Monsters, Aliens and Others in Pop Culture* (New Brunswick, NJ: Rutgers University Press, 2002).
16. It could be said that while Gaga is indeed missing the penis, what she does have is the *lesbian phallus:* 'When the phallus is lesbian, then it is and is not a masculinist figure of power; the signifier is significantly split, for it both recalls and displaces the masculinism by which it is impelled. And insofar as it operates at the site of anatomy, the phallus (re)produces the specter of the penis only to enact its vanishing, to reiterate and exploit its perpetual vanishing as the very occasion of the phallus', as Judith Butler has persuasively argued in *Bodies That Matter: On the Discursive Limits of 'Sex'* (New York, NY: Routledge, 1993), 89. In this way, what the prison guards do not see, cannot see, the butch prisoner (Marci Beck) in the yard can, because Gaga's anatomy signifies outside the heteronormative economy of signifiers. For instance, the prototypical phallic signifier in the cinema—the cigarette—is substantively resignified; it is not just split but multiplied and transformed from a singular object of an oral fixation into an apparatus for seeing. Gaga's smoking cigarette eyeglasses are a metonymy for the lesbian phallus, that 'site of desire', which functions not as a new body part but serves instead as 'a displacement of the hegemonic symbolic of (heterosexist) sexual difference'; indeed, I would argue that the women's prison in *Telephone,* anchored as it is to the lesbian phallic economy, is one possible 'alternative imaginary schema [. . .] of erotogenic pleasure' (Butler, *Bodies That Matter,* 91).
17. Julia Kristeva, *Powers of Horror: An Essay on Abjection,* tr. Leon S. Roudiez (New York, NY: Columbia University Press, 1982).
18. Halberstam, *Gaga Feminism,* 26.
19. Judith Butler, *Gender Trouble: Feminism and the Subversion of Identity,* 2nd edition (London: Routledge, 1999), 191.
20. Kaja Silverman, *The Threshold of the Visible World* (New York, NY: Routledge, 1996), 83.
21. *Ibid.,* 84.
22. *Ibid.*
23. Judith Butler, *Undoing Gender* (New York, NY: Routledge, 2004), 212.
24. The study of travesty, particularly in Marjorie Garber's *Vested Interests: Cross-Dressing and Cultural Anxiety* (New York, NY: Routledge, 1997), however, has shown this to be a much more complicated than a simple sartorial choice.
25. Butler, *Undoing Gender.* 213.
26. Lady Gaga, interviewed by Noah Michelson, *The Huffington Post,* 23 September 2011.
27. Butler, *Undoing Gender.* 214.
28. Silverman, *The Threshold of the Visible World,* 84–85.
29. Butler, *Gender Trouble.* 187.
30. I have discussed the significance of this interval in gender performance in corporeal feminism elsewhere, particularly in regards to Gilles Deleuze's elaboration of the interval as specific form of time-image. See 'The Cinematic Relations of Corporeal Feminism', in *The Becoming Deleuzo-guattarian of Queer Studies,* ed. Michael O'Rourke (Special Double Issue of *Rhizomes: Cultural Studies in Emerging Knowledge,* nos. 11/12 (Fall 2005/ Spring 2006), available at: http://www.rhizomes.net/issue11/geller.html).

31. Jeffrey Nealon, *Alterity Politics: Ethics and Performative Subjectivity* (Durham, NC): Duke University Press, 1998), 21.
32. Van Toffler, President of MTV, suggested that Gaga do 'something different, almost counterintuitive, and do a killer intimate version of "Yoü and I" as opposed to a massive, well-choreographed, full-of-explosions-and-tons-of-dancers kind of performance.' (Kyle Anderson, 'The VMAs' All-Time Wildest Moments', *Entertainment Weekly*, 14 September 2012).
33. Nigel Thrift, 'Understanding the Material Practices of Glamour', in *The Affect Theory Reader*, ed. Melissa Gregg and Gregory J. Seigworth (Durham, NC: Duke University Press, 2010 [2008]), 290.
34. *Ibid.*
35. *Ibid.*, 308.
36. Butler, *Gender Trouble*, 191.
37. Thrift, 'Understanding the Material Practices of Glamour', 297. Italics in original.
38. *Ibid.*, 304.
39. *Ibid.*, 305.
40. *Ibid.*, 299.
41. Eric Savoy, 'That Ain't All She Ain't: Doris Day and Queer Performativity', in *Out Takes: Essays on Queer Theory and Film*, ed. Ellis Hanson (Durham, NC: Duke University Press, 1999), 159–160.
42. Alexander Cho/FLOW Staff, 'Lady Gaga, Balls-Out: Recuperating Queer Performativity,' *FlowTV*, vol. 10, no. 5 (7 August 2009; available at: http://flowtv.org/2009/08/lady-gaga-balls-out-recuperating-queer-performativityalexander-cho-flow-staff/).
43. Carol-Ann Tyler, 'Boys Will Be Girls: The Politics of Gay Drag', in *Inside/Out: Lesbian Theories, Gay Theories*, ed. Diana Fuss (New York, NY: Routledge, 1991), 53.
44. Jean Baudrillard, *Seduction*, tr. Brian Singer (New York NY: St. Martin's Press, 1990 [1979]), 11.
45. *Ibid.*, 2.
46. *Ibid.*, 8.
47. *Ibid.*, 10.
48. *Ibid.*
49. *Ibid.*, 13.
50. *Ibid.*
51. *Ibid.*
52. *Ibid.*, 12.
53. This interview can be viewed at: http://www.youtube.com/watch?v=VE4L7SI-SwA <accessed: 4 April 2013>. It should be noted that she says to the journalist that the highlight of her success is her gay fans, who don't ask such dumb questions.
54. Butler, *Undoing Gender*, 213.
55. Thrift, 'Understanding the Material Practices of Glamour', 306.
56. Chris Holmlund, *Impossible Bodies: Femininity and Masculinity at the Movies* (New York, NY: Routledge, 2002), 83.
57. Joseph Bristow, *Sexuality* (New York, NY: Routledge, 1997), 129.
58. Judith Peraino, *Listening to the Sirens: Musical Technologies of Queer Identity from Homer to Hedwig*, (Berkeley, CA: University of California Press, 2006), 137.
59. *Ibid.*
60. *Ibid.* The lyric, 'a heart of gold', evokes another notably 'authentic' rocker, Neil Young.
61. Butler, *Gender Trouble*. 199.

62. *Ibid.*, 200.
63. *Ibid.*, 190.
64. Peraino, *Listening to the Sirens*, 137.
65. Lady Gaga, interviewed by Larry King, *Larry King Live*, CNN, broadcast: 1 June 2010.
66. Butler, *Undoing Gender* 218.
67. Jean-François Lyotard, 'Brief Reflections on Popular Culture', in *ICA Documents 4*, ed. Lisa Appignanesi (London: Institute of Contemporary Arts, 1986), 203.
68. *Ibid.*
69. Ben T. Singer, 'Towards a Transgender Sublime: The Politics of Excess in Trans-specific Cultural Production', in *The Transgender Studies Reader*, ed. Susan Stryker and Stephen Whittle (New York, NY: Routledge, 2006), 614.
70. *Ibid.*, 616.
71. *Ibid.*
72. Susan Stryker, 'My Words to Victor Frankenstein above the Village of Chamounix: Performing Transgender Rage', in *The Transgender Studies Reader*, ed. Susan Stryker and Stephen Whittle (New York, NY: Routledge, 2006), 246.
73. Stryker, 'My Words to Victor Frankenstein', 254.
74. Judith Halberstam, *The Queer Art of Failure* (Durham, NC: Duke University Press, 2011), 159.
75. Lady Gaga, 'Gaga Memorandum #4.'

12 Consuming Gaga[1]

Melanie L. Marshall

[Neil Strauss for Rolling Stone]: So, you're thinking, "I'm going to trick
    this idea down your throat"?

[Lady Gaga]: Or seduce people to be interested in something that is uncom-
    fortable Why are we still talking about "Don't ask, don't tell"?
    It's like, what fucking year is it? It makes me crazy! And I have
    been for three years baking cakes—and now I'm going to bake a
    cake that has a bitter jelly.

[NS]: Elaborate on that metaphor a little.

[LG]: The message of the new music is now more bitter than it was before.
    Because the sweeter the cake, the more bitter the jelly can be. If
    I had come out as who I was, no one would be listening. Now
    people are listening. So I can be inspirational, and I'm in a dif-
    ferent place in my life. I'm interested in different things. I've got
    fame now. So I don't want to write about it anymore.[2]

That's what everyone wants to know, right? "What's she gonna
look like when she dies? What's she gonna look like when she's
overdosed?" on whatever they think I'm overdosing on? Everybody
wants to see the decay of the superstar.

Lady Gaga.[3]

Marian McAlpin, the protagonist of Margaret Atwood's first novel *The
Edible Woman*, has a university degree, a job making market research
questionnaires intelligible to the general public, and a boyfriend who fan-
cies himself a bit of a catch. Following her engagement to Peter, Marian
feels consumed by her fiancé and his magazine-perfect desires. She sympa-
thizes with objects of consumption, and becomes unable to eat formerly living organisms, first cutting out meats, then vegetables, and eventually she
begins to wonder what is ground up to become vitamin pills. She becomes
unable to think of herself in the first person; she loses her sense of self, her
'I'. Even before Marian became anorexic, she often thought of herself in
relation to food, particularly cake and ice cream. Marian considered herself and her women colleagues to be the 'gooey layer in the middle' of an
ice-cream sandwich.[4] The 'upper crust' is the executives and psychologists
upstairs, all men, and the mimeo and IBM machines downstairs form the

bottom crust. It is only through baking (becoming a producer) that Marian regains her self and then her appetite for food. She bakes a light, white sponge cake, flavored with vanilla and lemon, arranges it into the shape of a woman, and decorates it with buttercream icing: a pink dress with floral pattern in silver balls, chocolate icing hair, and green eyes. Marian offers it to Peter as a substitute for her self, saying that he has been trying to destroy her, to assimilate her. In fact, Peter doesn't eat the cake at all. Marian eats some of it—'the cake, after all, was only a cake'—and her lover, Duncan, finishes it off, making for an uneasy ending. Through baking and eating the cake, Marian recovers her voice and re-enters consumer society.

Some have suggested the cake in Lady Gaga's 'Cake like Lady Gaga' refers to cocaine, or money, perhaps; it certainly indicates the general notion of excess outlined in the rest of the song.[5] In the teaser video by Terry Richardson, Lady Gaga writhes around in cake and icing. Even prior to this song, people consumed Gaga in cake form. Cupcakes by 'EclSpatial', one with white icing molded into a bow, like Lady Gaga's white blond hair bows in 'Poker Face' and 'Eh, Eh (Nothing Else Can I Say)' (2009), the other, also with white icing, reminiscent of the shoulder decorations on the Haus of Gaga's Origami Dress that Lady Gaga first wore in 2008.[6] Or a two-tier Lady Gaga cake by 'Charla Vail', with fondant Gagas, one in the white Origami Dress, one in Jeremy Scott's yellow jumpsuit and black Mickey Mouse sunglasses (Jeremy Scott X Linda Farrow) seen in 'Paparazzi', all on a predominately white background.[7] Jay Murphy of KAK (Kick Ass Kakes) worked on a different scale altogether. He marked the entertainer's visit to Phoenix, Arizona with a larger-than-life Lady Gaga (5'9" and weighing rather more than the singer at 180 lbs) made from a wooden frame covered with vanilla cake, vanilla buttercream and fondant icing.[8] Gaga has not only inspired cakes. Baby Gaga is the original name of a white, vanilla and lemon flavor artisan ice-cream, made in small quantities by The Icecreamists in London's Covent Garden from a top quality ingredient: human breast milk.[9] Despite (or owing to?) the high price tag (almost £15 [US $22] a scoop) and the unusual ingredients, the parlor allegedly sold out of Baby Gaga on the first day.

I am intrigued by these creations, the numerous Gaga cake images that can be found online, and what they may say about the relationship between celebrity, gender, fans and food. Ice cream and cake are calorie-laden, nutrient-light ways to consume Lady Gaga, to bring about the 'decay of the superstar'.[10] To point out that ice cream and cake are usually empty calories is not to imply that Gaga is meaningless fluff. Popular culture does important cultural work, both reflecting and shaping thought on current issues intriguing society. Perhaps most commented on in Gaga's case is the dynamics of gender and sexuality; she arguably exhibits a new approach to gender politics that Jack Halberstam has termed 'gaga feminism'.[11] But that is not the only work that Gaga does or allows others to do. The ice cream and many of the cakes have something in common: color. Baby

Gaga ice cream is white, and most of the cakes I have seen online have a white icing background. Baker Jay Murphy pointed out that white works well in the chosen medium, yet I would suggest it indicates something of Gaga's cultural signifying too.[12] She's hardly a vanilla entertainer: she qu(e)er(ie)s heteronormative white femininity, as many contributors to this volume have established, although this is not a consistent position. 'Born This Way' and Gaga's declaration of a body revolution may call for acceptance of physical difference but body is identity—a slight revision of biology is destiny—is not necessarily a progressive stance and it certainly lends itself to politically conservative arguments when it comes to gender and race, for example, since it prioritizes essentialism over cultural contingency and performativity.[13] This conservatism, though, may be entirely appropriate since, contrary to its propaganda, the music industry rarely takes risks, and since all of this takes place in a late capitalist, neoliberal context. Gaga offers a model of decadent consumption, offset with charitable work and actions, and continuing re-invention of the self that sits well with the neoliberal notion that individuals are responsible for themselves alone, and are entrepreneurs of the self. She sells the idea of an autonomous, creative individual while simultaneously being contractually beholden to her record company.[14] Stefani Germanotta is both a laborer in the music industry, and an entrepreneur selling products (Lady Gaga, records, lipstick, perfume, fashion).

Gaga has made being a misfit profitable. She appeals to an audience of young people who identify with her feelings of not fitting in.[15] She has championed gay rights, discussed the prevention of bullying with one of US President Barack Obama's staffers, and set up a foundation to 'foster a more accepting society,' which embraces differences and celebrates individuality.[16] In a sense, being a misfit, never belonging to one place, may be part of early twenty-first century neoliberalism. An identity tied to a job or a profession, for example, is not available to all, given that employers in so many sectors value the flexibility offered them by temporary hires and short term contracts. Identity is increasingly bound up with consumption.

My basic contention is that the Gaga brand is a form of Žižek's 'capitalism with a human face', one that enables the late capitalist phenomenon of commodity activism and commodity feminism.[17] By buying (into) Gaga, consumers can buy 'redemption from being only a consumerist' through identification with the social causes she champions and participation in her online community (littlemonsters.com) or other social networks (particularly Twitter).[18] Moreover, Gaga encourages her Little Monsters to share their own creative works and build their own narratives as consumer-producers; they contribute unpaid immaterial labor to produce web content and help to define and shape the Gaga brand.[19] Gaga is simultaneously a personal brand and a cultural product; although originally conceived by Germanotta, Lady Gaga is the product of a team of strategic thinkers and creators who maximize profit through careful management of brand partnerships, synchronization deals, merchandizing, and development and exploitation of a consumer-producer base though social media.[20] While Little Monsters may contribute to the brand on the social network without seeking the permission of Gaga first, the Gaga team protects the brand from commercial exploitation by others, as The Icecreamists discovered.

EXPLOITING GAGA

The Icecreamists created Baby Gaga breast milk ice cream to attract attention for the opening of their new boutique parlor in Covent Garden. They worked closely with PR firm Taylor Herring Ltd from the start. In fact, the PR company came up with the idea of a breast milk ice cream—it was one of several they put to their client—and their management of the launch garnered them an Event Award 2011 for best PR Event/Stunt.[21] After placing an advert on Mumsnet, The Icecreamists hired lactating mother and volunteer breastfeeding educator Victoria Hiley to supply breast milk. Despite the firm's description of Hiley as a donor, echoed in many of the news articles, she was compensated for her labor. The reported payment rate was £15 for 10 fluid ounces, which probably amounted to less than the minimum wage. (It takes some women 10–15 minutes to pump 1 oz.). Hiley's first batch of breast milk (30 fl oz) was mixed with cow milk cream and turned into a Madagascan vanilla and lemon zest ice cream. It was served in martini glasses by waitresses wearing costumes clearly reminiscent of Lady Gaga that were designed by a fashion student 'to keep overall costs to a minimum'.[22] The ice cream reportedly sold out the first day.

Not everyone was enthusiastic: food critic Zoe Williams concluded, 'At first I liked it; then I didn't mind it; then I hated it; then I wanted to be sick.'[23] The Food Standards Agency, the Health Protection Agency and Westminster City Council expressed concerns about the ice cream's suitability for human consumption—something the PR company had anticipated and built into their strategy—and council officers took samples for safety testing.[24] And many people find the concept of breast milk ice cream repulsive. Victoria Hiley, who initially provided the milk, said the ice cream was 'burlesque: It's sexy and unsexy; beautiful and repellent.' Hiley stated that she was pronounced 'revolting,' was accused of spreading disease, 'scolded for not donating to a milk bank [. . .] and [was] told to keep [her] fluids' to herself.'[25] Lady Gaga, or her lawyers, described it as 'deliberately provocative and, to many people, nausea inducing'.[26]

Like Lady Gaga, the controversial raw ingredient can be read as subversive or conservative. Breast milk has a complex social, racial, and transnational history. It is arguably the principal source for women's cultural association with food and nurturing, since a normally lactating woman can sustain her infant solely with breast milk for at least the first six months of the child's life. Human breast milk is often positioned as anti-capitalist or at least non-capitalist. It is something most women's (and some men's) bodies can make given certain hormones and physical stimulation; it is healthier than formula, and produced by women for their individual children rather than by vast food corporations for anonymous consumers.[27] Yet breastfeeding is considered and experienced by some in industrialized nations as tying a woman both to her child and to her home. Moreover, not all women are seen as producing equally healthy breast milk: in some states, women with addictions to legal substances and who are from underprivileged groups can be jailed for breastfeeding.[28] A state's emphasis on the importance of breastfeeding may potentially be a regressive step rather than a progressive step, unless it is accompanied by legal changes and social acceptance of breastfeeding in public and in the workplace.[29] In contemporary USA, the labor of breastfeeding has racial and socio-economic dimensions: within every subgroup, non-Hispanic black women are less likely than non-Hispanic white women to continue breastfeeding, while Hispanic women (whether black or white) and Asian women have the highest breastfeeding rates overall.[30] The majority of nursing women who have paid work outside the home are in professional or flexible service occupations, in part because these are the women who can arrange their schedules to enable the continuation of breastfeeding, or whose employers offer time and privacy for nursing or pumping.[31] And one of the ways a state may try to convince employers to support lactating workers is to argue that children fed breast milk are healthier than formula-fed babies, and therefore their parents take fewer days off to tend to sick kids. In other words, in a neoliberal economic climate, in order to justify giving lactating women who work outside the home the time and space to pump milk for their babies while at work, or to feed their babies directly, breastfeeding is given an economic value outside of the domestic sphere. This is not quite the same as creating a market for breast milk, although such a market does exist. Websites such as www.onlythebreast.com provide an unregulated space for women to sell breast milk to others for feeding infants, or even to supply the adult erotic lactation market (primarily men who like to drink human breast milk).

The ick factor of food for adults made with human breast milk is probably a combination of the potential for disease transmission and the taboo on consuming human bodily fluids—or perhaps it is more accurate to say anonymous consumption of human body fluids, since sexually active partners often share some bodily fluids—as well as the erotic connotations of breasts in Britain and the US, among other cultures, and the implied sexualized infantilization of the adult consumer.[32] The Icecreamists boutique is aimed at adults. The interior is decorated 'like a sex shop from the 80s' and they developed a line of 'Vice Creams' (ice creams and alcohol).[33] The intro to The Icecreamists website (www.theicecreamists.com) employs a by now standard image in eroticized marketing of ice cream: a woman's mouth open wide, licking ice cream from a spoon, in this case. (European adverts for Magnum ice cream employ similar images.) A subsequent image captioned 'sub zero medication' has a woman with her bust bursting out of a nurse costume feeding ice cream to an apparently naked and very happy young man. Hiley appreciated the burlesque concept behind the store, and apparently saw the breast milk ice cream and the resulting publicity as an opportunity to discuss breastfeeding more generally. Unfortunately for Hiley, lactation politics does not sell newspapers or ice cream; the 'tacky' quotes attributed to her in the official press release ('using my assets for a bit of extra cash?') were used in preference to her own words.[34]

Although there is an attempt to cast the breast milk ice cream as sexy burlesque, comments from the company illustrate the conflicted sexual politics and stray in to misogyny. They describe the milk as organic and free range—terms that normally refer to farm animals—and Matt O'Connor, the owner, claims to be 'challenging the preconceptions we have about food, about farming. [. . .] About ice cream.'[35] In one interview, O'Connor stated 'it [the boutique] looked more like a milking parlour than an ice cream parlour'[36]; in another, he asked '[w]ould you rather have a cheeky suckle of an attractive woman or a cheeky suckle of a cloven hoofed beast covered in dung?'[37] Indeed, The Icecreamists are not the first to draw a parallel between lactating women and cows: recently, PETA, an organization that is not known for its feminist politics, attempted to draw attention to the suffering of dairy cows by suggesting Ben & Jerry's should switch to human breast milk.[38] This is not anthropomorphizing cows but theriomorphizing women.

To associate this product with a woman celebrity, even one known for burlesque, for courting controversy through unusual uses of food stuffs, such as the meat dress, and, less charitably, for arguably playing along with the music industry's continued commodification of the female body, hardly seems to be intended as an honor.[39] It is not homage like Ben & Jerry's Cherry Garcia, and the 'nausea inducing' product reportedly earned them a cease and desist letter from Ate My Heart, Inc., Lady Gaga's publisher, on the grounds of trade mark infringement. The letter described the use of Gaga-themed costumes as 'clearly deliberate and intended to take advantage of her reputation and good will.'[40] O'Connor's response was to deny there was any reference to Lady Gaga, despite the similar name for the ice cream and the servers' costumes. He claimed the costumes were based on Jean-Paul Gaultier's cone bra designed for Madonna in 1990, and that Gaga did not have legitimate grounds for complaint since she also recycled pop culture.[41] He described the episode as a 'storm in a D cup' and said Gaga had no sense of humor.[42] While O'Connor took a dismissive tone in media interviews, in the end, he had to change the name of the ice cream: it is now called Baby Googoo.

BAKING GAGA

The Lady Gaga cakes I have found pictured on the Internet appear to be fan tributes that for the most part are hand made. In contrast, the majority of Beyoncé and Rihanna cakes were decorated with photographs printed with edible ink onto icing. This can be done via online mail order companies: the customer uploads a photo, the company prints it on to icing and posts it out for the customer to carefully transfer it to the cake. It appears that the DIY creativity of Little Monster culture extends from the costumes many fans make to wear to her live performances, and the poetry, photographs and artwork they share on littlemonsters.com, to the cakes they make or order. Even if some of these cakes are made by a professional baker, there seems to be a qualitative difference between printed images of a photograph and a molded fondant figurine in the implied personal touch. Cakes decorated by hand are still luxury items not because of the rarity and expense of the ingredients—sugar is now ubiquitous, especially in the form of corn syrup and high fructose corn syrup, and it is so cheap that it is used in many convenience foods, savory and sweet—but because of the time involved. A Lady Gaga made from fondant icing and details in food coloring does not only represent the time it took to make that specific Gaga, but also the time it took to develop the necessary skills. It is the result of productive labor: sugar work.

These cakes are a modern contribution to the history of food as art.[43] At least one was created by a professional. The life-size Gaga cake by Jay Murphy was multi purpose: a fan's commemoration of Gaga that extended and demonstrated his skill, attracted free publicity and therefore potentially brought in indirect business. It is thoroughly in keeping with a long tradition of sugar sculptures and with the history of theatrical window displays in confectioners' shops.

Murphy's Gaga is dressed in a white fondant frosting decorated with little silver sugar balls. The design is modeled on the white body suit by Somarta that Lady Gaga wore for Gagakoh, a collaboration with Terence Koh, hosted by MAC Viva Glam and KCD Worldwide at the Tabloid nightclub in Tokyo on 19 April 2010.[44] Gaga and Koh walked to the show in procession wearing white Shinto bridal headdresses by Balmung. In many ways, Murphy's creation owes something to US wedding traditions, namely the nineteenth-century ornamental bride cake. This was commonly made from angel food cake and covered with a hard white icing. The cake symbolized the pure, virginal bride, and thus the wedding couple holding the knife and cutting into the cake was analogous to the breaking of the hymen and consummation of the marriage. Murphy's vanilla cake Gaga is not intended for consumption but for display, for visual consumption.[45] And, like the untouched wedding cake in Dickens's *Great Expectations*, it will eventually decay. Said Murphy, 'I hate to say I'll throw her away, but she'll break down one way or the other.'[46] The life-size Gaga cake is decorative and transient, qualities that are, perhaps not coincidentally, attributed to many women pop stars whose work is presumed to be inconsequential and who are expected to have short careers.

CAKE LIKE LADY GAGA

To my knowledge, Lady Gaga has not baked a cake of herself, but she has used cake as a metaphor to discuss her work and herself. In an interview with Neil Strauss for *Rolling Stone*, for instance, she implied that initially she had to be 'sweet' to get attention (from the record company? from the public?) but that 'sweet' was not really her, or not completely her: 'I have been for three years baking cakes—and now I'm going to bake a cake that has a bitter jelly. [. . .] The message of the new music [presumably *Born This Way*] is now more bitter than it was before. Because the sweeter the cake, the more bitter the jelly can be. If I had come out as who I was, no one would be listening.'[47] Here, Gaga presents herself as an entrepreneur of the self who carefully disguised the less palatable aspects of her interiority in order to achieve success and the freedom to reveal her self, to come out as who she is. The idea that Lady Gaga had kept part of herself closeted is not one that Gaga normally pushes in interviews; she frequently insists instead that there is no inner identity hiding inside Gaga.

A recent rap song, 'Cake Like Lady Gaga', also known as 'Cake' or 'Trap', uses cake as a metaphor for wealth, luxury and excess. The kind of consumption the song outlines is also an investment in image and it illustrates Gaga's success in her neoliberal entrepreneurship of her self:

> Private plane like Lady Gaga
> Sip champagne like Lady Gaga
> Sold-out show like Lady Gaga
> Big bank roll like Lady Gaga
> Iced-out wrist, iced out chain
> [. . .]
> Diamond ring like Lady Gaga
> [. . .]
> Cake like Lady Gaga
> Cake like Lady Gaga

Gaga used the song in her work for the Mugler Spring/Summer 2013 show at Paris Fashion Week. It first appeared as an official 'leak'.[48] The usual narrative is as follows: DJ White Shadow, the producer, uploaded an incomplete sound file to SoundCloud and, on Twitter, announced a competition to provide a vocal track. Some hours later, the experiment in crowd sourcing was apparently over. Tara Savelo, Lady Gaga's make-up artist, used her Twitter account to share a link to another track on DJ White Shadow's

SoundCloud with an apparently male voice rapping about Gaga and cake. An unnamed fan realized the voice had been manipulated, altered its pitch and discovered it was Lady Gaga.

Gaga certainly plays with notions of white femininity by releasing a track that, according to *Spin*, sounds like rapper and producer Tyler, the Creator; she gave a cross-gender, black voice performance.[49] While this challenges notions of white feminine vocal performance, it does so through a pastiche of black macho masculinity. The performance does not work to dismantle racial categories although it does highlight their existence. She then employed the song in a collaboration with a major fashion house, thus gaining further cultural capital. While on the one hand this challenges notions of white femininity—white women singers just do not do black male voices—it depends upon and reinforces white supremacy.[50] The main beneficiaries are institutions that regulate hegemonic whiteness.

Gaga has released two teasers of the video directed by Terry Richardson. A photo from the shoot released on Twitter depicts a brunette Gaga in her underwear and high heel shoes, covered in cake and frosting with the caption: 'The real CAKE isn't HAVING what you want, It's DOING what you want'.[51] This undercuts the avarice voiced in the lyrics by emphasizing action over acquisition and fits with the mission of the Born This Way Foundation to 'celebrate individuality,' 'encourage self-expression' and help young people to 'feel empower[ed]'.[52] Yet empowerment has become a fuzzy notion, perhaps best illustrated by an article in the satirical newspaper *The Onion*, 'Women Now Empowered By Everything A Woman Does', which emphasized the idea that while women previously felt empowered by 'advancing in a male-dominated work world', contemporary women can feel empowered through consumerism: Banet-Weiser's consumer feminism.[53] Paradoxically, Gaga foregrounds the kind of neoliberal subjectivities that obscure the fact that there are structural barriers to everyone being able to do what they want: the idea that all individuals have the freedom to do what they want presupposes a level playing field that does not exist and cannot exist under neoliberal capitalism.

NOTES

1. I am grateful to Suzanne Cusick and Margaret McFadden for encouraging me to write about ice cream, and cake. I thank Jessica Allen for doing her job and directing me to resources, and, more personally, Catherine Watson Genna for her support.
2. Neil Strauss, 'The Broken Heart & Violent Fantasies of Lady Gaga', *Rolling Stone*, no. 1108/1109 (8–22 July 2010), 66–72, 74, 20.
3. 'Lady Gaga on "mastering the art of fame"', *60 Minutes* (online at: http://www.cbsnews.com/8301–18560_162–20066912.html?pageNum=2) <Last updated: 5 June 2011> <accessed: 31 March 2013>.
4. Margaret Atwood, *The Edible Woman* (New York, NY: Anchor Books, 1998 [1969]), 13.

5. Rap Genius, 'Lady Gaga—Cake Like Lady Gaga Lyrics' (online at: http://rapgenius.com/Lady-gaga-cake-like-lady-gaga-lyrics) <accessed: 30 April 2013>. This includes the verse Lady Gaga added for the Mugler Spring/Summer 2013 show at Paris Fashion Week.

6. EclSpatial, 'Lady Gaga Cupcakes-muffins' (6 February 2010) (online at: http://www.flickr.com/photos/47259637@N07/4331876071/) <accessed: 31 March 2013>. The Haus of Gaga Origami Dress is based on Thierry Mugler's Origami Dress (2008).

7. Charla Vail, 'Lady Gaga Cake' (5 February 2010) (online at: http://www.flickr.com/photos/charlavail/4336385478/) <accessed: 31 March 2013>.

8. Stella Inger, 'Life-size Lady Gaga Cake a Labor of Love for Phoenix Chef', *azfamily.com* (23 January 2013; updated 24 January 2013) (online at: http://www.azfamily.com/news/inger/Life-size-Lady-Gaga-cake—188070991.html) <accessed: 31 March 2013>. See also 'The Making of a Life Size Lady Gaga Cake', *Yahoo! Shine* (online at: http://shine.yahoo.com/photos/making-life-size-lady-gaga-slideshow/-photo-2573087–192900800.html) <accessed: 28 April 2013>.

9. Amy Fallon, 'Human Milk Ice Cream Goes on Sale', *The Guardian* (25 February 2011) (online at: http://www.guardian.co.uk/lifeandstyle/2011/feb/25/human-milk-ice-cream-sale/) <accessed: 23 March 2013>.

10. 'Lady Gaga on "mastering the art of fame"'.

11. J. Jack Halberstam, *Gaga Feminism: Sex, Gender and the End of Normal* (Boston, MA: Beacon Press, 2012).

12. See Burns and LaFrance, this volume.

13. Performativity, as I understand it, is one explanation of the cultural shaping of the person. My short version of Judith Butler's theory as laid out in *Gender Trouble* (2nd edition [London: Routledge, 1999]) and *Bodies that Matter* (New York, NY: Routledge, 1993) is as follows: a person comes into being through an ongoing, dynamic and complex process of interaction between various cultural norms, and through their own repetitive actions that are unconscious and based on a culture's existing repertoire of gestures and possibilities. A person might find themselves falling into the constitutive outside that defines the boundary of 'normal', in which case they are not culturally intelligible and officialdom may make existence in their own terms impossible. This does not mean that one has limitless freedom to choose what to be—it is not a personal choice that one makes at an arbitrary age—since much of the shaping is done while one is still a child without a concept of selfhood, at the stage when neural pathways are being laid down (hence the significance of interpellation). It does leave open the prospect that the cultural script might gradually change, which is what I believe is happening as more states and countries legally recognize same sex relationships, and as disability rights activists articulate the violence of neurotypical and able-bodied privilege.

14. Matt Stahl, *Unfree Masters: Recording Artists and the Politics of Work* (Durham, NC: Duke University Press, 2013) investigates this paradox. Stahl sees Gaga's success as buying her greater autonomy than less successful recording artists.

15. Melissa A. Click, Hyunji Lee and Holly Willson Holladay's article, 'Making Monsters: Lady Gaga, Fan Identification, and Social Media' (*Popular Music and Society*, vol. 36, no. 3 (July 2013), 360–379) investigates Gaga fans who self-identify as Little Monsters and demonstrates her signficance to them. The Little Monsters interviewed use Lady Gaga 'to reflect upon their own self-identities, to build self-confidence, and to embrace their differences from mainstream culture' (376); through their intense identification

with Lady Gaga, they find the resilience they need to survive being bullied and discriminated against.

16. Born This Way Foundation, 'Our Mission' (online at: http://bornthisway-foundation.org/pages/our-mission/) <accessed: 20 April 2013>.
17. Slavoj Žižek, 'First as Tragedy, Then as Farce', RSA, 24 November 2009. This talk is available in two separate videos: one 10' 57" version with an absorbing animation (4 August 2010, online at: http://www.thersa.org/events/rsaanimate/animate/rsa-animate-first-as-tragedy,-then-as-farce <accessed: 30 March 2013>), the other the full lecture (24 November 2009, online at: http://www.thersa.org/events/video/archive/slavoj-Žižek-first-as-tragedy,-then-as-farce <accessed: 30 March 2013>). On the origin and development of commodity activism, see Sarah Banet-Weiser, *Authentic: Political Possibilities in a Brand Culture* (New York, NY: New York University Press, 2012).
18. Žižek, 'First as Tragedy, Then as Farce'.
19. Banet-Weiser, *Authentic*. On the immaterial labor that produces cultural content, see Maurizio Lazzarato, *Lavoro immateriale: Forme di vita e produzione di soggettività* (Verona: Ombre Corte, 1997). Banet-Weiser discusses unpaid immaterial labor performed by consumer-producers on a Dove advertising campaign website.
20. For the recording industry's summary of its role in investing in music, including the opportunities for brand partnerships and 'synch deals', see the International Federation of the Phonographic Industry (IFPI), 'Record labels invest US$4.5 billion in new music', 12 November 2012 (online at: http://www.ifpi.org/content/section_news/investing_in_music.html) <accessed: 30 March 2013>. On the branding of women pop stars, including frequent discussion of Lady Gaga, see Kristen Lieb, *Gender, Branding, and the Modern Music Industry* (New York, NY: Routledge, 2013).
21. For Taylor Herring Ltd's account of the campaign, see Taylor Herring Ltd., 'The Icecreamists: Launching the World's First Breastmilk Icecream', [undated] (online at: http://www.taylorherring.com/case-studies/breast-milk-ice-cream/) <accessed: 30 March 2013>. For the award, see http://www.event magazine.co.uk/news/1093686/Event-Awards-2011-winners-announced/.
22. Taylor Herring Ltd., 'The Icecreamists'. The proportions of human milk to cow milk cream is mentioned in Zoe Williams, 'Breast Milk Ice-Cream: The Taste Test', *The Guardian*, 27 February 2011 (online at: http://www.guardian.co.uk/lifeandstyle/2011/feb/27/breast-milk-ice-cream-taste) <accessed: 22 April 2013>.
23. Zoe Williams, 'Breast Milk Ice-Cream'.
24. 'Baby Gaga Breast Milk Ice Cream Seized for Safety Tests', BBC News (London edition), 1 March 2011 (online at: http://www.bbc.co.uk/news/uk-england-london-12615353) <accessed: 23 March 2013>.
25. Victoria Hiley, 'Lady Gaga and My Breast Milk Burlesque', *The Guardian*, 6 March 2011 (online at: http://www.guardian.co.uk/theguardian/2011/mar/07/my-breast-milk-ilady-gaga/) <accessed: 23 March 2013>.
26. Bill Chappell, 'Breast Milk Ice Cream Back on Sale; Lady Gaga May Sue', NPR, 29 March 2011 (online at: http://www.npr.org/blogs/thetwo-way/2011/03/09/134389930/breast-milk-ice-cream-back-on-sale-lady-gaga-may-sue) <accessed: 23 March 2013>. The Icecreamists eventually changed the name of the ice cream to Baby Goo Goo.
27. The American Academy of Pediatrics, the World Health Organization, and other bodies recommend infants are exclusively breastfed for the first six months of their lives for reasons of nutrition and health. Many lactation activists (lactivists), anti-globalization protestors, and political entities proclaim the superiority of breast milk over formula on nutritional

and health grounds. New York City's Department of Health, for example, recently ran a multilingual pro-breast-feeding poster campaign in subway trains and hospitals (New York City Press Office, 'New York City Health Department Launches "Latch On NYC" Initiative to Support Breast-feeding Mothers', 9 May 2012 (online at: http://www.nyc.gov/html/doh/html/pr2012/pr013–12.shtml) <accessed: 24 March 2013>). However, many claims about infant feeding are not based on medical evidence; this is a discourse regulating women's bodies: see Jules Law, 'The Politics of Breastfeeding: Assessing Risk, Dividing Labor', *Signs*, vol. 25, no.2 (Winter 2000), 407–450. Aref Abu-Rabia, 'Breastfeeding Practices among Pastoral Tribes in the Middle East: A Cross-Cultural Study', *Anthropology of the Middle East*, vol. 2 no. 2 (2007), 38–54 has a brief discussion of historical and cross-cultural breastfeeding practices in Europe and the Middle East.

28. Kimberly Robertson places Native American breastfeeding in transnational contexts. Robertson points out that in the US, women with alcoholism who are breastfeeding their babies and are from underprivileged groups can find themselves jailed ('Globalization and the Politics of Native Breastfeeding', *Off Of Our Backs*, vol. 36 no. 4 (2006), 61–64).

29. For a thorough discussion, see Linda M. Blum, 'Mothers, Babies, and Breastfeeding in Late Capitalist America: The Shifting Contexts of Feminist Theory', *Feminist Studies*, vol. 19, no. 2 (Summer 1993), 291–311. Robertson's 'Globalization and the Politics of Native Breastfeeding' considers the effects of race and colonialism. Jacqueline H Wolf, 'Got Milk? Not In Public!', *International Breastfeeding Journal*, vol. 3, no. 11 (2008) (online at: http://www.internationalbreastfeedingjournal.com/content/3/1/11) <accessed: 20 August 2013> discusses the public health consequences of the sexualization of breasts in the US. That article is part of a special collection edited by Miriam H. Labbok, Paige Hall Smith, and Emily C. Taylor, 'Breastfeeding and Feminism: Reproductive Health, Rights and Justice', *International Breastfeeding Journal*, vol. 3 (2008) (online at: http://www.internationalbreastfeedingjournal.com/series/1746–4358-Fem) <accessed: 21 August 2013>. Wolf called for feminist support of breastfeeding in 'What Feminists Can Do for Breastfeeding and What Breastfeeding Can Do for Feminists', *Signs*, vol. 31, no. 2 (2006), 397–24.

30. The most recent sociodemographic breakdown is of data from births in 2007 (US Centers for Disease Control and Prevention, Division of Nutrition, Physical Activity, and Obesity, 'Breastfeeding Among U.S. Children Born 2000–2010, CDC National Immunization Survey' (online at: http://www.cdc.gov/breastfeeding/data/NIS_data/index.htm), <last reviewed: 31 July 2013>, <accessed: 16 August 2013>). For brief discussions, see Jessica A. Allen, Ruowei Li, Kelley S. Scanlon, Cria G. Perrine, Jian Chen, Erika Odom, and Carla Black, 'Progress in Increasing Breastfeeding and Reducing Racial/Ethnic Differences—United States, 2000–2008 Births', *Morbidity and Mortality Weekly Report*, vol. 62, no. 5 (8 February 2013), 77–80, (online at: http://www.cdc.gov/mmwr/preview/mmwrhtml/mm6205a1.htm), <accessed: 16 August 2013>; L. Gummer-Strawn, K. S. Scanlon, N. Darling, and E. J. Conrey, 'Racial and Socioeconomic Disparities in Breastfeeding—United States, 2004', *Morbidity and Mortality Weekly Report*, vol. 55, no. 12 (31 March 2006), 335–339 (online at: http://www.cdc.gov/mmwr/preview/mmwrhtml/mm5512a3.htm), <accessed: 16 August 2013>.

31. Rachel Tolbert Kimbro, 'On-the-Job Moms: Work and Breastfeeding Initiation and Duration for a Sample of Low-Income Women', *Maternal and Child Health Journal*, vol. 10, no. 1 (January 2006), 19–26.

32. Wolf, 'Got Milk? Not in Public!' briefly covers the cultural specificity of the idea that breasts are for sexual activity rather than for feeding a baby.

33. Williams, 'Breast Milk Ice Cream: The Taste Test'.

34. Jo, 'Baby Gaga Ice Cream: Victoria Hiley's Story', *The Babi Pur Blog*, 6 March 2011 (online at: http://www.ethicalshoppingforbabies.co.uk/2011/03/baby-gaga-icecream-victoria-hileys-story/) <accessed: 25 April 2013>.

35. Williams, 'Breast Milk Ice Cream: The Taste Test'.

36. Glynn Davis, 'Innovative Retailers Part 3—Where Ice Cream Is Much More than Just Ice and Cream', *Retail Insider*, 3 November 2011 (online at: http://www.retailinsider.com/2011/11/innovative-retailers-part-3-where-ice.html; and at: http://blog.theicecreamists.com/2011/11/420/) <accessed: 25 April 2013>.

37. The Icecreamists, 'Devilishly Good: Covent Garden Journal Interview with Matt O'Connor', 24 June 2011 (online at: http://blog.theicecreamists.com/2011/06/devilishly-good-covent-garden-journal-interview-with-matt-oconnor/) <accessed: 26 April 2013>.

38. The Associated Press, 'PETA Calls On Ice Cream Maker To Use Breast Milk', *LA Times*, 26 September 2008 (online at: http://articles.latimes.com/2008/sep/26/business/fi-icecream26) <accessed: 23 April 2013>; PETA, 'Breast Milk Headlines Explode After Ben & Jerry's Letter', *The PETA Files*, 10 October 2008 (online at: http://www.peta.org/b/thepetafiles/archive/2008/10/10/Breast-Milk-Headlines-Explode-After-Ben—Jerrys-Letter.aspx?PageIndex=3) <accessed: 25 April 2013>.

39. On the meat dress, see Lucy O'Brien's contribution to this volume.

40. By the time Gaga's lawyers contacted The Icecreamist with a cease and desist letter, the ice cream had been taken off the shelves by officers of Westminster Council who were concerned about the health implications. Alleged extracts of the letter were made available on the web: Hollywood Life Staff [Leigh Blickley with reporting by Jessica Finn], 'Lady Gaga Goes Gaga Over Breast Milk Ice Cream: "Spoon-to-Spoon Combat! Exclusive!"' (online at: http://hollywoodlife.com/2011/03/08/lady-gaga-breast-milk-ice-cream-interview-matt-o-connor/) <accessed: 26 April 2013>.

41. Owen Bowcott, 'Lady Gaga Takes On Baby Gaga in Breast Milk Ice-Cream Battle', *The Guardian*, 4 March 2011 (online at: http://www.guardian.co.uk/music/2011/mar/04/lady-gaga-baby-ice-cream) <accessed: 26 April 2013>.

42. This phrase appears in several reports, including Hollywood Life Staff, 'Lady Gaga Goes Gaga Over Breast Milk Ice Cream', and in an interview with the Covent Garden Journal which was cross-posted to The Icecreamists' blog: 'Devilishly Good: Covent Garden Journal Interview with Matt O'Connor'.

43. For discussion focused on confectionary in the US, see Wendy A. Woolson, *Refined Tastes: Sugar, Confectionery, and Consumers in Nineteenth-Century America* (Baltimore. MD: Johns Hopkins University Press, 2002).

44. The artists combined their names for the performance. Gagakoh is no doubt intended to be reminiscent of Gagaku. The proceeds of the Viva Glam cosmetics line are donated to the MAC AIDS Fund. This is in itself an example of 'capitalism with a human face'.

45. I borrow the idea of visual consumption from Woolson, *Refined Tastes*, 156.

46. Eatocracy Editors, 'Rah-rah oh yum yum: Fan Makes Life-Sized Lady Gaga Cake', *Eatocracy*, 24 January 2013 (online at: http://eatocracy.cnn.com/2013/01/24/life-sized-lady-gaga-cake/) <accessed: 26 April 2013>.

47. Neil Strauss, 'The Broken Heart & Violent Fantasies of Lady Gaga'.

48. Chris Martins, 'Lady Gaga "Leak" Fools Fans: Hear Cake Like Lady Gaga', *Spin*, 19 September 2012 (online at: http://www.spin.com/articles/lady-gaga-rap-leak-fools-fans-cake-like-gaga/) <accessed: 26 April 2013>.

49. On whiteness and femininity in US popular music history, see Laurie Stras, ed., *She's So Fine: Reflections on Whiteness, Femininity, Adolescence and Class in 1960s Music* (Aldershot: Ashgate, 2010); and Laurie Stras, 'White Face, Black Voice: Race, Gender and Region in the Music of the Boswell Sisters', *Journal of the Society for American Music* 1 (2007), 207–255.

50. The most significant text on the financial benefits of white privilege is George Lipsitz, *The Possessive Investment in Whiteness: How White People Profit from Identity Politics*, 2nd Edition (Philadelphia, PA: Temple University Press, 2006). On conceptions of whiteness and womanhood in the US, see Ruth Frankenberg, *White Women, Race Matters: The Social Construction of Whiteness* (Minneapolis, MN: The University of Minnesota Press, 1993).

51. Lady Gaga (@ladygaga), 15 November 2012 at 3.11pm (online at: https://twitter.com/ladygaga/status/269170781794213888) <accessed: 28 April 2013> (capitalization and punctuation as in original).

52. Born This Way Foundation, 'Our Mission'.

53. See Banet-Weiser, *Authentic*, and 'Women Now Empowered By Everything A Woman Does', *The Onion*, 19 February 2003 (online at: http://www.theonion.com/articles/women-now-empowered-by-everything-a-woman-does,1398/) <accessed: 28 April 2013>.

Supplement
Poker-faced. Revealing Nothing

Martin Iddon

All go unto one place; all are of the dust, and all turn to dust again.

Ecclesiastes 3:20

Elle, défunte nue en le miroir, encor
Que, dan l'oubli fermé par le cadre, se fixe
De scintillations sitôt le septuor.

'Ses purs ongles très haut . . . ', Stéphane Mallarmé

This final chapter is intended, in a wholly Derridean sense, as a supplement, rather than a conclusion. It does not, in and of itself, present anything 'new' about Lady Gaga; indeed, the evidence it relies on in terms of Gaga herself is precisely that which the previous chapters have presented. The reader looking for further insight, then, into Gaga *qua* Gaga will find this chapter, appropriately enough, empty. It is, as Derrida suggests the quality of a supplement ought to be, un-necessary, excess to that which is truly essential. Yet I hope that the reader looking for ways in which to debate what precedes this final contribution in a wider frame will also find a particular way in which it reflects upon the previous chapters, bringing together at least one of the strands which runs through them. Its interest is, on the one hand, to reflect upon what the evidence of the volume might be capable of saying in broader terms but, in a way which is, I hope, coherent with this chapter's more general thrust, not likely to reveal anything further about Gaga 'herself'. By contrast, Gaga here functions much more as a focus to talk about what she might be capable of showing about how aesthetics (and inaesthetics) can be held to function in the contemporary world. Gaga is, the reader should be warned in advance, palpably absent from the text of this chapter for much of its duration. Indeed, the reader might (rightly) suspect that she is only one of a number of potential examples that could have been marshalled here. That the example could have been a different one does not, I trust, take away from the degree to which Gaga is ideally suited to the purposes of this chapter.

Those purposes are, then, twofold. First, I seek to suggest, following Badiou (and, in a sense, Hegel), that art is a site where metaphysical enquiry takes place and that it is, by consequence, a site where truths can be revealed. Second, and as a further consequence, I aim to perform something of a reconciliation between modernist and postmodernist claims for the meaningfulness of the work of art. This argument is undertaken through the proposition that the ideas of modernist presence and postmodernist absence have often been elided with notions of plenitude and emptiness, respectively. This stance finds a close analogue in Badiou's claim at the outset of *Logics of Worlds* that the world of contemporary discourse admits only two sites: 'Today, natural belief is condensed into a single statement: *There are only bodies and languages.*'[1] The 'there is' of the world (indeed of worlds in Badiou's terms), then, is just this intermingling of bodies and languages, which is to say that contemporary thought broadly insists upon a (bodily) materialism suspended within (linguistic) discourse. Yet, vitally, Badiou insists that 'there isn't only what there is. And "truths" is the (philosophical) name of what interpolates itself into the continuity of the "there is"'.[2] The only obvious conclusion to be drawn from what Badiou suggests here is the 'truth' is therefore something that, in a sense, isn't. This is, indeed, exactly what Badiou *is* proposing: that the truth of what he calls the 'event' is always already absent from the situation, the 'way things are'. I will hope to clarify this position in what follows. By taking an approach developing from Heidegger's later reconfiguration of ἀλήθεια in *Parmenides* allied with Badiou's theorization of events, I suggest that the ways in which artworks reveal truths may remain constant, even where art becomes 'about' a sort of absence at its heart. In truth, it will become clear, I suspect, that I sympathize strongly with the idea that art ('real' art, perhaps even to the degree Hegel would have conceived of it, as I discuss below) is always about a revealing of a sort of absence; though I do not develop the point here, I suspect strongly that this may be a more generalizable idea, regardless of the historical epoch, and that 'real' art was ever thus: the idea of the birth to presence was always a fictional construct, the un-truth of which has only latterly become evident.

As Hegel puts it, '[f]ine art is not real art till it is [. . .] free, and only achieves its highest task when it has taken its place in the same sphere with religion and philosophy, and has become simply a mode of revealing to consciousness and bringing to utterance the Divine Nature, the deepest interests if humanity, and the most comprehensive truths of the mind.'[3] Thus the truth of art, from Hegel's perspective, art which has come to itself as it were, has several important characteristics in this description, although whether, in Hegel's terms they are ultimately dissociable from one another is certainly debatable. First, art must be 'free'. What Hegel means by this can be understood by his conception of what the world is. The world for Hegel is supra-sensuous, 'erected as a *beyond* over [and] against immediate consciousness and present sensation.'[4] The world, then, is unbounded by mere sensation, while the sensuous realm—which Heidegger would later distinguish as 'earth', rather than 'world'—is, by virtue of *being* sensuous, limited from the outset.[5] The unboundedness of the realm of thought—the world proper—is the quality of freedom Hegel ascribes to real art. In this sense, when Hegel demands that real art be free art, this is synonymous with his claim that real art's highest task—the task that moves it from being mere pastime to art proper—is to act as a way of revealing profound truths, ones which are concealed in the everyday realm of mere sensations. This, in turn, becomes synonymous with the other ways in which Hegel argues truth can be revealed, through religion and philosophy, though the synonymy is of a limited sort, to be sure, as discussed below. In any case, what is vital to the proper functioning of proper art is that its sensuous surface is shot through with something *else*, an arrow which points toward the world of Hegel's absolute.

Unsurprisingly, in such a context, Hegel is wary of art which is merely sensuous. In essence, much like Kant, Hegel is concerned by an aesthetics which would reduce the qualities of artworks only to its etymological root, to αἴσθησις.[6] As he describes it:

> Art liberates the real import of appearances from the semblance and deception of this bad and fleeting world, and imparts to phenomenal semblances a higher reality, born of mind. The appearances of art, therefore, far from being mere semblances, have the higher reality and the more genuine existence in comparison with the realities of common life.[7]

His conception of what art (true art, in any case) is is reliant upon a pulsation, a continual to-and-fro, re-sounding between the limited finitude of the senses and the unboundedness of infinite thought. It is this pulsation, from Hegel's perspective, which makes the artwork possible as such: the way in which art represents even the 'highest' thoughts in sensuous form allows those ideas to *appear* almost as if they were part of the world of phenomena. The artwork, Hegel suggests, reveals something of the character of infinite thought, then: it is a liminal site, where the phenomenal, sensual world of appearances and noumenal world of unbounded ideas are sutured. In this sense, Hegel's artwork is much like a neo-Platonic one. As Plotinus describes it,

> the Soul—by the very truth of its nature, by its affiliation to the noblest Existents in the hierarchy of Being—when it sees anything of that kin, or any trace of that kinship, thrills with an immediate delights, takes its own to itself, and thus stirs anew to the sense of its nature and of all its affinity.[8]

To be recognized—for these truths to be recognizable as truths—Plotinus suggests that they must, in some senses, already be known: we must, in at least some fashion recognize ourselves in them. This is precisely the same intuition on which Freud draws when he identifies the uncanny as 'that class of the frightening which leads back to what is known of old and long familiar.'[9] Not for nothing does Derrida cock a Hegelian snook when he says of the Spirit, the *Geist*, that 'it begins by coming back'.[10] Evoking Freud (and Derrida too) in this context is vital, precisely because of the way in which he nuances, doubtless without meaning to, Plotinus. For Plotinus, the recognition in question is certainly one of the beautiful. Not only does he observe that when the soul 'fall[s] in with the Ugly [. . .] at once it shrinks within itself, denies the thing, turns away from it, not accordant, resenting it',[11] but he also makes a core metaphor for the experience of art from the experience of falling in love:

> So with shape: granted beauty, the absence of shape or form to be grasped is but an enhancement of desire and love; the love will be limitless as the object is, an infinite love.
>
> Its beauty, too, will be unique, a beauty above beauty: it cannot be beauty since it is not a thing among things. It is loveable and the author of beauty; as the power to all beautiful shape, it will be the ultimate of beauty, that which brings all loveliness to be; it begets beauty and make it yet more beautiful by the excess of beauty streaming from itself, the source and height of beauty.[12]

Here again one finds shades of the Hegelian or, more properly, the reverse, in the freedom, the illimitability of that other sphere, the world itself. It is a reversal, too, which characterizes Freud's complaint at the outset of his consideration of the uncanny that '[a]s good as nothing is to be found upon this subject in comprehensive treatises on aesthetics, which in general prefer to concern themselves with what is beautiful, attractive and sublime— that is with feelings of a positive nature—and with the circumstances and objects that call them forth, rather than the opposite feelings of repulsion and distress.'[13] The idea that such expectations may be subject to a sudden reversal, while being *structured* in exactly the same way, is a recurrent theme of the present text. So, too, will be the question which Freud lets Plotinus pose with a tone which is no longer rhetorical: if it is nothing, what beauty can it be?

Yet, despite Hegel's broadly positive identification of art as a site where truths are revealed, he is far from positive about art's future. Indeed, the historical distance between Plotinus and Hegel helps clarify what Hegel, at least, thinks has happened in the interim. To be sure, the Plotinian perspective is one which Hegel might, perhaps, have felt adequate to Plotinus's own period, but the advent, first, of Christianity, and second, of modern philosophical thought, suggests to Hegel that there is 'a deeper form of truth, in which it is no longer so closely akin and so friendly to sense as to be adequately embraced and expressed by that medium [art].' [14] Precisely because art is sensuous, it is limited: while philosophy speaks of the unbounded ideas which are the proper content of thought and, thus, of the world on a level which is capable of engagement with them, art does little more than gesture, perhaps impotently, toward them.[15] Thus, even though art may point to the possibility of higher truths, 'art is, and remains for us, on the side of its highest destiny, a thing of the past.'[16] From Hegel's perspective, the proper activity of the consideration of art had become, in his own time, a broadly scientific one: 'Art invites us to consideration of it by means of thought, not to the end of stimulating art production, but in order to ascertain scientifically what art is.'[17] Art *qua* art, as Hegel would have it, had become in some senses a question of nostalgia, insofar as it survived in the present: 'it has further lost for us its genuine truth and life, and rather is transferred into our *idea* than asserts its former necessity, or assumes its former place, in reality.'[18] The best that was left for art, from Hegel's perspective, in his own time, was the memory of the time when art was the best method humans had for approaching immortal thoughts, if not thoughts of immortality.

Such a notion of memory might spur a divergence of thought, a splitting of what is under consideration here. On the one hand, one might think that Hegel prefigures—in this memory of art as the highest pursuit of truth—a sort of postmodern nostalgia for the time when presence *really was* presence. To be sure, there is good reason to think along such lines, and I shall turn to this view below, even if, by that point, it may look a little different from the sketch here. On the other hand, though, one's thoughts might rightly turn to Heidegger's thought on artworks. Both, it should be noted, are intimately involved with a particular rejection of the Hegelian teleologies which demand, axiomatically, that philosophy supplants religion and art, too, as the site of truth procedures *par excellence*, the former obviously because of the various ends of history intertwined with almost any conception of postmodernity, the latter both because Heidegger's site of truth *precedes* Western thought as ordinarily conceived—as Badiou notes in the Introduction to *Being and Event* that 'Heidegger is the last universally recognizable philosopher', so Heidegger might have said that Heraclitus was the last true thinker of what must be thought—and simultaneously proclaims that philosophy too has been superseded, or should be, with the overcoming of metaphysics.[19]

The key link between Hegel and Heidegger, in this context, is precisely the word Heidegger uses to describe the truth unveiled by artworks, ἀλήθεια. Were it not for the distinctiveness of Heidegger's expression, indeed, the following statement from Hegel might, almost, be mistaken for a Heideggerian thought, especially if ἀλήθεια or one of its inflections is substituted for the words true or truth:

> Beyond a doubt the mode of revelation which a content attains in the realm of thought is the truest reality; but in comparison with the show or semblance of immediate sensuous existence or of historical narrative,

the artistic semblance has the advantage that in itself it points beyond itself, and refers us away from itself to something spiritual which it is meant to bring before the mind's eye. Whereas immediate appearance does not give itself out to be deceptive, but rather to be real and true, though all the time its truth is contaminated and infected by the immediate sensuous element.[20]

To be sure, Heidegger's preferred readings of the word, at least in 'The Origin of the Work of Art' as 'unconcealment' or 'dis-closure' are vital. As he describes the knotty heart of this idea: 'Truth is un-truth, insofar as there belongs to it the reservoir of the not-yet-revealed, the un-covered, in the sense of concealment. In unconcealment, as truth, there occurs also the other 'un-' of a double restraint or refusal.'[21]

Yet ἀλήθεια has other dimensions too. Itself concealed, or enclosed, by other translations, when broken into its elements ά-λήθεια can be seen literally to read 'un-forgetting'.[22] Being as such, then, has been forgotten in Heidegger's terms and the clearing of art is a site where such a memory might be recalled. To be sure, one might consider the charge of mere nostalgia against Heidegger in such a context. As he himself describes it:

One can say that the further one moves away from the beginning of Western thinking, from *aletheia*, the further *aletheia* goes into oblivion; the clearer knowledge, consciousness, comes to the foreground, and Being thus withdraws itself. In addition, this withdrawal of Being remains concealed. In the *kryptesthai* of Heraclitus, that withdrawal is expressed for the first and last time. (*Physis krypsthesthai philei.* Nature loves to hide.) The withdrawal of *aletheia* as *aletheia* releases the transformation of Being from *energia* to *actualitas*, etc.[23]

Against the nostalgic charge, one might notice the clear hermeneutic circle at play in Heidegger's thought here: in order for a subject to recognize the truth of what has been enclosed or forgotten—what is un-forgotten, disclosed in the experience of art—that truth must already, in some senses, be known. One could not, to re-hash Meno's paradox, one might think, recognize a truth *as* a truth the truth of which one did not already somehow know. In the rethinking of these ideas, which follows below, it is worth noting that Badiou's understanding of the event that art is precisely posits a reversal of this aspect of Heidegger's thought. In any case, nostalgic or not, vitally, what is disclosed, uncovered, or, indeed, un-forgotten in the process Heidegger outlines in 'The Origin of the Work of Art' is born to *presence*. Krell's prefatory notes to the essay stress this aspect: 'For the Being of beings, the coming to presence of things, is the original self-showing by which entities emerge from hiddenness'.[24] The work of art is, in a sense, the site where the world is born from the earth, or the point at which the earth opens up, suturing itself to the far vaster world of infinite thought. Lee

Braver's exegesis of this aspect of 'The Origin of the Work of Art' doubtless captures the moment in ways which speak to musicians:

> My awareness of my emotional state listening to Bach's Cello Suites is heightened when I realize that my rapture, my sense of profound insight comes from rubbing horse hair across cat-gut bound to glued-together wooden boards. I cannot escape the feeling that such works express something profound about what it means to be human, yet they are 'really' just vibrations produced by rubbing strings together. This incongruity between the profound stirrings in my heart and their mundane cause, between art's meaningfulness and its medium's mean-inglessness, makes me aware of music as music, which helps me feel gratitude for what I had been taking for granted. I am grateful that I can hear and, by extension, that I am in the clearing at all.[25]

Heidegger thus creates the space which Badiou's view of artworks will occupy. At any rate, Badiou's conception of the sorts of truth procedures at play in artworks have a great deal to do with the clearing, a sort of empty space. For Badiou, philosophy *qua* philosophy has four conditions: art, science, politics, and love. In the case of art, one finds an strong echo of the Hegelian notion that art can, as it were, 'do' philosophy. It requires, Badiou suggests, a reversal of aesthetics in general and in principle. As he says,

> [b]y 'inaesthetics' I understand a relation of philosophy to art that, maintaining that art is itself a producer of truths, makes no claim to turn art into an object for philosophy. Against aesthetic speculation, inaesthetics describes the strictly intraphilosophical effects produced by the independent existence of some works of art.[26]

One might think, then, that Badiou repeats here a certain sort of autonomy for artworks, that the sphere of art is independent from the rest of the 'world'. Yet this is not the case. Or, at any rate, I do not think that what he says is so simple. In any case, since the other three spheres of activity that Badiou recognizes as conditions of philosophy are love, science, and politics, the notion that art would somehow exist in an autonomous sphere would seem surprising, at the very least.

Rather, Badiou suggests by inaesthetics a reversal of what aesthetics has, typically, claimed to do: philosophy does not, he seem to think, have the tools particularly to *interpret* artworks as such, to say what it is that they mean. It is not a privileged site in that sense at all. By contrast, Badiou holds that it is philosophical thought which is most capable of working symptomologically to *identify* that fact; here Badiou suggests that it is *within* the artwork that truths are produced, which is to say from a particular perspective that artworks themselves are capable of making philosophical arguments and considering philosophical questions. The artwork is not, as Badiou says, 'an object for philosophy'. In point of fact, what aesthetics (or inaesthetics at any rate) is placed to do, Badiou seems to suggest is, again, to symptomologize, to try to explain just what it is or may be in any particular art which produces a particular truth, which advances a particular philosophical line of enquiry. Thought is led by the artwork, rather than the artwork being interpreted by thought. If the point of philosophy in general is to change the world rather than interpret it, Badiou might well observe that just those philosophical effects *already occur* in artworks and the confusion arises, if confusion it is, because what writing about art is to interpret—to translate—are the philosophical effects which have *already taken place*.

Space hardly allows for a thoroughgoing consideration of each of these, though I shall consider Badiou's (in his terms essentially scientific) claim that mathematics is ontology below. In truth, this could hardly be avoided: a truth for Badiou is necessarily something new, an addition to the situation. What this means is that the event makes clear *that which was missing* from the situation. Events are always surprising, in this sense, because the very nature of the event is that it punctures a hole in what 'everyone knows to be true'. In essence, the event reveals that 'we all know' is a statement of opinion, not a statement of truth: it shows the hole in the argument. Events, for this reason, are always *voids* in Badiou's conception of being.

What can Badiou mean by this? The statement is surely paradoxical, since it seems that the one thing which an event *must* be is something which is present. As I will hope to show below, however, the confusion comes, I believe, from an elision of the ideas of fullness and emptiness with those of absence and presence. Indeed, as noted above, one of the fundamental aims of this chapter is to suggest that those four are no dyad, much less a dialectic, but more like a quartet of conceptions. The argument through Badiou must be founded upon the way in which the void— the null set—is deployed throughout his output, but especially in *Number and Numbers* and *Being and Event*. This latter, arguably his *magnum opus*, is, at least in part, an attempt to answer Plato's formulation of the issue of being in *Parmenides*: 'if the one is not, nothing is', which forms the epigraph to the whole of *Being and Event*. One might suspect that the common sense reading of this would be that being *qua* being cannot exist if 'things' (individual things, ones) do not exist. Badiou's reading is quite different. He is unconvinced that 'one' (as such) exists, but takes it that, if one follows Plato's argument, then a version of being *grounded on nothing* would follow. Paradoxical though this may seem, Badiou uses Zermelo-Fraenkel set theory to suggest that a wholly logical system *can* be created from a mode of thinking which decides, as one of its founding axioms, that 'nothing' exists (and makes of that a statement different from 'nothing exists'). This, it should be noted, is one of Badiou's key examples of the way in which his four spheres, the four conditions of philosophy, can produce truth events; that of Zermelo-Fraenkel set theory is the core example he gives of a scientific truth event.

It is two of the axioms of Zermelo-Fraenkel set theory that are most significant here (and, indeed, for Badiou): the Axiom of the Empty Set and the Axiom of Infinity. The former may be relatively simply expressed: there is a set such that no set is a member of it. The empty set, then can be notated either as { }, where the brackets denote the 'boundaries' of the set (and that nothing is contained within those boundaries), or as ø, which is to say null. Logically, *nothing* is contained within the empty set, which is to say, in more formal language that, as well as being { }, the empty set is, too, {ø}, since the set contains nothing. From this very simple manoeuver follow the natural numbers, according to the standard construction of the natural numbers. The successor of x in the standard construction is held to be $x \cup \{x\}$. Thus understood, one can construct the natural numbers:

$$1 = 0 \cup \{ø\} = \{ \} \cup \{ø\} = \{ø\}$$
$$2 = 1 \cup \{1\} = \{ø\} \cup \{1\} = \{ø,1\}$$
and so on.

The Axiom of Infinity follows this logical step, then: it argues that the operation of taking the successor ($n + 1$, in everyday language) necessarily ends in an infinite set, I, which contains all the natural numbers (and, by another proof, shows that this set I is directly coterminous with the smallest infinite ordinal, ω). Considered another way, since nothing is contained within the empty set—{ } becomes {ø}—then *all* sets contain the empty set. This means that one could, just as effectively write the motion of natural numbers toward infinity thus:

$$ø = \{ \}$$
$$1 = \{ø\} = \{\{ \}\}$$
$$2 = \{ø, \{ø\}\} = \{\{ \}, \{\{ \}\}\}$$
$$3 = \{ø, \{ø\}, \{ø, \{ø\}\}\} = \{\{ \}, \{\{ \}\}, \{\{ \}, \{\{ \}\}\}\}$$

In such a version—wholly licit within Zermelo-Fraenkel set theory—one can see that, in fact, number, denumerability *qua* denumerability, which is to say the *one*, never truly occurs. What one is left with are, in Badiou's terms, the limit conditions of the thinking of number—and by extension of thinking *qua* thinking—which is to say the empty set, zero or null (ø), and pure multiplicity (ω).[27] Yet null and pure multiplicity are folded in one on another. It is because of this that Badiou argues, if one allows his claim that mathematics *is* ontology to stand, that being *qua* being is—indeed *must be*—grounded on the void. For Badiou it is with Zermelo-Fraenkel set theory, at the beginning of the twentieth century, that the condition of science finally overthrew the hegemony of what he sees as the essentially

Greek thinking of number *as if* the truth of number was to be found in the counting of 1, 2, 3, 4, and so on, rather than in the intertwined boundary limits of ø and ω (even though, as he says, the axioms which ground those ideas pre-exist the point at which they become a truth-event by some three hundred years).[28] As Badiou regards the situation it is possible to 'observe a veritable *philosophical* desperation constantly putting these imperatives into reverse, whether through the intellectual dereliction of the theme of finitude or through nostalgia for the Greek ground of Presence.' Furthermore, since these *are* axioms, '[n]o argument can support them.' The system of ontology *qua* mathematics Badiou describes is self-consistent and elegant, but it does require, as he is the first to admit, that the reader *decide* upon the plausibility of the axioms. In this context Badiou also argues that it is only science which has come to terms with the ontological truth sited *within* the scientific sphere. Indeed, he goes so far as to argue that 'certain truth procedures, in particular politics, art and love, are not yet *capable of sustaining* such axioms, and so in many ways *remain Greek*. They cling to Presence (art and love), continually recusing the statement 'zero is the proper numeric name of being' in order to give tribute to the obsolete rights of the One.'[29]

Of this latter point, I am not wholly convinced. Indeed, I would argue that art certainly is capable of sustaining the axiom of the empty set and its consequences; the question is much more whether aesthetics is capable of identifying it for what it is. It is *aesthetics*, I might go so far as to argue, that clings to presence, rather than art, although as should already be clear, I believe the elision of the tetrad—presence/absence, plenitude/emptiness— into the dyad—presence/absence—to be at least a partial explanation for this situation. Indeed, Badiou himself confesses that, even if 'it would be pointless to set off in search of the nothing' nevertheless 'must be said that this is exactly what poetry exhausts itself doing; this is what renders poetry, even at the most sovereign point of its clarity, even in its peremptory affirmation, complicit with death.'[30]

In any case, the shifting sands might already make the reader think that Badiou's description of the contemporary subject is not *quite* as paradigmatically postmodern as a cursory reading might imagine:

> We are equally contemporaries of a *second epoch* of the doctrine of the Subject. It is no longer the founding subject, centered and reflexive, whose theme runs from Descartes to Hegel and which remains legible in Marx and Freud (in fact, in Husserl and Sartre). The contemporary Subject is void, cleaved, a-substantial, and ir-reflexive. Moreover, one can only suppose its existence in the context of particular processes whose conditions are rigorous.[31]

Arguably, the outer reaches of this span might be expanded—in Heideggerian fashion—to trace the boundary conditions of the sort of 'present' subject Badiou contrasts with the contemporary one from Socratic thought to (at least the early) Heidegger. Vitally, by this Badiou does not mean simply what he might at first blush be thought to mean. The contemporary subject he describes is not *only* to be conceived of as, variously, a collection of Whiteheadian processes, Deleuzian folds and knots, or the Lacanian mirrors of habit and repetition. Badiou stresses that the identity of the subject 'can only be grasped by attempting to think the subject *in its place*.'[32] The contemporary subject's genealogy is, though in once sense *displaced* from presence to absence, in another situated in the same nexus. Just as 'Freud can only be understood within the heritage of the Cartesian gesture,' so can Lacan only be conceived at the site of the Freudian fold, precisely in Lacan's 'return to Descartes'.[33] Though Lacan objects to Descartes's formulation of the *cogito* since 'in that which is thinking (*cogitans*), I am never doing anything but constituting myself as an object (*cogitatatum*)', he feels the objection can be overcome—and the site of thinking retained as the site of the subject—thus: *ubi cogito, ibi sum*.[34] Lacan is, to be sure, less straightforward in the clarification, a clarification which, nevertheless, makes the point that the *place* of the subject is as vital as the processes of subjectification which accrete around that site: 'I am not, where I am the plaything of my thought; I think about what I am, where I do not think I am thinking.'[35]

As Badiou summarises, in a description probably not much more immediate than Lacan's, '[w]hat *still* attaches Lacan (but this *still* is the modern perpetuation of sense) to the Cartesian epoch of science is the thought that the subject must be maintained in the pure void of its subtraction if one wishes to save truth.'[36] In short, the situatedness of the subject *survives* the shift from Cartesian to Lacanian self-identification. One, at least, of Badiou's key insights is that to posit a radical cleft between modern and postmodern subjects will not quite do: there is a sort of structural continuity which, not without a little irony, reaches across the postmodern divide. 'The choice here', Badiou insists, 'is between a structural recurrence [. . .] and a hypothesis of the rarity of the subject'.[37] Moreover, notable here is precisely the insistence that, to 'save truth' in the contemporary world, Badiou argues that the situatedness of the subject must persist from Descartes to Lacan, even if that motion is, too, one from presence to absence.

Baudrillard, in a rather different context, seems to hit on the same intuition, but in a mode which suggests that the link between fullness of presence and emptiness may not be at all simple:

> When the real is no longer what it was, nostalgia assumes its full meaning. There is a plethora of myths of origin and of signs of reality—a plethora of truth, of secondary objectivity, and authenticity. Escalation of the true, of lived experience, resurrection of the figurative where the object and substance have disappeared.[38]

Again, as in the Lacanian formulations disentangled by Badiou, there is, Baudrillard suggests, a certain species of the true which arrives in just this situation. One does not have to subscribe to the full-blooded version of Baudrillard's argument—where these species of the true nervously articulate the absence of any real behind them which would guarantee their meaning—to sense that there is something at stake in his claims, the implications of which Baudrillard does not himself fully follow through.[39] Svetlana Boym's version of nostalgia is more direct. Nostalgia is, first and foremost, 'a sentiment of loss and displacement, but it is also a romance with one's own fantasy' in the context of 'a longing for a home that no longer exists or has never existed.'[40] It is, then, the desire to return to an absence. If Baudrillard is taken at his word that, in the contemporary world—when the real is no longer what it was—, nostalgia indeed *has* assumed its *full* meaning, then that is to say that the qualities of nostalgia when they are in plenitude are precisely those of absence. In short, fullness and emptiness need not be collapsed with presence and absence in the way which one might often think. If this is the case, there is surely good reason to revisit what Heidegger, for one, has to say on the matter of the origin of the work of art, not least because his own, later *Parmenides* already points in the direction of what a version of the origin of the work of art might look like where what is unveiled might be a birth to absence, rather than the birth to presence seemingly implied by the earlier essay. It should go without saying that an example of what this model might have to do with actual artworks will be vital.

Though, to be sure, Heidegger's own concern in *Parmenides* is being *qua* being, rather than the ontic characteristics of artworks, the world-disclosing truths of artworks as outlined in 'The Origin of the Work of Art' surely gives sufficient license to think that, if ἀλήθεια has an intimate relationship with the truths of artworks, the explosion of the various configurations of truth in *Parmenides* may be considered to help refine Heidegger's own, more strictly artistic, envisioning of a particular site of truths. That ἀλήθεια cannot simply be left to mean 'truth' is signaled early on in Heidegger's re-examination of the notion in *Parmenides*. For ἀλήθεια to stand for 'truth' in modern fashion, Heidegger argues that one would expect the privative α to be removed, leaving τὸ ληθές to indicate 'the false'. Yet, as Heidegger stresses, 'nowhere do we actually find this word as the name for the false. Instead the Greeks call the false τὸ ψεύδος.'[41] Not only that, but the opposition between τὸ ψεύδος and τὸ ἀληθές is made more complex by the existence of just such a privative opposition being available in the formation of τὸ ἀψεύδος, which is to say, the un-false. Thus, the space available for such conceptions is fourfold: on the one hand, Heidegger has words which refer to that which is concealed or disclosed, τὸ ληθές and τὸ ἀληθές; on the other hand, he has the false and un-false, τὸ ψεύδος and τὸ ἀψεύδος. Vitally, then, ἀλήθεια and λήθη are intertwined on the side of (dis)closure, thus:

Disclosure	Falsity
τὸ ἀληθές	τὸ ψεῦδος
the disclosed	the false
τὸ ληθές	τὸ ἀψεῦδος
the undisclosed	the un-false

Heidegger's commentary here relies intimately on the very closing moments of Plato's *Republic*, the Myth of Er, which may help to show why, for Heidegger, forgetting and remembering, closure and disclosure, both fall on the side of the revealing of truths, rather than on the side of their dissembling:

> Then, without turning around, they went from there under the throne of Necessity and, when all of them had passed through, they travelled to the Plain of Forgetfulness in burning, choking, terrible heat, for it was empty of trees and earthly vegetation. And there, beside the River of Unheeding, whose water no vessel can hold they camped, for night was coming on. All of them had to drink a certain measure of this water, but those who weren't saved by reason drank more than that, and as each of them drank, he forgot everything and went to sleep. But around midnight there was a clap of thunder and an earthquake, and they were suddenly carried away from there, this way and that, up to their births, like shooting stars. Er himself was forbidden to drink from the water. All the same, he didn't know how he had come back to his body, except that waking up suddenly he saw himself lying on the pyre at dawn.[42]

As Heidegger interprets the passage:

> For the Greeks the divine is based immediately on the uncanny in the ordinary. [. . .] Everywhere there holds sway in advance for the Greeks the simple clarity of Being which lets beings arise in a lustre and sink down into darkness.
>   Therefore what belongs to the appearance of Being is still of the type uncanny, so that there is no need to ascribe to Being a divine character subsequently and to demonstrate it afterward. If now, however, ἀλήθεια belongs to the essence of primordial Being and so does its counter-essence λήθη, then each of these is primordially a θεῖον. [. . .] Should we then be offended if in Parmenides' primordial thinking ἀλήθεια appears as θεά, as goddess? We would now be more surprised if that were not the case.[43]

Heidegger's conclusion that ἀλήθεια and λήθη are both, in a particular sense, 'divine' is not immediately significant here. What is more obviously vital is the assertion that, on the level of (primordial) Being, ἀλήθεια and λήθη are (almost) one and the same thing. Or, more accurately, without both of them, primordial Being is not what it is. If the disclosing of the work of art is a world-disclosure, a disclosure of Being, the artwork might just as well disclose ἀλήθεια as λήθη. Yet, surely this results in tautology or paradox: ἀ-λήθεια is, precisely, dis-closure. Does it not make more sense to suppose that λήθη is the ground, the field of forgetfulness, in which revelation—by some process—takes place? Heidegger is not—or not any longer—so sure.

Heidegger's translation of 'τὸν δὲ ἀεὶ πιόντα πάντων ἐπιλανθάνεσθαι', (rendered 'as each of them [who were not saved by reason] drank, he forgot everything' by Grube and Reeve) begins to make clear just how distant he is from more traditional interpretations of the Myth of Er: 'However, for one who would constantly drink (this water) his relation to beings as a whole and to himself would stand in the concealment that withdraws everything and does not leave anything preserved.' Heidegger's response is unambiguous: 'On such a one further words should not be wasted. He could not be on earth as a man, since all beings would be concealed to him and there would be nothing unconcealed at all, nothing to which he could relate disclosively [. . .] and thereby be a man.'[44] In short, this absent ground, the ground of disclosure, is definitively not oblivion. On the contrary, 'since λήθη pertains to the essence of ἀλήθεια, un-concealedness itself cannot be the mere *elimination* of concealedness. The α in ἀλήθεια in no way means simply an undetermined universal "un-" and "not". Rather, the saving and conserving of the un-concealed is necessarily in relation to concealment, understood as the withdrawal of what appears in it appearing.'[45] The opening, then, is just as well an opening which reveals man *to* presence as one which reveals its own opening as grounded in withdrawing concealment. In short, the dis-closure of artworks intertwines dis- and closure in ways that cannot easily be disentangled. According to context what has often been thought of as the fullest capacity of a particular quality as revealed by an artwork might perfectly well be a revealing of its own ground—the ground of grounds, the absence which underpins it—as it might the explosion of energies sited there.[46] Put differently, Heidegger stresses that the close of *Republic* should not be read either literally or symbolically as such:

> What is preserved and secured is the legend of the essence of λήθη, the withdrawing concealment. [. . .] λήθη is πεδίον, field, region, the essence of the place and of the sojourn from which there is a sudden transition to a place and a sojourn that, as the unconcealedness of beings, envelops the mortal course of man. [. . .] The appropriate, i.e., the measured crossing of the river flowing through the place of λήθη consists in taking a drink of the water according to the fitting measure. Yet the *essence* of man, and not only the individual man in his destiny,

is saved only when man, as the being he is, harkens to the legend of concealment. Only in that way can he follow what unconcealedness itself and the disclosure of the unconcealed demand in their essence.[47]

If this reversal of Heidegger's earlier thought on being *qua* being is extended to the world of artworks, then it becomes clear that what is at the site of the artwork may not be, strictly, a birth to presence at all. By contrast, the true fullness promised by the artwork might perfectly well be a birth to absence, at least *as well as* a birth *from* absence. In any case, such an event would surely be worthy of the name, as either Badiou or Deleuze describe it. For Badiou

> [w]hat happens in art, in science, in true (rare) politics, and in love (if it exists), is the coming to light of an indiscernible of the times, which, as such, is neither a known or recognized multiple, nor an ineffable singularity, but that which detains in its multiple-being all the common traits of the collective in question: in this sense it is the truth of the collective's being.[48]

As so often, the particularities of Badiou's language make the sentiment require, at least, further explanation. What he means by the multiple here, as well as any potential relationship to the singularity of the evental site may perhaps be reached toward through Deleuze's conception of what an event might be. The conditions, for him, are straightforward: 'Events are produced in a chaos, in a chaotic multiplicity, but only under conditions that a sort of screen intervenes.'[49] Yet what Deleuze means by chaos moves him in the direction of Badiou:

> Chaos does not exist; it is an abstraction because it is inseparable from a screen that makes something—something rather than nothing— emerge from it. Chaos would be a pure *Many*, a purely disjunctive diversity, while the something is a *One*, not a pregiven unity, but instead the indefinite article that designates a certain singularity. How can the Many become the One? A great screen has to be placed in between them. Like a formless elastic membrane, an electromagnetic field, or the receptacle of the *Timaeus*, the screen makes something issue from chaos, and *even if this something differs only slightly.*[50]

Events, then, in Deleuze's terms come from a certain flattening, or framing, of the infinitude of being (or thought, or the world). Here, Deleuze follows a broadly traditional view, even, perhaps shockingly, an Aristotelian one, in which nature seems still to abhor a vacuum. The difficulty becomes clear: in the sort of pure infinitude which Deleuze imagines, *ones* must be produced. Deleuze's insistence of presence is captured in his statement that 'chaos would be the sum of all possibles, that is, all individual essences insofar as each tends to existence on its own account; but the screen only allows compossibles—and only the best combination of compossibles—to be sifted through.'[51] Here the problem is compounded, in order to produce the 'new', Deleuze relies on the sum of all possibles, a group of all that could be. Yet, the conception of that set denotes that it cannot, by default, contain anything new. It is for such reasons that Badiou is convinced that Deleuze is, against his own apparent intentions, finally a monadic thinker, since for Deleuze, following Leibniz and Whitehead,

> [t]he event is a vibration with an infinity of harmonics or submultiples, such as an audible wave, a luminous wave, or even an increasingly smaller part of space over the course of an increasingly shorter duration. For space and time are not limits but abstract coordinates of all series that are themselves in extension: the minute, the second, the tenth of a second . . . .

The Deleuzian question, then, is finally one of extension and, thus, of *series*. Badiou's view proceeds from a similar conception of multiplicity, but his understanding of and interest in set theory leads him to radically different conclusions, and ones which are germane for any understanding of the event horizon of the artwork.[52]

In short, in Deleuze's conception—resolutely classical—an event issues from the chaos, bending, but not puncturing the screen. This is, too, τὸ ἀληθές, the disclosed: the thing which is already part of the chaotic, singular multiplicity, revealed from within that multiplicity. Badiou's events breach the screen, tearing a hole even in its multiplicitous surface. That rupture, the void, reveals what is *un*-disclosed by the situation. It, too, *reveals*, but it reveals the absence within the situation, reveals that the situation was always already incomplete.

The relationship between events and the void in Badiou's conception might be perhaps more simply explained through the analogue of Gödel's incompleteness theories. As Shankar describes it: 'Gödel's first incompleteness theorem asserts of a theory such as formal number theory that is either inconsistent or contains an undecidable statement that can neither be proved nor disproved.'[53] This is to say that any self-consistent system contains *at least one* absence. For Badiou 'the ways things are' is a synonym for both the 'situation' and, broadly, ontology itself. This is why he can say, in a description strongly redolent of Gödel that

> [a]n event is linked to the notion of the *undecideable*. Take the statement: 'This event belongs to the situation.' If it is possible to decide, using the rules of established knowledge, whether a statement is true or false, then the so-called event is not an event. Its occurrence would be calculable within the situation. Nothing would permit us to say: here begins a truth.[54]

Thus, the long and short is that the event is strictly undecideable on the basis of the current situation. New events cannot be predicted, beyond the structural identification that they occur *at the points* where undecideability occurs.

Again, Badiou's description is heavy with his own terminology, but his stress on the *site* where events occur should recall the structural similarities outlined above with reference to the Cartesian and Lacanian subject, as well as to the site of art, in Heidegger's terms. Badiou determines that he define an '*evental site* an entirely abnormal multiple; that is, a multiple such that none of its elements are presented in the situation. The site, itself, is presented, but "beneath" it nothing from which it is composed is presented. As such, the site is not part of the situation. I will also say of such a multiple that it is *on the edge of the void*, or *foundational* [. . .].'[55] Put more simply: *creation* which is the hallmark of new events within art in Badiou's conception is founded upon precisely the site of absence in the present situation, exactly the point of incompleteness in the otherwise self-consistent system: the new is produced *precisely* out, and because, of the void, because of the incompleteness of the system. As far as ontology—identical with mathematics for Badiou—is concerned, 'non-contradiction is the *unnameable* of the mathematical. And it is clear that this unnameable is the *real* of the mathematical; for if a mathematical theory is contradictory, it is destroyed.'[56] Truth, Badiou insists, 'begins with a groundless decision—the decision to *say* that the event has taken place.'[57]

Just this theme, the revealing of absence, has run through this volume as a whole. Almost every commentator has noted points where Gaga has shown a site where absence—where the void of the situation—is presented. From the outset, for Hawkins, the question of drag is central. Of course, this is Butlerian drag: not only is this repetition of repetition which presupposes no center—those Lacanian mirrors, in which the self is no presence as such, but only the effect of repetition in a particular site—but it is drag which purposively refuses to do anything more than reveal absence. Not for nothing does Gaga let rumors of hermaphroditism resound and, indeed, foreground them in the video for 'Telephone'. Not only that but, as Hawkins stresses, she reveals too that the role of the celebrity is no more or less a performance—with no original—of that position. Precisely her awkwardness—discussed in terms of 'look' and of voice by O'Brien and Burns and Lafrance as well as Hawkins's insistence on the etymology of *patois*, leading to the idea of 'handling awkwardly'—make evident that she is, as a celebrity, only present insofar as she presents her own absence, an undecideability central to Owens too.

Hegarty also focuses on a particular sort of present absence in the way in which he, via Bataille, figures death and the erotic in the case of Gaga. The key, in this context, is his opinion that: 'I do not think that the dead women littered so crisply around the demesne are a critique of fashion, fame or overzealous fascination with celebrity. Oddly, these are almost faceless women, mostly suicides, it would seem.' It is just that juxtaposition of face-lessness with 'almost' that is the point, again, that the figured absence is starkly revealed for the absence that it (almost) is: the draw, as Hegarty has it, 'of the loss in eroticism and death'. Even the title of O'Brien's con-tribution makes the point: 'Not A Piece of Meat'. Gaga *is* what she *is not* (and, in this, distinguishes herself from Chrissie Hynde, Madonna, Bjork, M.I.A., Missy Elliott, Adele and Lily Allen, among others, in O'Brien's description). Of course, the question becomes literalized in this context too. In order to present the absence—to reveal that she is not a piece of meat—Gaga appears precisely *in one*, Fernandez and Formichetti's so-called 'meat dress'. This isn't to say, of course, that the manoeuver wasn't already suc-cessfully enacted by Sterbak or Kosianovsky, but it's the disclosure of the absence—and its very public nature, arguably—that helps to distinguish it here. It is, doubtless, a question of the event, which is not always—indeed hardly ever—coterminous with the first moment at which an idea is uttered or presented. Indeed, part of the purpose of what I have endeavored to outline here is exactly to suggest that what I read in the case of Gaga is not *merely* postmodern simulation, but is also, vitally, an approach to ensuring that the absence is always already *read* as such, that it is legible.

The notion that Gaga is going to 'take it all off' pervades Gray and Rutnam's account, but with a concomitant stress that, when that happens, it will reveal that there is nothing beneath or, at least, that what's beneath is far from the full, unambiguous presence one might have hoped for. In a sense, the striptease that Gray and Rutnam describe is precisely one which removes all the signifiers of presence that go with it: mere revelation, while tease and titillation is absent. Moreover, as Eva Barlow proposed it to O'Brien, the sexualized content of Gaga's presentation shows itself for what it is: 'Gaga's whole vision is hypersexualized for no one but herself. She is a sex symbol, but not for a male audience.'

Of course, the telephone, as presented by Colton, in the context of 'Tele-phone', is the very paradigm of present absence. Like signatures, as Der-rida examines them,[58] the purpose of the telephone is to create some sort of ghostly present out of the physically absent. Hardly surprisingly, in this context, Colton also stresses the cyborg entity which arguably results when the female voice is interlaced with the *idea* of the voice of the telephone—another ghost in the machine—in musical production. Colton's conclusion, too, focuses on the way in which the paradox comes about where the pres-ence of Gaga's (and Beyoncé's) absence, unveils the listener's own absence: 'Gaga's and Beyoncé's 'voices' are delivered to an absent, unlistening object, rather than being forced to respond through the mobile telephone tech-nology available to them. Paradoxically, the listener becomes that object through the mapping of telephone onto microphone/sound recording tech-nology that arguably occurs during telephone songs.' Television exhibits the same basic qualities as the telephone in this context, of course, but in the case of the 'Theatricality' episode of *Glee* it becomes even more notable that Gaga herself does not appear, but those things which define her—which *present* her—do, in the sense that the costuming which surrounds the centre of the Gaga assemblage is present, as it were, in full, from the bubble and Kermit dresses to Armani and McQueen.

Yet more technology becomes involved when Apolloni describes Gaga's stutter in 'Starstruck': it 'sounds like a digital skip in the record. It sounds like her unnatural voice is incapable of achieving the vocal authority and authenticity of the flesh, and is always threatening to collapse'. That same sense of figuring—literally presenting—the inauthentic is stressed in Burns and Lafrance's stress on the way in which Gaga reveals Pierrot, that figure of failure—the failure to win (or retain) Columbine or to find a place in the (modern) world as it is—often mute, voiceless, with the white pallor of the undead. Indeed, the cyborg body and (substitute) robot voice Apolloni describes very much imply the central absence of Gaga 'herself'. For O'Brien, Gaga is not even a cyborg as such (though O'Brien does explore the issue). More revealingly, O'Brien suggests that '[t]hrough her futuristic masque she reinvents Stefani Germanotta as a multimedia avatar': the avatar is, of course, the most contemporary symbol of revealed absence one could imagine. As O'Brien puts it 'Gaga has created a second life, her "new dimension", but it is one that involves a culture of forgetting.' Similarly, the stress Owens makes upon the figurative zombies which shamble through Gaga's intersections with celebrity emphasizes undeath. The elision, in turn, of this with the conspicuous consumption Marshall highlights makes it impossible for me, at least, not to remember both the fruitless desire to feed on the living of the zombies Owens mentions and that, as Peter, in *Dawn of the Dead* (1978) puts it: 'they're us, that's all'.

Vernallis makes this situation yet clearer, as she describes the mannequins of 'Paparazzi' as 'more an absence, than a presence', but one which is again fundamentally about disclosure—'they should display clothes'—while Geller's description of Jo Calderone repeatedly foregrounds another way in which Gaga presents her absence. As she says '"Lady Gaga" did not attend' the 2011 MTV Video Music Awards; those scare quotes are vital too: not only did Gaga, in some sense not attend, the figure of Calderone draws particular attention to the particular ways in which she was not there. Calderone, again, reveals the absence of Gaga, as he says, 'Gaga isn't here'. Nor is it for nothing that Geller posits 'glamour'—etymologically relating simultaneously to the vanishing power of magic *and* to the hidden force of the occult—as the *ground* of 'the subversive resignification that is figured in Jo Calderone'.

One might suggest that this argument might be generalized in particular ways, that I might be suggested nothing more, at heart, than that popular culture in the contemporary world is simply vapid, empty, that hidden here is some veiled slight on contemporary popular culture. After all, other examples of certain sorts of emptiness—of a wholly postmodern kind—might be found in, say, *The X Factor*, or any number of the international

Pop Idol formats, or *The Voice*. Yet this, I would argue is quite different from what happens at the site I have called here Gaga. Marshall makes the vital note that '[t]o point out that ice cream and cake are usually empty calories is not to imply that Gaga is meaningless fluff.' Here, I would argue, all is aimed at *concealing* the absence at the heart of those shows. Why else the insistence upon those signifiers of modernist presence: the invocation to 'keep it real', the stated desire to hunt down 'raw talent', the insistence upon the 'credibility' and 'believability' of the shows and its contestants alike, and the public upset on discovering that voices have been digitally altered (even while the narrative of the shows is precisely an *analogue* alteration in the presentation of the individuals involved to fit the appropriate—which is to say 'authentic'—model of an industry where digital treatment of the 'pitchy' is the norm). Gaga's absence is not of this type at all. Indeed, part of the point is the very fact that the *revealing* of the absent center which Gaga performs is staged on precisely the territory of the varied tropes and signifiers of modernism and postmodernism. To the many examples given throughout the volume, and summarized briefly above, I want to add a single, final illustration, no better, to be sure, than any of the others, but paradigmatic of my claims first, that the revealing of absence undertaken by Gaga is a disclosure where the modern and postmodern are intertwined and, second, that the unveiling itself is structured in the contemporary world in the same way in which it ever was, even though what is figured is the world-disclosure of absence.

The site that interests me here is the site of the Bath Haus of GaGa, figured in the video for 'Bad Romance' and it is literally the site, the Haus itself, that strikes me as vital. Not that there aren't all manner of other revealings going on here: the very opening of 'Bad Romance', the quasi-baroque synthesized harpsichord figurations, in combination with the static, pale, seemingly undead figures on screen, seems strikingly reminiscent to me at least of the opening of Goblin's score for Romero's *Dawn of the Dead*, underscoring the relationships drawn by Craig N. Owens. Other signifiers redolent of the undecideable pervade. The undead are the undecideable *par excellence* of course, but there are more undead creatures (or monsters, according to preference) here than zombies: the light sweeping across the space in the opening seconds is, first, rosy fingered dawn, sweeping across the caskets of the sleeping (now surely vampiric) undead, before being swapped for the glaring, artificial, white light which thereafter pervades the video. That the caskets—marked as such by the plain red cross with the word 'Monster' above it—are not really caskets, as Hegarty suggests, leads me, at least, to look at the space more carefully. The caskets, it seems to me, are not caskets at all, nor need they be thought of as 'futuristic' pods: they are much more banal than that; they are nothing more than automobile roof boxes. Yet their function is, without the car they 'ought' to be attached to, absent. In short, these sleek boxes state outright that they are functional—they reveal their functionality—but also demonstrate the absence of that function. What, then, of the space, the Bath Haus itself? It is slickly, sleekly white, with high-gloss tiled walls, evenly spaced lighting within those walls (even though the viewer might suspect that those lights conceal gazing eyes), a highly reflective, polished floor, and the sort of suspended, tiled ceiling that might make one think, again, of institutions or offices. It is, throughout, a space which signifies modernist functionality. Within the space, there are partitions, most reminiscent, for me at least, of the minimalist sculpture of Donald Judd: identical blocks, repeated at regular spatial distances. Again, these partitions seem to me to announce that same sort of clean, modernist function. There is even, on the wall which features these partitions, a repeated image, in black, which is redolent of the thick, black partitioning lines in Mondrian. Yet these are not graphic lines traced on the wall: they are pieces of pipework, and pipework which channels no water. Again, they are the most functional of signifiers, shorn of their function, revealing the absence of their own *point*. Indeed, the only thing which ever *looks* like water in the whole video is, it is signaled, vodka. The bath Gaga is seen to take certainly contains no water. What, then, of the cubicles? That pipework still suggests water *ought* to flow. Even this is not wholly decideable. At the song's midpoint, the viewer is presented with a seemingly naked Gaga, dancing in some sort of open framework of pipes within a cubicle like those described above. Like the bath, it is a function shorn of functionality; here, by rights, *ought* to be a shower. Yet this cubicle is exceptional. The rest are, surely, absent toilets. The space, the site of 'Bad Romance' is the most functional space imaginable: a public lavatory. Yet it is one which is vacant, void of that which would define it. Even the cat the viewer is presented with is bald and, seemingly, whiskerless. Little surprise that Gaga, when probed by the host of *Friday Night with Jonathan Ross* in 2009 as to her 'real name', insisted on the absence of Stefani Germanotta; indeed, at points the interview is conducted *as if* Gaga were another, third person who may or may not actually be present.[59] In a later interview on the same show, when pressed on the idea that there might be some other person, presumably Stefani Germanotta, who would slouch around the house, in loungewear, watching daytime TV, Gaga responded:

> For a very long time, I haven't really yet in my generation had, um, sort of a, a figure that was really an escapist figure for me that I could latch on to and have a, have the fantasy of the music and their life really inspire me and I, I guess I've always lived, since I've been in New York writing music, this very sort of art-centric glamorous life and, uh, it's important to me to always *be* that for my fans and the idea of showbiz; y'know, Michael Jackson, showbiz, and the, the sentiments of music and, uh, performance today with, with the media and the, the way that it is you see absolutely legendary people taking out their trash. It's something that we as a society don't really want to see but we, we keep buying into it and I think it's actually destroying show business. So, if

anything, there's absolutely no way I would ever give up my wigs and hats for anything.

Later in the interview, she summarized the point: 'I would rather die than have my fans not see me in a pair of high heels. And that's showbiz.'[60]

There is, in short, no 'behind the mask'; there is no 'real' Gaga to be revealed.[61] Yet, this is not the Baudrillardian simulacrum pure and simple, either. That is why I have sought throughout this chapter, up to and including this direct consideration of Gaga, the divisions which must be made between disclosure/enclosure, presence/absence, and plenitude/emptiness. If these stand as binary oppositions in any functional way, it can only be because they cannot, in and of themselves, be collapsed together. Consistently, just this absence is not only insisted upon, it is, itself, revealed. Where with Baudrillard, the simulacrum is still concerned with the hiding of the absent center, Gaga's art is revelatory: it *is* art, 'real' art, after all, just because it shows itself in this way. It discloses, in short, the world of the contemporary subject. As Hölderlin already knew:

The meaning of tragedies can most easily be understood in a paradox. For everything primal, because all potential is justly and equally divided, does not in fact manifest itself in its primal strength, but actually in its weakness, so that really and essentially the light of life and the manifestation of weakness are part of every whole. Now, in the tragic, the sign in itself is insignificant, ineffective, but the primal is straight out. For actually, the primal can only appear in its weakness, but insofar as the sign in itself is postulated as insignificant = 0, the primal, the hidden ground of every nature, can represent itself. If nature actually represents itself in its weakest gift, then the sign when it represents itself is its strongest gift = 0.[62]

NOTES

1. Alain Badiou, *Logics of Worlds*, tr. Alberto Toscano (London: Continuum, 2009 [2006]), 1.
2. Badiou, *Logics of Worlds*, 4–5.
3. G.W.F. Hegel, *Introductory Lectures on Aesthetics*, tr. Bernard Bosanquet (London: Penguin, 1993 [1818–29]), 9.
4. Hegel, *Introductory Lectures on Aesthetics*, 9.
5. See, for instance, Martin Heidegger, 'On the Origin of the Work of Art', tr. Albert Hofstadter, in Martin Heidegger, *Basic Writings*, ed. David Farrell Krell (London: Routledge, 2009 [1936]), 174–175.
6. As Bonds neatly summarizes: 'In his *Critique of Judgement*, Kant declared instrumental music to be "more pleasure than culture" (*mehr Genuß als Kultur*), for without a text, music could appeal only to the senses and not to reason.' (Mark Evan Bonds, *Music as Thought: Listening to the Symphony in the Age of Beethoven* (Princeton, NJ: Princeton University Press, 2006), 7) It must be remembered, however, as Parret stresses, that the aim of Kant's

third critique is precisely to do with a critical conception of αἴσθησις and that, consequentially, the fine arts *in general* appear only because they form a subsection of the argument: it is the argument, in the end, which is central, and art *qua* art marginal. See Herman Parret, 'Kant on Music and the Hierarchy of the Arts', *The Journal of Aesthetics and Art Criticism*, vol. 56, no. 3 (Summer 1998), 251.

7. Hegel, *Introductory Lectures on Aesthetics*, 11.
8. Plotinus, *The Enneads*, tr. Stephen MacKenna (New York, NY: Larson, 1992 [*ca.* 250–70 CE]), 65.
9. Sigmund Freud, 'The "Uncanny"', tr. Alix Strachey (rev. James Strachey), in Sigmund Freud, *Writings on Art and Literature* (Stanford, CA: Stanford University Press, 1997 [1919], 195.
10. Jacques Derrida, *Specters of Marx: The State of the Debt, the Work of Mourning, & the New International*, tr. Peggy Kamuf (London: Routledge, 1994 [1993]), 11.
11. Plotinus, *The Enneads*, 65.
12. Plotinus, *Ibid.*, 663.
13. Freud, 'The "Uncanny"', 194
14. Hegel, *Introductory Lectures on Aesthetics*, 11–12.
15. By way of riposte to Hegel in this context, one might recall Mendelssohn's argument that, far from music's meaning being 'too vague or indefinite to be stated in verbal form', in truth 'its meaning was far too precise and specific ever to be captured in words.' (See Christopher Norris, *Platonism, Music and the Listener's Share* (London: Continuum, 2006), 120).
16. Hegel, *Introductory Lectures on Aesthetics*, 31.
17. *Ibid.*
18. *Ibid.*
19. Alain Badiou, *Being and Event*, tr. Oliver Feltham (London: Continnum, 2007 [1988]), 1. See too Martin Heidegger, 'The End of Philosophy and the Task of Thinking', tr. Joan Stambaugh, rev. David Farrell Krell, in Martin Heidegger, *Basic Writings*, ed. David Farrell Krell (London: Routledge, 2009 [1936]), 427–449 (esp. 432–436).
20. Hegel, *Introductory Lectures on Aesthetics*, 11.
21. Heidegger, 'The Origin of the Work of Art', 185.
22. Indeed, this is the core definition of λήθη in Liddell-Scott-Jones (available online via: http://www.perseus.tufts.edu/hopper/).
23. Martin Heidegger, 'Summary of a Seminar on the Lecture "Time and Being"', tr. Joan Stambaugh, in Martin Heidegger, *On Time and Being*, ed. Joan Stambaugh (Chicago, IL: University of Chicago Press, 2002 [1962], 52.
24. David Farrell Krell's introductory notes to Martin Heidegger, 'The Origin of the Work of Art', tr. Albert Hofstadter, in Martin Heidegger, *Basic Writings*, ed. David Farrell Krell (London: Routledge, 2009 [1936]), 140
25. Lee Braver, *Heidegger's Later Writings: A Reader's Guide* (London: Continuum, 2009), 53.
26. Alain Badiou, *Handbook of Inaesthetics*, tr. Alberto Toscano (Stanford, CA: Stanford University Press, 2005 [1998]), xiv.
27. This is, in the latter case at least, an oversimplification. A further consideration must be given to the infinite in set theory. At the other end of the scale from the empty set one finds aleph which 'is the concept of sets whose members are sets—all the way down to nothing at all.' This means that, as Kauffman puts it 'any member of Aleph is a subset of Aleph' *and* 'as soon as you make a subset of Aleph, that set becomes a member of Aleph.' Kauffman's rather elegant description seems reminiscent of the functioning of the void,

however, to the extent that one might suspect that, even in this more complex case, the void and the infinite find themselves, in turn, infinitely intertwined: 'The reality of Aleph is a continual process of creation. No sooner have you written down a fragment of Aleph, then this fragment can be collected to form new members of Aleph. No matter how great Aleph becomes, she is always greater than that.

Aleph is the eye of the storm where thought can think itself and the world begins. When thought thinks itself and awareness becomes aware of awareness, then action occurs in the world and action being energy-through-time is physical. Pure thought and physicality are one in a creation that is a temporal eternity.' (Louis H. Kauffman, 'Virtual Logic: Cantor's Paradise and the Parable of Frozen Time', *Cybernetics and Human Knowing*, vol. 16, no. 1–2 (2009), 144).

28. Alain Badiou, *Number and Numbers*, tr. Robin Mackay (Cambridge: Polity, 2008 [1990]), 56–57.
29. *Ibid.*, 57.
30. Badiou, *Being and Event*, 54. Indeed, one might well hear the voice of the late Beckett in much of what Badiou has to say about presentation and the void. The way in which something—the dim—persists in the void in, above all, *Worstward Ho*, might well make one wonder whether Beckett already presents the sort of world of being Badiou imagines. The dim, in such a context, becomes an analogue to the brackets of set theory. The passage I am personally reminded of is the following: 'The dim. Far and wide the same. High and low. Unchanging. Say now unchanging. Whence no knowing. No saying. Say only such dim light as never. On all. Say a grot in that void. A gulf. Then in that grot or gulf such dimmest light as never. Whence no knowing. No saying. The void. Unchanging. Say now unchanging. Void were not the one. The twain. So far were not the one and twain. So far.' (Samuel Beckett, *Worstward Ho* (London: John Calder, 1999 [1983]), 16–17). It is surely significant that Badiou has himself dedicated a long essay to *Worstward Ho*; the title of that essay stresses the proximity of ideas in Beckett to Badiou's broader concerns: 'Being, Existence, Thought: Prose and Concept', tr. Alberto Toscano, rev. Nina Power, in Alain Badiou, *On Beckett*, eds. Alberto Toscano and Nina Power (Manchester: Clinamen, 2003 [1998]), 79–112.
31. Badiou, *Being and Event*, 3.
32. *Ibid.*, 431. Badiou's emphasis.
33. Jacques Lacan, 'Presentation on Psychic Causality', *Écrits*, ed. and tr. Bruce Fink (New York, NY: Norton, 2002 [1946]), 129. It should be noted, to be sure, that Lacan rapidly repudiated this particular Cartesian (re)turn, by 1949 explicitly splitting psychoanalytic experience from the *cogito*. See, in particular, Elisabeth Roudinesco, 'The Mirror Stage: An Obliterated Archive', tr. Barbara Bray, in Jean-Michel Rabaté, *The Cambridge Companion to Lacan* (Cambridge: Cambridge University Press, 2003), 32–33. Nevertheless, the comments on the *cogito* specifically highlighted by Badiou are drawn from 'The Agency of the Letter in the Unconscious or Reason since Freud', dating from 1957.
34. Jacques Lacan, 'The Instance of the Letter in the Unconscious, or Reason since Freud', *Écrits*, ed. and tr. Bruce Fink (New York, NY: Norton, 2002 [1957]), 429.
35. Lacan, 'The Instance of the Letter in the Unconscious', 430. It is surely not too difficult to hear the Heideggerian pulse of beings being in this passage.
36. Badiou, *Being and Event*, 432.
37. *Ibid.*

38. Jean Baudrillard, 'The Precession of Simulacra', *Simulacra and Simulation*, tr. Sheila Faria Glaser (Ann Arbor, MI: University of Michigan Press, 1994 [1981]), 6–7.

39. Paul Hegarty's revised translation of the second sentence of the given quotation indicates what might broadly be thought of as the 'essential' Baudrillardian view: '[There is] a plethora of second-hand truth, objectivity, and authenticity' (Paul Hegarty, *Jean Baudrillard: Live Theory* (London: Continuum, 2004), 53). As I hope is suggested above, with Badiou, I am unconvinced that the motion from presence to absence necessarily suggests that there is anything truly 'second-hand' in the situation.

40. Svetlana Boym, *The Future of Nostalgia* (New York, NY: Basic, 2001), xiii.

41. Martin Heidegger, *Parmenides*, tr. André Schuwer and Richard Rojewicz (Bloomington, IN: Indiana University Press, 1998 [1942–43]), 20–21.

42. Plato, *Republic*, 620e–621b, tr. G.M.A. Grube, rev. C.D.C. Reeve, in Plato, *Complete Works*, ed. John M. Cooper (Indianapolis, IN: Hackett, 1997 [*ca.* 380 BCE]), 1223.

43. Heidegger, *Parmenides*, 123.

44. *Ibid.* It is worth noting that Heidegger seems here to take the choice of the rarity of the subject, as Badiou proposed it, in a way which surely has troubling political overtones.

45. *Ibid.*, 124.

46. One might think this construction related to the distinction Agamben draws between ποίησις and πρᾶξις, quoting Plato's formulation in *Symposium* that 'any cause that brings into existence something that was not there before is ποίησις.' (Giorgio Agamben, *The Man Without Content*, tr. Georgia Albert (Stanford, CA: Stanford University Press, 1999 [1994]), 59). Indeed, Agamben himself makes just that link: 'The essential character of poiesis was not its aspect as a practical and voluntary process but its being a mode of truth understood as unveiling, ἀλήθεια.' (*Ibid.*, 69) Yet Heidegger's discussion really has little truck with such a conception, nor is his description really on the side of αἴσθησις. Though the immanent site at which truths are revealed in Heidegger's conception may be a product of ποίησις or πρᾶξις (indeed, either ποίησις or πρᾶξις may be a condition of the art work *qua* art work), neither is a necessary condition of the ontic characteristics of the art work, only a condition of the fact that there is an art work to *have* ontic characteristics. Indeed, even at his closest, here, Heidegger's interest is in *Handwerk*: πρᾶγμα, rather than πρᾶξις.

47. Heidegger, *Parmenides*, 126

48. Badiou, *Being and Event*, 17. It should be noted that, given the caveats appended to two of Badiou's four conditions of philosophy, it is clear that, like Hegel, Badiou is speaking here of 'real' art. Whatever ought *truly* to count as art would have characteristics like this.

49. Gilles Deleuze, *The Fold*, tr. Tom Conley (London: Continuum, 2011 [1988]), 86.

50. *Ibid.*

51. *Ibid.*, 87.

52. For all their common interests in the multiple, it is no surprise that Badiou asserts that, finally, '[t]he question posed by Deleuze is the question of Being. From beginning to end, and under the constraint of innumerable and fortuitous cases, his work is concerned with thinking though (its act, its movement) on the basis of an ontological precomprehension of Being as One.' Alain Badiou, *Deleuze: The Clamor of Being*, tr. Louise Burchill (Minneapolis, MN: University of Minnesota Press, 2000 [1997]), 20. It is important to recall, nevertheless, that Deleuze's position here may be closer to Badiou's

than Badiou suspects, in at least one key respect, which hinges upon precisely what Deleuze means by singularity. It seems likely, given Badiou's interests that, if he read singularity as meaning something more than a singular point, he will have thought of mathematical singularity. It is surely just as likely that Deleuze is thinking of gravitational singularities—especially since wavelengths are just what he immediately moves on to in his discussion—where infinite density is compressed into zero volume. Precisely this concatenation of the pure multiple and zero is that which one might expect to appeal to Badiou's thinking. The singularity, here common or garden, of Deleuze's infinitude perhaps still feels like a binary difference from a Badiouian perspective. Badiou's own reading of the distance between him and Deleuze on the subject of the event may be found in his review article 'Gilles Deleuze, The Fold: Leibniz and the Baroque', tr. Thelma Sowley, rev. Bruno Bosteels, in Alain Badiou, *The Adventure of French Philosophy* (London, Verso: 2012 [1989]), 241–267, esp. 248–255.

53. Natarajan Shankar, *Metamathematics, Machines, and Gödel's Proof* (Cambridge: Cambridge University Press, 1994), 2.
54. Alain Badiou, 'Philosophy and Truth', in Alain Badiou, *Infinite Thought*, ed. Oliver Feltham and Justin Clements (London: Continuum, 2006 [1999]), 62.
55. Badiou, *Being and Event*, 175.
56. *Idem*, 'Philosophy and Truth', 66.
57. *Ibid.*, 62.
58. See, in particular, Derrida's 'Signature Event Context', tr. Samuel Weber and Jeffrey Mehlman, in Jacques Derrida, *Limited Inc* (Evanston, IL: Northwestern University Press, 1988 [1972]), 1–24.
59. *Friday Night with Jonathan Ross*, BBC1, broadcast: 17 April 2009.
60. *Friday Night with Jonathan Ross*, BBC1, broadcast: 5 March 2010.
61. I am reminded here of a brief exchange between the supervillains Black Mask and The Joker in Grant Morrison and Dave McKean's graphic novel, *Arkham Asylum: A Serious House on Serious Earth* (London: Titan, 1990), 30. With Batman powerless, Black Mask wants to take off the cowl to reveal Batman's 'true' identity. He is refused by The Joker: 'Oh, don't be so predictable for Christ's sake. That *is* his real face.'
62. Friedrich Hölderlin, 'The meaning of tragedies . . . ', in *ibid.*, *Essay and Letters*, tr. and ed. Jeremy Adler and Charlie Louth (London: Penguin, 2009 [*ca.* 1802]), 316.

References

NB. *Non-scholarly web sources are given only within the footnotes associated with a particular chapter.*

Abu-Rabia, Aref, 'Breastfeeding Practices among Pastoral Tribes in the Middle East: A Cross-Cultural Study', *Anthropology of the Middle East*, vol. 2 no. 2 (2007), 38–54.

Agamben, Giorgio, *The Man Without Content*, tr. Georgia Albert (Stanford, CA: Stanford University Press, 1999 [1994]).

———, *State of Exception*, tr. Kevin Attell (Chicago, IL: University of Chicago Press, 2005 [2003]).

Allen, Jessica A., Ruowei Li, Kelley S. Scanlon, Cria G. Perrine, Jian Chen, Erika Odom, and Carla Black, 'Progress in Increasing Breastfeeding and Reducing Racial/Ethnic Differences—United States, 2000–2008 Births', *Morbidity and Mortality Weekly Report*, vol. 62, no. 5 (8 February 2013), 77–80, (online at: http://www.cdc.gov/mmwr/preview/mmwrhtml/mm6205a1.htm).

Alter, Gaby, 'Cyndi Lauper's "Girls Just Wanna Have Fun"', *MIX* (April 2004), 134–138.

Atwood, Margaret, *The Edible Woman* (New York, NY: Anchor Books, 1998 [1969]).

Auslander, Philip, 'Musical Persona: The Physical Performance of Popular Music', in *The Ashgate Research Companion to Popular Musicology*, ed. Derek Scott (Farnham: Ashgate, 2009), 303–16.

Badiou, Alain, *Deleuze: The Clamor of Being*, tr. Louise Burchill (Minneapolis, MN: University of Minnesota Press, 2000 [1997]).

———, 'Being, Existence, Thought: Prose and Concept', tr. Alberto Toscano, rev. Nina Power, in Alain Badiou, *On Beckett*, ed. Alberto Toscano and Nina Power (Manchester: Clinamen, 2003 [1998]), 79–112.

———, *Handbook of Inaesthetics*, tr. Alberto Toscano (Stanford, CA: Stanford University Press, 2005 [1998]).

———, 'Philosophy and Truth', in *idem, Infinite Thought*, ed. Oliver Feltham and Justin Clements (London: Continuum, 2006 [1999]), 58–68.

———, *Being and Event*, tr. Oliver Feltham (London: Continnum, 2007 [1988]).

———, *Number and Numbers*, tr. Robin Mackay (Cambridge: Polity, 2008 [1990]).

———, *Logics of Worlds*, tr. Alberto Toscano (London: Continuum, 2009 [2006]).

———, 'Gilles Deleuze, The Fold: Leibniz and the Baroque', tr. Thelma Sowley, rev. Bruno Bosteels, in Alain Badiou, *The Adventure of French Philosophy* (London, Verso: 2012 [1989]), 241–267.

Banet-Weiser, Sarah, *Authentic: Political Possibilities in a Brand Culture* (New York, NY: New York University Press, 2012).

Bataille, Georges, 'The Solar Anus', in *Visions of Excess: Selected Writings, 1927–1939*, ed. Allan Stoekl, tr. Allan Stoekl, Carl R. Lovitt, and Donald M. Leslie, Jr. (Minneapolis, MN: University of Minnesota Press, 1985 [1927], 5–9.

———, 'The Big Toe', in *Visions of Excess: Selected Writings, 1927–1939*, ed. Allan Stoekl, tr. Allan Stoekl, Carl R. Lovitt, and Donald M. Leslie, Jr. (Minneapolis, MN: University of Minnesota Press, 1985 [1929]), 20—23.

———, 'Attraction and Repulsion II: Social Structure' in *The College of Sociology, 1937–39*, ed. Denis Hollier (Minneapolis, MN: University of Minnesota Press, 1988 [1938]), 113–124.

———, *Inner Experience*, tr. Leslie Anne Boldt (New York, NY: State University of New York Press, 1988 [1954]).

———, *The Accursed Share*, vol. I., tr. Robert Hurley (New York: Zone, 1991 [1949]).

———, *Eroticism*, tr. Mary Dalwood (London: Penguin, 2001 [1957]).

———, *Guilty*, tr. Stuart Kendall (Albany, NY: State University of New York Press, 2011 [1944]).

Baudrillard, Jean, *Seduction*, tr. Brian Singer (New York NY: St. Martin's Press, 1990 [1979]).

———, 'The Precession of Simulacra', *Simulacra and Simulation*, tr. Sheila Faria Glaser (Ann Arbor, MI: University of Michigan Press, 1994 [1981]), 1–42.

Beckett, Samuel, *Worstward Ho* (London: John Calder, 1999 [1983]).

Bell, Chris, 'Introducing White Disability Studies: A Modest Proposal,' in *The Disability Studies Reader*, ed. Lennard J. Davis (New York, NY: Routledge, 2006), 275–282.

Berlant, Lauren and Michael Warner, 'Sex in Public', *Critical Inquiry*, vol. 24, no. 2 (Winter 1998), 547–566.

Betcher, Sharon, 'Putting My Foot (Prosthesis, Crutches, Phantom) Down: Considering Technology as Transcendence in the Writings of Donna Haraway', *Women's Studies Quarterly*, vol. 29, no. 3/4 (Fall/Winter 2001), 35–53.

Bezier, Janet L., *Ventriloquized Bodies: Narratives of Hysteria in 19th Century France.* (Ithaca, NY: Cornell University Press, 1994).

Blum, Linda M., 'Mothers, Babies, and Breastfeeding in Late Capitalist America: The Shifting Contexts of Feminist Theory,' *Feminist Studies*, vol. 19, no. 2 (Summer 1993), 291–311.

Bonds, Mark Evan, *Music as Thought: Listening to the Symphony in the Age of Beethoven* (Princeton, NJ: Princeton University Press, 2006).

Bordo, Susan, *Unbearable Weight: Feminism, Western Culture, and the Body* (Berkeley: University of California Press, 2003).

Bordwell, David and Kristin Thompson, *Film Art: An Introduction* (New York, NY: McGraw-Hill, 1997).

Bosma, Hannah 'The Death of the Singer: Authorship and Female Voices in Electronic Music', *Contact*, vol. 1, no. 3 (1998) (online at http://cec.sonus.ca/contact/Voice/Bosma.html) <accessed 19 July 2012>.

Boym, Svetlana, *The Future of Nostalgia* (New York, NY: Basic, 2001).

Bradby, Barbara and Dave Laing, 'Introduction to "Gender and Sexuality" Special Issue', *Popular Music*, vol. 20, no. 3 (October 2001), 295–300.

Braver, Lee, *Heidegger's Later Writings: A Reader's Guide* (London :Continuum, 2009).

Bristow, Joseph, *Sexuality* (New York, NY: Routledge, 1997).

Bronfen, Elisabeth, *Over Her Dead Body: Death, Femininity and the Aesthetic* (Manchester: Manchester University Press, 1992).

Butler, Judith, *Bodies That Matter: On the Discursive Limits of 'Sex'* (New York, NY: Routledge, 1993).

———, *Gender Trouble: Feminism and the Subversion of Identity*, 2nd edition (London: Routledge, 1999).

———, *Undoing Gender* (New York, NY: Routledge, 2004).

Callahan, Maureen, *Poker Face: The Rise and Rise of Lady Gaga* (New York, NY: Hyperion, 2010).

Carpenter, Alexander, 'Give a Man a Mask and He'll Tell the Truth: Arnold Schoenberg, David Bowie, and the Mask of Pierrot', *Intersections*, vol. 30, no. 2, 5–24.

Chion, Michel, *Audio-Vision: Sound on Screen* (New York, NY: Columbia University Press, 1994).

Click, Melissa A., Hyunji Lee and Holly Willson Holladay, 'Making Monsters: Lady Gaga, Fan Identification, and Social Media', *Popular Music and Society*, vol. 36, no. 3 (2013), 360–379.

Colton, Lisa, 'The Articulation of Virginity in the Medieval *Chanson de nonne*', *Journal of the Royal Musical Association*, vol. 133, no. 2 (2008), 159–188.

Cook, Nicholas, *Analysing Musical Multimedia* (Oxford: Oxford University Press, 1998).

Coon, Caroline, *1988: The New Wave Punk Rock Explosion* (London: Omnibus, 1977).

Davis, Angela, *Women, Race and Class* (New York, NY: Random House, 1983).

Davis, Lennard J., *Enforcing Normality: Disability, Deafness and the Body* (London: Verso, 1995).

Deleuze, Gilles, *The Fold*, tr. Tom Conley (London: Continuum, 2011 [1988]).

———and Félix Guattari, *A Thousand Plateaus*, tr. Brian Massumi (London: Athlone, 1988 [1980]).

Debord, Guy, *The Society of the Spectacle*, tr. Donald Nicholson-Smith (New York, NY: Zone, 1994 [1967]).

Derrida, Jacques, *Specters of Marx: The State of the Debt, the Work of Mourning, & the New International*, tr. Peggy Kamuf (London: Routledge, 1994 [1993]).

———, 'Signature Event Context', tr. Samuel Weber and Jeffrey Mehlman, in *Jacques Derrida, Limited Inc* (Evanston, IL: Northwestern University Press, 1988 [1972]), 1–24.

Dibben, Nicola, 'Vocal Performance and the Projection of Emotional Authenticity', in *The Ashgate Research Companion to Popular Musicology*, ed. Derek B. Scott (Aldershot: Ashgate, 2009), 317–333.

———, *Björk* (Bloomington, IN: Indiana University Press, 2009).

Dickinson, Kay, '"Believe?": Vocoders, Digitalized Female Identity, and Camp', *Popular Music*, vol. 20, no. 3 (October 2001), 333–347.

Doane, Mary Anne, *The Desire to Desire: The Woman's Film of the 1940s*, 2nd edition (Bloomington, IN: Indiana University Press, 1987).

Dolan, Jill, 'The Dynamics of Desire: Sexuality and Gender in Pornography and Performance', *Theatre Journal*, vol. 39, no. 2 (May 1987), 156–174.

During, Simon, 'Introduction', *The Cultural Studies Reader* (New York, NY: Routledge, 1993), 1–29.

Dyer, Richard, *Heavenly Bodies: Film Stars and Society*, 2nd edition (New York, NY: Routledge, 2004).

Eidsheim, Nina, 'Synthesizing Race: Towards an Analysis of the Performativity of Vocal Timbre', *Revista Transcultural de Musica*, vol. 13 (2009), n.p. (online at: http://www.sibetrans.com/trans/a57/synthesizing-race-towards-an-analysis-of-the-performativity-of-vocal-timbre) <accessed: 28 September 2011>.

Epstein, Marcy J., 'Eating Acts and Feminist Embodiment', *TDR*, vol. 40, no. 4 (Winter, 1996), 20–36.

Fischer, Claude S., 'Gender and the Residential Telephone, 1890–1940: Technologies of Sociability', *Sociological Forum*, vol. 3, no.2 (1988), 211–233.

Fiske, John, *Television Culture* (London: Methuen, 1987).

Foucault, Michel, 'A Preface to Transgression', tr. Donald F. Bouchard and Sherry Simon, in *Language, Counter-memory and Practice* (New York, NY: Cornell University Press, 1977), 29–52.

———, '22 January 1975', *The Abnormal: Lectures to the College de France 1974–1975*, eds. Valerio Marchetti and Antonella Solomoni, trans. Graham Burchell (Brooklyn, NY: Verso, 2003 [1975]), 55—80.

Frankenberg, Ruth, *White Women, Race Matters: The Social Construction of Whiteness* (Minneapolis, MN: The University of Minnesota Press, 1993).

Freud, Sigmund, 'The "Uncanny"', tr. Alix Strachey (rev. James Strachey), in Sigmund Freud, *Writings on Art and Literature* (Stanford, CA: Stanford University Press, 1997 [1919]), 193–233.

Frissen, Valerie, 'Gender is Calling: Some Reflections on Past, Present and Future Uses of the Telephone', in *The Gender-Technology Relation: Contemporary Theory and Research*, ed. Keith Grint and Rosalind Gill (London: Taylor & Francis, 1995), 79–94.

Frith, Simon, 'The Industrialization of Music', in *idem*, *Music for Pleasure: Essays in the Sociology of Pop* (Cambridge: Polity, 1998 [1987]), 11–23.

Garber, Marjorie, *Vested Interests: Cross-Dressing and Cultural Anxiety* (New York, NY: Routledge, 1997).

Garland-Thompson, Rosemarie, *Extraordinary Bodies: Figuring Physical Disability in American Culture and Literature* (New York, NY: Columbia University Press, 1997).

———, 'The Politics of Staring: Visual Rhetorics of Disability in Popular Photography', in *Disability Studies: Enabling the Humanities*, ed. Rosemarie Garland-Thomson *et al.* (New York, NY: Modern Languages Association, 2002), 55–75.

Geller, Theresa L., The Cinematic Relations of Corporeal Feminism', in *The Becoming Deleuzo-guattarian of Queer Studies*, ed. Michael O'Rourke (Special Double Issue of *Rhizomes: Cultural Studies in Emerging Knowledge*, nos. 11/12 (Fall 2005/ Spring 2006)), http://www.rhizomes.net/issue11/geller.html

Genz, Stephanie and Benjamin A. Brabon, *Postfeminism: Cultural Texts and Theories* (Edinburgh: Edinburgh University Press, 2009).

Gill, Rosalind, *Gender and the Media* (Cambridge: Polity, 2007).

Gillespie, Carmen, 'The N-word, the F-word and All that Jazz: Race, Sex and Transgressive Language in Contemporary American Literature and Popular Culture', in *Language in the Real World: An Introduction to Linguistics* ed. Susan J, Behrens and Judith A. Parker (Abingdon: Routledge, 2010), 123—135.

Gillett, Charlie, *The Sound of the City* (London: Souvenir, 1987).

Goldmark, Daniel 'Stuttering in American Popular Song, 1890–1930', in *Sounding Off: Theorizing Disability in Music*, ed. Neil Lerner and Joseph N. Straus (New York, NY: Routledge, 2006), 91–106.

Goodman, Lizzy, *Lady Gaga: Extreme Style* (London: HarperCollins, 2010).

Gorbman, Claudia, 'Aesthetics and Rhetoric,' *American Music*, vol. 22, no. 1 (Spring 2004), 14–26.

Gordon, Bonnie *Monteverdi's Unruly Women: The Power of Song in Early-Modern Italy* (Cambridge: Cambridge University Press, 2004).

Graham, Elaine L., *Representations of the Post/Human: Monsters, Aliens and Others in Pop Culture* (New Brunswick, NJ: Rutgers University Press, 2002).

Green, Lucy, *Music on Deaf Ears* (Manchester: Manchester University Press, 1988).

Green, Venus, 'Race, Gender, and National Identity in the American and British Telephone Industries', *International Review of Social History*, vol. 46, no. 2 (2001), 185–205.

Greer, Germaine, 'The Politics of Female Sexuality', *Oz*, no. 29 (May 1970), reprinted in *eadem*, *The Madwoman's Underclothes: Essays in Occasional Writings* (New York, NY: Atlantic Monthly, 1986), 36–37.

Gregg, Melissa and Gregory J. Seigworth (eds.), *The Affect Theory Reader* (Durham, NC: Duke University Press, 2010).

Gross, Larry, *Up From Invisibility: Lesbians, Gay Men, and the Media in America* (New York, NY: Columbia University Press, 2001).

Gummer-Strawn, L., K. S. Scanlon, N. Darling, and E. J. Conrey, 'Racial and Socioeconomic Disparities in Breastfeeding—United States, 2004', *Morbidity and Mortality Weekly Report*, vol. 55, no. 12 (31 March 2006), 335–339 (online at: http://www.cdc.gov/mmwr/preview/mmwrhtml/mm5512a3.htm),

Halberstam, J. Jack, *Gaga Feminism* (Boston, MA: Beacon Press, 2012).

Halberstam, Judith, *In a Queer Time and Place: Transgender Bodies, Sub-cultural Lives* (New York, NY: New York University Press, 2005).

——, *The Queer Art of Failure* (Durham, NC: Duke University Press, 2011).

Haraway, Donna, 'A Cyborg Manifesto: Science, Technology, and Socialist-Feminism in the Late Twentieth Century', in *Simians, Cyborgs, and Women: The Reinvention of Nature* (New York, NY: Routledge, 1991), 149–181.

Hawkins, Stan, *Settling the Pop Score: Pop Texts and Identity Politics* (Aldershot: Ashgate, 2002).

——, 'Dragging out Camp: Narrative Agendas in Madonna's Musical Production', in *Madonna's Drowned Worlds: New Approaches to Her Cultural Transformations, 1983–2003*, ed. S. Fouz-Hernández & F. Jarman-Ivens (Aldershot, Ashgate, 2004), 3–21.

——, *The British Pop Dandy: Masculinity, Popular Music and Culture* (Farnham: Ashgate, 2009).

Hayward, Susan, *Cinema Studies: The Key Concepts*, 2nd edition (London: Routldge, 2000).

Hegarty, Paul, *Jean Baudrillard: Live Theory* (London: Continuum, 2004).

Hegel, G.W.F., *Introductory Lectures on Aesthetics*, tr. Bernard Bosanquet (London: Penguin, 1993 [1818–29]).

Heidegger, Martin, *Parmenides*, tr. André Schuwer and Richard Rojewicz (Bloomington, IN: Indiana University Press, 1998 [1942–43]).

——, 'Summary of a Seminar on the Lecture "Time and Being"', tr. Joan Stambaugh, in Martin Heidegger, *On Time and Being*, ed. Joan Stambaugh (Chicago, IL: University of Chicago Press, 2002 [1962]), 25–54.

——, 'On the Origin of the Work of Art', tr. Albert Hofstadter, in Martin Heidegger, *Basic Writings*, ed. David Farrell Krell (London: Routledge, 2009 [1936]), 143–212.

——, 'The End of Philosophy and the Task of Thinking', tr. Joan Stambaugh, rev. David Farrell Krell, in Martin Heidegger, *Basic Writings*, ed. David Farrell Krell (London: Routledge, 2009 [1936]), 427–449.

Hölderlin, Friedrich, 'The Meaning of Tragedies . . . ', in *ibid.*, *Essay and Letters*, tr. and ed. Jeremy Adler and Charlie Louth (London: Penguin, 2009 [*ca.* 1802]), 316.

Holmlund, Chris, *Impossible Bodies: Femininity and Masculinity at the Movies* (New York, NY: Routledge, 2002).

Humann, Heather Duerre, 'What a Drag: Lady Gaga, Jo Calderone and the Politics of Representation', in *The Performance Identities of Lady Gaga*, ed. Richard Gray II, (Jefferson, NC: McFarland, 2012), 74–84.

Huyssen, Andreas, *After The Great Divide: Modernism, Mass Culture and Post-modernism* (Bloomington, IN: Indiana University Press, 1986).

Jarman-Ivens, Freya, 'Notes on Musical Camp', in Derek Scott (ed.) *The Ashgate Research Companion to Popular Musicology* (Farnham: Ashgate, 2009), 189–203.

Jones, Amelia, '1970/2007: The Return of Feminist Art', *X-Tra: Contemporary Art Quarterly*, vol. 10, no. 4 (Summer 2008) (online at: http://x-traonline.org/issues/volume-10/number-4/19702007-the-return-of-feminist-art/) <accessed: 18 March 2013>.

Kaplan, E. Ann, 'Madonna Politics: Perversion, Repression or Subversion? Or Masks and/as Master-y', in *The Madonna Connection: Representational Politics, Subcultural Identities, and Cultural Theory*, ed. Cathy Schwichtenberg (Boulder, CO: Westview, 1993), 149–165.

Kauffman, Louis H., 'Virtual Logic: Cantor's Paradise and the Parable of Frozen Time', *Cybernetics and Human Knowing*, vol. 16, no. 1–2 (2009), 143–151.

Kimbro, Rachel Tolbert, 'On-the-Job Moms: Work and Breastfeeding Initiation and Duration for a Sample of Low-Income Women', *Maternal and Child Health Journal*, vol. 10, no. 1 (January 2006), 19–26.

Klein, Bethany, *As Heard on TV: Popular Music in Advertising* (Farnham: Ashgate, 2010).

Klein, Naomi, *No Logo* (London: Flamingo, 2001).

Krell, David Farrell, introductory notes to Martin Heidegger, 'The Origin of the Work of Art', tr. Albert Hofstadter, in Martin Heidegger, *Basic Writings*, ed. David Farrell Krell (London: Routledge, 2009 [1936]), 140–142.

Kristeva, Julia, *Powers of Horror: An Essay on Abjection*, tr. Leon S. Roudiez (New York, NY: Columbia University Press, 1982 [1980]).

Kroker, Arthur, *Spasm: Virtual Reality/Android Music/Electric Flesh* (New York, NY: New World Perspectives/St Martin's Press, 1993).

Kuppers, Petra, *Disability and Contemporary Performance: Bodies on the Edge* (London: Routledge, 2003).

———, 'The Wheelchair's Rhetoric: The Performance of Disability', *TDR: The Drama Review*, vol. 51, no. 4 (Winter 2007), 80–88.

Lacan, Jacques, 'Presentation on Psychic Causality', *Écrits*, ed. and tr. Bruce Fink (New York, NY: Norton, 2002 [1946]), 123–158.

———, 'The Instance of the Letter in the Unconscious, or Reason since Freud', *Écrits*, ed. and tr. Bruce Fink (New York, NY: Norton, 2002 [1957]), 412–441.

Law, Jules, 'The Politics of Breastfeeding: Assessing Risk, Dividing Labor,' *Signs*, vol. 25, no.2 (Winter 2000), 407–450.

Lazzarato, Maurizio, *Lavoro immateriale: Forme di vita e produzione di soggettività* (Verona: Ombre Corte, 1997).

Lester, Paul, *Looking for Fame: The Life of a Pop Princess Lady Gaga* (London: Omnibus, 2010).

Levi-Strauss, Claude, *Myth and Meaning* (Toronto: University of Toronto Press, 1978).

Lieb, Kristen, *Gender, Branding, and the Modern Music Industry* (New York, NY: Routledge, 2013).

Lipartito, Kenneth, 'When Women Were Switches: Technology, Work, and Gender in the Telephone Industry, 1890–1920', *The American History Review*, vol. 99, no. 4 (1994), 1074–1111.

Loza, Susana, 'Sampling (hetero)sexuality: Diva-ness and Discipline in Electronic Dance Music', *Popular Music*, vol. 20, no. 3 (2001), 349–357.

Lyotard, Jean-François, 'Brief Reflections on Popular Culture', in *ICA Documents 4*, ed. Lisa Appignanesi (London: Institute of Contemporary Arts, 1986).

Maines, Rachel, *The Technology of Orgasm: Hysteria, the Vibrator and Women's Sexual Satisfaction* (Baltimore, MD: Johns Hopkins University Press, 1999).

Marcus, Greil, *In The Fascist Bathroom: Writings on Punk 1977–1992* (London: Viking, 1993).

Matthews, Glenna, Review of Lana F. Rakow, *Gender on the Line: Women, the Telephone, and Community Life* (Urbana: University of Illinois Press, 1992), in *The Journal of American History*, vol. 80, no. 2 (1993), 756–757.

McClary, Susan, *Feminine Endings: Music, Gender, and Sexuality*, (Minneapolis, MN: University of Minnesota Press, 1991).

McGrath, Tom, *MTV: The Making of a Revolution* (Philadelphia, PA: Running, 1996).

McNair, Brian, *Striptease Culture: Sex, Media and the Democratisation of Desire* (Abingdon: Routledge, 2002).

McQuiston, Liz, *Suffragettes to She-Devils* (London: Phaidon, 1997).

Miller, James, *Flowers in the Dustbin: The Rise of Rock and Roll, 1947–1977* (New York, NY: Simon & Schuster, 1999).

Mitchell, David and Sharon Snyder, *Narrative Prosthesis: Disability and the Dependencies of Discourse* (Ann Arbor, MI: University of Michigan Press, 2000).

Moore, Allan F., *Song Means: Analysing and Interpreting Recorded Popular Song* (Farnham: Ashgate, 2012).

Moran, Caitlin, *How To Be A Woman* (London: Ebury, 2011).

Morgan, Johnny, *Gaga* (New York: Sterling, 2010).

Morgan, Robert C., 'Carolee Schneemann: The Politics of Eroticism', *Art Journal*, vol. 56, no. 4 (Winter, 1997), 97–100.

Morrison, Grant and Dave McKean, *Arkham Asylum: A Serious House on Serious Earth* (London: Titan, 1990).

Morrison, Toni, *Playing in the Dark: Whiteness and the Literary Imagination* (Cambridge, MA: Harvard University Press, 1992).

Moylan, William, 'Considering Space in Recorded Music' in *The Art of Record Production*, ed. Simon Frith and Simon Zagorski-Thomas (Farnham: Ashgate, 2012), 163–188.

Murray Ormandy, Joanne, *Racing Critical Disability Discourse* (unpublished PhD dissertation, University of Toronto, 2008).

Nealon, Jeffrey, *Alterity Politics: Ethics and Performative Subjectivity* (Durham, NC): Duke University Press, 1998).

Niblock, Sarah and Stan Hawkins (*Prince: The Making of a Pop Music Phenomenon* (Farnham: Ashgate, 2011).

Nichols, Bill, 'Film Theory and the Revolt Against Master Narratives', *Reinventing Film Studies*, ed. Christine Gledhill and Linda Williams (New York, NY: Oxford University Press, 2000).34–52.

Norris, Christopher, *Platonism, Music and the Listener's Share* (London: Continuum, 2006).

Nyong'o, Tavia, 'Freddy Mercury Deconstructed Roundtable', 2010 Pop Conference, EMP Museum Seattle, WA, 16 April 2010.

O'Brien, Lucy 'The Woman Punk Made Me', in *Punk Rock: So What? The Cultural Legacy of Punk*, ed. Roger Sabin (London: Routledge, 1999), 186–198.

———, *She Bop II: The Definitive History of Women in Rock, Pop & Soul* (London: Continuum, 2002).

———, *Madonna: Like An Icon* (London: Bantam, 2007).

Parret, Herman 'Kant on Music and the Hierarchy of the Arts', *The Journal of Aesthetics and Art Criticism*, vol. 56, no. 3 (Summer 1998), 251–264.

Peraino, Judith, *Listening to the Sirens: Musical Technologies of Queer Identity from Homer to Hedwig*, (Berkeley, CA: University of California Press, 2006).

Peterson, Richard A., 'Why 1955? Explaining the Advent of Rock Music', *Popular Music*, vol. 9, no. 1 (January 1990), 97–116.

Plato, *Republic*, tr. G.M.A. Grube, rev. C.D.C. Reeve, in Plato, *Complete Works*, ed. John M. Cooper (Indianapolis, IN: Hackett, 1997 [*ca.* 380 BCE]), 971–1223.

Plotinus, *The Enneads*, tr. Stephen MacKenna (New York, NY: Larson, 1992 [*ca.* 250–70 CE]).

Rakow, Lana F. and Vija Navarro, 'Remote Mothering and the Parallel Shift: Women Meet the Cellular Telephone', *Critical Studies in Mass Communication*, vol. 10, no. 2 (1993), 144–157.

Riviere, Joan, 'Womanliness as a Masquerade', in, *Psychoanalysis and Female Sexuality*, ed. Henrik M. Ruitenbeek (New Haven, CT: College and University Press, 1966), 209–220.

Robertson, Kimberly, 'Globalization and the Politics of Native Breastfeeding', *Off of Our Backs*, vol. 36 no. 4 (2006), 61–64.

Ross, Andrew, 'Uses of Camp', in Fabio Cleto (ed.), *Camp: Queer Aesthetics and the Performing Subject: A Reader* (Edinburgh: Edinburgh University Press, 1999), 308–329.

Roudinesco, Elisabeth, 'The Mirror Stage: An Obliterated Archive', tr. Barbara Bray, in *The Cambridge Companion to Lacan* ed. Jean-Michel Rabaté (Cambridge: Cambridge University Press, 2003), 25–34.

Russo, Vito, *The Celluloid Closet: Homosexuality in the Movies*, revised ed. (New York, NY: Harper & Row, 1987 [1981]).

Savoy, Eric, 'That Ain't All She Ain't: Doris Day and Queer Performativity', in *Out Takes: Essays on Queer Theory and Film*, ed. Ellis Hanson (Durham, NC: Duke University Press, 1999), 151–182.

Schneemann, Carolee, 'The Obscene Body/Politic', *Art Journal*, vol. 50, no. 4 (Winter, 1991), 28–35.

Scott, Derek, *Sounds of the Metropolis: The 19th-Century Popular Music Revolution (in London, New York, Paris, and Vienna)* (New York, NY: Oxford University Press, 2008).

Shankar, Natarajan, *Metamathematics, Machines, and Gödel's Proof* (Cambridge: Cambridge University Press, 1994).

Siebers, Tobin, *Disability Theory* (Ann Arbor: University of Michigan Press, 2008).

Silverman, Kaja, *The Threshold of the Visible World* (New York, NY: Routledge, 1996).

Singer, Ben T., 'Towards a Transgender Sublime: The Politics of Excess in Trans-specific Cultural Production', in *The Transgender Studies Reader*, ed. Susan Stryker and Stephen Whittle (New York, NY: Routledge, 2006), 601–620.

Smith, Paul, 'Whiteness, Normal Theory, and Disability Studies', *Disability Studies Quarterly*, vol. 24, no. 2 (Spring 2004), (online at: http://dsq-sds.org/article/view/491/668) <accessed: 4 April 2013>

Snead, James, *White Screens, Black Images: Hollywood From the Dark Side*, ed. Colin MacCabe and Cornel West (New York, NY: Routledge, 1994).

Sontag, Susan, 'Notes on "Camp"', *Against Interpretation and Other Essays* (New York, NY: Anchor 1990 [1964]), 275–292.

Stahl, Matt, *Unfree Masters: Recording Artists and the Politics of Work* (Durham, NC: Duke University Press, 2013).

Stras, Laurie, 'The Organ of the Soul: Voice, Damage, and Affect', in *Sounding Off: Theorizing Disability in Music*, ed. Neil Lerner and Joseph Straus (New York, NY: Routledge, 2006), 173–184.

———, 'White Face, Black Voice: Race, Gender and Region in the Music of the Boswell Sisters', *Journal of the Society for American Music*, vol. 1 (2007), 207–255.

————, ed., *She's So Fine: Reflections on Whiteness, Femininity, Adolescence and Class in 1960s Music* (Aldershot: Ashgate, 2010).

Strauss, Neil, 'The Broken Heart & Violent Fantasies of Lady Gaga', *Rolling Stone*, no. 1108/1109 (8–22 July 2010), 66–72, 74, 20.

Stryker, Susan, 'My Words to Victor Frankenstein above the Village of Chamounix: Performing Transgender Rage', in *The Transgender Studies Reader*, ed. Susan Stryker and Stephen Whittle (New York, NY: Routledge, 2006), 244–256.

Tagg, Philip, *Fernando the Flute* (Liverpool: Mass Media Music Scholars' Press, 1991).

Terry, Jennifer and Melodie Calvert, 'Introduction', in *eadem, Processed Lives: Gender and Technology in Everyday Life* (London: Routledge, 1997), 1–19.

Thompson, Rosemary Garland, *Extraordinary Bodies: Figuring Physical Disability in American Culture and Literature* (New York: Columbia University Press, 1997).

Thrift, Nigel, 'Understanding the Material Practices of Glamour', in *The Affect Theory Reader*, ed. Melissa Gregg and Gregory J. Seigworth (Durham, NC: Duke University Press, 2010 [2008]), 289–308.

Tropiano, Stephen, *The Prime Time Closet: A History of Gays and Lesbians on TV* (New York: Applause Theater and Books, 2002).

Tyler, Carol-Anne, 'Boys Will Be Girls: The Politics of Gay Drag', in *Inside/Out: Lesbian Theories, Gay Theories*, ed. Diana Fuss (New York, NY: Routledge, 1991), 32–70.

US Centers for Disease Control and Prevention, Division of Nutrition, Physical Activity, and Obesity, 'Breastfeeding Among U.S. Children Born 2000–2010, CDC National Immunization Survey' (online at: http://www.cdc.gov/breastfeeding/data/NIS_data/index.htm), <last reviewed: 31 July 2013>.

Vernallis, Carol, *Experiencing Music Video: Aesthetics and Cultural Context* (New York: Columbia University Press, 2004).

Waldman, Diane, *Roy Lichtenstein* (New York, NY: Guggenheim, 1993).

Walters, Suzanne D., *All the Rage: The Story of Gay Visibility in America* (Chicago: University of Chicago Press, 2001).

Ward, Ed, Geoffrey Stokes and Ken Tucker, *Rock of Ages: The Rolling Stone History of Rock and Roll* (London: Penguin, 1987).

Warner, Simon, 'Sifting the Shifting Sands: "Howl" and the American Landscape in the 1950s', *Howl for Now: A Celebration of Allen Ginsberg's Epic Protest Poem*, ed. Simon Warner (Pontefract Route, 2005), 25–52.

Watney, Simon, 'The Spectacle of AIDS', in *AIDS: Cultural Analysis, Cultural Activism*, ed. David Crimp (Cambridge, MA: MIT Press, 1989 [1987]), 71–86.

Whiteley, Sheila, Andy Bennett, and Stan Hawkins (eds.), *Music, Space and Place: Popular Music and Cultural Identity* (Aldershot: Ashgate, 2004).

Wilbur, Kenneth C., 'How the Digital Video Recorder Changes Traditional Television Advertising', *The Journal of Advertising*, vol. 37, no. 1 (Spring 2008), 143—149.

Wolf, Jacqueline H., 'Got Milk? Not In Public!', *International Breastfeeding Journal*, vol. 3, no. 11 (2008) (online at: http://www.internationalbreastfeedingjournal.com/content/3/1/11).

————, 'What Feminists Can Do for Breastfeeding and What Breastfeeding Can Do for Feminists', *Signs*, vol. 31, no. 2 (2006), 397–424.

Woolson, Wendy A., *Refined Tastes: Sugar, Confectionery, and Consumers in Nineteenth-Century America* (Baltimore, MD: The Johns Hopkins University Press, 2002).

Wosk, Julie, *Women and the Machine: Representations from the Spinning Wheel to the Electronic Age* (Baltimore, MD: The Johns Hopkins University Press, 2001).

Wright, Lee, 'Objectifying Gender: The Stiletto Heel', in *Fashion Theory: A Reader*, ed. Malcolm Barnard (Oxford and New York: Routledge, 2007), 197–207.

Zagorski-Thomas, Simon, 'The Stadium in Your Bedroom: Functional Staging, Authenticity and the Audience-led Aesthetic in Record Production', *Popular Music*, vol. 29, no. 2 (May 2010), 251–266.

Žižek, Slavoj, *Looking Awry: An Introduction to Jacques Lacan through Popular Culture* (Boston, MA: MIT Press, 1992).

Contributors

Alexandra Apolloni holds a Ph.D. in Musicology from UCLA. Her research focuses on the relationship between vocal timbre and constructions of race and gender in performances by women pop vocalists from 1950 to the present. Her dissertation, *Wishin' and Hopin': Whiteness, Femininity, and Voice in 1960s British Pop*, was completed with the support of an Alvin H. Johnson AMS-50 Fellowship from the American Musicological Society. She has taught courses on popular music, music and gender, and music writing, and served as Editor-in-Chief of *Echo: A Music-Centered Journal* from 2011–2013. She is currently working on a project about Jamaican singer Millie Small.

Lori Burns is a Professor of Music at the University of Ottawa. Her interdisciplinary research merges cultural theory and musical analysis to explore representations of gender in the lyrical, musical, and visual texts of popular music. She has published articles in edited collections published by Oxford, Garland, Routledge, and the University of Michigan Press, as well as in leading journals (*Popular Music, Popular Music and Society, The Journal for Music, Sound, and Moving Image, Studies in Music, Music Theory Spectrum, Music Theory Online* and *The Journal for Music Theory*). Along with co-researcher Marc Lafrance, Burns is the recipient of an Insight Grant from the Social Sciences and Humanities Research Council of Canada (2013–2018).

Lisa Colton is Subject Leader for Music at the University of Huddersfield, where she lectures in musicology. Her research focuses on early and contemporary music from various critical perspectives. Dr Colton's journal articles include studies of women's roles in the cultivation of fourteenth-century polyphony (*Early Music*) seventeenth-century keyboard music (*Music and Letters*), gender and virginity in motets relating to nuns (*Journal of the Royal Musical Association*), and of the music of Judith Weir (*Contemporary Music Review*). Her forthcoming work includes a chapter in the *Oxford Handbook of Music and Queerness*, entitled 'Queer Sensibilities in Medieval Musical Culture', and a chapter on perceptions of sound and music in the Middle Ages as part of the collection *Noise, Audition, Aurality: Histories of the Sonic Worlds of Europe c.1500–1918.*

Theresa L. Geller is Assistant Professor of Film Theory and History at Grinnell College. Her research on women directors has appeared in *Biography, Senses of Cinema, Oxford Bibliographies Online,* and the collection, *There She Goes: Feminist Filmmaking and Beyond.* She has published on film, TV, and critical theory in *Rhizomes, Frontiers: A Journal of Women Studies,* and *Spectator,* and has chapters in the critical anthologies, *Gender After Lyotard,* and *East Asian Cinemas: Exploring Transnational Connections on Film.* Professor Geller is currently completing a monograph on *The X-Files* for Wayne State Press and co-editing the critical anthology, *An Indelible Mark: Women and the Work of Todd Haynes.*

Sally Gray is a Visiting Scholar in Cultural History at the College of Fine Arts, at the University of New South Wales, Sydney. Her work on fashion and art history appears in leading journals and edited volumes and she is currently completing a book, *You Are It!,* on self-fashioned creative lives, funded by a three-year Australian Research Council Postdoctoral Fellowship. She taught Art History and Fashion History and Theory at the University of New South Wales between 2002 and 2009 and has been an independent curator of art and design exhibitions since the early 1990s. Her latest curatorial project is 'When This You See Remember Me', a retrospective exhibition of the work of the queer artist David McDiarmid, at the National Gallery of Victoria, Melbourne. Her website is http://www.sallygray.com.au.

Stan Hawkins is Professor of Musicology at the University of Oslo and Adjunct Professor at the University of Agder. He has led a project, *Popular Music and Gender in a Transcultural Contect,* funded by the Norwegian Research Council (2010–2014). He is author of *Settling the Pop Score* (2002), *The British Pop Dandy* (2009), and *Prince: The Making of a Pop Music Phenomenon* (2011). His edited books include *Music, Space & Place* (2004), *Essays on Sound & Vision* (2007), *Pop Music & Easy Listening* (2011) and *Critical Musicological Reflections* (2012). He is also a composer, and his works include string quartets, symphonies, a clarinet concerto, electro-acoustic, and live arrangements, and numerous solo and ensemble pieces.

Paul Hegarty studied Languages, Economics and Politics at what was then Kingston Polytechnic for his first degree, including a year at the Institut d'Etudes Politiques at Bordeaux, then taking a master's degree in Critical Theory at the University of Nottingham, which was followed by a

PhD thesis on Jean Baudrillard, Georges Bataille and photography. He joined the staff at University College Cork in October 1996, and has since taught courses on cultural studies, philosophy, politics, feminism in France, the Enlightenment, Music and Culture, twentieth-century art, as well as literary seminars on transgression, the City, writing and sexuality. His publications include *Georges Bataille* (2000), *Jean Baudrillard* (2004), and *Noise/Music* (2007).

Martin Iddon is Professor of Music and Aesthetics at the University of Leeds. He is the author of *New Music at Darmstadt: Nono, Stockhausen, Cage, and Boulez* and *John Cage: Correspondence on Interpretation and Performance* (both Cambridge University Press). He has published widely on musical modernism, experimental music, and musical aesthetics, amongst other topics, for journals including *Contemporary Music Review*, *Performance Research*, and *Musical Quarterly*.

Marc Lafrance is an Assistant Professor of Sociology at Concordia University. Informed by an intersectional approach, his research on popular media culture explores issues of self, body, and society and how they are bound up with the cultural politics of identity. Lafrance's work has been published in a variety of refereed journals such as *Body and Society* and *Popular Music and Society* and edited collections such as *Revealing Bodies, Unveiling Representations* as well as in the biggest online men's lifestyle magazine *AskMen.com*. Along with co-researcher Lori Burns, Lafrance is the recipient of an Insight Grant from the Social Sciences and Humanities Research Council of Canada (2013–2018).

Melanie L. Marshall is a musicologist at University College Cork specialising in sixteenth-century Italian music, gender and sexuality. During her Marie Curie International Outgoing Fellowship (2011–2014) she held visiting scholar positions at UCLA and NYU. Her articles and reviews appear in *Early Music*, *Renaissance Studies*, and *Women and Music: A Journal of Gender and Culture*. A co-edited volume, *Sexualities, Textualities, Art and Music in Early Modern Italy* is forthcoming from Ashgate.

Lucy O'Brien has been writing on music, feminism and popular culture, and creating fiction since the early 1980s. She grew up in Southampton, played in all-girl punk band The Catholic Girls, and graduated from Leeds University in 1983. Since starting out on *NME*, she has written for a range of titles including the *Sunday Times*, *Marie Claire*, the *Guardian*, *Q*, and *Mojo*. She's the author of *Madonna: Like An Icon*, *She Bop* and *She Bop II* and biographies of Dusty Springfield and Annie Lennox. A regular 'pundit' on TV and radio, she also co-produced the

Channel 4 (UK) film *Righteous Babes* on rock and new feminism. She teaches in Media & Communications at London's Goldsmiths' College and Westminster University, and is currently working on a memoir that combines music, mysticism, and magic.

Craig N. Owens teaches drama and performance studies, playwriting, poetics, and critical theory at Drake University, in Des Moines, Iowa, where he directs the Center for the Humanities. He has written and spoken extensively on the work of George Bernard Shaw, Samuel Beckett, and Harold Pinter; American film, popular music, and television; and the symbolic importance of vodka in *The Big Lebowski* and the *James Bond* franchise. He is past-president of the Midwest Modern Language Society, a founding member of SteinSemble Performance Group, and author of the award-winning domestic drama *Open House*.

Anusha Rutnam studied Fashion History and Theory at the University of New South Wales and wrote her History Honours thesis, at The University of Sydney, on the foundation of Australian Fashion Week. She is currently studying applied fashion design at the Sydney Institute of TAFE NSW, Sydney. Her fashion blog is http://pavement-frippery.blogspot.com.au/.

Carol Vernallis teaches at Stanford University in Film and Media studies. Her first book, *Experiencing Music Video* (Columbia University Press), attempts to theorize an aesthetics of the genre. Her second, *Unruly Media: Youtube, Music Video, and the New Digital Cinema*, will be in press fall 2013. She is co-editor of *The Oxford Handbook of New Audiovisual Aesthetics*, and *The Oxford Handbook of Sound and Image in Digital Media*.

Simon Warner is a lecturer, writer and broadcaster on popular music issues. A member of Leeds University's School of Music since 1994, he takes a particular interest in the ways in which social, political and cultural history connect with the evolution of pop and rock styles in the post-war period. A History graduate of Sheffield University, he took and gained the first ever MA in Popular Music Studies at Liverpool University in 1993, and was awarded his PhD by Leeds University in 2010. A former journalist—he was a live reviewer for *The Guardian* in the early 1990s—he published *Rockspeak: The Language of Rock and Pop* in 1996, and edited *Howl for Now*, a study of Allen Ginsberg's groundbreaking poem, in 2005 and *Summer of Love: The Beatles, Art and Culture in the Sixties* in 2008. His latest book, *Text and Drugs and Rock'n'Roll*, which considers the links between the US Beat poets and subsequent rock culture, was published by Bloomsbury in 2013. He makes frequent contributions to the BBC and wrote and presented the 2010 radio documentary on the jazz poet Michael Horovitz. His obituaries of key members of the American counterculture have appeared in *The Guardian* and *The Independent*. Currently he is working on *New York, New Wave*, a title that will consider the rise of punk in Manhattan in the 1970s.

Index

443660